D0906726

History

of

BREVARD COUNTY

Volume 1

By

Jerrell H. Shofner

Brevard County Historical Commission

Library of Congress Card Catalog Number
95-079892

ISBN
0-9646660-0-6

Designed and produced by richworks • Stuart, Florida
Printed by Southeastern Printing Co., Inc. • Stuart, Florida

Contents

Acknowledgments

This history of Brevard County is the result of a project initiated by the Brevard County Historical Commission when Robert Whitney was president and Douglas Hendriksen was chairman of the committee on publications. I am obliged to them for transforming the idea of a history of the county into a practical project. I would like also to express my appreciation to them and the entire membership of the commission for their forbearance and assistance while I was gathering information and writing the manuscript.

It is impossible to name all the people to whom I am obliged for assistance along the way, but I must express my thanks to all of those individuals named in the Interview section of the bibliography. I am especially indebted to Robert Whitney of Indian Harbour Beach and Fred Hopwood of Melbourne for reading portions of the manuscript and making valuable suggestions. Weona Cleveland of Melbourne generously shared with me her time, her library, and her extensive knowledge. Since the Melbourne Times was not available for research until the manuscript was completed, Ms. Cleveland's large clipping file was invaluable. Mr. and Mrs. Henry U. Parrish, Jr. welcomed me into their home and held me spellbound for hours. Hugh's recounting of his personal experiences and Ada's stories gleaned from area history were most helpful. She also made available to me a large number of books and documents from her voluminous collection of both primary and secondary materials. Mrs. Fred Woelk, my colleague in the University of Central Florida history department and a native of Merritt Island, was always available to answer questions. She probably at times wished she was not so accessible, but I am grateful for her tolerance in assisting me in numerous ways. Kyle S. VanLandingham of Riverview, Florida shared with me his collection of materials relating to the southern part of the county. Dr. Robert Dean of New Smyrna Beach also shared his insights with me and permitted me to borrow from his collection of primary sources. I would like to thank Vera Zimmerman of Merritt Island for generously sharing with me her knowledge of the archaeology of the county.

Miss Elizabeth Alexander of the P. K. Yonge Library of Florida History at the University of Florida once again assisted me in many ways. I wish to thank her for this and for many favors over the past 30 years. David Coles of the manuscript division of the Florida State Archives searched out and brought to my research table great volumes of primary documents during my visit to Tallahassee. He then went the extra mile and responded to several telephone calls for additional information. I owe him for his kind assistance. I must also acknowledge my indebtedness to the staffs of the Southern Historical Collection at the University of North Carolina at Chapel Hill, the National Archives and the Manuscript Division of the Library of Congress in Washington, D. C., and the special collections divisions of the Florida State University and the University of South Florida. I wish also to acknowledge the assistance of the library staff at my own school, the University of Central Florida. John Walters of the documents division and Cheryl D. Walters of the interlibrary loan office at this school deserve special mention.

I am most grateful to Carole Gonzalez and Kimberly Hillyard of the University of Central Florida history department for their careful editing and typing of the manuscript.

—*Jerrell H. Shofner*

Foreword

The concept for a history of Brevard County, Florida was first presented to the Brevard County Historical Commission (BCHC) by Douglas G. Hendriksen, newly appointed to the BCHC in 1987. The BCHC designated Douglas Hendriksen as a committee of one to pursue this endeavor - to survey Florida historians and to determine the historian most qualified to undertake this task. After surveying qualified Florida historians, Dr. Jerrell Shofner, Chairman of the History Department at the University of Central Florida, was selected due to his stature in the Florida historical community, previous historical accomplishments, and proximity to Brevard County. Dr. Shofner, under contract with the Brevard County Board of County Commissioners (BCBCC), was given the task of writing the "History of Brevard County." This history was to encompass all of Brevard County and its communities from its earliest beginnings to the present. After five years in research and writing, the final draft of the book was submitted to the BCHC by Dr. Shofner. The BCHC then went to work proofreading, editing and selecting the most appropriate drawings, maps and photos to best illustrate Dr. Shofner's narrative. Vera Zimmerman took charge of collecting and editing the photos and captions.

BCHC members responsible for contributing most heavily of their time and talents to the History are Douglas G. Hendriksen, James E. Ball, past BCHC chairman John M. Rawls, Vera Zimmerman, James Culberson, past BCHC member Clyde Field, and Brevard County employee, Todd Peetz, and former Brevard County employee, Jennifer Goulet.

Brevard County Historical Commission

Douglas G. Hendriksen, District 2, Chairman
James E. Ball, District 1, Vice Chairman
Vera Zimmerman, District 2, Secretary
John Rawls, District 1
A. Brooks Humphrys, District 1
Gregory Jones, District 2
Margaret Senne, District 3
Debbie Palmer, District 3
Orlando Ramirez, District 4
Ada Parrish, District 4
Georgiana Kjerulff, District 5
Yvonne Shingler, District 5
James Culberson, District 5

1

The Land and Its Original Inhabitants

Mammoth and mastodon were extant when the first humans arrived in the area some 12,000 years ago. By 1763 Native American populations were decimated by European colonial struggles.

The Ais, who lived along the Indian River, are believed to have been among the Indians who emigrated to Cuba when Spain left Florida in 1763. (Etching © Vera Zimmerman, 1987)

Stretching for 72 miles along Florida's Atlantic coast from just north of the Haulover between Mosquito Lagoon and the Indian River to Sebastian Inlet, Brevard County reaches about 20 miles inland to the St. Johns River. It has not always been that way. During the nearly 150 years of its existence as a political subdivision of the state of Florida, it has undergone numerous boundary adjustments. Even its name has not always been the same.

A part of Mosquito County until Florida became a state in 1845, the county was first named St. Lucie. It was then a huge expanse of territory reaching southward until it adjoined Dade County in the Lake Okeechobee area and westward to

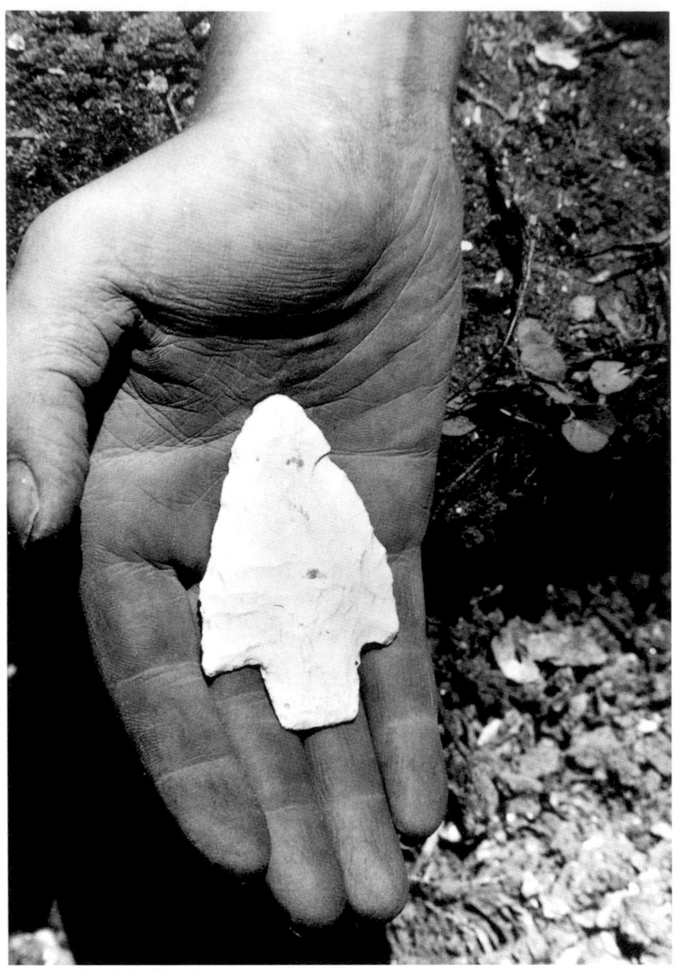

Florida Archaic stemmed points date from 5,000 *to* 1,000 B.C. *and are found throughout Brevard County.* (*Photo by Vera Zimmerman*, 1979)

its border with Manatee County. A sizable portion of Lake Okeechobee was included in its boundaries. Renamed Brevard County in 1855, it was reduced somewhat in size but still stretched along the Atlantic Coast for about 150 miles and extended to the Kissimmee Valley on the west. Additional boundary changes came in 1861 when some land was made part of Polk County and in 1873 when other territory was joined to Orange County. There were other boundary adjustments with Dade and Manatee counties in 1874. An important change came in 1879 when the southern portion of Volusia County, which included Titusville, was added to Brevard. At that time the county extended from the head of the Indian River just north of the Haulover to Jupiter on the south and westward to the area around Fort Drum. This was the configuration of the county during the 1880s when it began experiencing its first extensive settlement. Then, in 1887, the western portion of the county was detached and made part of Osceola County. As more and more people settled in the southern portion of Brevard they complained of the distance to the county seat at Titusville and began pressing for a county of their own. They were rewarded by the state legislature in 1905 when St. Lucie was created out of the southern portion of Brevard. In 1959 the county acquired its present boundaries when the area south of Sebastian Inlet was transferred to Indian River County.

As in the case of its political boundaries, Brevard County's physical characteristics have also changed, albeit over a much longer period of time. While much of the available information about the county's geologic development is speculative, there are areas of general agreement among geologists and archaeologists. Most accept the premise that the Florida peninsula first rose from the sea at least 20 million, and perhaps 40 million, years ago. In either case it is the youngest part of the land mass which presently comprises the United States. Geologists also agree that the peninsula's relationship to the sea has changed from time to time, especially during the Ice Age when the water level rose and fell as the ice cap grew and receded. Several shorelines on the Florida peninsula have been identified which mark the changing water levels. In addition to the oscillations of the water level in relation to climatic changes, there has also been a cumulative drop over time so that land which was once covered with water is now exposed.

These geologic and climatic changes over time have left present-day Brevard County with three main geographic features. The Indian River Lagoon itself is the dominant one. Separated on the north from the Mosquito Lagoon by a narrow spit of land known as the Haulover, the Indian River is a little over five miles wide just below that point. On its east bank is Merritt Island, a low land mass more than 30 miles long. The island is in turn bordered on the east by the Banana River and on the north by Mosquito Lagoon. On its southern end Merritt Island forms two small peninsulas which enclose Newfound Harbor. Further to the east is a long, low barrier island. It widens into Cape Canaveral just east of Merritt Island and then narrows again. Rarely more than ten feet above sea level and usually no more than a half mile wide, this barrier peninsula extends far to the south, separating the Indian River from the Atlantic Ocean. Just south of Sebastian and the present southern boundary of Brevard County is a ten-mile stretch known as the Narrows. Filled with many oyster beds and mangrove marshes, the river is narrow and tortuous until it emerges again into another wide stretch of water which extends for many miles along what was still Brevard County until 1905.

Artifacts tell archaeologists about the area's original inhabitants from the stone points of the earliest Paleo Hunters to the pottery fragments of the St. Johns and Malabar cultures. (Etching © Vera Zimmerman, 1987)

West of the Indian River are the Five Mile Ridge, also known as the Atlantic Coastal Ridge, and the Ten Mile Ridge, so called because of the distance from the coast. Cut in several places by valleys caused by Crane, Turkey and Sebastian Creeks, the Atlantic Coastal Ridge is about a mile or so wide and averages about 30 feet above sea level.[1]

On its western side the Ten Mile Ridge slopes into the St. Johns River valley. The St. Johns is a slow moving body of water which flows northward through a series of shallow lakes. It has also been described as a chain of lakes

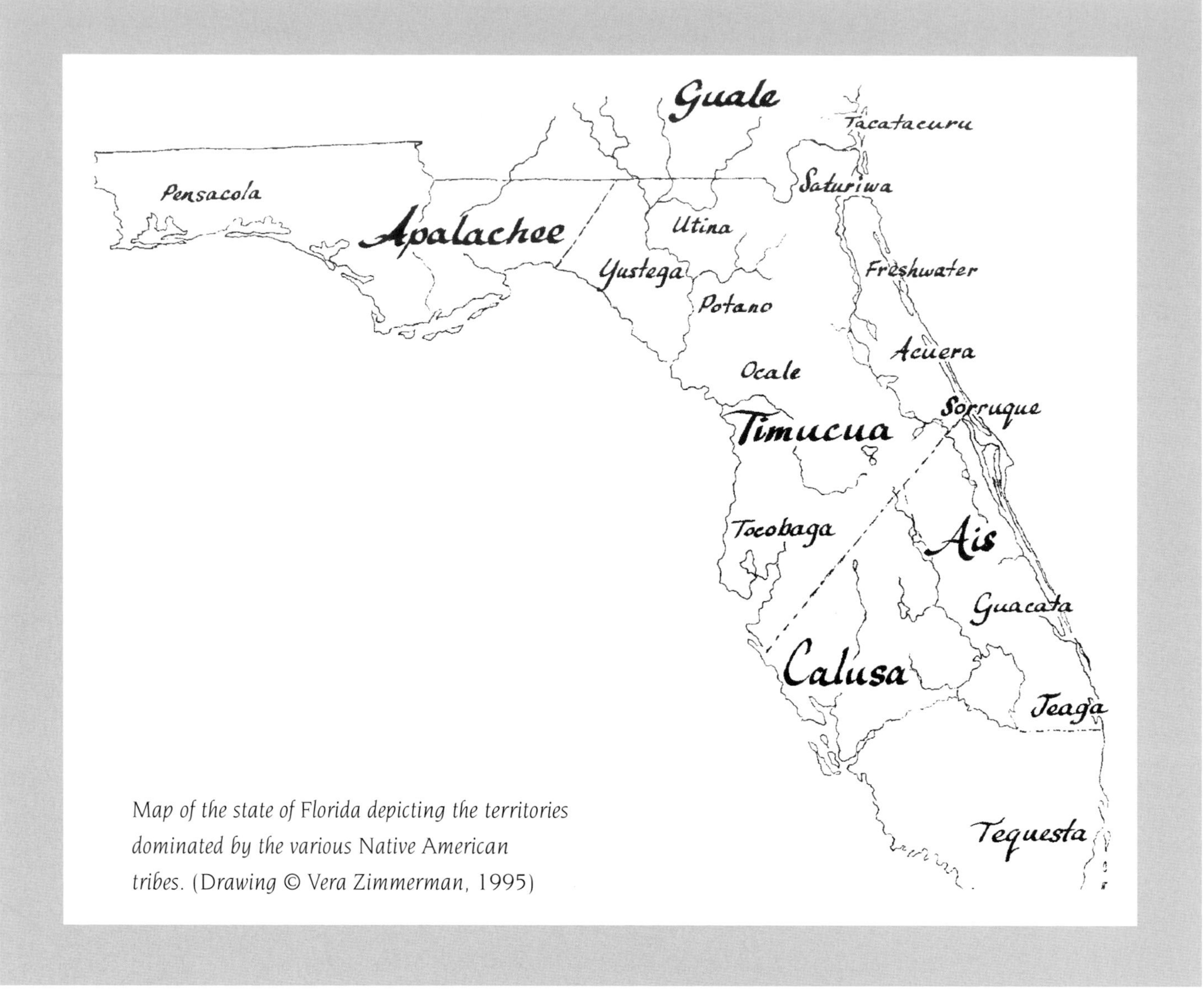

Map of the state of Florida depicting the territories dominated by the various Native American tribes. (*Drawing* © *Vera Zimmerman, 1995*)

connected by a channel. From the south those lakes are Helen Blazes, Sawgrass, Washington, Winder, Poinsett, Cone, and Puzzle. Since the river is only 15.73 feet above sea level at Lake Winder, it is easy to see why it moves so sluggishly on its northerly course to its outlet into the Atlantic Ocean east of Jacksonville.

Most of Brevard County was submerged at one time or another during the Ice Age. The Atlantic Coastal Ridge and the Five Mile Ridge, for example, are thought to have been formed as offshore bars comparable to the barrier peninsula which presently lies east of the Indian River. It may have been formed by sand carried from the north by a current running counter to the Gulf Stream.[2] Such fluctuation of the water level would explain the existence of the many sites of prehistoric villages which have been found in the St. Johns valley and along the Indian River, both above and below the present water level.

As the Florida peninsula was forming, it was inhabited by numerous species of prehistoric animals including the now-extinct mammoth, mastodon, saber-toothed cat, horse and giant ground sloth. There were also spectacled bears, wolves, and alligators. Remains of mastodon and other species have been recovered from deep springs around the state, including Rock Springs in neighboring Orange County, as well as from many Brevard sites. Many of these animals were extant when the first humans came to the peninsula some 12,000 years ago. These Paleo-Indians were nomadic hunters and gatherers who used spears to kill even some of the larger animals. Some authorities believe that the Paleo-Indians were such successful hunters that they may have caused the extinction of some species. Camping near water holes or river crossings frequented by their prey, these early Floridians stalked and killed them for the necessities of life. The meat supplied food, the skins provided clothing, and the bones and sinews were fashioned into tools. These early inhabitants gathered nuts, berries, and wild plants for food. This nomadic style of life lasted several thousand years.

Pot sherds are often used to date archaeological sites.
Row 1: *Incised and Plain Fiber-tempered, Orange Period,* 2,000 – 1,200 B.C.
Row 2: *Fiber and Sand-tempered, Transitional period,* 1,200 – 500 B.C.
Row 3: *St. Johns Incised and Plain, St. Johns I/Malabar I Period,* 500B.C. *to* A.D. 800
Row 4: *St. Johns Check-Stamped, St. Johns II/Malabar II period,* A.D. 800 – A.D. 1565.
(*Bense and Phillips,* 1990; *Photo by Vera Zimmerman,* 1994)

Whether from human or other causes, most of the larger animals disappeared about 8,000 or 9,000 years ago, bringing changes in the way the Indians lived. While they still hunted smaller game and gathered nuts and berries, these Archaic Indians depended more and more on snails, mollusks, and shellfish for their food. They became less nomadic, living in villages on lake shores and along streams for much longer periods. At times they still moved, sometimes perhaps to permit depleted shellfish to replenish themselves or to find better hunting grounds. Even while maintaining

The discovery of Early Archaic burials in Titusville in 1982 and the ensuing archaeological excavation attracted international attention. Dramatic finds produced new information about the biology, diet, textiles and environment of the period. (Photo by Vera Zimmerman, 1985)

semi-permanent villages, they frequently established temporary campsites for gathering nuts in season, hunting, or fishing. Living in the same places for longer periods than their predecessors, they accumulated more waste material and left a better record for archaeologists.

Archaeologists are continually revising their estimates of the date of the arrival of Brevard County's first inhabitants. The present prevailing evidence suggests that they came as early as 8000 B.C. Their preceramic culture included the use of flint and bone projectile points, bone awls and pins, and shell gouges.[3] Arriving during a relatively dry period when the water level was lower than it is today, they settled primarily in the St. Johns River valley.

The ability of the prehistoric inhabitants to remain longer in their villages was advanced by a technological innovation about 4,000 years ago. The invention of fired-clay pots, tempered with palmetto fibers or Spanish moss made it possible to store supplies. Food gathering remained the same but it became possible for villages to be occupied year-round.

Pottery designs and use became quite diverse during the 1,500 year epoch which anthropologists call the Orange Period. Toward the end of the Orange Period, north Florida's early inhabitants began to learn the advantages of agriculture. Squash was the first crop but

Dr. Glen Doran, Director of the WindoverArchaeological Project, explains the importance of the pond's peat deposits in the preservation of material and in providing a record of environmental change during the past 11,000 years. (Photo by Vera Zimmerman, 1985)

Indian River Anthropological Society crew with archaeologist Dr. David Dickel investigate a shell mound along the Indian River in Palm Bay. Left to right: Walt Hersing, Mary Carroll, David Dickel, Tamaria Bishop and Michael Bishop. (Photo by Vera Zimmerman, 1992.)

Jeff Goulet, T. C. Bishop, Dr. Judith Bense, Dean Zimmerman, Jennifer Goulet (Photo by Vera Zimmerman, 1992)

maize followed soon afterward. Although the inhabitants of the Indian River Area developed fiber-tempered pottery, they never engaged in agriculture as did their neighbors to the north.

The people of the St. Johns and Malabar Periods scattered along the St. Johns and crossed the ridge to the Indian River. In both areas they lived in semi-permanent villages and left evidence of their existence in great shell mounds as well as middens. Numerous burial sites have been found in both circumstances. There is ample evidence as well of temporary campsites where they hunted and fished. Apparently the insects on the offshore islands made that area uninhabitable except during the cooler periods. Archaeologists have concluded that villages and temporary hunting and fishing sites followed the food sources as the water table changed. Some sites were abandoned permanently and some were reoccupied after long absences. But there is considerable evidence that some sites were continuously occupied, leaving the belief that there is a historical continuity from the earliest settlements and that the first inhabitants are the ancestors of the natives who occupied the region when the first Europeans arrived.[4]

Although information about the natives who met the first European explorers along the Atlantic Coast is still quite fragmentary, much more is known about them than their ancestors. While historians have drawn some distinctions between the Sorruque, who inhabited the Cape Canaveral area, the Ais, who lived in the area just to their south, the

In 1992, Dr. Judith Bense began a project to nominate sites along the St. Johns River to the National Register. From left to right: Dr. Judith Bense, Jennifer Goulet, Dean Zimmerman, Greg Jones, Jeff Goulet. (Photo by Vera Zimmerman, 1992)

Guacata, a smaller group which inhabited the area around St. Lucie, and the Jeaga, who lived near Jupiter, anthropologists tend to look at them as a common group identified generally as the Ais. However they are viewed as cultural groups, there is considerable evidence that the chief of the Ais was the dominant figure among all of the groups and some homage was paid him by the chiefs of the Sorruque, Guacata and, perhaps, the Jeaga.

According to the anthropologists who have studied the evidence of prehistoric as well as early historic life in the Brevard County region, some general observations can be drawn about the habits of the natives who met the first Europeans. There was some loose political organization involving a chief (or cacique as the Spanish called him) who presided over a village and sometimes received homage from smaller and less powerful settlements. Some authorities compare this arrangement to what sociologists call extended households. The chiefs had more than one wife and their residence served as the center of the community. This perhaps explains the extended household arrangement. The sizes of the villages are undetermined, but they were made up of wooden framed houses covered with palmetto thatch. Furniture consisted of low wooden benches. There was usually a council of the most important men and a religious figure. Both political and religious ceremonies were celebrated at the homesite of the chief and residents from neighboring villages attended. Sometimes the visitors brought gifts. The economy was based on fishing and gathering. No agriculture was practiced. Diet consisted of fish, shellfish, deer, manatee, palm berries, and sea grapes. The men fished, usually in pairs in canoes. The women were responsible for gathering, cooking and infant care. Locally produced items included baskets, nets, ropes, wooden canoes and paddles, bone projectile points, awls and ornaments from deer, shark teeth for cutting, deer skins for clothing and drums, and shell celts, picks, dippers, and pendants. The presence of tobacco, chert, gourd dippers, hematite, and brass, gold and silver ornaments suggest some trade with other groups.[5]

Whether they are identified collectively as Ais or separately as Sorruque, Ais, Guacata, and Jeaga, the Indians of the region are regarded by all authorities as distinct from the Timucua to the north and the Calusa and Tequesta to the south. The only exception is perhaps the Sorruque who are sometimes identified with the Timucua. They were sometimes friendly and more often hostile to the Europeans who began arriving in the 16th century as will be shown in the next chapter. They seem to have resisted for some time the infusion of European culture, but gradually succumbed to it. Ultimately becoming enmeshed in the European colonial struggles in North America, their ranks were decimated and a handful of survivors may have emigrated to Cuba when the Spanish relinquished control of Florida in 1763.

End Notes

1. Irving Rouse, A Survey of Indian River Archaeology (New Haven, 1951), p. 18.
2. Ibid., p. 23.
3. Ibid., p. 262.
4. Barbara A. Purdy (editor), Wetsite Archaeology, Caldwell, New Jersey, 1988) pp. 302-303.
5. Ibid., pp. 303-304.

Page 10 Map: A photo mosaic of satellite images from Landsat 5. (Image processed by General Electric Digital Image Analysis Laboratory)

NOUA
Canada
Novelle
Biscaie
FRANCIA
NIEU NEDERLAND
VIRGINIA
Mangook
MARE
VIRGIVIUM
FLORIDA
INSVLÆ BARLOVENTO
D E L
Golfe del S
Louys
Golfe d. S
Laurens
Terre neufve
Accadie
I. de Sable
La Bermuda
C. Cod
C. Charle
Port Royal
R. de May
R. de Dolphins
C. de Canaveral
B. de Carlos
De groote Vlacte
Cuba
Espanola
Mayaguana
Noorder Caicos
Abreojo O Baxos de Babueca
Hollantsche bay
Laeghe hoeck
Blanc Sablon
Belisle
C. de Grat
C. rouge
Orange Bay
F. Orange
Rensselaers hoeck
Evorhaven
Barra de madre de Dios
Trinitie harbor
B. de la Madalena
C. de Trafalgar
Caio de Sal
Coxumel
Caiman grande
Tortugos
Barbada
Guadalupa

2

Florida and the European Struggle for the New World

Florida's strategic proximity to the route of the Spanish treasure fleet made it a pivotal feature in the struggle between the European powers for control of the New World.

The first documented contact between Spanish and Ais was by Ponce de León who went ashore at a village south of Cape Canaveral in 1513. (*Etching* © *Vera Zimmerman*, 1994)

Within less than a half century after the discovery of the New World in 1492, Spaniards were transporting great quantities of precious metals from Mexico and Peru to Spain. By the mid-1550s a system had evolved whereby treasure fleets made semi-annual voyages from the western Caribbean following the Gulf Stream through the straits of Florida and up the Atlantic Coast to a point near present-day Jacksonville where the current turned seaward. Given the rivalries between Spain, France, and England in the 16th century, the value of its cargo, and its vulnerability to attack while so close to shore, the Spanish fleet became a centerpiece in the struggle between the European powers for control of the New

World. Florida's strategic proximity to the route of the treasure fleet made it a pivotal feature of that struggle. Its land mass pointed dagger-like into the evolving Spanish-American empire. Even had Spain had no interest in occupying Florida, it could ill afford one of its European antagonists to do so. Another reason for Spain's covetous attitude toward Florida was the problem of survivors of the frequent shipwrecks in the Gulf Stream who were subjected to the hostilities of inhabitants of the sandy peninsula.

As the Spanish exploration of the Western Hemisphere progressed, stories about an island called Bimini somewhere to the north had created curiosity and not a little active interest. Ponce de León had already chosen to investigate this matter and had discovered and named Florida in 1513. He had apparently stopped in Ais territory on his voyage along the Florida coast. The only other contacts between Europeans and the natives along the Atlantic Coast until the 1560s resulted from the all-too-frequent shipwrecks caused by the hazardous navigation in the Gulf Stream and the destructive hurricanes which sometimes devastated the treasure fleets. In the meantime, there were several expeditions of exploration on Florida's west coast following de León's discovery. They expanded existing knowledge of Florida's dimensions but also demonstrated that not only was there no precious metal to be found but also that establishing a permanent settlement was extremely difficult. It was largely strategic considerations having to do with protecting the bullion fleets rather than a desire for settlement that prompted Spain's royal decree of 1557 authorizing colonies to be established at Pensacola on the Gulf and Port Royal on the Atlantic. When that enterprise ended in abject failure in 1561, Phillip II decided that there would be no further efforts to colonize Florida. If Spain could not do it, then he had little to fear from any other nation, he apparently reasoned.

He was not to enjoy that satisfaction for long. The French had already begun planning a settlement in Florida when Phillip decided to abandon his efforts. Although they suffered severe privations, the French led by Rene de Laudonnière built and manned Fort Caroline on the river which would soon become known as the St. Johns. Phillip II then turned to Pedro Menéndez, his successful commander of the treasure fleets. Naming him adelantado of Florida, the king charged Menéndez with the task of driving the French out, settling Florida, converting the natives to Christianity, and providing refuge stations for shipwreck survivors along the Atlantic Coast.

Menéndez' remarkable feats in Florida are well known. In a series of daring military maneuvers, he drove the French from the peninsula, founded St. Augustine, and for a brief period maintained a string of outposts where Jesuit missionaries tried to convert the Indians to the Catholic faith. Some of his French adversaries became shipwrecked at Cape Canaveral where Menéndez found them building both a fort and a vessel with which they were planning to put to sea. About 150 Frenchmen surrendered to Menéndez and some 20 others reportedly escaped into the woods.[1] Menéndez then ordered his three vessels to sail southward while he marched with a column of men along the shore of what he called the Rio de Ays. Apparently looking for a suitable spot where he might leave some of his men while he sailed to Cuba for supplies, Menéndez arrived on November 4, 1565 at the settlement of Ais, so-called because that was the name of the chieftain, or cacique, there. The chief was friendly and gave the Spaniards food in return for mirrors, knives, scissors, and bells, items greatly prized by the chief and his people. After four days of exploration, Menéndez failed to find a place he thought suitable for a settlement. Wishing to leave a detachment on the coast but fearing subsequent trouble with the natives, he marched about three leagues southward from the village of Ais and left a detachment under the command of Captain Juan Velez de Medrano.[2]

Medrano's tour in Ais country was not a happy one.

From Havana, Menéndez sent a caravel with supplies for the outpost. When the vessel arrived, a number of dissident soldiers seized it and set sail. Both Medrano and his assistant, Lieutenant Gabriel de Ayala, were wounded while trying to stop the mutiny. Sailing toward Havana, the rebels were intercepted and apprehended by Menéndez. In the meantime, the soldiers remaining with Medrano, enduring extreme hunger and discomfort, abandoned the post. Although many died on the way, the surviving soldiers reached an inlet from the sea and established a post which became Fort Santa Lucia. There, Menéndez found them and established a settlement.[3] The natives of the Santa Lucia area were apparently the Guacata, who may have been subject to the Ais on the north although that was not certain. Whatever the case, they at first seemed friendly to the Spaniards, but after a while that changed. One day about 500 Indians attacked the fort without warning and killed at least 15 Spaniards. One of the surviving soldiers complained that the "savages" escaped unharmed because of their "manner of fighting." According to him, they could fire 20 projectiles while a Spanish soldier was firing a single shot.[4] Although there were other armed confrontations, the fort at Santa Lucia lasted about three years, during which time its population was increased markedly by a number of

In 1605, the Spanish governor of St. Augustine sent Alvaro Mexia on a mission to the Ais resulting in the first map of the area and ushering in an era of improved relations. Shipwreck survivors in the area still reported inhospitable treatment. (Etching © Vera Zimmerman, 1987)

Spaniards who had abandoned their own outpost at Tequesta as a result of hostile Indian attacks. The post was permanently abandoned in 1568, by which time the efforts of Menéndez and the Jesuit missionaries had ended in failure. The Jesuits abandoned Florida for the more amenable fields of South America. After Menéndez died, his successors largely left peninsular Florida to its native inhabitants for several decades, despite the continuing problem of the plight of sailors who survived the shipwrecks along the coast. The boundary of the Spanish mission system, which was resumed by the Franciscans, nominally continued to include the area between Cape Canaveral and Santa Lucia, but little was done about it.[5]

Shipwrecked Spanish sailors continued to endure "inhospitable treatment" when marooned on the Atlantic Coast in Ais territory and, eventually, some of the Spanish governors of Florida attempted to improve the situation. Contact was reopened in 1597 when Governor Gonzalo Méndez de Canzo was on his way back to St. Augustine from Havana. His vessel apparently accidentally crossed paths with the Ais chief and about 80 men aboard 15 canoes. A seemingly friendly conversation ensued during which gifts were exchanged. The Indians provided fish, wood, and water while Canzo offered the usual trade goods as well as a piece of his own clothing as a special show of good faith. The chief then asked Canzo to send to him a Spanish interpreter who could explain to his people the wishes of the Spanish government. Governor Canzo was pleased at this overture and shortly dispatched Juan Ramirez de Contreras and two mission Indians to Ais territory. Contreras was familiar with the language and had conducted similar missions in the past.

Contreras and his two companions set off with a load of gifts. News soon came back that the three had been summarily executed upon their arrival in Ais. An infuriated Canzo wrote the king that "this spring I shall make war on them and attempt to punish them in order that they may be an object lesson to others."[6] In defending his harsh plans, Canzo informed the king that these Indians were not only guilty of the latest atrocity, but had frequently killed shipwrecked sailors and several messengers sent out by former governors. Since the "cacique of Sorruque" lived only about 20 leagues from St. Augustine, Canzo felt that he could not allow him to "act in so bold a manner, with so many crimes to his credit."[7] The attack was carried out by Spanish soldiers and Indian allies under cover of darkness. Canzo wrote that the surprise attack was successful but that it had been difficult to tell whether those killed were men, women or children. The missionaries, who were often at odds with the governors over Indian policy, were displeased. Father Lopez condemned the affair as unjust and mourned the death of the "seventy innocent victims." Father Pareja was generally critical of Canzo for his dealings with the Indians, but chose not to "judge in this case."[8]

Regardless of the displeasure of the religious leaders, Canzo seemed pleased with the results. According to him, the effect was that "those who were not friends became friends after the punishment, and those who were friends became stronger friends." He added that the Indians along that part of the coast were guilty of "a thousand treacheries and misdeeds," and only after punishment would they "live peacefully and quietly."[9]

A different sort of problem confronted Governor Pedro de Ybarra in 1603. He continued to cultivate a friendly relationship with the coastal Indians, but the situation seems to have remained quite tenuous. He had sent a vessel to the Ais with gifts and an invitation for the Ais leaders to come to St. Augustine to discuss friendly relations.

Although the Indians promised to accept the invitation, they were not in a hurry to do so. In the meantime, seven black slaves escaped from St. Augustine and headed toward Sorruque. Ybarra's search party captured five of the runaways, but the other two reached Ais territory. There, they were permitted to marry two Indian women. Ybarra was alarmed. In the first place, he wanted to recover the escapees because of their economic value. But, perhaps more important, he desired their return because they could provide valuable information in case the Indians should decide to attack St. Augustine. The governor sent Juan Rodríguez de Cartaya in a launch loaded with gifts to open new relations with the Ais. He was told specifically to speak with one Capitán Chico. This so-called "little captain" was an important figure since he was the interpreter for the entire Ais region and had influence with most of the chiefs, including the principal Ais chieftain, to whom the Spaniards referred as Capitán Grande. He was instructed to induce Chico to visit St. Augustine voluntarily, but if that failed he was to bring him by force. Rodríguez was obliged to use the latter method. At St. Augustine, however, Chico was showered with gifts for himself as well as others which he was to take back to the Capitán Grande and the chiefs of Sorruque and Oribia.[10] Leaving St. Augustine, Chico promised to bring the other chiefs as well as the two escaped slaves back with him. That did not happen.

Rodríguez was ordered back to Ais in early 1605 with orders to induce Capitán Grande to accompany him to St. Augustine and to return the two slaves. Grande willingly accepted the gifts showered upon him, but he was absolutely unwilling to visit St. Augustine. He did release the slaves and Rodríguez returned to the presidio with them but without the Ais chief.[11]

The situation unexpectedly changed much for the better. Capitán Chico suddenly appeared in St. Augustine with 30 warriors and offered his services to Governor Ybarra on behalf of Capitán Grande. He said the Ais had heard the governor was "engaged in fighting the English" and thought his warriors might be of assistance. Not long afterward the chiefs of Sorruque and Oribia arrived at St. Augustine and declared their wishes to become vassals of Spain. They said that Capitán Grande had the same wish and would soon come to the presidio. There were more delays during which the governor and the Capitán Grande exchanged gifts from the distance of their respective residences. Then, Ybarra was again surprised on September 2, 1605 when the Capitán Grande, the chiefs of Sorruque and Oribia, and 20 other high-ranking Indians appeared in St. Augustine. The elated Governor Ybarra welcomed them and gave a feast in their honor in his home. He wrote that Spanish diplomacy had won even though it had taken much patience and "watchful waiting."[12] He made no comment on the possible effect that Canzo's actions might have had.

This was apparently the beginning of an era of improved relations, if not outright friendship, between the Spanish and the coastal Indians. During the extended negotiations between Governor Ybarra and the Ais leaders, Alvaro Mexia made a carefully documented journey through the northern portion of Ais territory. During his travels he noted the locations of several Indian villages of the time. He placed both Sorruque and Oribia (sometimes spelled Urribia) at the southern end of Mosquito Lagoon but quite near the Haulover. According to him, Ulumay was the first town in "the province of the Ais" and was located on the Banana River on present-day Merritt Island. He noted "many other encampments in the winter-time," suggesting fishing camps which were inhabited only when the insects were at a minimum. The town of Savochequeya was located on Newfound Harbor. Further south was the winter town of Pentoaya, directly across the river from which was the summer site of the same town. It was at the present site of Eau Gallie. Mexia located the principle town of Ais across the river from the present-day town of Vero Beach.[13]

Mexia seems to have been a successful emissary to the Indians since Governor Ybarra reported that he became the first European ever to be made an Indian chief. Relations between the Ais and their lesser neighbors on the one hand and the Spaniards on the other remained more friendly during the 17th century, although there does

Spanish coins from the 1715 Spanish treasure fleet wrecked in a hurricane along the East Coast from South Brevard to Ft. Pierce. (*Photo Brevard County Historical Commission Archives*)

not seem to have been much contact between them.

When Jonathan Dickinson and his group of English Quakers were shipwrecked near Jupiter in 1696, the party made its way up the coast, eventually reaching St. Augustine. Subjected to harsh treatment by several Indian groups, probably including the Jeaga and the Guacata, they were apparently befriended by the principal Ais chief. During their ordeal they noted that the Indians evinced friendship toward the Spanish while showing definite hostility toward Englishmen. Continually attempting to detect evidence that the shipwrecked group was English, they seem never to have been able to do so. Although only one of their group spoke Spanish, he and his fellow Englishmen successfully posed as Spaniards. Most authorities believe that had there been much contact with the Spanish during the 17th century, the Indians would have been easily able to see through the subterfuge. In any event, Dickinson and most of his fellow survivors eventually made their way through the Indian River region. They lost all their material possessions and were subjected to some quite unpleasant experiences.[14]

In the meantime, the Spanish continued a nominal but apparently diminishing relationship with the Ais. In 1703 Governor José de Zuñiga was directed to attempt to convert the Ais to Christianity and there was continuing concern about establishing a relief station for shipwreck survivors on the coast, but little was done about either of these.[15]

The Spanish were increasingly occupied with the English advances on the northern frontier of Florida. As the English had moved down the Atlantic coast, the Spaniards had withdrawn to the south side of the St. Marys River but without recognizing the legitimacy of the English occupation of the Carolinas. As the English settlers extended their trade with the Indians into Apalachee territory, the Spaniards attacked South Carolina. The English then retaliated. Both sides committed sizable numbers of Indian allies whose ranks were severely reduced by the continuing conflict.

About the time Governor Zuñiga was directed to renew missionary activities among the Ais, Spain and England went to war in Europe. South Carolina Governor James Moore took this opportunity to attack St. Augustine. He destroyed the town but was unable to capture the stone fort. Apparently humiliated by his failure, Moore then marched with a handful of English soldiers and over a thousand Creek allies into Apalachee territory, laying waste to the extensive mission system which the Spanish had maintained across northern Florida. Most of the Indians who survived the devastation wrought by Moore's raid went with him when he returned to South Carolina, although a handful sought refuge near St. Augustine.

A diver brings up a clay jar from one of the Spanish shipwrecks along Brevard's coast. (Photo Brevard County Historical Commission Archives)

Moore's conquest of Apalachee, completed by 1704, essentially ended the Spanish mission system in Florida.

A kind of uneasy peace was restored between Spain and England in Europe by the 1713 Peace of Utrecht, but there was continual tension and occasional conflict in the New World.

When Georgia was established in the 1730s as a buffer between Spanish Florida and English South Carolina, it was only a question of time before hostile action resumed. The catalyst for war turned out to be English pirate activity against Spanish shipping in the Caribbean. English sailors complained to their government of cruel treatment from Spanish corsairs who were trying to suppress the attacks on their shipping. When a British sailor displayed what he claimed to be one of his ears allegedly cut off by the Spaniards, the so-called War of Jenkins Ear broke out in 1739. Hostilities lasted on and off between Spain and England until the Treaty of Paris in 1763. According to that treaty Spain ceded all of the Floridas to England. When Spain left the peninsula, the few remaining Ais still inhabiting the Atlantic coast followed the Spaniards to Cuba. Peninsular Florida was then left almost completely unpopulated, but that was not to last very long.[16]

Increasing pressure from the advancing line of white settlement along the Carolina frontier was causing several southeastern Indian groups to begin moving into Florida about the middle of the 18th century. The Alachuas and Oconees, for example, were already in the central Florida area around present-day Gainesville and Payne's Prairie while the Spanish still possessed Florida. By the time Spain relinquished the colony in 1763, the nucleus of the Seminoles was already in the peninsula. During the two decades that Britain controlled Florida, there were two important developments. The British attempted to settle the peninsula with European immigrants through several large grants of land. Lord Egmont received a grant in the Fernandina area. Francis Philip Fatio acquired land on the St. Johns where he established his New Switzerland. Rollestown was the site of a major settlement effort also on the St. Johns River. The best-known of these undertakings, however, was Andrew Turnbull's colony at New Smyrna. All of them eventually failed, but the concept of large land grants to potential developers who would bring in settlers was firmly implanted by the time the Spanish returned in 1784.

The other important development was English policy toward the Indians. Although both England and Spain had treated the Indians with equal degrees of cruelty in the early years of their struggle for the New World, the former had been far more successful in establishing trade with the native tribes. English trade with the Indians had often

The Panton, Leslie Company developed a lucrative fur and deer hide trade with the Seminoles who were extending their activity up the St. Johns River. (*Etching* © Vera Zimmerman, 1987)

been the cause of the confrontations between English South Carolina and Spanish Florida. Now in control of Florida, the English applied the same trading policies which had worked earlier in the Carolinas. Although Governor James Grant's official dealings with Cowkeeper and his band was a propitious beginning for good relations with the Florida Indians, it was Panton, Leslie and Company which provided the substance. William Panton was a South Carolinian who had long been engaged in the Indian trade. With John Leslie, he formed the Panton, Leslie Company to trade out of St. Augustine with Florida Indians. During the period of British occupation of the peninsular colony, the firm solidified its relations with the emerging Seminoles whose numbers were growing considerably. From a store on Lake George, Panton, Leslie developed a lucrative fur and deer hide trade with the Indians who were extending their activity farther and farther up the St. Johns valley.

When Florida was returned to Spain in 1784 after the American Revolution, Panton, Leslie was permitted to remain in Florida and continue its profitable trade, this time under Spanish hegemony. A beleaguered Spain, much diminished in wealth and power since the heady days of the great treasure fleets, attempted to manage the peninsula along the lines established by Britain rather than return to the exclusionary policies it had followed before 1763. In addition to Catholic Spaniards, people of various nationalities and religious preferences would be permitted to take up Florida land. Governor Vicente Manuel de Zéspedes had originally recommended opening up Spanish Florida to foreigners, he also wanted to exclude Americans on the ground that they would come in great numbers and eventually bring the United States flag with them. His successor in 1790 disagreed and Americans were included in the new generous land policy. It seems that Zéspedes had been correct. Hearing of the policy, Thomas Jefferson expressed his pleasure because it would provide a way of delivering to the United States peaceably, what might otherwise have cost a war. Between 1790 and 1804 hundreds of parcels of land were granted to Americans who soon comprised a majority of the inhabitants of the area between the St. Marys and St. Johns rivers. The Spaniards belatedly stopped permitting Americans to take up Florida lands, but it was already too late. A group of Americans, perhaps but not certainly, with the support of President James Madison, staged a revolution and declared the area between the St. Marys and the St. Johns an independent state in 1812. Although they were not successful at the time, their audacity demonstrated the inability of Spain to control Florida at a time when Napoleon had driven the legitimate Spanish monarch into exile.

During the next several years various filibusterers attempted to occupy portions of Spanish Florida and the United States eventually ran them out of the Fernandina area and occupied it, ostensibly until such time as the Spanish could take it back. The rationale for this action was the continued exile of the Spanish king. While that was happening the United States was engaged in the War of 1812 with England and General Andrew Jackson was fighting the Creek Indians in Alabama. After he destroyed the fighting capability of the Red Stick Creeks at the Battle of Horseshoe Bend, the survivors fled to Florida where they joined with Mikasukis already occupying the hilly region around what would soon become Tallahassee. Along with the other Indian bands already in Florida, they would soon be referred to as Seminoles.

The vacuum left in Florida by the absence of an effective Spanish government had other deleterious influences. Escaping black slaves from adjacent American plantations into Florida and frequent Indian raids out of Spanish Florida into Georgia were creating an intolerable border condition. Eventually, Andrew Jackson returned to active duty and marched into Florida in what became known as the First Seminole War in 1818. Having defeated the Indians, captured two Spanish garrisons, and hanged two British citizens, Jackson seemed to have quieted the border situation, but created an international uproar. There was discussion of punishing Jackson for his aggressive action, but Secretary of State John Quincy Adams interceded on his behalf.

Secretary Adams had been engaged in seemingly endless negotiations with the Spanish government over the future of Florida. Unable to get an answer from his Spanish counterpart, Adams suggested that the United States government's support of Jackson's foray into Spanish Florida would convey to the reluctant Spanish government the strong impression that it might expect

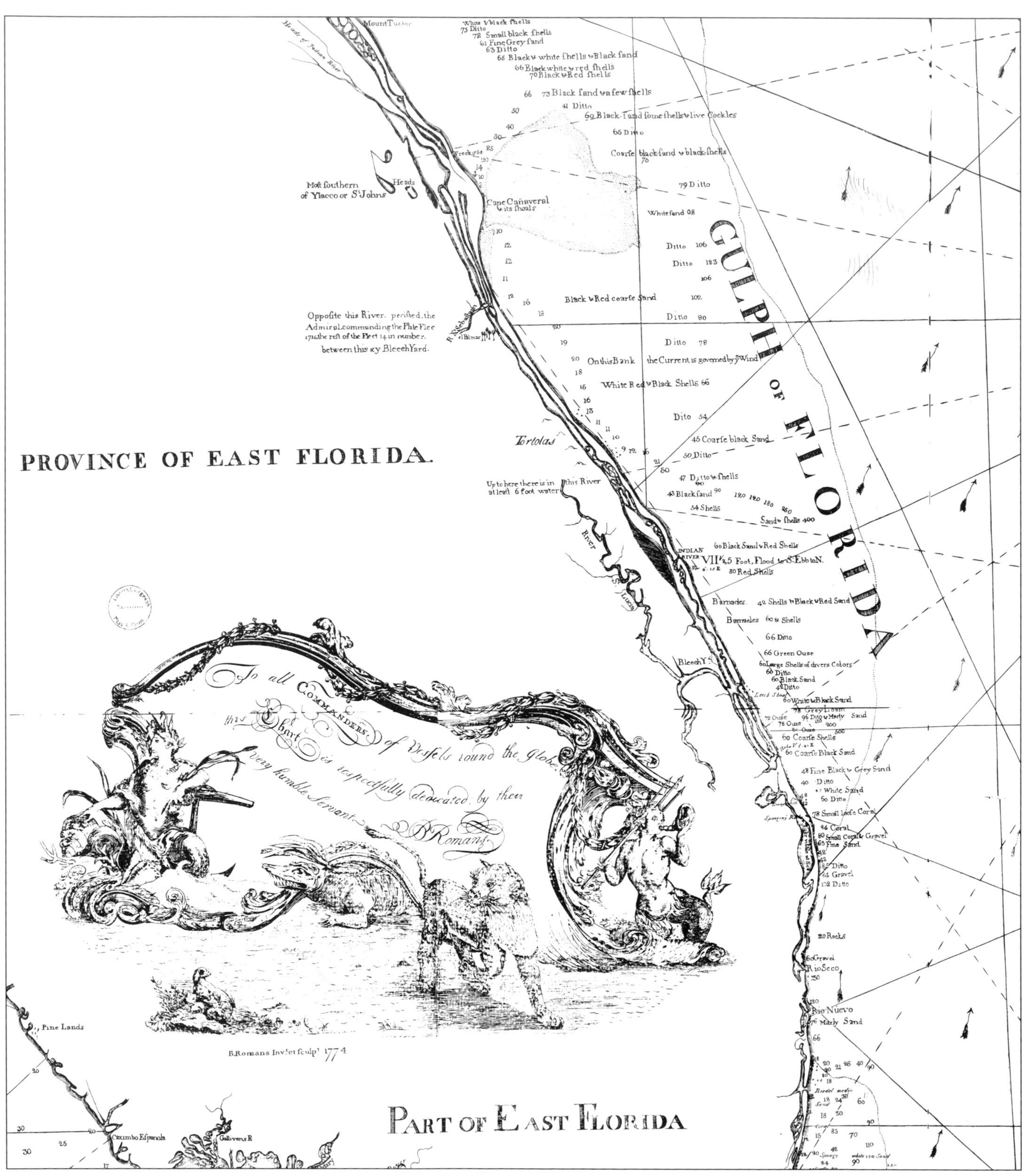

When the British took over Florida in 1763, Bernard Romans was sent to survey and map the area. (Library of Congress)

more of the same unless something was done to pacify the border situation. In other words, Adams seemed to be saying either govern Florida or get out of it.

The Spanish government, still reeling from the ravages of the Napoleonic occupation of its territory and dealing with incipient revolution at home, chose to cede Florida to the United States. During the negotiations which still took some time, the Spanish government was busily granting quantities of Florida land to numerous private parties. Apparently Spain was anxious to alienate as much territory from use by the United States government as was possible, while the United States was just as anxious to limit the land which was passing into private hands. An important provision of the treaty accordingly stated that only Spanish grants dated prior to 1818 would be recognized by the United States. The question of these Spanish grants filled the negotiating rooms and the courts for decades afterward, but in the end only seven of them affected Brevard County and five of those were in the territory which was transferred from Volusia County in 1879. The latter five were the Acosta, Fontaine, Garvin, Pouchard and Segui grants. In the southern part of present-day Brevard County near Sebastian was the Fleming grant. The largest and most troublesome one in terms of future litigation was the Delespine grant located just south of present-day Titusville.

The Adams-Onis Treaty was completed in 1819 and, after several delays, Florida was transferred to the United States in 1821.

End Notes

1. Bartolomé Barrientos, Pedro Menéndez de Aviles, Founder of Florida (Gainesville, 1965) p. 71; Solís de Merás, Gonzalo, Pedro Menéndez de Aviles (Gainesville, 1964) p.126.
2. Solís de Merás, p. 153.
3. Barrientos, p. 91; Daniel G. Brinton, Notes on the Florida Peninsula (Philadelphia, 1859) p. 154.
4. Barrientos, p. 91.
5. Verne de Chatelain, Defenses of Spanish Florida, 1565-1763, (Washington, 1914) p. 79.
6. Maynard J. Geiger, The Franciscan Conquest of Florida, 1573-1618 (Washington, 1937) p. 138; John R. Swanton, The Indians of the Southeastern United States (Washington, 1946) p. 84, 187.
7. Ibid., p. 139.
8. Ibid., p. 134.
9. Ibid., p. 138.
10. The Capitán Grande was apparently the Ais chief who held sway over the entire area and to whom the lesser chiefs of Sorruque and Oribia owed homage. Oribia was a village just slightly south of Sorruque (north of Cape Canaveral).
11. Geiger, pp. 177-78.
12. Ibid., p. 181.
13. Charles D. Higgs (trans.), The Derrotero of Alvaro Mexia, 1605, which appears as Appendix A to Irving Rouse, Survey of Indian River Archaeology, Florida (New Haven: Yale University Press, 1951).
14. Evangeline Walker Andrews and Charles McLean Andrews, Jonathan Dickinson's Journal (Stuart, Florida; Valentine Books, 1975), pp. 42-57.
15. Andres Gonzalez Barcia, Chronological History of the Continent of Florida (Gainesville: University of Florida Press, 1951), p. 351; Chatelain, p. 79.
16. Swanton, p. 84.

Page 20 Map: 1650 map of the North Atlantic Ocean. (Collection of Historic Urban Plans, Ithaca, New York)

MAP OF FLORIDA according to the Latest Authorities.

SCALE.
10 20 30 40 50 100 150 MILES.

Longitude West 7 from Washington.

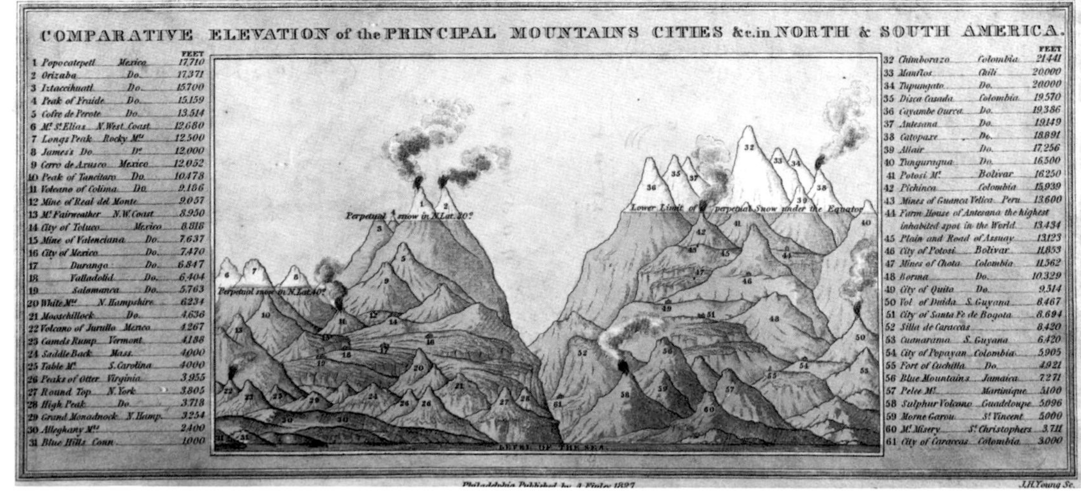
COMPARATIVE ELEVATION of the PRINCIPAL MOUNTAINS CITIES &c. in NORTH & SOUTH AMERICA.
FEET
1 Popocatepetl Mexico 17,710
2 Orizaba Do. 17,371
3 Iztaccihuatl Do. 15,700
4 Peak of Fraide Do. 15,159
5 Cofre de Perote Do. 13,514
6 Mt. St. Elias N. West Coast 12,680
7 Longs Peak Rocky Mts. 12,500
8 James's Do. Do. 12,000
9 Cerro de Axusco Mexico 12,052
10 Peak of Tancitaro Do. 10,478
11 Volcano of Colima Do. 9,186
12 Mine of Real del Monte 9,057
13 Mt. Fairweather N.W. Coast 8,950
14 City of Toluco Mexico 8,818
15 Mine of Valenciana Do. 7,637
16 City of Mexico Do. 7,470
17 Durango Do. 6,847
18 Valladolid Do. 6,404
19 Salamanca Do. 5,763
20 White Mts. N. Hampshire 6234
21 Mooschillock Do. 4,636
22 Volcano of Jurullo Mexico 4,267
23 Camels Rump Vermont 4,188
24 Saddle Back Mass. 4000
25 Table Mt. S. Carolina 4000
26 Peaks of Otter Virginia 3,955
27 Round Top N. York 3,805
28 High Peak Do. 3,718
29 Grand Monadnock N. Hamp. 3,254
30 Alleghany Mts. 2400
31 Blue Hills Conn. 1000
Perpetual snow in N. Lat. 40°
Perpetual snow in N. Lat. 20°
Lower Limit of perpetual Snow under the Equator
LEVEL OF THE SEA
FEET
32 Chimborazo Colombia 21441
33 Manflos Chili 20,000
34 Tupungato Do. 20,000
35 Disca Casada Colombia 19,570
36 Cayambe Ourca Do. 19,386
37 Antesana Do. 19,149
38 Catopaxe Do. 18,891
39 Altair Do. 17,256
40 Tunguragua Do. 16,500
41 Potosi Mt. Bolivar 16,250
42 Pichinca Colombia 15,939
43 Mines of Guanca Velica Peru 13,600
44 Farm House of Antesana the highest inhabited spot in the World 13,434
45 Plain and Road of Assuay 13,123
46 City of Potosi Bolivar 11,853
47 Mines of Chota Colombia 11,562
48 Borma Do. 10,329
49 City of Quito Do. 9,514
50 Vol. of Duida S. Guyana 8,467
51 City of Santa Fe de Bogota 8,694
52 Silla de Caraccas 8,420
53 Cuanarama S. Guyana 6,420
54 City of Popayan Colombia 5,905
55 Fort of Cuchilla Do. 4,921
56 Blue Mountains Jamaica 7,271
57 Pelee Mt. Martinique 5100
58 Sulphur Volcano Guadeloupe 5,096
59 Morne Garou St. Vincent 5000
60 Mt. Misery St. Christophers 3,711
61 City of Caraccas Colombia 3,000

Philadelphia Published by A. Finley 1827.
J.H. Young Sc.

3
Territorial Florida and the Second Seminole War

Having migrated over many years in the face of advancing white settlement, many Indian groups had come to Florida as a safe haven. Now, as Seminoles, they found themselves confronted with just the problem they had attempted to escape.

Capt. John Rogers Vinton of the Third Artillery sketched Fort Taylor which was built atop an Indian mound on Lake Winder.

After a stormy transitional period during which Territorial Governor Andrew Jackson threw the outgoing Spanish governor in jail, Florida finally became part of the United States and a territorial government was established in 1822. Two counties, Escambia and St. Johns were created. The latter encompassed the entire Florida peninsula and, of course, the territory from which Brevard County would ultimately be carved. Jackson soon left Florida never to return. Richard Keith Call was appointed to work out the question of the Spanish land grants, an undertaking which would require many years. Several were confirmed in the territory which eventually became Brevard County. The territorial government busied itself with the many logistical matters confronting it, not the least of which was the question of where to locate the seat of government. With both St. Augustine and Pensacola jealously claiming that distinction and neither being suitably located in a day when transportation was so difficult, it was decided that the more centrally located Tallahassee would become the capital of territorial Florida. That was a reasonable compromise between the two distant settlements but it immediately focused attention on another and more serious problem.

When they fled Alabama after the Battle of Horseshoe Bend, some of the surviving Red Stick Creeks had settled in the area around Tallahassee where they became neighbors of the Mikasukis who had suffered Andrew Jackson's wrath in 1818. Neither of these groups looked with much favor upon the decision to establish the Florida territorial capital in the red hills of Middle Florida. For that matter, all of the Indians then living in Florida were extremely anxious about their situation. Having migrated over many years in the face of advancing white settlement, they had come to Florida as a safe haven. Now they found themselves confronted with just the problem they had tried to escape. Whether they were Alachuas and Oconees living in the peninsula, Mikasukis and Red Stick Creeks living in Middle Florida, or Lower Creeks inhabiting the Apalachicola River valley, they were all becoming Seminoles whose most common bond was antipathy toward the whites who were continually taking their lands from them. The Adams-Onis Treaty provided that the inhabitants of the territory would become citizens of the United States, but the wary Seminoles had little faith in that part of the agreement. Their lack of faith was well-advised, for the officials of the United States had no intention of honoring that part of the treaty.

For several months, Indian leaders had been trying to find out what they could expect. Repeated delegations to St. Augustine had brought no information. The United States government was itself undecided and was discussing two possibilities. Some individuals believed that the simplest solution was to concentrate the Indians on a reservation in Florida – that part which was not then desired by whites – while others were in favor of total removal to territory in the west which had been set aside for that purpose. The thousands of white settlers then rushing into Florida strongly favored the latter solution.[1]

It was decided that the Seminoles should be offered a reservation in the Florida peninsula where they would be free of association with white settlers or, much more important, where white settlers would not come into contact with them. William P. Duval, who had succeeded Andrew Jackson as territorial governor, Bernard Segui of St. Augustine, and James Gadsden, who had campaigned with Jackson during the First Seminole War before settling on a plantation near Tallahassee, were named commissioners to complete a treaty with the Seminoles. Gadsden was in agreement with General Jackson about how to handle Indians while Duval was considerably more sympathetic with them. But all three commissioners were determined to effect a treaty which would remove the Seminoles from their present habitats in northern Florida. In 1823 the commissioners met a few miles south of St. Augustine with a number of Seminole chiefs and completed the Treaty of Moultrie Creek. According to it, the Indians accepted a reservation comprising about four million acres in the Florida peninsula. It was to extend no closer than fifteen miles toward the Gulf and about 20 miles from the Atlantic. The chiefs agreed to permit United States citizens to pass through their reservation on official business and the commissioners agreed in turn to protect the Seminoles from interference by other parties. The United States would provide farm implements and livestock worth $6,000, furnish annuities of $5,000 annually for 20 years, and assist in the migration. Rations for one year in the new location would be provided. There were other minor provisions which were to run for a 20 year period.

The migration began in 1824 but was never fully carried out. Some Indians were not required to move while others who were expected to never did. A number of them actually went to the reservation and shortly left because it proved to be an unsatisfactory place for them to sustain themselves. Bands returned to Middle Florida where they roamed among the white settlers. There was some friendly trade, but confrontations were frequent. Individuals from both sides acted violently. The chiefs tried to cooperate with white officials but justice was invariably one-sided. Governor Duval said that he was ashamed to have to urge the Indians to give up their property when he had no power to see that their rights were observed. "To tell one of these people that he must go to law for his property, in our courts, with a white man is only adding insult to injury," the frustrated governor complained.

When Andrew Jackson acceded to the presidency in 1829, Floridians and others were demanding removal of the Indians from the southeast to the trans-Mississippi territory which had been set aside for them. Although the Seminoles interpreted the Fort Moultrie Treaty to mean they had the right to remain in Florida for twenty years, many of them were facing starvation by the early 1830s when the United States government reopened negotiations concerning their rapid departure. At a meeting with James Gadsden, some of the chiefs agreed to go to Indian Territory at least to see for themselves whether or not it was suitable for their relocation. At Fort Gibson in that territory, those chiefs signed an agreement to move. Whether they were coerced into the decision is a matter for speculation, but upon their return to Florida they were immediately and furiously denounced by a group of younger Seminoles led by Osceola and Coacoochee. All of the signers except one repudiated the treaty and the lone holdout was assassinated while leading his band toward Fort Brooke on Tampa Bay where ships were waiting to take him west.

General Wiley Thompson, who had recently received the dubious commission as agent in charge of the Seminole removal, inherited the incendiary relocation problem. At his Fort King headquarters near Ocala, eight chiefs agreed to take their people west, but Micanopy, Jumper, Alligator, Black Dirt, and Sam Jones (Arpeika), adamantly refused. Angered by their defiance, Thompson arrogantly removed the chiefs from their positions as heads of their respective bands. Realizing the explosive nature of such an insult to the proud Indians, Washington officials overruled Thompson who then agreed to a second meeting with the Seminole leaders. This time he quarreled with the defiant Osceola and lodged him in jail. Having thus demeaned the young Indian, Thompson then made the fatal mistake of setting him free after a brief incarceration. During several tense weeks, United States authorities continued planning for removal while the Indians generally decided to resist. On December 28, 1835, Thompson took his customary stroll outside the fort late in the evening. He and a companion were cut down by a volley fired from ambush by Osceola and a small band of allies. Major Francis Dade and his column of troops on their way from Fort Brooke to Fort King were ambushed on the same day. The column was annihilated by warriors led by Micanopy, Alligator, and Coacoochee. Thus began the Second Seminole War, setting in motion a series of events which led to the first white settlements along the Indian River in what was to become Brevard County.

The outbreak of hostilities followed directly from the assassination of Wiley Thompson and the Dade Massacre, but serious depredations of the sugar plantations in Mosquito County had already occurred three days earlier. Despite the efforts of General Joseph Hernandez, the militia commander of the St. Augustine area, five plantations east of the St. Johns River were laid waste on Christmas Day, 1835, and one more the following day. Sixteen more were destroyed in January 1836. On January 17, 1836 the St. Augustine Guards, commanded by Major Benjamin A. Putnam, and a company from Mosquito Inlet commanded by Douglas Dummett and soon to become known as the "Mosquito Roarers," marched to Dunlawton on the Halifax River to salvage some supplies from the fire-ravaged Anderson plantation. A sharp fire fight ensued when the volunteers encountered about 120 Indians. When four of their number were killed and 13 more were wounded, these Floridians learned quickly of the seriousness of the Seminole uprising.[2]

The war effectively depopulated Mosquito County. Formed in 1828, it had experienced a modest growth until 1835 when first a severe freeze occurred and then the Indian uprising began. In 1838, there was so little activity in Mosquito County that the clerk of St. Johns County was designated as the keeper of the county's records.[3]

Mosquito did have its own officials by 1840. Henry A. Crane was county clerk, Douglas Dummett was the judge, and John C. Houston of Enterprise was sheriff, but their duties must certainly have been few. The county recorded only three votes in the elections of that year.[4]

While inhabitants of other outlying areas followed the example of their Mosquito County neighbors and fled to what they considered safer places, both the territorial militia and the United States army prepared to contain the Seminoles. Both were initially determined to remove the Indians entirely from Florida soil. Although the United States army subsequently ameliorated that resolve, Florida citizens never relented. It was to be a huge undertaking. Before it was over, a third of the generals then on active duty with the United States army would have served in Florida at one time or another and volunteers from many states, including distant Missouri, would have participated.

With authority to call upon the governors of South Carolina, Georgia, Alabama, and Florida for as many citizen soldiers as he deemed necessary, Brevet Major General Winfield Scott became the first to direct the Florida war. Despite a well-conceived, but poorly executed campaign in 1836 and many small skirmishes along the way, Scott failed to come to grips with the Seminoles. He was briefly superseded as commander by Territorial Governor Richard Keith Call who was no more successful. It was to be General Thomas S. Jesup who eventually brought the war to the St. Johns and Indian River areas. After exhausting considerable energy in attempting to get the principal chiefs to agree to peaceful removal and receiving calumny from an outraged nation by capturing Osceola and Coacoochee while they were under a flag of truce, General Jesup began an elaborate campaign in the fall of 1837. Estimating that no more than 200 Indians remained north of Lake Monroe, he intended to converge his forces on the Seminoles south of that point.

With about 4,000 effectives, the general launched his campaign. Colonel Zachary Taylor was to march between the Kissimmee River and Pease Creek. It was during this campaign that Taylor built Fort Gardner and Fort Bassinger in the Kissimmee Valley. Lieutenant Levi N. Powell of the United States Navy was to take a mixed force of sailors, artillerymen, and volunteers into the Everglades, and Colonel Persifor F. Smith was to march eastward from the mouth of the Caloosatchee. The main force was itself divided into four columns. The one commanded by General Joseph Hernandez was to move by steamer to Mosquito Lagoon and await instructions. He subsequently built Camp Hernandez on the mainland near the headwaters of Indian River before marching into the St. Lucie and Okeechobee areas. Colonel John Warren with a combined force of militiamen and regular dragoons was to move southward between the Atlantic and the St. Johns. General Abraham Eustis was to take his force up the St. Johns by boat. A fourth column was to move between the Oklawaha and the St. Johns and eventually join Eustis at Fort Mellon for the campaign southward.[5]

Dr. Jacob Rhette Motte, a surgeon with a naval force

Brig. Gen. Joseph M. Hernandez (1792–1857) was a native of St. Augustine and the first congressional delegate from the Territory of Florida. In December of 1837, he and his troops encamped near Titusville at Camp Hernandez. ▶
(Drawing © Vera Zimmerman, 1993)

©1993
Zimmerman

Fort Ann
at the location of the Old Haulover.....
Yolanda Fiorentino Schofield
©...anno domini 1993......

Dr. Jacob Motte writes: "Lt. Irwin of the 1st Art. was ordered to superintend the erection of some kind of fortification at the haulover, capable of being defended by one company, which were to remain as a guard when we had left." Whether Fort Ann was earthwork or pine pickets Motte does not say, but he does mention that it was named by Lt. Irwin "after the prettiest girl in Pennsylvania." (Drawing © Yolanda Schofield, 1993)

assigned to proceed to the Haulover between Mosquito and Indian River to meet General Hernandez, left an account of his experiences in the Florida war. According to Motte, the sailors were obliged to drag their boats across the Haulover and into the Indian River just as the natives had been doing for centuries. A detachment was left at Fort Ann while the main body joined General Hernandez on a southward march beginning in early December 1837. While at the Haulover, Motte's expedition was overtaken by Lieutenant Powell's combined force on its way to the Everglades, but with orders to explore the Indian River on the way. Motte was amused by Powell's troops as they spent several days moving their vessels across the Haulover. "When drawn up in line," he wrote, "they presented a curious blending of black and white, like the keys of a piano forte; many of the sailors being colored men. There was also an odd alternation of tarpaulin hats and pea-jackets, with forage caps and soldiers trip round-abouts; soldiers and sailors, white men and black, being all thrown into the ranks indiscriminately, a beautiful specimen of mosaic, thus modifying sailor's ardour with soldier's discipline." The route used by Hernandez was at the site of what became known as the Old Haulover. The New Haulover was subsequently laid out by the

United States Coast Survey in 1887. The canal completed there in 1888 substantially improved navigation along the East Coast.[6]

While Hernandez's column marched southward on the mainland, the naval force moved along the Indian River, arriving at the inlet on December 31. Four miles south of the inlet on a low bluff, a blockhouse was erected and named Fort Pierce, after Lieutenant Colonel Benjamin K. Pierce, one of the few regular army officers who managed to win the esteem of the Florida citizenry. When General Hernandez arrived a few days later, Colonel Pierce was almost immediately dispatched with a force to continue on along the Indian River. By that time, Lieutenant Powell was also moving along the coast on his way into the Everglades. The trail which General Hernandez and his troops hacked through the wilderness southward from the Haulover to the St. Lucie area appeared on subsequent Brevard County maps as the Hernandez-Capron Trail and was used by cattlemen to move their herds for years.[7]

In the meantime, Colonel Zachary Taylor had been busy with his own assignment. Having constructed Fort Gardner on the Kissimmee River, he set out on December 19 with 1,032 men to search for the Indians. As he marched southward several bands came in and surrendered. One of them was Jumper and his 63 followers. Taylor built Fort Bassinger on December 21 as a place to store his artillery and heavy equipment. With rations for only five days he set out again. A single Indian was captured who told Taylor where the main force was dug in for battle. The captive was probably a plant since the Indians had prepared well. They were in a hammock with nearly a half mile of sawgrass swamp in front of them. Mud and water were about three feet deep and the sawgrass was above the soldiers' heads. The Indians had cut the grass in front of them so as better to see the attacking soldiers. Sam Jones, an old Mikasuki chief, was in command of about 200 warriors. Alligator led 120 more. Coacoochee, having just made his famous escape from Fort Marion, was dug in with about 80 of his people, still smoldering with anger at General Jesup's treachery. With such a favorable advantage, the Indians chose to stand and fight even though they were outnumbered more than two to one.

Never one to evade an issue, Colonel Taylor ordered a frontal assault and the Battle of Lake Okeechobee, probably the largest and bloodiest single battle of the Second Seminole War, ensued on Christmas Day, 1837. Taylor was victorious but at a heavy cost. The Seminoles lost 11 dead and 14 wounded while Taylor's casualties numbered 26 killed and 112 wounded. The Indians retreated toward the big lake without pursuit for Taylor had his work cut out in evacuating his casualties. His battle-weary column started back toward Fort Bassinger on December 27, and arrived at Fort Gardner the next day. He had with him 180 Indian captives, 600 head of Indian cattle and about 100 of their horses.[8]

Convinced more than ever that the bulk of the Indian population was concentrated in the area south and east of Lake Monroe, General Jesup prepared to press his campaign in that region. On the same day that Taylor was fighting at Okeechobee, Jesup's forces built Fort Christmas about 80 miles due north of the battle site. It was intended to be a temporary replacement for Fort Mellon as a supply depot until better arrangements could be made. Jesup had intended to move his main supply depot to Indian River Inlet and even ordered a road cut from that point to the headwaters of the St. Johns. But, when the water at the inlet proved too shallow for the available vessels, he was obliged to retain the St. Johns River supply line.[9]

Marching south from Fort Christmas with his main force, Jesup soon understood the enormity of a campaign in Florida even in the winter. It was 103 degrees when he left Fort Christmas and, as John Mahon summed it up, "heat, sawgrass, and insects made living itself a hopeless toil."[10] Fort Taylor was built on Lake Winder and Camp Lloyd (also known as Fort Floyd) was thrown up about 30 miles west of Fort Pierce. Leaving part of his troops there to await the arrival of General Abraham Eustis who was marching south from Fort Mellon, Jesup went on to Fort Pierce, arriving on January 14.[11] While the general waited at Fort Pierce, gathering oysters on the one hand and information about the difficulty of the terrain he was about to face on the other, Lieutenant Powell was engaging the enemy.

After several running skirmishes, Powell's force encountered its fiercest opposition on January 15, 1838. Having captured an Indian woman near Jupiter and forcing her to act as a guide, Powell's troops were suddenly met with heavy gunfire. Forced to retreat toward their boats, the soldiers and sailors fought a costly rear-guard action. Five men were killed and 15 wounded. Among the slain was Dr. Frederick Leitner, a naval surgeon who had been a classmate of Dr. Motte's.[12] The so-called Battle of Jupiter Inlet had been a costly one for Lieutenant Powell's combined army and naval force.

With the erection of Fort Floyd, Jesup had completed a line of forts across the peninsula from Tampa Bay to Fort Pierce. This string of forts had long been advocated by various commanders and would subsequently become the line of separation between the Seminoles who remained in Florida and the advancing white settlers. In early 1838, however, that was still far in the future.

Having been joined by both Colonel Taylor's column and General Abraham Eustis' force, Jesup marched south of the St. Lucie River and soon found that the intelligence he had gathered about the countryside was correct. Without either roads or identifiable trails, his army moved forward in three columns. With the wagon train in the center and a line of troops on each side, men and animals struggled through swampy ground. Sawgrass cut the horses' legs, shredded clothing and literally demolished shoes. The natural environment seemed to be challenge enough, but the army was there to seek out the enemy. On January 24, an Indian force was reported to be dug in ahead and prepared for a fight at a place not far from where Lieutenant Powell had recently fought. The Battle of Loxsahatchee was soon underway. Perhaps 300 Indians fought a sharp, brief engagement before slipping away into the wilderness. Seven soldiers were killed and 31 were wounded. The Indian casualties were unknown. By that time more than 400 soldiers in Jesup's command were completely without shoes because of the sharp sawgrass. The general was obliged to halt his army at Fort Jupiter and await the arrival of new shoes.

By this time, Jesup had come to agree with most of his military colleagues who questioned the necessity of removing the Indians at such great cost from an area which was neither worth the price nor then needed for white settlement. Despite his knowledge that Floridians and their representatives in Washington were adamantly insisting that every Seminole be removed from the territory, he decided to seek a compromise. On February 8, he conferred with two important chiefs, promising to inquire of the United States government whether they might remain in Florida. Pending an answer, the Indians agreed to camp near Jesup's headquarters.[13]

After more than a month of waiting, Jesup received his answer on March 17. His request was categorically denied. The dejected general called a council to announce the bad news. The Indians seemed to have sensed the answer for none of them even bothered to attend. In a manner characteristic of him, Jesup then seized the opportunity to prevent the Indians from returning to the field. Colonel David E. Twiggs was ordered to disarm and arrest all those who had been voluntarily encamped awaiting the answer from Washington. Over 500 Indians, including 150 warriors, were thus apprehended. This was the largest number the army had captured in a single group since the outbreak of hostilities.[14]

The 1839 Mackay map was compiled by order of Brig. Gen. Zachary Taylor and shows the locations of Seminole War forts. (Courtesy Jim Ball) ▶

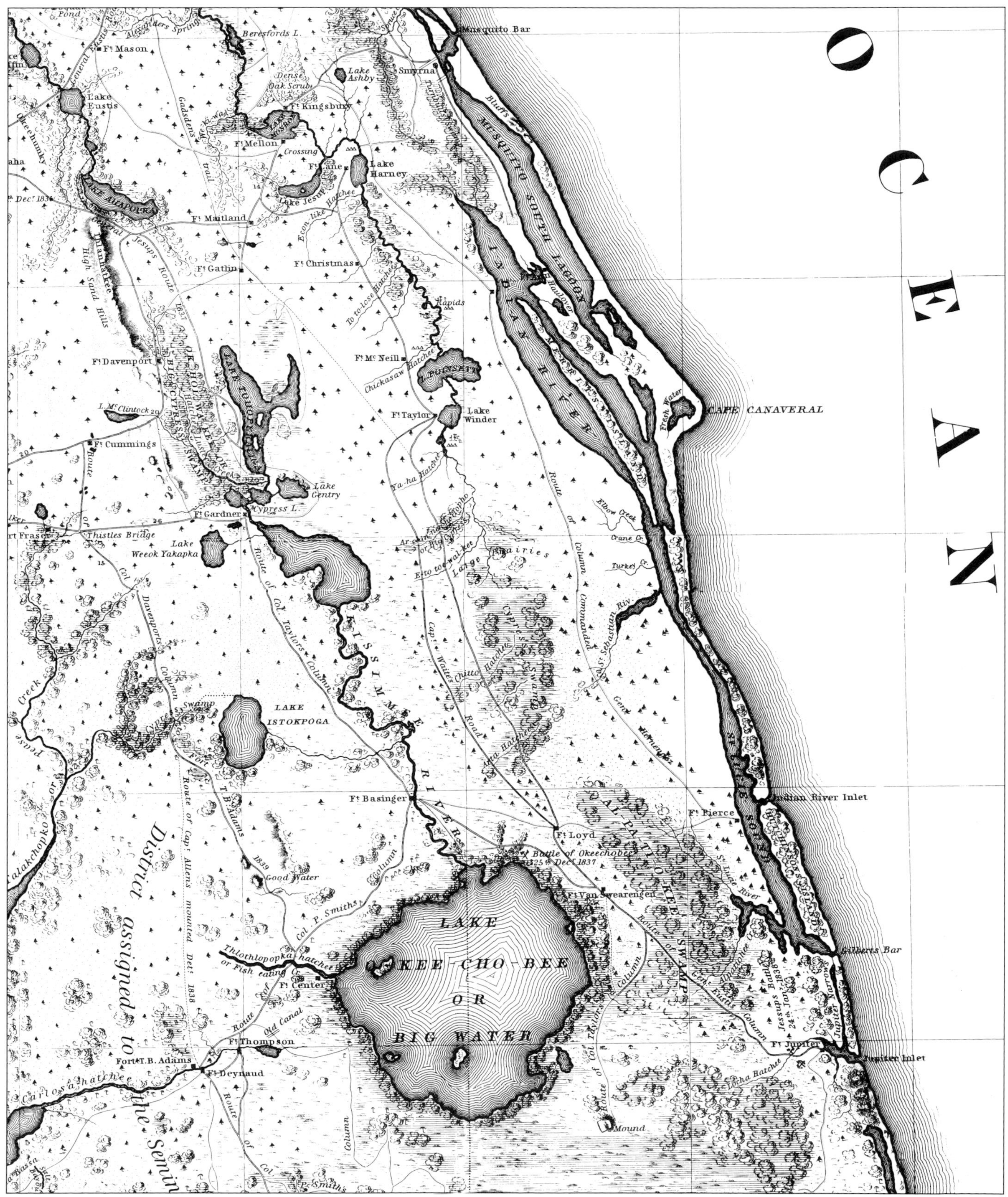
OCEAN
Mosquito Bar
Beresfords L.
Ft Mason
Lake Eustis
Lake Ashby
Smyrna
Dense Oak Scrub
Ft Kingsbury
Ft Mellon
Crossing
Ft Lane
Lake Harney
Lake Jesup
Ft Maitland
LAKE AHAPOPKA
MUSQUITO SOUTH LAGOON
INDIAN RIVER
Ft Gatlin
Ft Christmas
Rapids
Haulover
Ft Davenport
Ft Mc Neill
Chickasaw Hatchee
Ft Taylor
Lake Winder
Fresh Water
CAPE CANAVERAL
L. Mc Clintock
Ft Cummings
LAKE TOHOPKALIGA
Lake Gentry
Cypress L.
Ft Gardner
Thistles Bridge
Lake Weeok Yakapka
Elbow Creek
Crane Cr.
Turkey Cr.
Large Prairies
St Sebastian Riv.
KISSIMMEE RIVER
LAKE ISTOKPOGA
Cypress Swamp
Ft Basinger
Indian River Inlet
Ft Pierce
Ft Loyd
Battle of Okeechobee 25th Decr 1837
District assigned to the Semin
Good Water
Ft Van Swearengen
St Lucie River
LAKE OKEE-CHO-BEE OR BIG WATER
Thlothlopopka hatchee or Fish eating Cr.
Ft Center
Old Canal
Gilberts Bar
Ft Thompson
Fort T.B. Adams
Ft Deynaud
Ft Jupiter
Jupiter Inlet
Carlos a hatchee
Mound

The war resumed over a wide area as several bands eluded Jesup's army and moved back toward Middle Florida. But the Indians were now destitute. Having been on the run too frequently either to tend their cattle or cultivate crops, most of them were facing starvation. As they had awaited the answer from Washington, several of Jesup's soldiers had observed Indian women picking up single kernels of corn which the army horses had dropped while they were eating. Realizing the futility of their situation, Alligator and 88 followers walked into Fort Bassinger and surrendered. Small bands followed suit from time to time during the following months. When Jesup left Florida in May 1838 to be succeeded by Zachary Taylor, he reported that 2,900 Indians had been captured and about 100 killed during his campaign. But, it was not a proud situation. Just before he left his command, he had requisitioned bloodhounds to ferret out the remaining Seminoles. Happily for the Indians, the idea failed. The bloodhounds, trained to run down blacks, would not follow Indian sign. Nor were relations between Floridians and regular army soldiers very wholesome. At a banquet in Tallahassee an irate Floridian toasted the army: "The Army of the United States, paralyzed and powerless. Too feeble to chastise one tribe of wandering savages. How hath the mighty fallen." At about the same time Andrew Jackson had expressed corresponding disdain for Floridians and said, "Let the damned cowards defend their country."

Into this happy situation stepped Zachary Taylor, recently promoted to general after his victory at Okeechobee. Like his predecessors, Taylor insisted that the war could be brought to a close only by allowing the Indians to remain in Florida. Over the protests of most Floridians, General Alexander Macomb came from Washington with a compromise offer for the Seminoles. After conferring with several Indian leaders at Fort King, General Macomb issued an order on May 20, 1839, which declared the war ended. Two of the Indian leaders whom Macomb believed to speak with authority agreed to withdraw south of Pease Creek by July 15, 1839, and remain there pending final arrangements.[15] From his stronghold near Fort Lauderdale, Sam Jones agreed to abide by the proposal by remaining where he was. Elsewhere, however, hostilities continued through 1839 and "final arrangements" were not soon forthcoming.

General Taylor was eventually granted permission to leave Florida in April 1840 and he was replaced by General Walker K. Armistead who was in turn succeeded the following year by Colonel William J. Worth. In the meantime, more Indians surrendered and went to Fort Brooke for removal to the west. Even Coacoochee surrendered to Lieutenant William Tecumseh Sherman.

Colonel Worth first declared his determination to bring in all the remaining Indians, but he had a difficult task. Sam Jones continued to elude his pursuers. A combined column of soldiers and sailors led by Lieutenant John T. McLaughlin suffered exhaustion merely from the difficulty of marching up the Caloosatchee toward Lake Okeechobee on to the Atlantic Ocean and it encountered no Indians at all. Major Thomas Childs was surprised to find cultivated fields along the Indian River which were so extensive that it took 80 men two days to destroy them.[16] It was a slow and difficult undertaking but the army seemed to be slowly gaining some ground. In February 1842, Colonel Worth reported that he had just shipped 230 Indians west. He estimated that only about that many more remained in the peninsula, but he also admitted that they could not be removed by force.

Worth's suggestion that the remaining fugitives be allowed to remain where they were once again evoked the wrath of Floridians. The citizens of St. Johns County, for example, memorialized Congress in fervent opposition. It would be a calamity, they declared, to cede to the Indians "the most desirable portion of East Florida." Such an act would extinguish the hope of those who had looked forward to the restoration of peace, and a return to their homes. They could "feel no security in the vicinity of those frantic and merciless savages." The memorialists added that "the country which it is intended to grant to the Indians comprises the finest portion of East Florida."[17] It is doubtful that Lieutenant McLaughlin and the others who had struggled through the difficult terrain of southern Florida would have agreed with the enthusiasts of St. Augustine, but it apparently did not matter at the time. The national government had decided. On May 10, 1842, Colonel Worth was told to end hostilities against the Seminoles as soon as possible.

An order was issued on August 11, 1842, delineating a reservation for the Indians, although it was so worded as to imply only a temporary arrangement. "By arrangement with the few Indians remaining in the south portion of Florida between whom and the whites hostilities no longer exist, they are permitted for a while to plant and hunt on the lands included within the following boundaries," the order began. The boundaries were the same as earlier proposed by General Macomb. Beginning at the mouth of Pease Creek the line ran up to the head of Lake Istokpoga, then eastward to the stream which emptied from the lake into the Kissimmee River. It continued down the left bank of the Kissimmee to Lake Okeechobee, through the lake and the Everglades to the Shark River, and westward to the Gulf.[18] It may be noted that the reservation boundary along the Kissimmee River and into Lake Okeechobee coincides with the southwestern boundary of Brevard County as it was established in 1855.

The United States army had been unable to remove all the Seminoles from Florida, but it had reduced their number to a handful of refugees residing deep in the Everglades, a territory which, despite the claims of the St. Johns County memorialists, white men still found undesirable. Floridians continued to clamor for the removal of every last Indian, but the United States government had had enough.

A new method of dealing with the Indians and, perhaps, of placating some of the Floridians was enunciated in an act of Congress passed in August, 1842, about the same time the order was issued establishing the Indian reservation. The Armed Occupation Act was not actually original, since such a plan had been advocated at least as early as 1838 by then Territorial Governor Richard Keith Call. But, it was now national policy. The legislation provided that any head of a family could acquire title to a quarter section of land if certain conditions were met. Those conditions were that the land had to be south of a line running just north of Palatka, that the recipient must live on the land for five years, that he must build a house and clear at least five acres, and that he must settle at least two miles from the nearest military post. The idea was to settle the land with citizens who would then presumably have an interest in defending it. It was this law which stimulated the first substantial white settlement of the Brevard County area.

End Notes

1. John K. Mahon, History of the Second Seminole War, 1835-1842, (Gainesville, 1967) pp. 29-34.
2. John Lee Williams, The Territory of Florida (Gainesville, 1962), p. 224; Mahon, pp. 137-138.
3. Titusville Star Advocate, November 23, 1940.
4. Florida State Archives, Record Group 156, Series 259, Mosquito County Officials, 1841.
5. John T. Sprague, Origins, Progress and Conclusion of the Florida War (Gainesville, 1964) p. 190; Mahon, pp. 219-220.
6. Motte, p. 168; John W. Griffin and James J. Miller, "Cultural Resource Survey of the Merritt Island Wildlife Refuge," August 1, 1978. It should also be noted that Native Americans as well as Spanish soldiers had sometimes made the haulover from Mosquito Lagoon to the Banana River.
7. Sprague, p. 190; Motte, p. 176.
8. Mahon, pp. 227-229.
9. Ibid., pp. 231-232.
10. Ibid., p. 232.
11. Motte, pp. 178-179.
12. Mahon, p. 232.
13. Sprague, p. 192; Mahon, p. 235.
14. Mahon, p. 237.
15. Ibid., p. 257.
16. Clarence E. Carter, Territorial Papers of the United States, 1839-1845, Volume 26 (Washington, 1960) p. 386, Mahon, p. 304.
17. Carter, pp. 265-266
18. Ibid., p.1081; Mahon, pp. 315-316.

Page 32 Map: 1827 Finley map showing "Musquito County" (Florida State Archives)

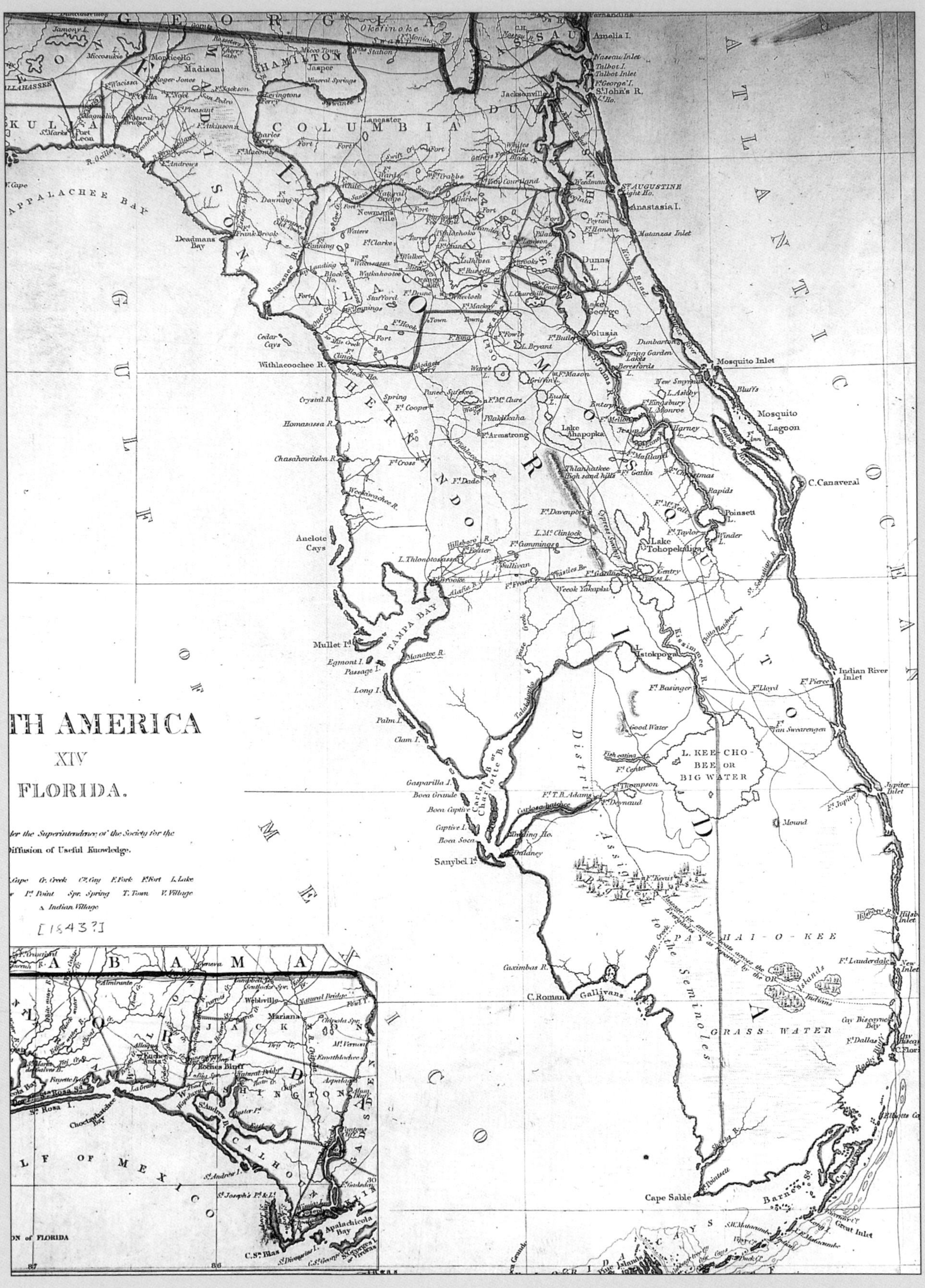

TH AMERICA
XIV
FLORIDA.
der the Superintendence of the Society for the
Diffusion of Useful Knowledge.
Cape Cr. Creek Cy. Cay F. Fork Ft. Fort L. Lake
Pt. Point Spr. Spring T. Town V. Village
Indian Village
[1843?]
GEORGIA
ALABAMA
ATLANTIC OCEAN
GULF OF MEXICO
APPALACHEE BAY
COLUMBIA
HAMILTON
MADISON
Okefinoke
Fernandina
Amelia I.
Nassau Inlet
Talbot I.
Talbot Inlet
St. John's R.
Jacksonville
Monticello
Madison
Jasper
Mineral Springs
Lancaster
St. Marks
Port Leon
St. AUGUSTINE
Light Ho.
Anastasia I.
Matanzas Inlet
Deadmans Bay
Suwanee R.
Newnansville
Dunns L.
Lake George
Volusia
Cedar Cays
Withlacoochee R.
Dunbarton
Spring Garden Lakes
Mosquito Inlet
New Smyrna
L. Ashby
Mosquito Lagoon
Crystal R.
Homasassa R.
Chasahowitska R.
Lake Ahapopka
Harney L.
Ft. Mellon
Ft. Armstrong
Ft. Cross
Ft. Dade
Ft. Gatlin
Ft. Davenport
L. Mc. Clintock
C. Canaveral
Poinsett L.
Winder L.
Anclote Cays
Lake Tohopekaliga
L. Thlonotosassa
TAMPA BAY
Mullet Id.
Egmont I.
Passage I.
Long I.
Palm I.
Clam I.
Manatee R.
L. Istokpoga
Ft. Basinger
Ft. Lloyd
Ft. Pierce
Indian River Inlet
Good Water
L. KEE-CHO-BEE OR BIG WATER
Ft. Van Swearengen
Jupiter Inlet
Ft. Jupiter
Mound
Gasparilla I.
Boca Grande
Boca Captive
Captive I.
Boca Soca
Sanybel Id.
Ft. Dulaney
Charlotte H.
District Assigned to the Seminoles
PAY HAI-O-KEE
GRASS WATER
Ft. Lauderdale
New Inlet
Caximbas R.
C. Romano
Gallivans B.
Ft. Dallas
Cape Sable
Great Inlet
Webbville
Mariana
Mt. Vernon
Roches Bluff
St. Rosa I.
Choctawhatchee Bay
St. Andrew I.
St. Joseph's Pt. & I.
Apalachicola Bay
C. St. Blas
ON of FLORIDA

4
The Armed Occupation Colony and More Indians

Under the Armed Occupation Act, one hundred twelve patents were issued for locations along the Indian River between Merritt Island and Lake Worth. These settlements became known as the Indian River Colony.

The houses of the early settlers were mostly constructed of wood and palmetto, scavenged from the clearing of the land. The Smith brothers build a palmetto house at Mullet Creek. (Photo Brevard County Historical Commission Archives)

While the questions of Florida statehood and racial slavery were receiving increasing attention and causing more than a little anxiety in both Tallahassee and Washington, settlers were taking advantage of the Armed Occupation Act. During the one year it was in effect, 942 patents were issued at Newnansville and 370 at St. Augustine. One hundred twelve were issued for locations along the Indian River between Merritt Island and Lake Worth. While the largest concentration of settlers was around Fort Pierce, numerous others took up land along the coast of what subsequently became Brevard County. The exact number of people who actually moved to their land grants is not certain. Frederick Weedon did take up

his land at Fort Pierce while Frederick Weedon, Jr., settled on the south end of Merritt Island. Others whose tracts were on Merritt Island included Douglas Dummett, Nathaniel C. Scobie, Charles Scobie, William Heath, and John P. Zystra. Some of those who figured prominently in the colony were Ossian B. Hart, whose land was near Fort Pierce on the west side of the river; Samuel H. Peck, three miles south of Gilbert's Bar; and Mills O. Burnham, eight miles from Fort Pierce. Others were John Barker, on the east side of Indian River near Sebastian; John P. Hermans, on the west bank of St. Lucie Sound; John W. Hutchinson, six miles south of Fort Pierce; James H. Russell, eight miles from the head of Lake Worth; and Thomas T. Russell, five miles northwest of Lake Worth.[1]

Just moving their belongings and their families to the new land posed enormous problems to say nothing of the need for transportation to and from markets and supply centers. There were three ways to reach the Indian River region from the settled parts of the United States. Some people sailed the outside route past Cape Canaveral and through the Indian River Inlet, the only natural waterway into the river along the coast. That route involved the dangerous open sea and shallow water at the inlet. Others came up the St. Johns River to Enterprise on Lake Monroe and made the tortuous journey to Salt Lake or one of the other lakes in the upper reaches of the river. From there, they crossed over to the Indian River and proceeded southward to their destination. This was unsatisfactory since the land was too marshy for wagons and the water often too shallow for boats. The other route was by way of Mosquito Lagoon, across the Haulover, and into the Indian River. Indians had long used this route and the army had emulated them during the recent war. At times, more than 800 soldiers had been stationed at Fort Ann to assist in the portage of supplies for the soldiers operating in the areas of the St. Johns River, Lake Okeechobee, and the Everglades.

◀ *Douglas Dummett filed a claim under the Armed Occupation Act on March 16, 1843 for land near the site of Fort Ann. He and his common-law wife, Leandra Fernandez, who was part Negro and part Indian, began developing orange groves at Dummett's Cove. (Drawing © Vera Zimmerman, 1993)*

Since none of these routes were satisfactory, suggestions for improved access were offered from all quarters. The territorial legislative council cast its suggestion in terms of future development of the peninsula. Its resolution noted that "the various maps of Florida" showed that "the waters of the Indian River and of the River St. Johns" were very near each other. The council believed that a canal of "six or seven miles might be made to connect the navigable waters of the two said Rivers." Such a canal would be of great importance since it would "have a tendency to increase very rapidly the population of the southern part of Florida." No action was taken on the ensuing request for a Congressional appropriation for such a project, but the state legislature continued to press the matter.[2] Although no such canal was ever built, Florida legislators and Congressmen were still pushing the project nearly a hundred years later.

Ninety citizens of East Florida also implored Congress to authorize and finance a road from St. Augustine to St. Lucie Sound by way of New Smyrna. The petitioners, among whom were Samuel Peck, Ossian B. Hart, Oscar Hart, E. J. Dummett, Robert Robertson, and Thomas Telfair Long, based their request on the grounds of the success of the Armed Occupation Act. According to the petitioners, "about 1,200 souls" had settled around St. Lucie Sound and were encountering "incredible privations and hardships." Persons with limited means but enterprising spirits and indomitable courage, they had cheerfully abandoned the comforts of the "old fireside." The inland passage through Mosquito Lagoon and Indian River was unsatisfactory because of its numerous marshes and mangrove islands and "several haulovers." The route around Cape Canaveral was dangerous, expensive, and "equally as objectionable as the inland route." The courageous settlers deserved something better and an improved road was the answer.[3]

Although it would prove just as difficult to accomplish and would still be an objective of both public and private enterprise until well into the 20th century, the army's transportation proposal appeared more realistic if only because some funds were available. Emphasizing the ease by which an inland waterway for light draft vessels might be opened up between the Mosquito Lagoon and St. Lucie, Colonel Worth wrote that the haulover at Fort Ann was only 720 yards wide and could be easily cut through. Using troops in his command during the winter months, Worth promised to open up "immense facilities to the settlers now studding the South Atlantic coast of the Peninsula." His project would bring public lands into the market and "greatly facilitate the transmission of military supplies in respect to time, expense, and avoidance of hazardous navigation and the active energies of an enemy's cruisers." He thought the project could be completed for about $5,500, which was already available to him. His officers would benefit from being busy with a useful project instead of merely serving garrison duty. Perhaps best of all, Lieutenant Jacob E. Blake possessed the skills to oversee the project.[4]

Lieutenant Blake was exuberant in detailing his plans for the canal across the Haulover. He would enable vessels drawing up to three feet of water to gain access to "the rich lands on Indian River and St. Lucie," well adapted for the cultivation of sugar, cotton, tobacco, and the various kinds of tropical fruits which were at present "rendered almost useless and bearing but a nominal value" because of the difficulty of getting there. He proposed a canal of 725 yards length for an expenditure of about $4,000. About 400 yards of the cut would be through hard coquina overlaid with red sand. The remainder was sand and shell which would "easily yield to the pick." He recognized, as did many of his successors in this project, that the sand at each end of the cut would quickly fill in unless artificially reinforced. That was no problem for Blake who planned to stabilize the outlets of the canals with two inch planks affixed to eight inch pilings. The manpower was to come from the troops garrisoned at St. Francis Barracks in St. Augustine.[5] Whether Blake actually made the cut is unlikely, but if he did, it was unsuccessful. Fourteen months later, in March 1845, he was still offering plans to open a canal through the Haulover. He was to have many successors, most of whom accomplished no more than he.[6]

While the many schemes for improved transportation were being pursued, the settlers along the Indian River were adapting to the frontier. Fort Pierce was approximately the geographic center of the colony which actually spread for miles along the river in both directions. Situated on a low bluff above the river, the first community in what became Brevard County evolved at the site which was later named Ankona. Among the inhabitants was Mills Burnham, who is credited with the introduction of pineapple cultivation to the area where it would become so important many years later. A versatile individual determined to provide for his family, he also became one of the area's first commercial fishermen. Purchasing a schooner which he named "The Josephine," he began catching green turtles in the river and transporting them to Charleston where he sold them to a firm which ultimately marketed them in England. Because he took good care of his catch on the way to Charleston, most of his turtles arrived in good condition. Burnham's reputation for providing a good product apparently grew and he was always able to dispose of his catch for a good price.[7]

Most of the inhabitants of the region depended upon the river for a good part of their livelihood. James Price, an English sailor, spent considerable time fishing on the river. James Middleton was a ship's carpenter whose skills were quite valuable to his neighbors. Most of the men also took advantage of the abundance of wild game to supply their tables, but Daniel E. Bowen was recognized as the most

Lieutenant Jacob E. Blake was exuberant in detailing his plans for a canal at the Haulover, the place where boats had long been portaged between Mosquito Lagoon and the Indian River. (*Drawing* © *Vera Zimmerman*, 1994).

skilled hunter among them. The game and fish constituted the basic and by far most dependable part of the food supply, but all of the families engaged in some sort of agriculture. Markets were too far and transportation too difficult for much in the way of commercial production, so most of the crops were grown for local consumption. All in all, the community was adequately fed. There were even some supplies such as coffee and sugar brought in by vessels engaged in the coasting trade.[8]

Housing was generally crude, mostly constructed of wood with palmetto roofs. Such windows as they had were usually covered with oiled paper. Candles, lightwood knots and a few whale-oil lamps provided lighting. One exception was the house which Samuel Peck had framed in Savannah and transported by schooner to his homestead. Peck left the area in 1845 and sold his fine house to Mills Burnham.[9]

Social life was typical of the frontier. Shared fishing trips, hunting, house-raisings, helping each other with field work and tending to the sick were common occasions for social intercourse, but it was not all work and no play. There were festive occasions and the community was fortunate to have some musical talent among its inhabitants. In addition to his skills as a sailor and fisherman, James Price was also a fine singer with a great voice which he was quite willing to use. Another accomplished musician was Ossian B. Hart, a promising young attorney who, having been born in Jacksonville in 1822, was one of the few native Floridians around. After the Indian difficulty of 1849, he moved to Tampa and in 1873 became governor of the state.

One of the common projects undertaken by the settlers resulted from dissatisfaction with the shallowness of the Indian River Inlet. Deciding that better access to the sea could be made available by cutting through a narrow spit of land almost directly in front of the mouth of the St. Lucie River, all hands pitched in to dig. Apparently the water in the river was quite high at the time due to heavy rains in the back country. Having exhausted themselves during a day of shoveling sand, the crew pitched camp and retired for the night. Ossian Hart subsequently reported that he was awakened during the night by the sound of rushing water. He called to his friends and they all moved quickly from their encampment just in time to see it swept away. They had retired for the day leaving a small portion of the sand in place. During the night a strong wind came up and forced the high water in the river through the remaining sand. By morning the force of the water gushing from the river into the Atlantic had made a wide cut through Gilbert's Bar. Although they had narrowly escaped a dangerous situation, the men were at least spared further digging. The cut improved the quality of water in the Indian River and made fishing much better, but it soon closed up again and left navigation in the river as it had been before.[10]

In light of what happened later, it is perhaps worth mentioning that there was a friendly relationship with Indians who from time to time visited the various homes up and down the coast. The Burnhams remembered even loaning cooking utensils to some of them.[11] Continuing complaints about the Indians were still heard from some quarters, however. From Fort Gatlin, where Orlando later emerged, Aaron Jernigan sounded frequent alarms. Jernigan seems to have had an irresistible compulsion to lead an expedition against the Indians, which he eventually did. In response to his complaints, John T. Sprague of the United States army made an extensive investigation of the frontier, including the Indian River area. He reported that "from the Atlantic to the Gulf...no fears were entertained by citizens generally of Indians in that quarter, nor has there been seen, for more than a year past, an Indian over the line within which they promised to remain."[12]

Although there was no way Sprague could have known at the time, his report was not entirely correct. There were Indians living outside the reservation. A self-proclaimed chief named Charley had renounced the authority of Billy Bowlegs and Sam Jones and led about 20 renegades to a camp on the Kissimmee River about 40 miles west of the Indian River colony and just outside the reservation boundary.[13]

There was also an incipient problem of which neither Sprague nor any other officials could have known at the time. John Barker had opened a store at what became known as Barker's Bluff where a few Indians occasionally traded. It seems that Barker had gained a reputation among the Indians for dealing unfairly with them and some bore a grudge toward him.[14]

Difficulties with the Indians were not a matter of serious concern among the Indian River settlers as they went about the business of earning a living from the sea and the soil of their frontier home in the mid-1840s. Everyone seemed to be looking to a brighter future with improved transportation from one or more of the various proposals already mentioned and from increased settlement as more land was opened up. Land was not available under the Armed Occupation Act after August of 1843, but surveyors were working diligently to open other land for purchase from the government. Valentine Y. Conway was appointed surveyor general for United States lands in Florida in 1843 and immediately set to work. From his office in Tallahassee he expressed enthusiasm about the Atlantic coast. He wrote that the lands near Mosquito Lagoon, Indian River, and St. Lucie Sound were of excellent quality and would command a ready sale if surveyed and opened to the public. He recommended for immediate attention the land lying east of the lines dividing Ranges 35 and 36 and Ranges 36 and 37 and received an appropriation of $10,000 to undertake the survey. By mid-1844 his surveyors were hard at work in the Indian River area and "moving on in fine health and spirits." He did mention that "Indians occasionally afford a little diversion by offering a harmless menace – some time since a deputy found painted on one of his blazed line trees a rifle and cross – designed I suppose to indicate the penalty of violating their reserved rights."[15]

Another government official who was enthusiastic about the region was Timber Agent Hezekiah Thistle, whose persistence in protecting government timber from private poachers kept him in constant controversy with both timber companies and his superiors. In a report condemning the firm of Palmer and Ferris for illegally cutting live oak from government land, he added his analysis of the timber assets of the upper St. Johns and Kissimmee valleys as well as the Indian River area. He reported good timber at Lake Poinsett "and at intervals to the head of the river St. Johns" which "at trifling expense" could be made accessible to vessels drawing from two to two and a half feet of water. He also noted "choice timber for naval purposes" at St. Sebastian, St. Lucie, and points south. He added his endorsement of Lieutenant Blake's canal across the haulover which he thought would make this timber easily available for use.[16]

Despite the difficulties that General Jesup and others had encountered with shallow water at Indian River Inlet, there was also official interest in the possibilities of a commercial port there. Augustus Walker wrote the Secretary of the Treasury in 1842 that a settlement was rapidly forming there and that trade could be expected. He suggested that a customs inspector be assigned to the place.[17] Nothing was done about the inspector until an incident occurred more than a year later. The Schooner Ellen, a vessel of about 50 tons out of Jacksonville, dropped off several passengers at Indian River on its way to Nassau with a load of lumber. On the return voyage it stopped again and unloaded salt, sugar, and coffee. While in the river, the Ellen was accosted by the United States Revenue Cutter Crawford whose crew discovered that the ship's manifest did not list all the cargo on board. Smuggling was clearly implied. It was reported to the secretary of the treasury that both Indian River Inlet and Gilbert's Bar afforded opportunity for smuggling contraband articles from the West Indies into the United States as the Ellen incident demonstrated. The secretary was apparently impressed and the revenue inspector's office at Charlotte Harbor was relocated to the Indian River in mid-1844.[18]

The settlement on the Indian River seemed to be permanent. Some people moved away from time to time, but there were also new arrivals. Then everything changed on July 12, 1849 when four young Indians arrived at the Indian River settlement, outfitted as if they had been hunting. Two of them were known to the settlers by the names of Sammy and Eli. The other two were unfamiliar. All acted in their usual friendly manner during the morning. They ate at the home of W. A. Russell, the customs official for Indian River. In the early afternoon Russell and John Barker, his brother-in-law, were standing in a field near his home when the young Indians walked toward them. At a distance of about 40 yards, two of them opened fire. Both white men were wounded and immediately fled in opposite directions. The Indians overtook Barker and stabbed him to death. Russell escaped with an arm wound. While the settlers were sounding the alarm, the Indians pillaged the homes of both Barker and Russell and burned the house of D. H. Gettis. The only other house in the immediate vicinity was left undisturbed.[19]

Events moved swiftly after the killing of Barker. The same group of Indians killed more people at Payne's store on the Peace River on July 17. Settlers all across the peninsula were alarmed, but not all reacted as had those along the Indian River. Captain J. C. Casey, an official who was especially sympathetic with the Indians wrote from his post at Fort Brooke that many of the frontiersmen were "flying like sheep, abandoning everything." But, he added, there were others who were collecting their families in blockhouses in each neighborhood and organizing scouting parties to protect their cattle and fields. Unlike their counterparts on the Indian River, many of those in southwest Florida remained on their land.[20]

Although 27 people from the settlement where Russell, Barker, and Gettis lived left immediately by boat for St. Augustine, there was apparently extended discussion among their remaining neighbors about the wisdom of abandoning their homes. The wounded Russell finally prevailed and all decided to leave. Mills Burnham was absent on one of his trading trips to Charleston and some writers have lamented that had he been present he might have talked some of the settlers out of their determination to leave. However that may have been most of the inhabitants left. The Armed Occupation colony on the Indian River, as it had existed during the past six years, ended in the summer of 1849. It is incorrect, however, to say that all of the settlers left permanently. Several of the individuals whose names appeared on the lists of homesteaders under the Armed Occupation Act were still active in the affairs of Brevard County in the 1850s.

One of the first reports of the incident came from Nathaniel Scobie, then keeper of the Cape Canaveral lighthouse, who was quite upset when the 27 refugees stopped at his place. Writing to Douglas Dummett at New Smyrna, he pleaded, "For God's sake come with your boat as soon as possible and help us get away. The Indians have broken out at Indian River, and I am obliged to take to the light house."[21] Colonel Smith at St. Augustine received the information and quite calmly reported the affair to his superior officer. As soon as a boat could be made ready, he said, a detachment would be sent to Cape Canaveral and on to Indian River.[22]

While some residents agreed with Colonel Smith, many others were anything but calm. Having implored the government for years to remove the Indians from southern Florida, they now saw opportunity in the latest affair. Governor W. D. Moseley wrote President Zachary Taylor that he "had fully anticipated" what had happened. He and other Floridians had been insisting that something be done about Indians violating the reservation boundaries for the past three years. As a temporary measure of defense he was calling out two companies of mounted men, but he fully expected the national government to take action. He then reiterated his belief that the only solution was complete Indian removal.[23]

Most of the military officials believed that the murders at both Indian River and Payne's Landing were isolated incidents and not the responsibility of either Bowlegs or Sam Jones. Several citizens of St. Augustine expressed similar sentiment to Colonel Smith. When Senator David L. Yulee demanded action from Secretary of War George Crawford, the secretary responded that "the violence and outrage exhibited in the vicinity of Fort Pierce, and at the house on Pease Creek, were done by the same party of Indians, which did not exceed five."[24]

Whether it was a general uprising or the act of a handful of criminals, it was still a sensitive matter and the army undertook a thorough investigation. Aware of the delicate political climate, Colonel Smith wrote that although "fully impressed that the outrage is an isolated case for revenge or plunder...I have nevertheless deemed it the better policy to send this detachment, with the view of inspiring confidence in the settlers,...and thus try to counteract the ...unreasonable panic that seems to pervade the settlements on the coast."[25]

Lieutenant R. S. Ripley and eleven soldiers were sent to the Indian River. Nothing had been touched at the scene. They buried Barker's body and reported the plunder of the Russell and Barker houses and the complete destruction of the Gettis house. Nothing else had been touched. Neither Ripley's detachment nor anyone else had seen any sign of Indians since the July 12 incident. Ripley reported that two parties of settlers were removing their belongings in preparation for departure. When the Davis and Gates parties left, according to Ripley, there would not be a white man left between New Smyrna and Biscayne.[26]

It soon became clear that Colonel Smith had correctly assessed the situation. At Charlotte Harbor, three messengers from Billy Bowlegs reported to Colonel David E. Twiggs that only five renegades had committed the crimes and that they were in the chief's custody. Anxious to turn them over to the military authorities and be done with it all, Bowlegs and several other chiefs went to Charlotte Harbor and worked out an agreement whereby the fugitives would be delivered. Then, on the following day, the embarrassed chief admitted that one man had escaped, but he delivered three of the fugitives and the hand of a fourth whose escape attempt had been unsuccessful. With incredible perseverance, Twiggs accepted the prisoners and immediately took up the issue of Bowlegs migration to the west. The chief demurred, but promised to think it over.[27]

Twiggs accomplished nothing on the subject of further removal of the Indians and Florida officials continued to press the national government. Despite Bowlegs' swift justice, rumors continued to circulate in southern Florida about "further Indian depredations on Indian River." Governor Thomas Brown, who had succeeded Moseley, wrote President Taylor in late 1849 accusing the United States army of failing to afford protection for the settlers against the Indians. One may question the sincerity of the Florida governor when he continued to complain in the fall of 1850 that "all activity has ceased on Indian River and the people do not plan to return." By that time he had full knowledge that Fort Capron had been constructed and manned in March of that year. The Capron Trail was built from that point across the peninsula to Fort Brooke and became the line beyond which Indians were not permitted to roam. Despite the governor's assertions, a few hearty souls were drifting back to the area around Fort Pierce by that time.[28]

Although Fort Capron was garrisoned until 1858, Florida officials and their constituents continued to complain about the Indians straying off the reservation. It was probably true that some were hunting and perhaps even grazing cattle and hogs in the Kissimmee valley beyond the reservation boundary, but they showed no interest in contacting the white settlers. Aaron Jernigan was more vocal than most about his beliefs that Indians were poaching off the reservation. He and a handful of neighbors proved their point by locating an Indian camp and driving off a herd of hogs. On a return visit with additional assistance, he captured several Indians. On his way back to Fort Gatlin with his prisoners, however, all escaped except a woman and child. This was evidence enough to convince Governor Brown that the army was not competent to deal with the Indians and that only native volunteers were equal to the task. Whether to contain Jernigan or drive the Indians back into the reservation or both, Governor Brown called out a militia force under the command of General Benjamin Hopkins in the spring of 1852. Hopkins marched out of Mellonville up the St. Johns apparently with plans for returning by way of the Kissimmee. His force of between forty and fifty men was supplied by boats which were able to move up the waters of the St. Johns as far as Lake Winder. Hopkins located at least one band of Indians living outside the reservation

and captured eleven of them. In reporting the expedition, Governor Brown again demanded the removal of all Indians from Florida.[29]

The Indian controversy continued, but the pressure on them to go west was accelerated by Secretary of War Jefferson Davis in 1854. Davis wrote Lieutenant John C. Casey in May of that year that efforts were to be made to prevent the Indians from continuing to trade with whites and that the Department of Interior was planning to open up for sale much of the land on the frontier to accelerate settlement. "The privations consequent upon the cessation of their trade with the whites and the gradual contraction of their limits by the advance of the white settlements may possibly induce some of the Indians to accept the terms heretofore offered," he wrote. Even if it did not work, Davis continued, the change would "place the Department in a better position to apply force whenever the season and other circumstances will permit of its so doing in order to effect their removal."[30]

The policy change at least temporarily affected Fort Capron. On the west coast, roads were to be built from Fort Myers or the head of navigation on the Caloosahatchee River to Lake Okeechobee. On the east coast, Fort Capron was to be closed and its soldiers were to be reassigned to a site at or near old Fort Jupiter. From that point roads were to be constructed toward Lake Okeechobee. The purpose of these changes was to establish a line of communication between Jupiter Inlet and Fort Myers and "circumscribe the Indians in their limits as much as possible."[31]

During early 1855, Lieutenant A. P. Hill located what was thought to be a suitable site near Jupiter Inlet and began building a military post. Labor was supplied by the troops from Fort Capron and lumber and hardware was

Fort Capron was manned until 1858 for the protection of settlers who continued to complain about Indians straying off the reservation. (*Drawing* © Vera Zimmerman, 1994)

shipped from Jacksonville. But, by summer nearly all the soldiers were afflicted with malaria. In early October, Major J. A. Haskin removed the entire detachment from Fort Jupiter and returned it to Fort Capron where both he and the post surgeon were primarily concerned with keeping an adequate supply of quinine for the ailing command.[32]

It was agreed that the Fort Jupiter site should be abandoned for reasons of health, but Major Haskin soon found himself in difficulties of another nature at Fort Capron. The land upon which the post was situated belonged to William F. Russell. Although soldiers had been stationed there since 1850, Russell decided in 1855 that the army should pay him rent. He and his wife offered to lease the site to the United States for $800 per year for as long as it was needed for military purposes. When informed of the offer, Major Haskin was irate. "I do not think it possible to occupy this post with any peace so long as that family live so near and have any claim on the place," he wrote. He suggested that the post be relocated to the old Fort Pierce site which was owned by Thomas Hite of St. Augustine. At first amenable to the idea, Hite offered the land on any terms the army desired, but that soon changed. It seems that Hite was a joint owner with the same William F. Russell. After the two conferred, Hite suggested that the army might be willing to pay "a few hundred dollars" annual rental. Haskin still thought it unnecessary to pay rent on lands to be used as a military post to protect the same settlers who were charging the rent. He suggested that the post be relocated to lands along the river which were still in the public domain.[33]

While the matter was still being considered by the army, Russell obtained a writ of ejectment but Judge Hermans refused to serve it. Russell then offered to rent the land for $300 per year. Haskin still advised against a contract with Russell and urged that "if any new buildings are to put up here by the Government that they be erected on Government land." At about the same time that Haskin's letter arrived at Fort Brooke, another was received from Susan Russell saying that the land known as Fort Capron "and as much land as you wish" was available to the army "at what you think is a fair compensation." Her husband also wrote Colonel Monroe at Fort Brooke explaining that he had gotten along well with the soldiers at Fort Capron from 1850 until 1854 when Major Haskin arrived and that he was "not only willing but anxious to aid in any way the Government operations here, Brev. Major Haskin's statements to the contrary notwithstanding."[34]

Whether it was personal animosity between two individuals or a genuine difference of opinion about compensation for use of the land, the feud affected Fort Capron. On December 8, 1855, Colonel Monroe wrote Mrs. Russell that "orders have been given to abandon the post" and "the differences which have already existed between some members of your family and the troops...may have had some weight in dictating the present movement."[35]

The quarrel mattered little. About the time the army decided to abandon Fort Capron, a detachment of troops marched into the Indian reservation from Fort Myers and apparently maliciously destroyed some property belonging to Billy Bowlegs. The chief retaliated and several soldiers were killed. This incident grew into the Third Seminole War, sometimes also called the Billy Bowlegs War. It aroused the usual anxieties of Floridians although it resulted in few casualties and never reached the Indian River area. Probably as a result of the renewed hostilities, Fort Capron continued to be manned until 1858. It is not clear whether Russell was ever compensated for its use. When peace was restored, a few more Indians were removed to the west. The remainder were deep in the Everglades and ceased to be a central concern as Floridians began to deal with the sectional crisis which led to Civil War.

End Notes

1. U. S. House of Representatives, Document No. 70, 28th Congress, 1st Sess. (All of the 112 land patents and their locations may be found in this document.) More information on the Armed Occupation Colony may be found in Joseph D. Cushman, Jr., "The Indian River Colony: 1842-1849," Florida Historical Quarterly, XLIII (1964), pp. 21-35.
2. Clarence E. Carter, Volume 26, p. 1012; Florida State Archives, Record Group 101, Letter book 5, James Broome to F. L. Dancy, November 29, 1853.
3. Ibid., p. 975.
4. Ibid., p. 780, William J. Worth to Colonel J. J. Abert, November 10, 1843.
5. Ibid., pp. 803-805, Jacob E. Blake to Worth, December 11, 1843.
6. Ibid., p. 1023, Blake to Chief of Engineers, March 3, 1845.
7. Robert Ranson, East Coast Florida Memoirs, 1837-1886 (Port Salerno, Florida, 1989), p. 14.
8. Carter, pp. 808-810, Chandler S. Emery to Secretary of the Treasury, December 14, 1842; Ranson, pp. 9, 11.
9. Ranson, Memoirs, p. 9.
10. Ibid., pp. 12-13.
11. Ibid., p. 14.
12. U.S. House, Document 90, 29th Cong., 2nd Sess., John T. Sprague to Governor W. D. Moseley, January 10, 1846.
13. U.S. Senate, Executive Document 49, 31st Cong., Ist Sess., C. F. Smith to General R. Jones, August 3, 1849.
14. Ranson, Memoirs, pp. 14-15.
15. Carter, pp. 776, 928, 1077, Valentine Y. Conway to Thomas H. Blake, July 12, 1844, Conway to Blake, October 24, 1843, Conway to James Shields, May 19,1845.
16. Ibid., pp. 695-696, Hezekiah L. Thistle to Secretary of the Navy, July 20, 1843.
17. Ibid., p. 577, Augustus W. Walker to Secretary of the Treasury, December 2, 1842.
18. Ibid., pp. 808-810, Chandler S. Emery to Secretary of the Treasury, December 14, 1843 and William J. Worth to Adjutant General, August 19, 1844.
19. U. S. Senate, Executive Document 49, 31st Cong., Ist Sess, C. F. Smith to General R. Jones, July 18, 1849; Original Census Schedules, 7th Census, 1850, Florida, St. Lucie County, Mortality Records.
20. U. S. Senate, Executive Document 49, J. C. Casey to General George Gibson, July 29, 1849.
21. Ibid., Secretary of War George W. Crawford to D. L. Yulee, August 9, 1849.
22. Ibid., C. F. Smith to R. Jones, July 18, 1849
23. Florida State Archives, Record Group 101, Series 32 Carton 5, W. D. Moseley to President Taylor, July 29, 1849.
24. U. S. Senate , Document 49, Secretary Crawford to Yulee, August 9, 1849.
25. Ibid., C. F. Smith to R. Jones, July 18, 1849.
26. Ibid., R. S. Ripley to C. F. Smith, August 9, 1849, and Ripley to R. Jones, August 18, 1849.
27. Ibid., David E. Twiggs to Secretary of War, September 6, September 23, October 19, 1849.
28. Florida State Archives, Record Group 101, Letterbook 5, Thomas Brown to Zachary Taylor, November 29, 1849, and Brown to Millard Fillmore, September 5, 1850, and Samuel Spencer to Orlando Brown, October 1, 1849; Microfilm 185L (Typescript on Fort Pierce), P. K. Yonge Library of Florida History.
29. Florida State Archives, RG 101, Series 577, Carton 2, Arthur Ginn to Governor Brown, February 11, 1852, Ginn to Brown, April 3,1852, Brown to Secretary of the Interior, September 8, 1852.
30. National Archives, Record Group 393, Records of the United States Army Commands, 1821-1900, Jefferson Davis to John C. Casey, May 10, 1854.
31. Ibid., Wayne C. Cooper to Colonel John Monroe, September 21, 1854.
32. National Archives, Record Group 393, Register of Letters Received, M-1084, Roll 4, A. P. Hill to J. A. Haskin, January 14, 1855; Haskin to T. J. Haimes, October 1, 1855.
33. Ibid., William F. Russell to Haimes, November 1, 1855.
34. Ibid., Haskin to T. M. Vincent, November 24, 1855; Russell to Monroe, November 25, 1855.
35. Ibid., Monroe to Susan Russell, December 8, 1855.

Page 44 Map: The 1843 Tanner map shows the eastern boundary of the "District Assigned to the Seminoles" running along the Kissimmee River. (Florida State Archives)

FLORIDA
PUBLISHED BY S. AUGUSTUS MITCHELL,
N.E. corner of Market & 7th Streets Philada. 1846.
Scale of Miles.
10 20 40 60 80 100
Explanation.
Routes of the Army during Seminole War
Forts
Battle Grounds
Capital
County Towns
Common Towns
WATER ROUTES.
PENSACOLA
a Market House
b Custom House
c Chappel
d Court Ho. & Jail
e Old Callaboza
f Public Store
Smith & Ralmsons Tract
King & Haines Claim
TALLAHASSEE
a Methodist Church
b Public Church Masonic Hall & Academy
Gov. Duvals Residence
HARBOUR OF ST. AUGUSTINE
The Soundings are in Fathoms taken at high water
ATLANTIC OCEAN
GEORGIA
TALLAHASSEE
APPALACHEE BAY
TAMPA BAY
LAKE OKEECHOBEE
CAPE CANAVERAL
CAPE SABLE
FLORIDA KEYS
REEFS

5

Florida Statehood and the Origins of Brevard County

The huge Mosquito County was reduced in size and renamed Orange County in 1844. The territory which would eventually become Brevard County was carved from it and officially named St. Lucie County in 1845.

By 1860 the county was still sparsely settled with 300 inhabitants including 31 slaves. (Photo Brevard County Historical Commission Archives)

The Second Seminole War was a calamity for the settlers of territorial Florida in the late 1830s for many reasons, but most of all because of its interruption of their hopes and plans for the future. Florida became a United States territory at a time of great optimism and belief in a better future. Settlers had poured into Middle Florida to grow cotton and sugar cane and build a social and economic structure similar to the ones they had left in Georgia, the Carolinas, Virginia, Maryland and other such places. It seemed to them that the recalcitrant and belligerent Indians stood in the way of progress. The issue of Florida statehood had already been raised before the war began. That the state's population was too small for statehood was only a temporary matter. Floridians fully intended to encourage and accomplish the growth which would make their new home a state and they wished to do so without delay.

The issue of statehood also converged with several other difficulties which not only interfered with those plans, but also eventually made Floridians almost as anxious to get out of the United States as they had first been to become part of it.

While General Jesup was conducting his 1837 campaign, the nation was falling into one of its periodic depressions. The entire country was adversely affected, but the Florida territory was especially vulnerable. Not only had the Seminole confrontation interrupted the economy but the national depression had destroyed the infant banking system and thrown the territorial government as well as most citizens into deep debt. One wag in Tallahassee wrote that the entire territory was "covered with judgments." This condition would continue through most of the 1840s until cotton prices finally recovered.

Although the advocates of statehood pushed ahead despite the economic collapse, they encountered two other problems which, each in its own way, would affect the infant Brevard County. Of more immediate significance was the question of whether Florida should be admitted as one state or two. East Floridians – those residing south of the Suwannee River and in the peninsula – whose population center was around St. Augustine, favored two states, or even better, no state at all. If the cotton moguls of Middle Florida desired statehood, then the East Floridians were happy to see them go. It would be perfectly all right for East Florida to remain a territory. That question concerned legislators in both Tallahassee and Washington right up to the time when Florida was admitted in 1845 as a single state. People continued to speak of the unnatural connection between peninsular – or East – Florida for years and even as late as the first decade of the 20th century many in that part of the state were still supporting attempts to cede part of West Florida to Alabama.

Of greater significance in the long run was the question of racial slavery in the United States. Floridians sent delegates to a constitutional convention at St. Joseph in 1838. A constitution was completed which called for a single state of Florida. That document was narrowly ratified by the voters of the entire territory, but it was opposed by a majority of those of East Florida. The dispute over statehood continued, but it was actually the slavery issue which delayed Florida's admission to the Union until 1845. Since the Missouri Compromise of 1820, Congress had followed an implicit policy of keeping a balance in the Union between slave and free states. Since Florida was to be a slave state, a counterbalancing free state was needed. Iowa, the only prospect, was not yet ready to apply for statehood. Floridians consequently waited seven years until Iowa was ready.

The Union which the two new states joined was one whose affairs were colored by the question of racial slavery until it was torn apart in 1860, but in the meantime Floridians went about the business of making a state. The Democrats defeated the Whigs in 1845 and Democrat William D. Moseley of Jefferson County became the first governor. While he and the legislature were busily making the necessary changes from territorial status to sovereign statehood, they were also busy creating local political units to meet the needs of a growing population. The huge Mosquito County was renamed Orange County in 1844 and was reduced in size. The territory which would eventually become Brevard County was carved from it and named St. Lucie County. Only a quick look at the loose definition of its boundaries is sufficient to understand why there were so many uncertainties about county lines in central Florida in later years. The legislative assembly defined the new St. Lucie County as extending from the Atlantic Coast "near Cape Canaveral," then south to the "line run by Colonel Washington," then west to the Hillsborough County line, then south to Lake Okeechobee, then east to

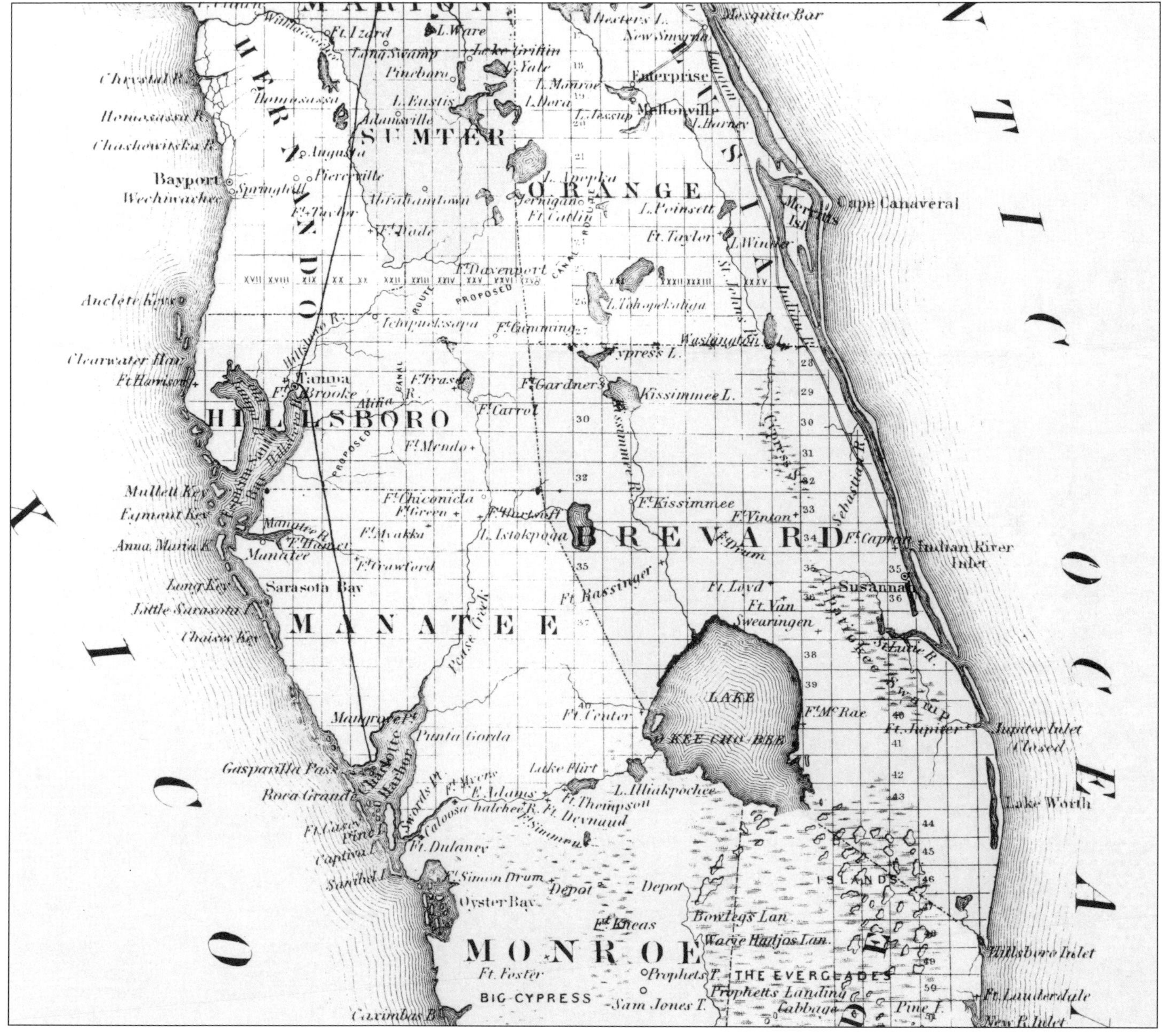

The Colton map with revisions through 1859 shows the new Brevard County. (Brevard County Historical Commission Archives)

Hillsborough Inlet, then north to the beginning. Because of difficulties with the first election of officers, the original territorial act of 1844 was repealed and replaced with one enacted by the state legislature in 1845. According to the records, a delegate from St. Lucie County was allowed a seat in the 1844 session of the assembly, but since he was not compensated for his travel, it seems unlikely that one actually went to Tallahassee that year.[1]

The new county's seat was at St. Lucie but the clerk of the court was permitted to keep the public records in his home except when the courts were in session. Joseph S. Osborne was the first clerk, but the 1847 legislature combined the offices of clerk of court for St. Lucie and Orange counties. J. C. Hemming was then elected to succeed

Osborne. Hemming apparently served in that capacity until 1850, but the St. Lucie County records were kept in the home of D. H. Gettis. They were completely destroyed during the Indian affairs of 1849 when the Gettis house was burned to the ground. Henry A. Crane, who had earlier been an official of Mosquito County, became clerk in 1850 and is the last person to serve in that capacity until the county was renamed.[2]

The first county commissioners were William B. Davis, John Barker, and Ossian B. Hart. They were succeeded in 1847 by Levy M. Crawford, William F. Russell, James S. Grant, W. D. Ward and Jasper J. Papy. No elections were held in 1849 during the Indian troubles. Order was restored the following year and William F. Russell was re-elected, along with D. H. Gettis, and Manuel Navarro. The commissioners in 1852 were D. G. Brewer, C. L. Brayton, John S. Hermans, and Nathaniel C. Scobie. They were succeeded in 1853 by Henry Wilson, George Davison, William F. Russell, and Manuel Navarro. The last county commissioners for old St. Lucie were William F. Russell, William B. Davis, Henry Wilson, and Henry P. Arlington. They served until 1855 when Brevard County was organized.[3]

Mills Burnham was St. Lucie County's first sheriff. He was followed in 1847 by F. M. K. Morrison. C. L. Brayton succeeded Morrison in 1850 and apparently remained in that office until 1855. Judges of probate were John S. Hermans, who served until 1851; D. H. Gettis whose term was from 1851 to 1853; and Hermans again until 1855. At various times between 1845 and 1854 several persons served as justices of the peace. They included James P. Lightburn, Reuben H. Pinkham, William B. Davis, John Bulloch, W. D. Ward, William F. Russell, C. L. Brayton, D. F. Jones, N. C. Scobie, and George C. Stowell. These same individuals, and only two others, filled all other county offices, including those of coroner, assessor of revenue, tax assessor and collector, auctioneer, and notary public. The others were Sebastian Ortega who served as coroner, and James S. Grant who was tax assessor and collector for one term.[4]

It is unlikely that any of them were overwhelmed with work. According to the 1850 census, the population of St. Lucie County was 139. This number included 54 soldiers stationed at Fort Capron. Of the remaining 81, 53 were free whites, one was a free black, and 27 were black slaves. The names of the 20 heads of families show clearly that some of the original Armed Occupation colonists had either remained in the county or had returned shortly after the Indian difficulties. In light of their subsequent roles in Brevard County history, however, some of them listed interesting occupations in 1850. Douglas Dummett was shown as a pilot and Mills O. Burnham gave his occupation as gunsmith. Nathaniel C. Scobie and Daniel Sinclair were merchants and Isaac Tyson was a butcher. D. H. Gettis and Peter Johnson were the only farmers. Others included Vincent Bowers, laborer; James T. Lighthouse, mariner; Theodore Mead, clerk; Calab C. Brayton, mail contractor; John S. Hermans, probate judge; William F. Russell, customs inspector. Elizabeth Bevins listed no occupation. Six other heads of families were officers and non-commissioned officers stationed at Fort Capron. Total valuation of real estate was $277,000 and personal property was valued at $41,300.[5]

The 1854 legislature changed the name of St. Lucie County to Brevard County to be effective in 1855. Volusia County was carved from Orange at the same time. The boundary between Volusia and Brevard was the south line of township 23, near present-day Sharpes. Other boundaries were the same as they had been for St. Lucie County. The statute creating the county called for the seat of government to be at "a place known and designated as Fort Pierce, and the name of said county site shall be Susannah." Although it appears occasionally in correspondence and a few historical sources, the name seems never to have caught on. Both the post office and the county seat were usually referred to as Indian River.[6]

In a letter declining a new term as probate judge in 1854, John S. Hermans modestly asserted that "I have thus far kept the county together." He went on to explain, however, that the population was increasing and there were others "better qualified and younger and do not live so far from the place of business." He seems to have been right about the increasing population, since a number of new names appear on the rosters of county officials after 1855. Among the county commissioners between 1855 and 1860 were George Davison, Allen W. Estis, and David Stone. Oliver H. Perry was county judge, but no clerk was listed for the period, probably because Orange and Brevard were still being served by the same official. James A. Armour was sheriff from 1855 to 1857 and was succeeded by William B. Davis. Justices of the Peace included George E. Stowell, John S. Hermans, William E. Ransom, and James Armour.[7]

The original lighthouse at Cape Canaveral, built in 1848, used a whale-oil lamp. (Etching © Vera Zimmerman, 1987)

Brevard County was still a long way from the rest of the state and nation through the 1850s. C. L. Brayton was the contract mail carrier along a route from New Smyrna through Indian River to Miami in 1851. Mail was supposed to be delivered twice monthly, but Brayton's job was a difficult one. He used a boat from New Smyrna to Indian River, but from that point southward he attempted to ride a horse along the beach. It was difficult to find water for the horse and all its feed had to be carried along. Brayton complained that he had "ruined a horse each of the two last trips." The legislature of 1851 had appropriated $1,000 for construction of a road from Indian River to Miami, and Brayton was imploring Governor Thomas Brown, apparently without success, to see that it was built. The difficulty of the terrain was not the only problem with the mails. Writing three years later in 1854, John Hermans complained to the secretary of state that the Tallahassee post office often sent Indian River mail by way of Key West and then to Miami, requiring as long as three months for delivery. The bi-monthly mail could be delivered to Indian River in only three weeks by way of the St. Johns River.[8]

The problem of mail delivery was related to the general need for improved transportation, a matter which had

In 1854 Dr. George E. Hawes, using slave labor, completed a canal three feet deep and about fourteen feet wide between Mosquito Lagoon and the Indian River. (Etching © Vera Zimmerman, 1987)

concerned everyone connected with the Indian River region since the late 1830s when the Second Seminole War was being waged. The transportation issue soon became entwined with the larger issue of drainage of the swamp and overflowed lands of peninsular Florida. The idea of a canal across the Haulover between Mosquito Lagoon and Indian River, promoted by Colonel Worth and attempted by Lieutenant Blake in the 1840s, evolved into action in 1854. The United States government made available $5,000 for the project and a contract was awarded to Dr. George E. Hawes. Using slave labor, Hawes completed a canal three feet deep and about fourteen feet wide to improve the inland passage between New Smyrna and Indian River.[9]

Much more was to be heard of the Haulover Canal in the future. In the meantime, the question of making the lands of southern Florida available for use was under discussion and was integrated with that of the need for transportation. Both were significant to the future of Brevard County. Florida's first legislature called on its Congressional delegation to obtain a survey of south Florida with a view to making it habitable for settlers. At the insistence of Senator James D. Westcott, Jr., the secretary of the treasury commissioned Buckingham Smith of St. Augustine to explore and report on the peninsula of Florida. Smith reported that the Everglades could be easily drained with "two or three small canals" and that drainage would attract enough people to form a new state within a few years. Westcott followed up on this over-simplified report and called upon Congress to make available land which could be sold to finance drainage projects. After David L. Yulee, Florida's other senator, became involved, Congress enacted the Swamp Land Act in 1850. It eventually made available to Florida nearly 20,000,000 acres to be used for development. The state legislature created the Internal Improvement Fund with a Board of Trustees to manage the land. It was not only to be drained and made available for settlement, but it could also be used to provide incentive to private developers to build transportation facilities. Railroads across the state and down the peninsula as well as an inland waterway along the Atlantic Coast were specifically named as projects suitable for such state assistance. While the Internal Improvement Fund and its vast lands were to be enormously important in the development of Brevard County, little was done until well after the Civil War.[10]

The Swamp Land Act did attract some attention in the 1850s. The 1853 legislature passed a resolution calling on the state engineer to, among other things, investigate and report on the practicability of "draining the main Savannah in St. Lucie County." Intent on complying with the resolution, F. L. Dancy, the state engineer, asked for a small appropriation with which to purchase the necessary surveying equipment for the project. It is unclear whether Governor Brown authorized Dancy to proceed.[11]

John S. Hermans was also intrigued by the possible drainage of the interior of Brevard County. In a letter to the secretary of state in 1855, he asked for information about the "submerged land fund." It was his understanding that the legislature had made potentially available $3,000 for draining Brevard County's "main savanna." The money was to come from the first sales of land which had been made available by Congress. It was of great consequence to the county, Hermans wrote, to have the savanna drained. There was not at that time 160 acres in the interior of the county "that is not more or less flooded save a small but short ridge near the River." Drainage of the main savannah would incidentally drain the entire back country and make available an expanse of desirable land which would soon be taken up by settlers.

Mills Burnham, one of the original Indian River colonists, was appointed keeper of the Canaveral Light in 1853 and served until his death in 1886. (Photo courtesy Robert Hudson, North Brevard Historical Society)

"I am anxious myself to have a quarter section," he added, "and know of others who want as much and more." Hermans wrote again in 1856 about the possibility of drainage, even offering to undertake the task himself, but he received no encouragement.[12] Nothing more was heard of drainage in the region until several years after the Civil War, but ultimately the topography of the county would be vastly altered by it.

Although the population of Brevard County in 1860 was nearly twice what St. Lucie's had been in 1850, there were still only 267 people there. Fort Capron was closed in 1858, taking away the soldiers. John Houston brought his family from Enterprise and settled in 1859 at what eventually became Eau Gallie. James Paine, Sr., is credited with having founded St. Lucie in 1856. In the portion of Volusia County which was subsequently adjoined to Brevard there was some activity. Although he continued to live at New Smyrna for a while, Douglas Dummett was cultivating the grove which he had started on the northern end of Merritt Island several years earlier. The founding of a settlement at the Haulover is credited to Dummett by

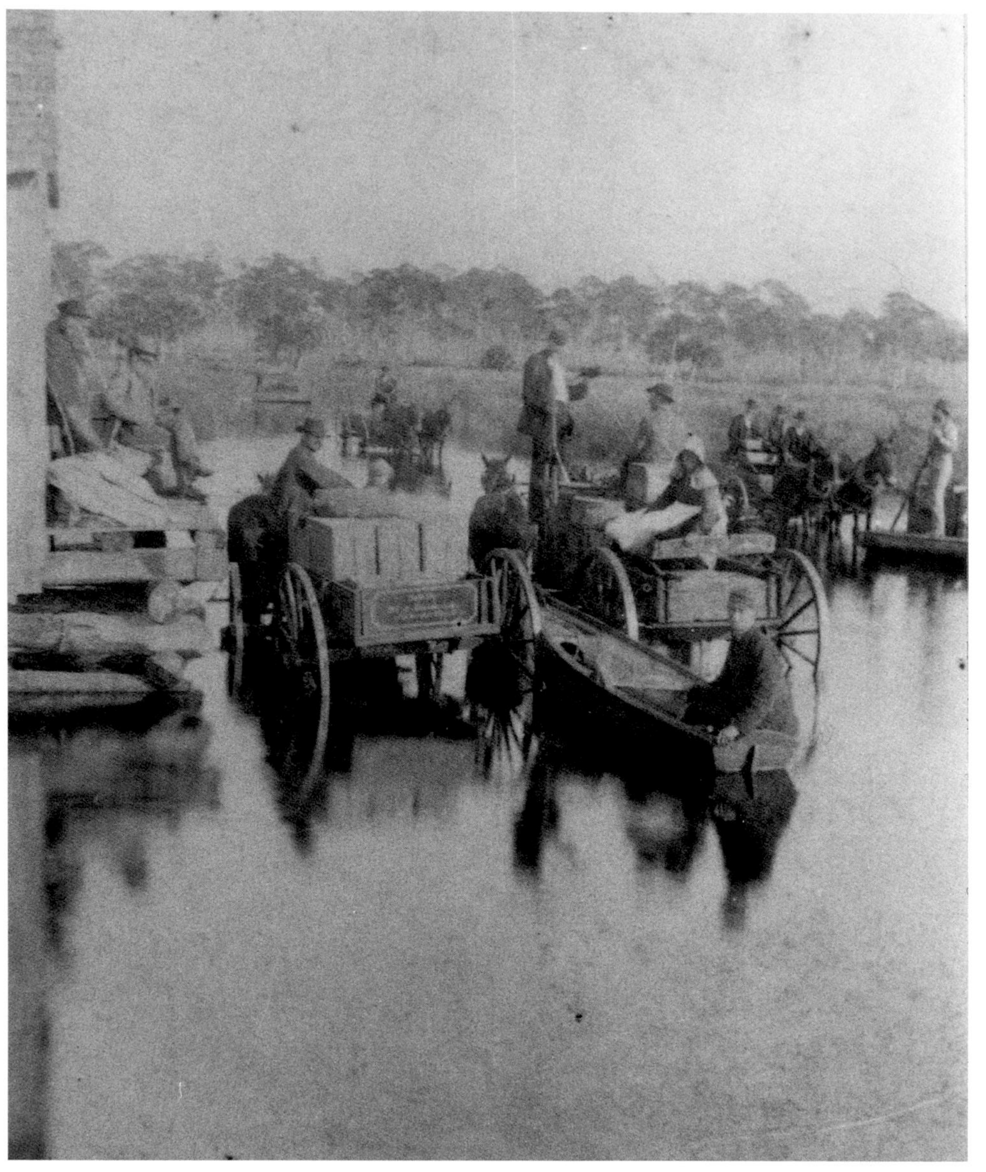

Early settlers, such as these at Lake Poinsett, drove wagons to the St. Johns to meet supply boats. (Photo courtesy Doug Hendriksen)

some authorities. The Cape Canaveral lighthouse was built in 1848 and manned by Nathaniel C. Scobie until the early 1850s. Mills Burnham succeeded him in 1853 and remained in that position for more than 30 years. In the mid-1850s, he was joined by Henry Wilson who shortly afterward became his son-in-law. The two planted and cultivated a grove of about 15 acres on the Banana River, about four miles from the lighthouse. Questioned by his superiors about how many settlers he was protecting, the commander at Fort Capron gave a detailed account in 1854. "Below the post there are five settlements," he wrote. The most southerly one was Judge Hermans' place, 12 miles from the post. About nine miles away was another settlement where three men lived. Next was a place belonging to the man who furnished beef for the soldiers, but he actually lived at the post. Then, about eight miles south was William B. Davis' settlement with three men, one woman, and one child. Just north of that place, was C. L. Brayton's home. There were three men, one woman, two children, and one slave who lived there, but two of the men were mail carriers and were frequently absent. One other male settler lived about a mile south of the post.[13]

The economic development of Brevard County along the Indian River was still in the future in 1860. A few people grew subsistence crops, but cattle constituted the preponderance of production. Several immigrants, mostly from Georgia, had driven herds into the western portion of the county by the late 1850s. According to William B. Watson, the 1860 census taker, no individual or firm was then producing any manufactured product valued at as much as $500 per year. The county still had only two merchants, Thomas Autman and Herman W. Ross. There was one mechanic and four carpenters. John W. Whitfield was the only physician. There was one mail carrier and one individual who classified himself simply as "gentleman." Only 31 slaves were owned by four different individuals. There were, however, 39 people who owned cattle and several of the herds were quite large. James Johnson was grazing 10,500 head while Jackson Raulerson had 8,000. Two other owners of large herds were Needham Yates with 7,600 and Samuel B. McGuire who had 7,000. Thomas Jarvis claimed 3,500 while William F. Russell and William Shiver had 700 each. Most of the others had only small herds, but some of them who figured in the later history of Florida's range cattle industry were James Whitten, James Paine, James Yates, Henry Yates, William B. Yates, Isaac Jernigan, Elias Jernigan, Ely P. Jernigan, James Paget, Quinn Bass, and Henry Overstreet.[14]

As the few inhabitants of Brevard County went about their business of earning livelihoods and perhaps building for the future, events from which they were far removed were about to interrupt their affairs and delay the growth of the county. The issue which had delayed Florida's admission as a state in the Union in the 1840s continued to divide the nation. The question of legal slavery accelerated in the late 1840s when the United States acquired from Mexico a huge expanse of land, including the territory from Texas to California. When gold was discovered in California and its population mushroomed to more than 100,000 within a short time, those people began clamoring for statehood. Since California's admission as a free state would have upset the balance in the United States Senate between free and slave states, resistance to California statehood was tremendous. A compromise was worked out whereby California became a free state, but concessions were given to the southern states. During the 1850s, both sides became dissatisfied with the compromise. Opponents of slavery gradually became the majority in northern states while southerners dug in their heels and defended the institution with more and more determination. When John Brown unsuccessfully attempted to set off a slave insurrection in 1859, southerners were not only outraged but also began doubting that they should remain in the Union. They came to believe by 1860 that the election of Abraham Lincoln as president of the United States was sufficient cause for them to leave the Union. He was elected and, within a few months, 11 southern states had seceded and formed the Confederate States of America. Florida, the third state to secede, became part of the Confederacy. The state which had struggled to join the United States only 15 years earlier became engaged in a military struggle against it. Brevard County, only five years old and with fewer than 300 inhabitants, was faced with the vagaries and uncertainties of Civil War.

End Notes

1. Clarence E. Carter, Volume 26, pp. 878-879, 994, 996.
2. Florida State Archives, WPA Roster of State and County Officers, 1845-1868, and Record Group 101, Series 32, Letterbook 5, W. D. Moseley to Sir, July 3, 1845.
3. FSA, WPA Roster.
4. Ibid.
5. Original Census Schedules, 7th Census, 1850, Population, Florida, St. Lucie County.
6. Titusville Star Advocate, July 9, 1926, and November 29, 1940.
7. FSA, Record Group 150, Series 24, Secretary of State Correspondence, Box I, John S. Hermans to F.L. Villepigue, March 7, 1854.
8. FSA, Record Group 101, Series 577, C. L. Brayton to Thomas Brown, June 11, 1851; and Record Group 150, Series 24, John S. Hermans to F. L. Villepigue, March 7, 1854.
9. Alfred Jackson Hanna and Kathryn Abbey Hanna, Florida's Golden Sands (Indianapolis and New York, 1950), p. 246.
10. Hanna and Hanna, pp. 54-57.
11. FSA, Record Group 101, Series 577, F. L. Dancy to Governor, February 5, 1853.
12. FSA, Record Group 150, Series 24, John S. Hermans to F.L. Villepigue, April15, 1855, and Record Group 593, Series 914, Internal Improvement Fund General Correspondence, 1855-1856, Herman to Villepigue, May 27, 1856.
13. Ranson, pp. 19-20; National Archives, Record Group 393, Records of the United States Army Commands, 1821-1900.
14. Original Census Schedules, 8th Census, 1860, Agriculture, Industry, and Population, Florida, Brevard County; FSA, Record Group 1020, Series 1201, Florida Census, 1860.

Page 58 Map: The 1846 Mitchell map shows the new State of Florida. (Florida State Archives)

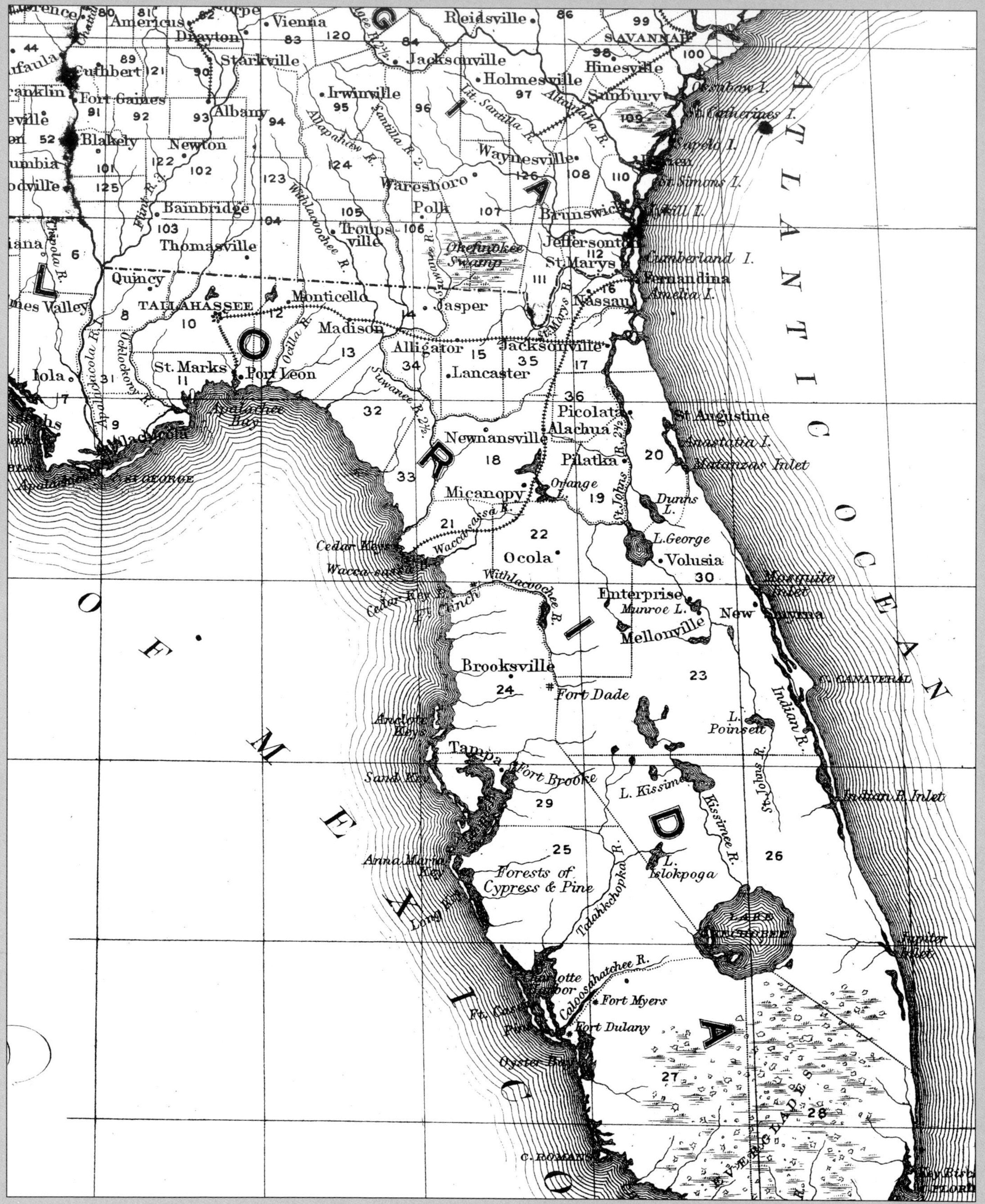

Americus
Drayton
Vienna
Reidsville
SAVANNAH
Cuthbert
Starkville
Jacksonville
Holmesville
Hinesville
Fort Gaines
Irwinville
Sunbury
Albany
St. Catherines I.
Blakely
Newton
Waynesville
Waresboro
Bainbridge
Polk
Brunswick
Troups-ville
Thomasville
Okefinokee Swamp
Jeffersonton
Cumberland I.
St. Marys
Quincy
Fernandina
Amelia I.
TALLAHASSEE
Monticello
Jasper
Nassau
Madison
Alligator
Jacksonville
Lancaster
Iola
St. Marks
Fort Leon
Apalachee Bay
Picolata
Alachua
St. Augustine
Anastatia I.
Newnansville
Pilatka
Matanzas Inlet
Micanopy
Orange L.
Dunns L.
L. George
Volusia
Cedar Keys
Ocola
Enterprise
Munroe L.
Mellonville
New Smyrna
Brooksville
Fort Dade
C. CANAVERAL
Indian R.
L. Poinsett
Tampa
Fort Brooke
Sand Key
L. Kissimee
Kissimee R.
Indian R. Inlet
Anna Maria Key
Forests of Cypress & Pine
L. Islokpoga
Long Key
LAKE
Jupiter Inlet
Caloosahatchee R.
Fort Myers
Fort Dulany
Oyster Bay
C. ROMANO
ATLANTIC OCEAN
O F M E X I C O
F L O R I D A

6
The Era of Civil War and Reconstruction, 1861 – 1880

When George F. Thompson toured the area on behalf of the Freedmen's Bureau in 1865, he reported more than 100,000 cattle grazing on the vast stretches of open land. He described them as "wild and fleet of foot as the deer..."

This team of long horn oxen were photographed on Titusville's Main Street around 1880. (Photo courtesy Jim Ball)

When Florida seceded from the Union and joined the Confederacy in early 1861, the few inhabitants of Brevard County and the southern portion of Volusia County which was destined to be adjoined to it in 1879 reacted in much the same way as their fellow Floridians elsewhere. Most followed their state government and supported the Confederacy while a few were more or less active Unionists. Most of the younger men marched off to war and eventually participated in battles in Virginia, Tennessee, and elsewhere. Mills Burnham's son-in-law, Henry Wilson, for example, was wounded in Tennessee while one of his sons was killed on a distant battlefield. Henry A. Crane, who had held offices in both Mosquito

John Quincy Stewart (above and in group below) was a Representative from Hamilton County in the Florida Legislature that supported secession in 1861. He moved to Brevard with his father and brothers soon after the War and served as Representative from Brevard County in 1879. (Photo courtesy Jim Ball)

County and St. Lucie County before moving to Tampa, remained loyal to the Union and acted as a pilot aboard the U. S. S. Sagamore in the United States blockading squadron which patrolled the Indian River region. The cattlemen whose herds ranged between the St. Johns and Kissimmee rivers were divided. Some tended to favor the Union while others were more sympathetic with the Confederacy.

The state of Florida and the infant Confederate States of America spent much of 1861 in preparing for war, organizing new governments, and establishing procedures by which the central government and the states could cooperate in a common effort. Brevard County residents followed suit, cooperating when they could, and resorting to their own initiatives when necessary. When Confederate Secretary of the Navy Stephen R. Mallory ordered all lighthouses closed and their lights extinguished, James A. Paine, Oswald Long, Frances A. Ivey, and John Whitten, all residents of the Fort Capron and St. Lucie areas, readily complied. They reported in August 1861 that both the Jupiter Inlet and Cape Florida lights had been extinguished. Mills Burnham, a confirmed Unionist, dismantled the Cape Canaveral light, carefully packing the lamp and mechanisms in boxes which he buried in his orange grove.[1]

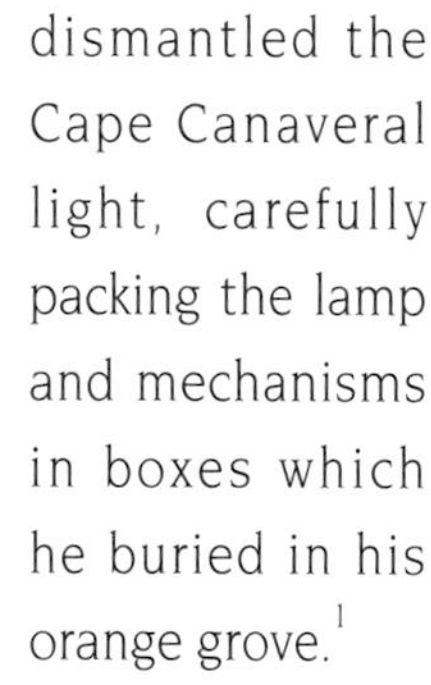

Brevard Countians met at the home of James A. Paine and made plans for their protection. William B. Davis and James A. Armour led a discussion about how "to provide for the safety and protection of this community in view of the expected invasion of our coast." While it is doubtful that Abraham Lincoln's government ever considered using its military forces to occupy such a sparsely settled region, it was natural that the settlers were concerned about their homes. Paine, John S. Hermans, and Frances Ivey were named a committee to draft appropriate resolutions addressing the matter. The committee advised Governor Madison Perry that "we are sparsely settled and at a distance of 100 miles of coast and our young men are now in Virginia, so we ask for protection." Assuring the governor that "we adhere to the Constitution of the Confederate States of America" they asked him to protect the Indian River Inlet with a company of soldiers. While two companies of Florida troops were stationed at New Smyrna in the early months of the war, Governor Perry was unable to send soldiers to Indian River. The local residents had to be satisfied with a home guard company commanded by Captain James A. Paine.[2]

Although a military invasion at Indian River Inlet was unlikely, the United States Navy was serious about blockading the coast to prevent the export of cotton and timber products and, even more important, the importation of supplies such as weapons, ammunition, food, and medicine. From Cape Canaveral northward, the Florida coastal waters were patrolled by the South Atlantic Blockading Squadron while the Eastern Gulf Blockading Squadron was responsible for the remainder of the coast from Cape Canaveral southward and around the peninsula to St. Andrews Bay. Between 1862 and 1865, 32 vessels were captured along the Atlantic coast from New Smyrna southward. The Confederates established a supply line from New Smyrna to the St. Johns River and into the interior with the result that much of the blockade action occurred in that area. The Confederate government discussed the possibility of a blockade running operation through the Indian River Inlet, but both Confederate Agent Samuel Swann and Brigadier General Joseph Finegan discouraged it. They were successful in convincing Confederate authorities that the lack of either roads or navigable waterways rendered the undertaking unwise.[3]

While the Confederacy never followed through on its plan to use the Indian River Inlet, this did not prevent individual blockade runners from attempting to run goods in and out of the Indian River. Most of them were small vessels able to carry only a bale or two of cotton and a small amount of turpentine on the outbound voyage. On the return trip, these vessels usually carried salt, food, and general merchandise. The U. S. S. *Gem of the Sea* captured the *Maggie Fulton* in the Indian River in April 1863. It was inbound with a load of merchandise which included buttons, belts, buckles, ribbons, paper, scented soap, and similar goods. The only military supplies were 12,000 gun caps. As was the case with all such captures, the *Maggie Fulton* was taken to Key West where it was declared a prize by the admiralty court. This meant that the vessel and its cargo could be sold at auction. Since the captors shared in the proceeds of such sales, there was considerable incentive for them to be vigilant in guarding the coastal waters. The *Gem of the Sea* also captured the *Ann*, the *Petie* and the *Inez*, but these were so unseaworthy that they were destroyed at sea. The *Gem of the Sea* was the most successful blockading vessel in taking prizes in the Indian River, but other ships which guarded the southern Florida coast included the *Beauregard*, the *Roebuck* and the *Sagamore*. The *Sagamore* captured the British sloop *Julia* in early 1863 in the Atlantic waters between Indian River Inlet and Jupiter Inlet. In early 1864, the *Roebuck* took the Confederate schooner *Rebel* in the Indian River. The Confederate sloop *Nina* was captured in the river shortly afterward. Both vessels carried salt, liquor, coffee, and boxes of sundries and were destined for Sand Point. The last blockade runner captured along the Florida coast was the *Mary*, taken in the Indian River just a few weeks before General Lee surrendered in April 1865.[4]

This 1913 postcard shows the ruins of the old Gleason home in Eau Gallie. (Photo courtesy Doug Hendriksen)

It was customary in the 19th century for seagoing vessels to carry salt in ballast when sailing empty, but that was not the reason that so many of the inbound blockade runners carried that bulky item. Salt was a scarce commodity in the Confederacy and it frequently sold for as much as thirty dollars a bushel and sometimes even more. To increase the salt supply both the Confederate and Florida state governments as well as many individuals went to the coast to manufacture it from sea water. It was a simple process. The saltmaker had simply to boil quantities of sea water in large vats over fires made from the readily available supply of wood. When the water evaporated the salt remaining in the vats was shoveled out and spread to dry. The resulting product was a dirty brownish color but it served its intended purposes. The fires of the saltmakers were easily located by the blockading squadrons and the equipment was easily destroyed. It was also easily replaced. Many salt works were destroyed by the enemy forces, but the manufacture of salt continued until the end of the war. Salt was made both at Sand Point and at the Indian River Inlet. People frequently came from considerable distances to engage in the simple but profitable enterprise. Peter and Joseph Buchan and other members of their large family came from Apopka (then known simply as "The Lodge") to make salt at Sand Point. William Willingham, who was grazing a large herd at Kissimmee Island, travelled more than 45 miles to Indian River to obtain salt for his cattle. Whether he actually made his own salt or bought it from others is not clear.[5]

The cattlemen who began moving into the prairies west of the St. Johns River in the mid-1850s had developed sizable herds by the time the Civil War began. They were already accustomed to driving their cattle over the Capron Trail to Tampa where they were usually sold to James McKay for about four dollars a head. McKay loaded the cattle aboard boats and shipped them to Cuba where they were sold for gold coin. When the war began, the direction of the cattle drives changed. At first Jacob Summerlin, and then James McKay, acted as commissary agent to procure and deliver cattle for the Confederacy. The Yates, Overstreets, Parkers, Basses, Barbers, James F. P. Johnston and other Brevard County cattlemen cooperated with the commissary agents, driving their herds over the difficult terrain to north Florida railheads where they received from eight to ten dollars a head for their stock. By 1863, Confederate authorities estimated that three-fourths of the cattle which Florida was supplying to the Confederacy was coming from Brevard and Manatee counties. By the latter years of the war, Florida was supplying nearly all the beef being consumed by Confederate troops.[6]

The main trail out of the Kissimmee prairies was through Orlando, northward to Payne's Prairie, and then to Waldo, Madison, or Baldwin where the cattle were loaded on trains. The cattle were driven at a slow pace – usually about eight miles a day – so that they could forage on the way. It was a grueling trip for both cowmen and cattle.

Some beeves lost as much as 150 pounds on the way, but some of that could be recouped at Payne's Prairie where the grass was always good. At Orlando and at intervals along the way, pens were built for holding the cattle overnight. If the drovers managed to get their herds to a pen, then their task of tending the skittish animals was simplified. If, on the other hand, they were obliged to hold them in the open, night watches reduced their rest. Difficult though the operation was, it was profitable for the cattlemen and the Confederacy desperately needed the beef.[7]

The infant county government functioned without serious interruption during the war. Elections were held for county and state officials, although not all offices were occupied at all times. The growing influence of the cattlemen was probably the reason for relocating the county seat to Bassville in the western part of the county in 1864. The legislative act making Bassville the county seat was repealed in 1865 and the voters were allowed to choose a new location. It was apparently at this time that nearby Lake View became the seat of Brevard County government.[8]

Between 1860 and 1865, Brevard County was represented in the state assembly in turn by Needham Yates, Henry Overstreet, James F. P. Johnston, and then Henry Overstreet again. A part of the 19th senatorial district, the county was represented in the upper house by J. D. Starke, W. C. Roper, and Francis A. Hendry in turn.[9] Among those who served as commissioners were Quinn Bass, John Barber, Jesse Long, A. M. Jernigan, James Harrell, James Yates, Eli P. Jernigan, A. J. Sullivan, W. B. Yates, and James Herndon. James G. Benton was county judge, William Cook was clerk of the court, and Thomas M. McDaniel was the sheriff.[10]

The end of the war in the spring of 1865 was followed by uncertainty and confusion. Lincoln was killed at about the same time Lee surrendered. Confederate soldiers in Florida surrendered in May 1865 by which time Andrew Johnson had become president. While the soldiers were drifting back home from the battlefields, Johnson announced his policy for putting the Union back together. He chose a non-punitive course by which the former Confederate states could rejoin the Union if they renounced slavery, recognized that secession had been illegal, and repudiated all debts incurred in support of the Confederacy. He made no mention of the future status of the freed slaves, an omission which was to set off a bitter dispute with a group of Congressmen who would soon be known as Radical Republicans. Johnson appointed a provisional governor to oversee the formation of a new government in Florida and asked local officials to remain in their positions until new elections were held. Among Brevard County's interim officials were commissioners Needham Yates, William B. Yates, Francis Gregg, and Quinn Bass; County Judge John Barber; Clerk of the Court James Padgett; and Sheriff Jackson Clifton. James F. P. Johnston represented Brevard County at the constitutional convention.[11]

After a brielf and turbulent term as lieutenant governor in 1868, William Henry Gleason acquired thousands of acres of land between Eau Gallie and Melbourne and proposed location of an agricultural college in Eau Gallie. (Florida State Archives)

While the so-called Johnson government was being organized, opposition to the president's program was growing in Congress. Determined to see that something was done to protect the freedmen before the former Confederate states were readmitted to the Union, Radical Republicans stopped the Johnson program by refusing to seat the senators and representatives from those states.

Johnson's plan was thrown out in early 1867 by legislation which called for new constitutions to be drawn up in the Southern states by electorates which included adult male blacks. When new constitutions were written, approved by Congress, and ratified by the people, Florida and the other seceded states could be readmitted to the Union. The supervisor of elections for delegates to the new constitutional convention in Florida was Ossian B. Hart, one of the settlers of the old Armed Occupation Colony. Hart first appointed Thomas J. Cockshutt, who would later emerge as a leading citizen of the LaGrange community, as supervisor of registration for Brevard County. Apparently because of his prior association with the Confederacy, Cockshutt was unable to take the required oath to qualify for office. He was then replaced by W. S. Norwood, another recent arrival in the county.[12]

The new constitution which was written and implemented in July 1868 provided for appointment of all local officials by the governor. Republicans swept all the statewide offices with Harrison Reed becoming governor and William Henry Gleason becoming lieutenant governor. With such extensive appointive powers, Reed tried to build a harmonious coalition government by including in it many former Confederates who were then identifying themselves as Conservatives.[13] He failed mostly because there was too much opposition among the older Floridians to black suffrage, but also because it was so difficult to obtain reliable advice from the counties about appointments. Reed's administration was marred by numerous incidents of racial violence and general disorder. While there were few blacks in Brevard County, it was not spared lawlessness. Its trouble stemmed from a full-fledged range war which raged through the central Florida area in the late 1860s and early 1870s.

When George F. Thompson toured South Florida on behalf of the Freedmen's Bureau in 1865 he reported more than 100,000 cattle grazing on the vast stretches of open land. According to him they were "wild and fleet of foot as the deer and only those who are trained to the business could succeed in finding them." He described those "trained to the business" as a "class entirely destitute, ignorant and generally ambitious only for enough to eat regardless of quality to satisfy their hunger." Thompson grossly under-estimated the cattlemen of the region, but he was correct about the nature of their business.[14] Herds then ranged over many miles of open territory. Moses E. Barber's nearly 10,000 head, for example, roamed from his headquarters in western Brevard County northward into Orange County and southward almost to Lake Okeechobee. Other herds intermingled with his cattle. It was easy enough for honest men to mistakenly brand the wrong calves, but some people were more careless than others with their branding irons. The court dockets of the central Florida counties in the period following the Civil War are filled with indictments for "altering the brand of an animal." While indictments were frequent, prosecutions were less so, and convictions even more rare. Angry cattlemen often resorted to their own measures. An outgrowth of one such incident disturbed the peace of central Florida for several years and caused Harrison Reed's administration continuing embarrassment.

In August, 1868, Moses E. Barber, Moses B. F. Barber, and Thomas Johnson approached George Bass and placed him under arrest at gunpoint for allegedly stealing some of Barber's cattle. There was apparently little disagreement about whether or not Bass had committed the act since he promised to stop stealing if the other cattlemen would do the same. He also said he would pay for the cattle if Barber could prove that they were his. His captors were apparently not interested in what Bass had to say. They told him to quit the country within thirty days or suffer the consequences. "Being overpowered," Bass testified, "I said I would leave the state in 30 days if they would not hang me."[15]

When he was released, Bass filed a complaint for false imprisonment and threats of injury. A disagreement immediately ensued over jurisdiction. Since the incident occurred "about a mile east" of William Cook's house and he had once been clerk of court for Brevard County, it would seem reasonable to assume that Bass had been assaulted in that county. But, it was not that simple. Several witnesses testified at the trial that no one was sure where the county line was. One witness asserted that William Cook had refused to pay taxes in Orange County because he claimed to live in Brevard. All of the confusion may have resulted from a boundary definition made by the 1866 legislature. At that time the line between Brevard and Orange was declared to be located at the line between townships 27 and 28 from its intersection with the Polk County boundary on the west, then running east along that line to the St. Johns River. Since this was a much more precise delineation than the one which had been described in 1845, it seems that honest persons may have honestly disagreed about the location of the county boundary.[16]

The boundary dispute apparently arose because Bass had filed his charges at Orlando in Orange County, leading Sheriff David W. Mizell to take the initiative in arresting the Barbers and Johnson. Brevard County Sheriff Dempsey Cain, who lived on the coast at the site of what became Roseland seems to have had no objection to Mizell handling the arrests. In fact, Cain resigned as sheriff in early 1870 at about the time the range war reached its most violent proportions. It also became clear that Brevard County's population was too small to assemble a jury to try the resulting case. Preparations were made for trial at the October 1868 term of the circuit court at Orlando. Prominent Jacksonville attorneys arrived in town to represent the defendants. Then, the courthouse mysteriously burned to the ground and the trial was postponed.[17]

During the next few months Sheriff Mizell pursued his job with impressive diligence. Many charges were lodged against a number of Brevard and Orange residents for "altering mark on an animal," but his persistence in pursuing charges against the Barbers and their friends suggests that a bitter feud had developed. Moses E. Barber was charged with polygamy. Moses B. F. Barber and Bathsheba Sheffield were indicted for adultery and Sheffield was additionally charged with arson. Murder charges were filed against Barber's friends, Needham Yates and James F. P. Johnston. The docket was so full that a special term of court was called for April 1869.[18]

Having failed to show up for trial at the spring term, Moses E. Barber made bond in July to appear in the fall. His guarantors were Needham Yates and Andrew J. Barber. When he again failed to come before the court, Sheriff Mizell set out to arrest him. As he crossed Bull Creek near Kenansville deep in Brevard County on February 21, 1870, he was shot and killed. His brother, Judge John Mizell gathered a posse which consisted of some of the most prominent citizens of Orange County and set out to find the Barbers. During the next several months a virtual war was fought in the cattle country of Brevard and Orange counties. Isaac Barber and Needham Yates were both shot to death, Moses B. F. Barber was brought back to the Orlando area and thrown into Lake Conway with a plowshare tied to his neck. When he managed to swim to shore, the posse riddled him with bullets. By May, 1870, at least seven men had been killed either in Brevard or Orange. Although there are various legends about what happened to Moses E. Barber, the major figure in the manhunts, the Tampa Florida Peninsular reported that he had been killed on May 10, 1870, making him the seventh victim of the range war. The newspaper condemned Governor Reed for failing to declare martial law or otherwise address the lawlessness in the cattle country. Ocala attorney Robert W. Bullock, who was handling some of the Barber herds at the time, wrote a friend in late April that he was "going south in about two days provided there is any one left to go to. If they keep on killing they will kill out my party pretty soon, I will have a gay time among the widows..."[19]

The violence abated after the spring of 1870, but the grand jury in the fall still reported "the disorderly conduct of those men who were running their horses through crowds of men on the streets, then into homes, stores and churches."[20]

Perhaps because of the range violence, the legislature changed the boundary between the two counties again in 1873. The boundary was then to run from the St. Johns River westward along the line between townships 25 and 26 to Little Lake Tohopekaliga, around the western side of the lake to Cross Prairie, then along the northern edge of the prairie to Lake Tohopekaliga to the same township line, continuing west along that line to the division between ranges 25 and 27 east.

Brevard County's population was then increasing along the Indian River, which may have been the reason for yet another relocation of the county seat. The 1872 legislature empowered the voters of counties to change seat by majority vote which Brevard County electors soon did. The 1874 legislature proclaimed Eau Gallie as the permanent seat of Brevard County.[21]

Alexander A. Stewart, born in 1840 near Jasper, Florida, served as an officer in the Confederate Army and moved to Brevard soon after the War. He was appointed Clerk of the Circuit Court in 1871 and served in the post until 1912. (Photo and document courtesy Jim Ball)

As elsewhere in the state, Governor Reed tried mightily to establish a civil government in Brevard, but it was a difficult task in view of the sparse population, the distance between Tallahassee and the county, and the exceedingly slow communications. These problems were exemplified by the appointment of Henry L. Parker as county judge in 1872. Parker lived at Fort Drum, but his post office address was St. Lucie, about 40 miles from his residence. James Paine, Sr., seems to have emerged as political advisor for the county and recommended numerous appointments to Reed as well as his successor, Ossian B. Hart. But it was a difficult task to fill the various offices and even a greater problem to keep them filled. When a number of officials resigned in 1871, Paine wrote that "Frank Smith is doing all he can to deter those I have recommended from accepting offices. He wants to prevent organization of a county government so as to delay collection of taxes and opening of courts." In the same letter he recommended Alexander A. Stewart for clerk of court and Charles McLane for county judge.[22]

Paine continued to advise the chief executive about appointments and himself served in several offices during the period. Both Harrison Reed and Ossian Hart tried to pursue bipartisanship in their appointments, but their intentions sometimes backfired. For example, Paine had recommended John Houston of Eau Gallie for justice of the peace in early 1872. When he became governor in 1873, Hart assumed that Houston was a good choice for office and offered him the positions of tax assessor and collector of revenue. When Houston declined, the governor extended the same offer to Minor S. Jones of Indian River. Jones first accepted, but when he learned that he was the second choice after Houston, he wrote a blistering letter saying that "my object in first consenting

Executive Department.

IN THE NAME AND UNDER THE AUTHORITY OF

THE STATE OF FLORIDA.

Whereas, A. A. Stewart hath been duly appointed by the Governor, according to the Constitution and Laws of said State, to be Clerk of the Circuit Court for Brevard County, from the 23d day of September A D 1873, until the End of the next Ensuing Session of the Senate unless an appointment be sooner made and Confirmed

Now, Therefore, Reposing especial trust and confidence in the loyalty, patriotism, fidelity, and prudence of the said A. A. Stewart, I,

MARCELLUS L. STEARNS,

Lieutenant-Governor of the State of Florida, acting Governor, under and by virtue of the authority vested in me by the Constitution and Laws of the said State, **DO HEREBY COMMISSION** the said A. A. Stewart to be such Clerk of the Circt Court according to the Laws and Constitution of said State, for the time aforesaid, and **In the Name of the People of the State of Florida,** to have, hold, and exercise such office, and all the powers appertaining thereto, and to perform the duties thereof, and to enjoy all the privileges and benefits of the same, in accordance with the requirements of Law.

In Testimony Whereof, I do hereunto set my hand, and cause to be affixed the Great Seal of the State, at **Tallahassee, the Capital,** this 23d day of September A. D. 1873, and of the Independence of the United States the ninety seventh year.

M L Stearns

Acting Governor of Florida.

By the Acting Governor. Attest:

Sam B McLin

Secretary of State.

to take [the positions] was to republicanize the county, but now that the governor has 'given first refusal of them' to an illiterate democrat (Jno Houston), no consideration could induce me to such a violation of self respect..." Jones apparently had no such problems with his acceptance in the same letter of an appointment as county judge. There is no record that he was confirmed in the latter position, however. And, despite Jones' animosity, John Houston continued to serve as a county commissioner during the Reed and Hart administrations as well as that of Marcellus L. Stearns who succeeded the latter after his untimely death in 1874. It is somewhat ironic that Houston was subsequently removed from office after he was criticized for being a Republican.[23]

Others who served as commissioner during the years of Republican hegemony were O. J. Pettit, Gardner S. Hardee, John L. Casper, A. Hendry, Thomas L. Paine, R. A. Hardee, William H. Sharpe, William Shiver, Berrien Sullivan, William F. Richards, John P. Varnum, and William Simms. County judges included James Paine, Sr., Charles McLane, Henry L. Parker, Charles B. Magruder, and Abner D. Johnston. Frank Smith, Aaron Smith, Joseph Smith, Alexander A. Stewart, and John M. Lee were clerks of court. Dempsey Cain was succeeded as sheriff by John Quincy Stewart, Charles Bass and Abner J. Wright. James Paine, Sr., John Quincy Stewart and Thomas A. Bass each served as collector of revenue, and Quinn Bass was county treasurer for a time. James Paine, Sr., was superintendent of schools until he was succeeded by William H. Sharpe in 1874. Robert C. May was surveyor for at least part of the period. Brevard was in the 21st senatorial district with Dade and William H. Hunt of the latter county served in the senate until he was succeeded by the controversial E. T. Sturtevant in 1873. Brevard County was not represented in the assembly from 1868 to 1870. It is not clear whether or not James Paine, Sr., was the representative from 1870 to 1872, but R. A. Hardee went to Tallahassee in that capacity in 1873 to be followed by Quinn Bass for the following term.[24]

The extensive appointive powers accorded the governors by the 1868 constitution were a mixed blessing to Reed, Hart and Stearns, all of whom had difficulty in maintaining a balance among the various shadings of political opinion in the sparsely settled county, but there was controversy over the elective offices as well. The Republicans had achieved sizable majorities in both houses of the legislature in 1868, but by 1872 the two parties were approaching a balance. As the Democrats gained strength in the legislature, county elections received more and more scrutiny. Constituting a single senatorial district, Brevard and Dade counties were casting about a hundred votes by 1872 when Israel Stewart of Brevard ran against E. T. Sturtevant of Dade for the seat. In an election which emphasized informality in conforming with the election laws, Stewart received a majority on the face of the returns in both counties, but that was before the election officials had their say.

Thirty votes had been cast in Dade and 69 in Brevard. Sturtevant received 14 and Stewart 17 in Dade. Stewart received 39 of the Brevard votes while Sturtevant received none. But majorities were not what they seemed in the 1870s. Sturtevant had been an inspector at Dade's only voting precinct. As county judge he was also a member of the county canvassing board which reviewed the precinct returns and reported them to the state. As a candidate he contested three votes which had been cast against him on the grounds that the electors had been ineligible. He had permitted the votes to be cast at the precinct, but he and the other two board members threw them out at the county level, showing the state election board a Sturtevant majority of 14 to 13. The state board declared Sturtevant elected because Brevard's returns were received too late to be counted. Despite a long and heated dispute in the senate, Sturtevant retained his seat and served the entire term. The seat was politically crucial, since the seating of Stewart instead of Sturtevant would have given the Democrats a majority of one in the senate.[25]

The struggle over the Sturtevant-Stewart election had aroused partisan anger and raised tempers as people began to anticipate the 1876 presidential election. The assassination of Republican Senator Elisha G. Johnson of Columbia County, which left the Democrats a majority in the upper house, created even more hostility. The hard feelings between political parties, which had abated somewhat since 1872, were exacerbated once more and at a time when the nation was almost evenly divided in its politics. After a mud-slinging campaign of many months the national press reported in November 1876 that Republican Rutherford B. Hayes had received 176 electoral votes to 184 for Democrat Samuel J. Tilden. With 185 required to elect, Tilden needed only one of the nineteen contested votes which were in Florida, Louisiana, and South Carolina. The electoral votes of Florida, Louisiana, and South Carolina were too close to call. The nation looked toward these states, especially Florida where the two candidates were divided by fewer than 100 votes. In a series of maneuvers involving the state election board and the Congress of the United States, Hayes was declared elected president by an electoral vote of 185-184.

After the national partisans left Florida, the Democratic candidate for governor, George F. Drew, obtained a ruling from the state supreme court which awarded him the election over incumbent Republican Marcellus L. Stearns. Drew's inauguration in early January 1877 was hailed as the "end of Reconstruction," since Democrats acquired the extensive appointive powers which had been previously enjoyed by the Republicans as long as they held the governorship. Unfortunately, the political acrimony of the previous decade did not end with the election. While the Democrats had acquired hegemony in the state, the Republicans controlled the national government which had authority to investigate national elections in the former Confederate states and would use it frequently. Brevard County, which had cast 104 votes for Drew and 63 for Stearns in 1876 and had not been directly involved in the disputed presidential election, was not to be exempt from the continuing disputes over Congressional elections.[26]

Only when the House of Representatives investigated the contested Congressional election between Republican Horatio Bisbee, Jr., and Democrat Jesse J. Finley was the conduct of Brevard County's 1876 election revealed. There were seven voting precincts in the county at the time: Fort Pierce, No. 1; Eau Gallie, No. 2; City Point, No. 3; Fort Drum, No. 4, Lake Marion, No. 5; Bassville, No. 6, and Yates, No. 7. Returns were tabulated from all of them except Fort Drum where no election was held. It was alleged that the inspectors at Fort Drum were Democrats who had refused to open the polls because they believed a majority of the estimated 25 voters there were Republicans. Since electors could vote at any precinct in the county by swearing that they were qualified, two of the Fort Drum residents voted elsewhere, but the others were denied opportunity to cast their votes. At City Point, Finley charged that 38 votes had been cast for Bisbee by persons whose names were not on the registration lists and who had not taken oaths of qualification. Furthermore, no poll lists had been kept. Although such loose procedure was illegal, it was not in fact unusual in the county in 1876 or during subsequent elections. What was unusual in 1876 was that 21 votes had been tabulated from Lake Winder which was not a polling place at all.[27]

The irregularities of the 1878 election were comparable to those of 1876, but the consequences were more serious. In a Congressional investigation of the contest between Republican Horatio Bisbee, Jr., and Democrat Noble A. Hull it was made clear that the election had once again been quite informal, but this time the United States marshals interceded. John M. Lee, a 25-year-old resident of Lake View, was clerk of the circuit court, having been appointed to that position in 1875. His assistant was Eugene Gaulden. Gaulden had altered the tabulation of the votes from the precinct and the marshal alleged that the crime had been committed with Lee's knowledge. Lee, Sheriff Abner J. Wright and Justice of the Peace Johns were charged with violations of federal election laws and Lee and Wright were convicted. Lee was sent to a prison at Albany, New York, served his sentence, and returned to the county to hold public office again. Wright escaped from authorities at Jacksonville and fled. Eugene Gaulden was also charged but he escaped prosecution by fleeing the county. It was estimated that 157 votes had been cast in the county; 117 for Hull and 46 for Bisbee. The state election board had thrown the votes out, but the Congressional committee apparently agreed to count them.[28]

The Congressional investigative process was repeated in 1880 when Horatio Bisbee again contested the election of Jesse J. Finley, but this time no one was charged with a crime. The leading witness was James A. McCrory, a 26-year-old resident of Titusville who was serving both as county judge and deputy clerk of the court. By this time the county seat had been moved to Titusville and the county had twelve voting precincts. Those east of the St. Johns were LaGrange, No. 1; Titusville, No. 2; City Point, No. 3; Eau Gallie, No. 4; Fort Pierce, No. 5; Georgiana, No. 6; Burnhams, No. 7; and Haulover, No. 12. On the west side were Crab-Grass, No. 8; Fort Drum, No. 11; Bassville, No. 9, and Lake View, No. 10. McCrory's testimony made it clear that once again there were several irregularities and that most of them were at the distant precincts west of the river. The testimony of Sheriff Richards also demonstrated how difficult it was to comply with the election laws in such a large county where transportation was so primitive. As the person responsible for delivering the ballot boxes and voter registration lists to all the precincts, he testified that he had managed to reach all of them except Fort Pierce, but had run out of time before he got there. The entire county vote was 222 for Finley and 74 for Bisbee.[29]

George F. Drew's inauguration as governor brought no sudden sweep of county offices, but there was a change of emphasis which eventually brought Democratic majorities. Abner Johnson, Abner J. Wright, and John M. Lee continued to serve as county judge, sheriff, and clerk respectively, although Alexander Tindall replaced Lee as superintendent of schools. Drew named three new county commissioners – William Simmons, T. H. Whaley, and Elijah Padgett – all of whom lived in the western part of the county. In 1879 the commissioners were John H. Trimble of Lakeview, R. A. Hardee of Rockledge, P. E. Wager of Titusville, and Alexander Bell and Henry L. Parker of St. Lucie. Parker still lived at Fort Drum. Israel Stewart was elected to the senate from the 21st district in 1876, but died before the 1877 session was held. William H. Sharpe was seated for the 1879 session. A. C. Bass of Bassville was Brevard's representative in 1877 followed by John Quincy Stewart of Georgiana in 1879.[30]

As will be shown in the next chapter, there was considerable population growth along the Indian River in the years following the Civil War. Titusville had become the transportation gateway to the settlements along the river as well as a growing community in its own right by 1880. Led by Henry T. Titus, several residents of southern Volusia County began advocating annexation to Brevard. They found a willing ally in Charles Dougherty, a young legislator from Volusia who supported the change as a way of building political support for his career plans. Dougherty pushed a bill through the legislature which brought about the desired change in 1879. "An Act to define the Boundary Line Between Volusia and Brevard" changed the line to run between townships 19 and 20 westward to the line between ranges 33 and 34, then south to the line between townships 21 and 22, then southward along the middle of the St. Johns River. Another enactment of the same legislature provided that "whereas the county seat of Brevard County has never been legally located," the voters were empowered to locate the county seat. Although it might be argued that the county seat had been "legally located" several times, the Brevard County voters chose Titusville as the county seat and it has remained there since 1880.[31]

END NOTES

1. Florida State Archives, Record Group 101, Series 577, Correspondence of Madison S. Perry, Box 1, James A. Paine, et al, to Madison S. Perry, August 28, 1861; Robert Ranson, East Coast Memoirs, p. 25.
2. FSA, RG 101, Perry Correspondence, Citizens of Brevard County to Governor, August 28, 1861.
3. Alfred Jackson Hanna and Kathryn Abbey Hanna, Florida's Golden Sands (Indianapolis and New York, 1950), p. 156; Alice Strickland, "Blockade Runners," Florida Historical Quarterly, XXXVI (1957), pp. 88-90.
4. Hanna and Hanna, pp. 154-156; Strickland, p. 86.
5. Jerrell H. Shofner, History of Apopka and Northwest Orange County (Tallahassee, 1982), p. 14; Joe A. Akerman, Jr., Florida Cowman (Kissimmee, 1976), p. 47.
6. Akerman, pp. 85-87.
7. Ibid., pp. 87-89.
8. Laws of Florida, 1864, pp. 21-22, and 1865-66, pp. 91-92.
9. Florida State Library, Roster of State Legislators.
10. Florida State Archives, WPA Roster of State and County Officers, 1845-1868.
11. Ibid.; Journal of the Constitutional Convention of 1865.
12. FSA, RG 1020, Series 626, Correspondence of O. B. Hart, 1867.
13. Before the Civil War, Florida's political parties were Whigs and Democrats and they had opposed each other with considerable vigor. After the war they were anxious to resist the infant Republican Party and its black constituency with as much strength as possible. To avoid offending members of either of the ante bellum parties, the leaders of the post-war coalition which opposed the Republicans called themselves Conservatives. This new group came to represent the white population of the state. It was first the Conservatives, then the Conservative-Democrats, and, finally, the Democrats.
14. George F. Thompson,"Journal...as Inspector, Bureau of Refugees, Freedman and Abandoned Lands, on a tour of Central Florida and the Lower East Coast," December 1865, in P. K. Yonge Library, University of Florida.
15. Orange County, Circuit Court Records (Criminal), Moses B. F. Barber Papers, 1868-1870.
16. Ibid., Minute Book A, p. 273; Laws of Florida, 1866, p. 82
17. FSA, RG 150, Series 24, Correspondence of Secretary of State, Box 61, James Paine to Jonathan C. Gibbs, March 18, 1870.
18. Orange County, Circuit Court, Minute Book A, pp. 277-308.
19. Tampa Florida Peninsular, May 25, 1870; Robert W. Bullock to Edward M. L'Engle, May 18, 1870 Edward M. L'Engle Papers, University of North Carolina; FSA, RG 1020, Florida Census, 1870, Mortality.
20. Orange County, Circuit Court, Minute Book A, p. 59.
21. Laws of Florida, 1873, p. 36, and 1874, p. 96.
22. FSA, RG 101, Reed Correspondence, Box I, James Paine to Harrison Reed, May 19 1871.
23. Ibid., RG 150, Series 24, Box 5, Minor S. Jones to Samuel B. McLin, May 9, 1873.
24. Ibid., RG 150, Series 259, Commission Director; Laws of Florida, 1868, 1873, 1874.
25. Florida, Senate Journal, 1875, pp. 262-63; Tallahassee Weekly Floridian, February 2, 1875; Laws of Florida, 1873.
26. Titusville Florida Star, November 17, 1880.
27. United States, House of Representatives, Miscellaneous Document No. 10, 45th Cong., 1st Sess., pp. 22-23, 442, 445.
28. Tallahassee Weekly Floridian, January 28, 1875, November 30, 1880; U. S., House, Misc. Doc. No. 26, 46th Cong., 1st Sess., pp. 487, 614-617, and Doc. 86, 46th Cong., 3rd Sess., p. 3; FSA, RG 101, Series 577, Correspondence of George F. Drew, Senate Confirmation of Appointments, 1877; and RG 156, Series 259, Commission Directory, 1879; Andrew Jackson Hanna and Kathryn A. Hanna, Florida's Golden Sands (Indianapolis and New York,1950), pp. 176-179.
29. U. S., House, Report No. 11, pp. 403-405, and Report No. 1066, p. 17, 47th Cong., 1st Sess.
30. Laws of Florida, 1877, 1879; FSA, RG 156, Series 259, Commission Directory; RG 150, Series 24, Correspondence of Secretary of State, Box 6.
31. Laws of Florida, 1879, pp. 140, 142.

Page 68 Map: 1860 map of Florida and adjoining states, published in McNally's Geography Textbook. (Courtesy Jim Ball)

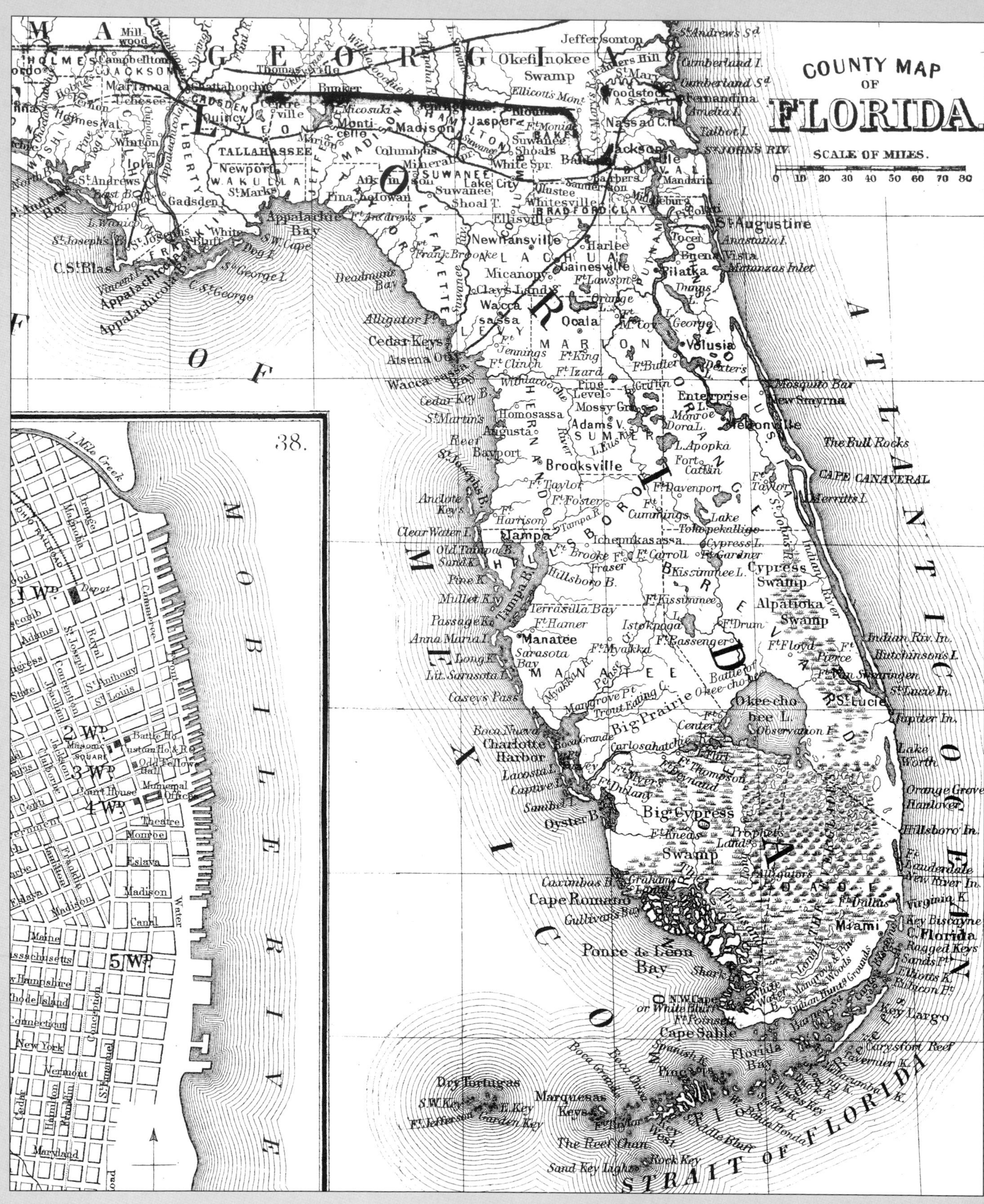

COUNTY MAP OF FLORIDA.
SCALE OF MILES.
0 10 20 30 40 50 60 70 80
38.
GEORGIA
FLORIDA
GULF OF MEXICO
ATLANTIC OCEAN
STRAIT OF FLORIDA
MOBILE RIVER
TALLAHASSEE
Jacksonville
St. Augustine
Tampa
Key West
Dry Tortugas
Okee-cho-bee L.
Cape Sable
Cape Canaveral

7
A Developing Riverine Community, 1865 – 1880

Permanent settlers and winter visitors transformed the county from a sprawling cattle range to a string of settlements bound together by the waters of the Indian River Lagoon. Population rose from 300 in 1865 to 1,497 in 1880.

The sender of this postcard from Sand Point (Titusville) wrote, "This is the only street in this wonderful city." (Photo courtesy Doug Hendriksen)

The Civil War stimulated the post-1865 growth of Brevard County in at least two ways. On the one hand, the political and social unrest in northern Florida and the neighboring ex-Confederate states after the war caused many Southerners to seek new homes. On the other, the Civil War had brought prosperity and wealth to a large number of Northerners who were thus enabled to think of vacation homes in warmer climates. Both groups learned of the vast open lands and favorable climate of central and southern Florida through such reports as the one circulated after Colonel George F. Thompson made his tour on behalf of the Freedmen's Bureau in 1865-1866. Some of the more adventurous

Above and left: Dr. and Mrs. William Wittfeld *developed beautiful gardens and groves at* Fairyland *on* Honeymoon Lake. *(Photos courtesy* Margaret Peterson *and* Mrs. J. M. Field, *Brevard County Historical Commission Archives)*

individuals from both sides decided to brave the physical isolation and lack of transportation and visit the Indian River country. Some came as permanent settlers and others as winter visitors. Though their numbers were small at first, they eventually transformed the county from a nearly empty, sprawling cattle range to a string of settlements bound together by the waters of the Indian River lagoon.

Most of the first settlers reached the Indian River region by way of the St. Johns River from Jacksonville or Palatka to Enterprise or Lake Harney. From those points they travelled by a rough wagon road to the coast or, if the water was sufficient, by shallow draft boat up the St. Johns to Salt Lake and then overland for about six miles. Either way was difficult. In the first few years, these settlers were also obliged to travel to Enterprise for whatever supplies they required. As more people arrived, a few stores appeared along the river and trade boats were visiting some of the more remote locations by the latter 1870s, but satisfactory transportation had to await the railroads in the mid-1880s.

Having lived in the county briefly before the war, Dr. William Wittfeld returned with his brother in 1866 to find that the homesteads they had started were no longer available for settlement. It was probably fortunate for Wittfeld who chose a new homestead on the southern end of Merritt Island. There he built and cultivated Fairyland which ultimately became one of the famed showplaces along the river. Douglas Dummett continued to cultivate his grove on the northern end of the island and employed several people there. One of them was a black man named Andrew Jackson who had survived a shipwreck on the nearby coast and spent the rest of his life in Brevard County. Jackson married Dummett's mixed-blood daughter and eventually developed a fine grove of his own. He became a substantial grove owner and shipped oranges from his place for nearly fifty years. William E. Futch had a home and grove on the site of old Fort Ann in 1868. J. Sykes lived nearby. Both Mills Burnham, the lighthouse keeper, and his son-in-law, Henry Wilson, were still tending their groves near Cape Canaveral. Wilson soon became a mail contractor for the route between New Smyrna and Fort Pierce. He carried the mail from the latter point by boat to the Haulover, crossed it on foot, and continued in another boat which he kept there. T. J. Carlisle settled in 1865 at the place which became LaGrange. John M. Feaster came from South Carolina about a year later. They were joined about 1867 by T. J. Cockshutt and Jacob N. Feaster.[1]

John Quincy was one of many former slaves who moved to Brevard after the Civil War. He delivered mail by boat along the Indian River and maintained close ties with his former owners, the Stewarts. (Photo courtesy Jim Ball)

Albert and Lawrence Faber came in 1866 to the area which became Sharpes. William H. Sharpe, who gave his name to the place, arrived in 1868. John Wesley Joyner left Jefferson County in 1866 and brought his family to Dixon's Point not far from Sharpes. He shortly moved to Titusville and the southern part of that town was for a time known as Joynerville. Dixon's Point was named for Robert Dixon who moved his family there from Kentucky in 1869. Israel Stewart moved to the area which later became Bonaventure in 1866. John Quincy and A. A. Stewart arrived about two years later. Benjamin C. Willard came to City Point in 1868 and eventually settled at Cocoa where he ran a store. Gardner S., R. A., and Thomas Hardee settled in 1868 near Rockledge. They were soon joined by A. L. Hatch, H. S. Williams, R. C. May and M. Delannoy. Cephas B. Magruder set out a grove and then brought his family from Georgia in 1870. Rockledge was taking shape as a progressive community by 1875. Joseph E. Gruber and his wife arrived from South Carolina in 1868 and settled at Sand Point. Other South Carolinians who came in the early years were the Sams and LaRoche families. Five of the LaRoche brothers

Israel Stewart and members of his family began moving from Hamilton County, Florida, to Brevard in 1866. This palmetto thatched house was built by his son Alexander at Bonaventure about 1868. (Photo courtesy Jim Ball)

Brothers John Robert and Samuel Joseph Field of Macon, Georgia served in the Confederate Army. They arrived on Merritt Island at the place which became Indianola in 1866. (*Photo courtesy Clyde Field*)

stories about the future of Brevard County, the loaded rifle which lay in his lap as he surveyed his holdings from the veranda of his hotel, and the tall stories which he told with gusto and obvious relish.

Although he gave his stories appropriate embellishment, they were derived from his own career as a soldier of fortune and professional Southerner. Titus had first come to national attention in 1851 when he raised a force of Floridians to assist the filibusterer, Narciso Lopez, in his third attempt to free Cuba from Spanish control. In the fall of that year he set out from the St. Johns River in the *Pampero* with arms and ammunition and about 75 men. When news reached him that Lopez had been captured and executed, Titus headed back to the St. Johns with a United States vessel in

lived for a time at the Narrows and Johns Island is named for one of them, but both families finally settled at Courtenay on Merritt Island. Phineas D. Wesson came from Rhode Island in 1870 and lived near Salt Lake until he purchased a grove from Mills Burnham on the Banana River. John R. and Samuel Field arrived on Merritt Island at the place which became Indianola in 1866. Their neighbor, William R. Sanders, arrived a year later, accompanied by his three brothers.[2]

There had been a post office at Sand Point just before the Civil War. It was reestablished in 1869 with John P. Harvey as postmaster.[3] Having arrived at Sand Point about 1867, Henry T. Titus would eventually lend his name to the growing town and become its most memorable citizen. Confined to a wheel chair for several years before his death in 1881, Titus was widely known for his promotional

hot pursuit but he managed to unload his cargo before he was arrested. He was brought to trial but United States authorities were unable to disprove his assertion that he had merely been on a pleasure excursion. Titus was next heard from when he went to Kansas to help make that territory into a slave state. He was with the proslavery force which attacked and burned much of Lawrence, Kansas, an act which enraged John Brown. Brown retaliated by executing five proslavery settlers and setting off a two-year period of violence which earned the territory the name of "Bleeding Kansas." Titus was captured by the abolitionist forces and eventually freed in a prisoner exchange. His wife and friends described his actions in the battle as heroic while his adversaries had other things to say. Whatever the case in Kansas, Titus was not yet finished.[4]

In early 1857 he arrived in Nicaragua with about 100

men and offered his services to William Walker, another American filibusterer, who had set himself up as president of that central American state. His military feats there served only to anger both William Walker and his own followers. Titus boarded a vessel in Panama which was sailing for San Francisco. He was not heard from again until the Civil War began. During that conflagration he was active in providing the Confederate army with supplies as well as freight service.[5]

Titus next made news in 1866 in Jacksonville where he was brought into court for assaulting a Union man during a heated discussion. Titus told the mayor's court "I had a political discussion with this fellow...he used some language that did not suit me and I knocked him in the head with my stick."[6]

At the time of this incident, Titus was engaged with Dr. John Westcott and several New York investors in a fishing venture at New Smyrna. As the New York and Indian River Preserving Company, they were employing ten men to catch fish, turtles, and oysters.[7]

While Titus was at New Smyrna rumors began circulating that enterprising Southerners were kidnapping freed blacks and taking them to Cuba where they were being sold back into slavery. Perhaps because of his flamboyant reputation, Titus was frequently mentioned as one of the persons so engaged. Lieutenant D. M. Hammond of the Freedmen's Bureau was detailed to investigate the activities at New Smyrna. Hammond found the fishing business at a standstill because the company's ship had been wrecked and he concluded that there was nothing to indicate a kidnapping operation there "except for the previous character of Titus, the commander of the fishing party."[8]

After the New Smyrna venture failed, Titus may have engaged in another fishing venture which took him to Sand Point. A company formed in Liverpool, England, and known as the Florida Provision Company acquired a 73 acre tract there in 1867. Its purpose was to establish a

Eliza A. Field, *wife of* John R. Field, *was faced with life in an isolated new settlement at* Indianola. (*Photo courtesy* Clyde Field)

cannery for turtle, fish, oysters, meats, fruits, and vegetables. The products were to be preserved in hermetically sealed cans which was the same process that Titus had used at New Smyrna. The venture was unsuccessful, but the firm deeded its land at Sand Point to Mary E. Titus (Mrs. Henry T. Titus) in June 1868. With the establishment

THE UNITED STATES OF AMERICA,

To all to whom these presents shall come, Greeting:

Homestead Certificate No. 619

APPLICATION 3297

Whereas There has been deposited in the General Land Office of the United States a Certificate of the Register of the Land Office at Gainesville, Florida, whereby it appears that, pursuant to the Act of Congress approved 20th May, 1862, "To secure Homesteads to actual Settlers on the Public Domain," and the acts supplemental thereto, the claim of Israel M. Stewart has been established and duly consummated, in conformity to law, for the [illegible]

according to the Official Plat of the Survey of the said Land, returned to the General Land Office by the Surveyor General:

Now know ye, That there is, therefore, granted by the United States unto the said Israel M. Stewart the tract of Land above described: To have and to hold the said tract of Land, with the appurtenances thereof, unto the said Israel M. Stewart and to [illegible] heirs and assigns forever.

In testimony whereof, I, [illegible] President of the United States of America, have caused these letters to be made Patent, and the Seal of the General Land Office to be hereunto affixed.

Given under my hand, at the City of Washington, the [illegible] day of July, in the year of our Lord one thousand eight hundred and [illegible], and of the Independence of the United States the [illegible]

BY THE PRESIDENT: U. S. Grant

By [illegible], Secretary.

Recorded, Vol. [illegible], Page 76 [illegible], Recorder of the General Land Office.

Homestead certificate given to Israel M. Stewart signed by President U. S. Grant and dated July 1, 1875. (Courtesy Jim Ball)

of a post office the following year, Sand Point was on its way to becoming Titusville.[9]

John W. Joyner had already relocated to Sand Point when Titus arrived and James Peckham came shortly afterward. Joyner subsequently opened a store in partnership with P. E. Wager. Titus not only offered supplies and general merchandise in his own store, but also had an extensive liquor inventory in connection with his hotel. Other early settlers of Titusville included Daniel O'Hara, John Simonson, William B. Hatter, W. H. Churchill, and Albert Becker. B. Einig started a small sawmill soon after his arrival. Andrew Gibson was the first black man to settle at Titusville. He came about 1870 and opened a barber shop which was the only such facility available to local residents for many years. Gibson also ran a restaurant and became one of the leaders of the black community which became known as Colored Town in later years. When Henry Maxwell arrived in 1880, he found a black population of about 13 already there. Some of the others were Dick Wright, Ned Gibson, and Betsy Thomas.[10]

Nearby LaGrange was a viable community which slightly preceded Sand Point. The Roberts family had settled just north of the Carlisles after the war ended. The first church in Brevard County was erected at LaGrange in 1869. Adhemar Brady started a store in the 1870s and a post office was opened in 1880. The settlement was then described as about 40 miles from Enterprise and about three miles from Titusville. The nearest post office on the north was Oak Hill, some 16 miles away. Frank Smith was the mail contractor and W. S. Norwood was the subcontractor. John P. Harvey was the proposed postmaster for the village which was estimated to encompass about 175 people. Harvey had also been the first postmaster at Sand Point.[11]

Casper Neil Mims arrived in 1876 and settled at the place north of LaGrange which soon became Mims. He recalled that there then were no roads except for a dirt affair to Enterprise over which a wagon travelled bi-weekly to carry produce to market and return with supplies. Most of Mims' visiting, like that of his neighbors along the river was done by sailboat. He later opened the first dry goods and grocery store at the town which bore his name.[12]

John Houston had settled at what became Eau Gallie just before the Civil War. Known at first as Arlington, the place was named Eau Gallie at least as early as 1871 when a post office was established there. Houston became the first postmaster. He was joined by a few families in the early 1870s, among whom were John and Andrew Chauncey from Jefferson County. Alexander Hodgson was also an early settler.[13]

The prime mover of Eau Gallie, however, was William Henry Gleason, who first purchased land there in 1869, although he did not settle there for a number of years. After a brief and turbulent term as lieutenant governor in 1868, Gleason turned his considerable abilities and energies to the promotion and development of peninsular Florida. His work with the Southern Inland Navigation and Improvement Company will be discussed in another chapter, but it was through his drainage plans in connection with that company that he acquired thousands of acres of raw land including much of the area between Eau Gallie and Melbourne. Gleason spent several years in Dade County where he and his partner, William H. Hunt, promoted the development of the area and also exercised extensive political influence. He was interested in opening an inland waterway from Biscayne Bay to the Halifax River as a part of his work with the Southern Inland Navigation and Improvement Company. He expected by this undertaking to drain about three million acres of land and make it available for sale and settlement, but he also intended to connect the waterway with the St. Johns River at Lake Washington and make Eau Gallie accessible as well.[14]

With his plans for a canal from Lake Washington to Eau Gallie and title to large tracts of land there, Gleason saw opportunity when the state decided to open an agricultural college. The Morrill Act of 1862 (popularly known as the Land Grant College Act) made available to the states 30,000 acres of land for each member of their Congressional delegations to be used for establishing a college. After Florida was restored to the Union, its allotment of 90,000 acres became available. A college was incorporated in 1872 although no site was then selected. While still a member of the legislature from Dade County, Gleason proposed location of the incipient agricultural college at Eau Gallie. Noting that Florida was the only semi-tropical state in the nation, he argued that the west bank of the Indian River was an ideal location for botanical experiments with tropical plants because:

> The air south of Cape Canaveral is soft and balmy, and vegetation assumes immediately a tropical character...I think that Eau Gallie is the most eligible for the College, all things taken into consideration. Biscayne Bay is more tropical, and the only objection to it is its inaccessibility. Eau Gallie is about 40 miles south of Cape Canaveral, and is as far north as the college can be located and have the advantage of a semi-tropical climate.

Before anyone noted that Eau Gallie was almost as inaccessible as Biscayne Bay, Gleason called attention to his plans for a canal from Lake Washington to the site.[15] In the spring of 1875, Governor Marcellus L. Stearns, John P. Varnum, and Dr. W. W. Hicks were named a committee to select a site for the college. Accompanied by Gleason, Stearns and Hicks visited Eau Gallie in April and subsequently recommended locating the college there. Gleason's offer of 2,320 acres of land supplemented by the offer of another 1,000 from W. R. Anno probably aided them in their choice.[16]

Varnum was made superintendent of construction of the college and by 1876 he had completed a two-story building with ten rooms and a hall, a two-room dormitory, and several outbuildings. Coquina from the immediate area was the basic construction material. The college never opened, probably because the Republicans were ousted from control of the state in early 1877 and Gleason lost his legislative seat at the same time. The 1877 legislature authorized the new school trustees to relocate the institution which opened in the early 1880s at Lake City. The buildings were converted into the Granada Hotel a few years later. Gleason tried other ways of attracting settlers to Eau Gallie. About 1880 he published a broadside describing the fine natural harbor situated about 40 miles south of Titusville at a point where the river was two miles wide. He offered a free lot to each of the first 20 people who built houses there. He also announced that he had another 16,000 acres of raw land for sale near Eau Gallie and Melbourne.[17]

When Eau Gallie got its post office in 1871 it was the only one between Sand Point, about 40 miles to the north, and St. Lucie, 53 miles to the south. Gleason obtained the mail contract in 1875 for the route between Titusville and Eau Gallie, but it is not likely that he delivered the mail himself. He did not move from Biscayne Bay to Eau Gallie until 1883 and even then he maintained his law offices in Jacksonville.[18]

Hunters had been using Crane Creek as a route to the interior for several years before the first settlers of Melbourne arrived in the mid-1870's. (Photo Brevard County Historical Commission Archives)

Hunters had been using Crane Creek as a route to the interior for several years before the first settlers of Melbourne arrived in the mid-1870s. First to arrive were three black men, Peter Wright, Wright Brothers, and Balaam Allen. Richard W. Goode brought his family from Chicago in early 1877 and Cornthwaite J. Hector came shortly afterward. A few others settled in the area and Melbourne was named in 1880 when a post office was established in Hector's general store.[19]

E. B. Arnold, who settled at the site of Malabar in 1873, was one of the few who lived along the river south of Melbourne before 1880. Another was August Park, a German immigrant who came to the Sebastian area in the 1860s. Gottlob Kroegel, another German immigrant, settled at Barker's Bluff. A post office was opened at St. Lucie in 1868 with James Smith as the first postmaster. Alexander Bell came from Hamilton County in 1871 to join the handful of people who were already living near the Indian River Inlet and Fort Pierce.

Gottlob Kroegel built his home on Barker's Bluff, site of an early trading post and an earlier Indian mound. His daughter-in-law, Ila Lawson Kroegel, stands under the large oak atop the mound. (Photo by Rodney Kroegel, Brevard County Historical Commission Archives)

C. B. Magruder wrote in the 1870s that "It seems generally not known that there are families scattered all along from Sand Point to Fort Capron, houses in many places less than half a mile apart." He did not add that there were also places where houses were much farther than half a mile apart.[20]

Although the territory west of the St. Johns extending to Fort Bassinger near the western boundary of the county remained the center of the range cattle industry, several cattlemen were moving closer to the coast. Archibald Hendry came in 1872 and a few years later Reuben Carlton began ranging cattle near Fort Pierce. Francis M. Platt was herding near Melbourne by 1878.[21]

Emily Lagow arrived with her family about 1876. It was at her father's place near Fort Pierce that Benjamin Hogg landed his trade boat in 1879. The Lagows welcomed Hogg, his wife and four children who remained there for several days until cattlemen and Indians from the interior had had time to come to the coast and trade with Hogg. He soon opened a store nearby which was eventually purchased and operated by P. P. Cobb. First Hogg, and then both Cobb and Alexander Bell engaged in a steady

Gottlob Kroegel (1837 - 1923) (Photo courtesy Rodney Kroegel, Brevard County Historical Commission Archives)

trade with the Indians who brought their pelts and hides to exchange for supplies.[22]

Several of the first post-Civil War settlers and a number of the visitors, left accounts of the difficult travel facilities into Brevard County. Perhaps none had more reason to deal with the adversities of the region than Confederate Secretary of War John C. Breckinridge who chose that route to escape the fallen Confederacy while his colleague, Secretary of State Judah P. Benjamin, chose a westerly route through Tampa Bay. Breckinridge reached the St. Johns via Madison to Lake George. He and his guide, John Taylor Wood, went up the river to Enterprise and then overland to the Indian River, hauling a boat all the way. Complaining of swarms of flies and maddening "chiggers," Breckinridge is said to have been unimpressed with both the land and the people. "I never saw such people...This is awful country," he was quoted as saying. Nevertheless, he reached the Atlantic Ocean and eventually landed in Cuba. The people to whom he so disparagingly referred, must have been few in 1865, but, as has been shown in the preceding paragraphs, a trickle of immigrants were braving the difficult transportation routes and the adversities of the frontier to join them.[23]

Nancy Dixon recalled that in 1869, "we had no transportation," except that T. W. Lund came as far as Lake Harney or Salt Lake every three to six months in his light draft vessel. On a trip in 1872, Charles Hallock found that he could travel from Jacksonville to Enterprise by steamer for $12 and that it cost about six dollars more to go to Salt Lake. From that point it was about six miles to Indian River, "the great game section." Writing in 1874, John L. Edwards saw it a little differently. He reached Salt Lake by steamer from Jacksonville and then went by stage the remaining six miles to Sand Point. There, he found "a comfortable house...kept for visitors," but he concluded that "you are now as far south as pleasure seekers need go."[24] The majority of visitors seem to have agreed with Hallock rather than Edwards and overcame the difficulties of travel in order to enjoy the outdoors with its excellent hunting and fishing many miles south of Titusville.

On one of his visits to the Indian River, Hallock set out from New Smyrna and crossed the Haulover by way of the canal which was then half a mile long, from seven to twelve feet wide, and only about 12 inches deep. His party spent the night at Andrew Jackson's place which was described as "the neatest little orange grove on the river." He next described the buildings of the Aurantia Grove about seven miles from the Haulover which had been laid out – and eventually abandoned – by Bliss and Company of New York. After a delay in calm water, Hallock and his party arrived at LaGrange, where there was a store and a small boarding house. From there they went on about two miles to Titusville, "the northernmost of the four post-offices on the river." It was ostensibly served by a weekly mail, which "really arrives and leaves with the wind." Titusville, according to Hallock, was "only noteworthy as a point of the arrival and departure for more interesting points on the river" and owed "all of its present prosperity to the indefatigable energy of its proprietor, Colonel H. T. Titus." Boatmen and guides could be hired there for any point on the lagoon or the interior. He recommended James Stewart, captain of the *Blonde*, or Jim Russell, who had lived on the river for more than 20 years. On the way south, Hallock passed Gardner Hardee's grove of "three-year-old trees" which he described as the finest he had seen. Jim Russell guided the party through the Narrows and called attention to Pelican Island on the way. Russell took them to Fort Pierce, from which point they set out for a visit to Lake Okeechobee.[25]

Hallock was favorably impressed with the Indian River region, but he thought its proper development depended on either a railroad southward to Lake Harney, which he regarded as the head of navigation on the St. Johns or a new canal to Mosquito Lagoon enabling light draft steamers to ply between the Indian River and Jacksonville. He believed the railroad to be the more feasible. He also recommended a small steamer on the Indian River and three good hotels, one at the head of the river, one midway, and one near the southern end. With these improvements, "this delightful climate might be enjoyed by the thousands now kept away by the difficulties attending transportation and lack of accommodations. The present route, via Salt Lake, is very tedious, and uncomfortably long."[26]

Tedious though it may have been, it was the latter route which brought James A. Henshall on his trip to the Indian River in the late 1870s. On the third day out of Jacksonville, he wrote, Henshall's party left the St. Johns a few miles above Lake Harney and entered Snake Creek, arriving at Salt Lake in late morning. At that point he changed to a "car" which stood several hundred yards from shore in shallow water. The car was on a wooden tramway which ran from Salt Lake to Titusville and was drawn by two mules. The tram was owned and operated by Samuel J. Fox whom Henshall thought was going to extend it to Lake Harney, "some twenty miles" away. His reasoning was that such products as oranges, limes, pineapples, bananas, cane syrup, early vegetables, green turtle, oysters, venison, skins, and hides were already being shipped to Jacksonville via Salt Lake, and return cargoes of groceries, provisions, clothing, and household goods were much in demand as settlement of the Indian River country accelerated.[27]

Settlers engaged in trade with the Seminoles who brought their pelts and hides to exchange for supplies. (Photo courtesy Vera Zimmerman)

With a much better appreciation of Titusville than Hallock, Henshall called it "the emporium for the entire country south for a distance of two hundred miles." With the usual complementary notice of Henry Titus, he went

One of two hotels in Titusville, the Lund House *was owned by* T. W. Lund *of the* Jacksonville *and* Salt Lake *Line of steamers.* (*Photo courtesy* Robert Hudson, North Brevard Historical Society)

on to describe it as the "distributing and shipping point for Southeast Florida." There were two hotels, the Titus Hotel and the Lund House, both of which were "good houses." The latter was owned by T. W. Lund of the Jacksonville and Salt Lake Line of steamers. The Lund House was anticipating the introduction of pleasure boats "in charge of competent skippers, who will take parties of guests on camping and fishing excursions down the river, at no additional expense to the regular per diem rate of the hotel." Where Mrs. Joseph Gruber had been obliged only a few years earlier to travel to Enterprise for supplies, Henshall reported several stores, including those of Titus and John W. Joyner in Titusville where "grub" could be obtained at reasonable prices. "Self-raising flour, bacon, coffee, sugar, canned goods of every description, and the great Florida staple, hominy, or 'grits,'" were available at Jacksonville prices. He advised, however, that the hunter would have to bring his ammunition and fishing tackle since those items were unavailable on the river.[28] From Titusville, Henshall set out in the *Blue Wing* with a group of youngsters on their way around the tip of Florida to the Gulf. On the way they fished, explored the interior and shot at everything in sight, including pelicans which were used for target practice.

George W. Parsons and his brother reversed the usual trip on the Indian River lagoon. The young New Yorkers had spent several months at Key West and along the Miami River before returning home in a small boat in early 1875. Having made their way on the outside – that is, in the Atlantic Ocean – from Biscayne Bay to Jupiter, they proceeded up the river from that point. At Fort Pierce they found no one except Alexander Bell and his family. Bell explained that the land around Fort Pierce was poor and the insects made habitation difficult. Bell took his family to the interior during the summer months to avoid the chills and fever. He also grew sugar cane there where he found the soil to be much better than on the coast. At Fort Capron, the Parsons met James Paine who was then operating a boarding house which would accommodate 14 persons. There was also a port of entry there and Paine was collector. Paine told them that there were plans for a small steamer to make regular runs from Sand Point to the Indian River Inlet beginning in 1876. They landed at Barker's Bluff to ride out a storm. Finding no one there, they pitched a tent for shelter. On March 11, they stopped at John Houston's place near Eau Gallie and heard the news that Governor Stearns' party had been there to select the agricultural college site. When told that all of the land between Eau Gallie and Sand Point had been taken up, George Parsons commented that "all I have to say is that they have selected a poor country to come to..." He was equally disdainful of Sand Point – although the place had been renamed Titusville, it continued to be known by its older name as well – which he thought "a miserable place." He estimated that about 300 families "at present reside on Indian River and have to fight mosquitoes and insects which are very bad and injure the crops...In fact everything is so different from what I had been led to believe... no one need ever whisper Indian River to me after this."[29]

A traveller in 1880 *described the mule-drawn train from Salt Lake to Titusville as a "wooden tram, dignified by the title of railroad."* (Stereo view, Florida State Archives)

Parsons was more favorably impressed with Henry Titus who agreed to have the brothers transported to Lake Harney for $10. He thought this a remarkably low price "as twice that amount besides charge for luggage and passengers is the regular price." He noted that Titus had some freight to bring back from Lake Harney which probably explained the bargain price. In any event, the Parsons departed Titusville seated in their boat aboard a wagon being pulled by mules.[30]

Talk of a tram road from Titusville to Lake Harney was quite enthusiastic when Parsons was there in 1875, but it was never built. In fact, the existing line to Salt Lake had apparently fallen into disuse by 1880. A traveller using the pseudonym "Friar Tuck" wrote that he arrived at Salt Lake in 1880 and spoke with W. H. Churchill who was managing the "wooden tram, dignified by the title of railroad, only to find that it had not been 'officially' open for some time because of repairs in progress." "For old times sake," however, Churchill agreed to transport Friar Tuck's boat and equipment to the Indian River.[31]

Visitors and settlers alike enjoyed hunting alligators. These two men have killed an eight and a half footer. (Photo by C. F. Conkling, Brevard County Historical Commission Archives)

The idea of a wooden tram road was apparently replaced by plans for a more substantial railroad, more and more of which were being advocated by 1880. In the meantime, the primary avenue of transportation to and from the Indian River country continued to be up the St. Johns to Enterprise or Lake Harney and then either overland by wagon or by way of the river to Salt Lake or Lake Poinsett. T. W. Lund and S. J. Fox, and a few others, made the difficult water voyage. Some of the vessels engaged in the traffic were the *Darlington*, *Wekiva*, *Fox*, *Volusia*, *Marion*, *Osceola*, *Astatula*, and *Waunita*. The *Volusia* was operated by the Pioneer Line which maintained connections with the Mallory Line at Jacksonville.

Friar Tuck spent the night at the Titus House which he found "as good as any hotel on the St. Johns." From there, he went to St. Lucie where he found the Paine family to be the only inhabitants. One son was the postmaster, another was deputy collector, and the elder Paine was still keeping the boarding house. He found a group of fisherman busy at the inlet. Headed by Silas B. Latham of Connecticut they were catching and shipping fish on weekly runs to Savannah aboard the schooner *Lillian*. While on the river, Friar Tuck was impressed with the services of Frank Strobhar of Eau Gallie and Charles Carlin of Titusville, whom he found to be good guides as well as good boatmen. As was usually the case of hunters who visited the area, Friar Tuck travelled from the Indian River to the St. Johns prairie where he "shot dozens of alligators, pelicans, spoonbills, and anything else that made a target." That kind of hunting was the routine rather than the exception in the early days long before there was much thought of conserving wild game.[32]

Just before he died in 1881, Henry Titus had occasion to undertake one more battle, but this time his weapons were words. The Florida Dispatch Line was then operating out of Jacksonville as a kind of commission merchant for Florida produce on its way to northern markets. It published the Florida Dispatch as an extension of its business and the newspaper served as a clearinghouse for information about the happenings of peninsular Florida. When a visitor to the Malabar area fired off a letter boasting of the superiority of a transportation route from Rockledge by way of Lake Poinsett and disparaging Titusville as a "dreary waste of white sand," the old warrior rose in wrath. In a letter to the Dispatch in August, four days before his death, Titus dismissed the "Knight of the Quill" with an "imbecile nature" and went on to plug his town one more time. Titusville, he declared, was "the grand center of all trade and will so continue to be. No slanderous article from any irresponsible person will change or alter its destiny."[33]

Brevard County had made measurable progress since the end of the Civil War. With the change of county lines in 1879 and removal of the county seat to Titusville, it had begun regular tax collections to the point that its circulating scrip was approaching par value. People were discussing with some reason the possibility of railroad connections with the outside world. Settlers were becoming more numerous along the Indian River lagoon and on Merritt Island. The 1880 census showed a population of 1,497 in the county. Perhaps more revealing was the fact that 932 people lived east of the St. Johns while only 565 were on the west side. The county realignment of 1879 had reduced the numerical strength of the cattlemen as more and more growers of citrus, pineapples, and vegetables came to the east side of the St. Johns. Although there were still numerous cattle herds on both sides of the river, the census showed that there were about three times as many growers as cattlemen in Brevard County in 1880.[34]

End Notes

1. Titusville East Coast Advocate, Illustrated Supplement, 1913; Robert Ranson, East Coast Florida Memoirs, 1837-1886 (Port Salerno, Florida, 1989), passim; Titusville Star Advocate, April 24, 1928; C. J. Maynard, "A Naturalists Trip to Florida," The American Sportsman, July 1874; John W. Griffin and James J. Miller, "Cultural Resource Survey of Merritt Island Wildlife Refuge," August 1, 1978.
2. Melbourne Times, August 3, 1877; Letter of Nancy J. Dixon, March 24, 1896, MSS Box 70, P. K. Yonge Library; Titusville East Coast Advocate, Illustrated Supplement, 1913; Titusville Star, March 8, October 4, 1888, February 22, March 29, 1895; Titusville Star Advocate, April 27, 1928, April 25, 1933; Clara Edwards, History of the Rockledge Presbyterian Churchy, 1877-1953 (Cocoa, 1953); Brevard County Historical Commission, Historical Book, 1830-1920 [Hatch Journal], 1870.
3. Post Office Site Locations, Microfilm 1126, Roll 88.
4. Alfred J. Hanna and Kathryn A. Hanna, Florida's Golden Sands (Indianapolis and New York, 1950), pp. 172-178.
5. Ibid., pp. 178-182.
6. National Archives, Records Group 105, Records of the Bureau of Refugees, Freedmen and Abandoned Lands, Florida, Andrew Mahoney to Charles Mundee, September 2, 1866.
7. Jerrell H. Shofner, Nor Is It Over Yet: Florida in the Era of Reconstruction, 1863-1877 (Gainesville, 1947), p. 138.
8. National Archives, Record Group 94, Adjutant Generals Office, John G. Foster to G. L. Hartsuff, March 6, 1866; St. Augustine Examiner, March 9, 1867.
9. Titusville Star Advocate, May 25, 1934.
10. Ibid., July 2, 1929, January 1, May 1, 1930.
11. Post Office Site Locations, April 5, 1880, M 1126, Roll 88.
12. Titusville Star Advocate, July 1, 1938.
13. Ibid., April 27, 1928. (Site location - June 2, 1871 - Microfilm 1126 Roll 88)
14. Lewis H. Cresse, "A Study of William Henry Gleason: Carpetbagger, Politician, Land Developer," (Unpublished Ph. D. Dissertation, University of South Carolina, 1975), p. 69.
15. Quotation is from Cresse, Gleason, p. 91.
16. George W. Parsons Diary, May 11, 1875, P. K. Yonge Library; Cresse, Gleason, p. 91.
17. William Henry Gleason, Broadside, n/d, MSS Box 69, P. K. Yonge Library.
18. Hanna and Hanna, Florida's Golden Sands, p. 165; Cresse, Gleason, p. 113.
19. Melbourne Area Chamber of Commerce Centennial Committee, Melbourne: A Century of Memories, (Melbourne, 1980), p. 1.
20. Charles Hallock, Camp Life in Florida (New York, 1876), p. 110.
21. Kyle S. Van Landingham, Pictorial History of Saint Lucie County (Bicentennial Project of Saint Lucie County Historical Society), p. 14; Florida State Archives, Record Group 150, Series 24, J. Q. Stewart to George F. Drew, August 26, 1878. Charlotte Lockwood, 1975, Florida's Historic I.R. County (Vero Beach, 1975), p. 5.
22. Emily Lagow Bell, My Pioneer Days in Florida, 1876-1898 (n. p., n. d.), pp. 29-30.
23. Georgianna Kjerulff, Tales of Old Brevard (Melbourne, 1972), p. 27.
24. Hallock, Camp Life, p. 71; John L. Edwards, Gratuitous Guide to Florida, 1874, Microfilm 1851, P. K. Yonge Library.
25. Hallock, Camp Life, pp. 228-231.
26. Ibid., pp. 229-230.
27. James A. Henshall, Camping and Cruising in Florida (Cincinnati, 1888), pp. 11-13.
28. Ibid., pp. 12-14.
29. Parsons, Diary, 1875.
30. Ibid.
31. Gazenovia (New York) Republican, September 2, 1880.
32. Ibid.
33. Jacksonville Florida Dispatch, August 3, 1881. Hanna & Hanna, Golden Sands, pp. 184-185
34. FSA, RG I020, Series 1203, Florida Census, 1880, Population, Agriculture.

Page 82 map: 1870 County Map of Florida by S. Augustus Mitchell, Jr. (Courtesy Jim Ball)

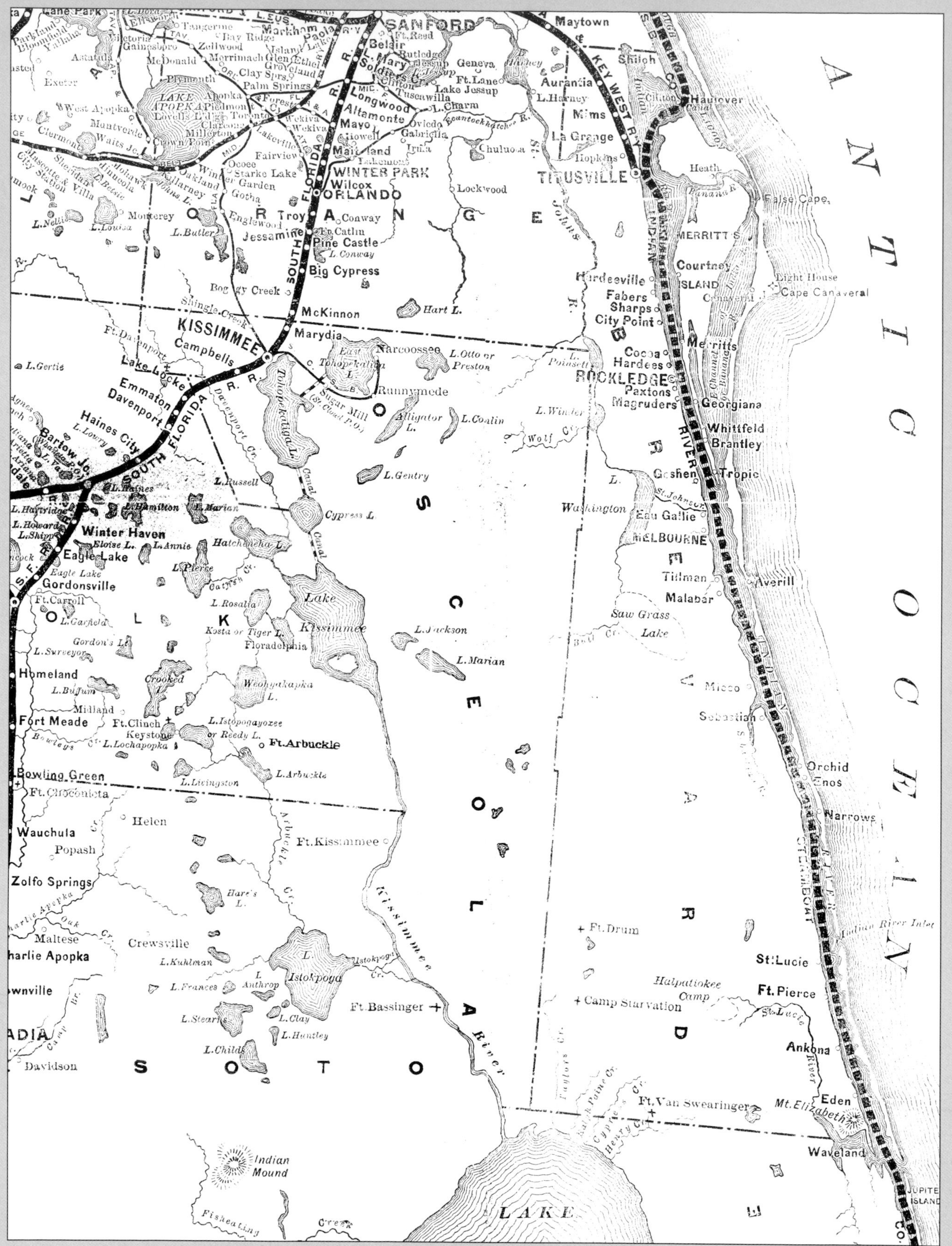

SANFORD
Maytown
Ft. Reed
Belair
Markham
Paola
Tangerine
Victoria
Gaineshoro
Zellwood
McDonald
Merrimach
Clay Sprs
Palm Springs
Plymouth
Astatula
Exeter
LAKE APOPKA
Apopka
West Apopka
Montverde
Clermont
Waits Jc.
Crown Point
Oakland
Winter Garden
Killarney
Ocoee
Starke Lake
Gotha
Fairview
Lakeville
Wekiva
Rutledge
Soldiers Cr.
Geneva
Ft. Lane
Lake Jessup
Aurantia
L. Harney
Mims
Clifton
Tuscawilla
Longwood
L. Charm
Altamonte
Oviedo
Gabriella
Mayo
Howell
Maitland
Chuluota
La Grange
Hopkins
TITUSVILLE
Shiloh
Haulover
Heath
WINTER PARK
Wilcox
ORLANDO
Lockwood
Monterey
L. Louisa
L. Butler
Englewood
Troy
Conway
Jessamine
Pine Castle
L. Conway
Big Cypress
Boggy Creek
Shingle Creek
McKinnon
Hart L.
O R A N G E
Banana R.
False Cape
MERRITTS
INDIAN
Courtney
ISLAND
Light House
Cape Canaveral
Hardeeville
Fabers
Sharps
City Point
Cocoa
Hardees
Merritts
ROCKLEDGE
Paxtons
Magruders
Georgiana
Whitfield
Brantley
Goshen
Tropic
Washington
Eau Gallie
MELBOURNE
Tillman
Averill
Malabar
Saw Grass Lake
Micco
Sebastian
Orchid
Enos
Narrows
INDIAN RIVER
Indian River Inlet
St. Lucie
Halpatiokee Camp
Ft. Pierce
Camp Starvation
Ft. Drum
Ankona
Eden
Mt. Elizabeth
Ft. Van Swearingen
Waveland
JUPITER ISLAND
A T L A N T I C O C E A N
KISSIMMEE
Campbells
Marydia
Narcoossee
East Tohopekaliga L.
L. Otto or Preston
Runnymede
Tohopekaliga L.
Sugar Mill
Alligator L.
L. Coalin
L. Winder
L. Gertie
Ft. Davenport
Lake Locke
Emmaton
Davenport
Haines City
SOUTH FLORIDA R. R.
Bartow Jc.
L. Lowery
L. Gentry
L. Russell
L. Haines
L. Hamilton
L. Marian
Cypress L.
Canal
Winter Haven
Hatchineha L.
Eloise L.
L. Annie
Eagle Lake
Gordonsville
L. Pierce
Ft. Carroll
P O L K
L. Rosalia
Lake Kissimmee
L. Jackson
L. Marian
Kosta or Tiger L.
Floradelphia
Homeland
Crooked L.
Weohyakapka L.
Midland
Fort Meade
Ft. Clinch
Keystone
L. Lochapopka
L. Istopogayozee or Reedy L.
Ft. Arbuckle
L. Arbuckle
Bowling Green
Ft. Choconikta
L. Livingston
Wauchula
Helen
Popash
Ft. Kissimmee
Zolfo Springs
Hare's L.
Kissimmee River
Maltese
Crewsville
Charlie Apopka
L. Kuhlman
L. Istokpoga
L. Frances
L. Anthrop
Ft. Bassinger
L. Stearns
L. Clay
L. Huntley
L. Childs
Davidson
D E S O T O
O S C E O L A
B R E V A R D
Indian Mound
Fisheating Creek
LAKE

8
Transportation and Communication in Early Brevard

Whether they arrived by wagon or by steamer, travellers endured many experiences which they were quite willing to forego when train travel eventually became available.

Just a few days before his death in 1881, Henry Titus declared that "the Enterprise and Titusville Railroad is a fixed fact" and predicted that it would be completed by the last of the year. (*Etching © Vera Zimmerman 1987*)

Railroad fever was strong in Brevard County by 1881. Just a few days before his death, Henry Titus, the county's most enthusiastic advocate, declared that "the Enterprise and Titusville Railroad is a fixed fact" and predicted that it would be completed by the last of the year. He declared with equal confidence that the Coast Canal Company would finish its work on the Haulover Canal and other navigational obstacles in the Indian River with comparable alacrity. "Your transit will soon be perfected and our Indian River country will be a continuous city from Titusville to Eau Gallie," he promised. The Florida Star was more hopeful than optimistic when it noted three months later that seven railroad companies had been

The steamer Astatula *provided service on the St. Johns River from Lake Poinsett to Sanford where the Rockledge Line connected with the Independent Line for Jacksonville.* (*Photo courtesy Doug Hendriksen*)

organized with Titusville as their termini and "we surely ought to get one out of seven." Titus had identified the two avenues by which the Indian River country would eventually be connected with the highways of commerce and travel, but the newspaper had also called attention to the difference between boosterism and railroad construction. It was to be several years before a locomotive steamed into Titusville and even longer before the intracoastal waterway could be depended upon by vessels of any size.[1]

While grander schemes awaited fruition, people continued to travel to and from the county by the best available means while continuing to try to improve them. W. H. Churchill, who had been operating the tram road from Salt Lake to LaGrange since the mid-1870s, became president of the Indian River Railway and Transportation Company in 1881 with expectations of building a railroad westward to Lake Harney. W. S. Norwood's hack line was running from Titusville to Enterprise where connections could be made with the DeBary Line. Fare was three dollars to Enterprise and another three from there to Jacksonville. Thomas W. Lund's Pioneer Line transported passengers and freight from Titusville to Salt Lake by hacks and wagons where connections were made with vessels bound for Sanford as well as Jacksonville. When his Steamer *Volusia* blew up at the docks in Jacksonville he relied upon the *Wekiva* and the *Fox*, both of which plied the waters of the Indian River as well as the St. Johns at various times. By the mid-1880s Lund was also running the *Fox* as far as Lake Washington during the winter season. W. A. Ostrander's *Cinderella* and *Duchess* were carrying the mail between Titusville and Lake Worth in 1882, but in 1884 he was also plying between Salt Lake and Enterprise and Sanford with smaller vessels. The Steamer *Osceola*, also no stranger to the Indian River trade, was making bi-weekly trips between Sanford and Salt Lake in 1883. E. H. Rice had a hack and freight service which brought passengers and goods from the Salt Lake landing to Titusville.[2]

Residents of Rockledge and neighboring settlements were not content with the transportation available by way of the Indian River from Titusville. Some sought a railroad to the county seat while others tried to establish direct connections with Sanford through Lake Poinsett. In early 1882 the Titusville and Rockledge Railroad Company was incorporated by Joseph N. Wilkinson, Gardner S. Hardee, Charles A. Hentz, William H. Sharpe, James D. Spratt, and C. B. Magruder. Another rail line was proposed by J. A. McRory, Minor S. Jones, and A. A. Stewart. Their Indian River and Northern Transportation Company was to run between Rockledge and Lake Poinsett. Neither road was ever built, but passengers and freight were transported between Sanford and Rockledge by way of Lake Poinsett. Gardner Hardee, A. L. Hatch and others built a wharf to navigable water on Lake Poinsett in the late 1870s. Hatch was soon transporting supplies from there to his store at City Point. In 1883 the steamer *Tuskawilla* was running from Lake Poinsett to Sanford where it connected with the Independent Line for Jacksonville. The Rockledge Line offered comparable service aboard its *Astatula* and *Waunita* in 1885. By that time D. W. McQuaig and others were employing 15 teams and wagons to transport passengers and freight between Rockledge and the lake. As late as 1887 plans were still being made for "a good steel rail tram road across from river to river" to serve Rockledge and Cocoa.[3]

Whether they arrived by wagon or by steamer from Enterprise and Sanford in the early 1880s, travellers endured many experiences which they were quite willing to forego when train travel eventually became available. Herman Herold complained of his 1884 trip aboard the *Astatula* which, according to him, was filthy and cramped. Arriving at Willard's dock on Lake Poinsett, he was transferred to a wagon for a "terrible three mile ride" to the Del Monico Hotel at Rockledge. Travel by land could be even more memorable. Arriving by wagon from Enterprise just a few months before the railroad was completed, V. F. Hankins explained why the mail arrived wet. The wagon was crossing a slough when it struck a large alligator. The wagon was upset and mail and passengers were dumped into about 18 inches of water. It was little wonder that the railroad received such enthusiastic support from Brevard County residents.[4]

Traffic on the Indian River itself was often unreliable and sometimes dangerous. Inadequate water in the Haulover canal, tortuous channels through the Narrows, and the constant difficulty of navigating shallow water so near the unpredictable winds of the Atlantic Ocean presented continuing challenges. But the river offered the best means of transportation and communication and everyone used it. Nearly every settler on the river had a wharf from which small vessels came and went much as automobiles do today. Although scheduled steamer traffic was uncommon until the mid-1880s, mail contractors could be relied upon to keep loose schedules, subject to weather on the river and delays at Enterprise and other points. Although they certainly kept no schedule, a number of trade boats provided a valuable service as well as opportunities for social intercourse for residents along the river.

These trading vessels were literally travelling stores, selling goods for cash or produce. Stopping at every landing along the river, they traded with single families or groups of people depending upon the population. They sometimes remained at a landing for several days while people came from the interior to buy, sell, or exchange. Most of the traders carried groceries, dry goods, canned goods, clothing and shoes, toilet articles and notions.

The river offered the best means of transportation and communication and everyone used it. Nearly every settler on the river had a wharf from which small vessels came and went. Kroegel dock, Sebastian. (Photo by Paul Kroegel, courtesy Rodney Kroegel, Brevard Historical Commission Archives)

The Steamer Indian River maintained a schedule of two round trips weekly from Titusville to Eau Gallie, Melbourne and Sebastian. (Photo courtesy Doug Hendriksen)

They also carried penny candy for the children and liquor for the men. Whiskey was also traded to Indians from the interior for otter pelts and deer hides.

Benjamin Hogg, one of the earliest trade boat captains, obtained his supplies from the Bahamas, but most bought their stock at Jacksonville, Daytona, or Titusville. John McLean traded on the river in his sloop *Agnes* for many years beginning about 1880. He operated out of Daytona although he frequently encountered difficulty at the Haulover canal. W. S. Norwood and Company sold goods on the river on the *Osceola*. G. B. Rumph of Titusville operated the *Irene* for several years, but sold it to the Florida Canning Company which continued to trade on the river after 1890. Described as "one of Indian River's business women," a Mrs. Chase had a store boat in the 1890s which sold dry goods and millinery on the river. Some of the other trade boat operators were Alfred Michael, Walter Kitching, and Cornthwaite J. Hector. The *Mary B* was owned by Mary Baird who operated it with her two sons. There was also the *Norma* with Captain McNeil as master and the *Merchant* owned and operated by the Travis Supply Store of Cocoa. The trade boats provided a valuable service during the late 19th century and were gradually replaced by stores in the river towns which were better supplied as transportation improved after the mid-1880s.[5]

Small steamers such as T. W. Lund's *Pioneer* had been on Indian River waters since the late 1870s, but the first large passenger steamer was W. A. Ostrander's *Cinderella* which arrived in 1882. Too large to navigate the Haulover canal, the *Cinderella* carried the mail on the Indian River and transferred its cargo to the *Duchess* which operated on the Mosquito Lagoon. Emphasizing the need for an improved inland waterway, the *Cinderella* spent nearly a month in the spring of 1883 struggling over the shoals of the lower Indian River. After a few more equally difficult voyages, the steamer was removed to the St. Johns in November 1883.[6]

Jacob Lorillard of New York City provided a steamer service in the early 1880s with the *Indian River* and the *Haulover*, both of which were 60 feet long and 12 feet wide and too large to pass through the Haulover canal. The *Haulover* operated on the Halifax, meeting the *Indian River* at the Haulover. With C. F. Fischer as master, the *Indian River* hauled both freight and passengers up and down the waterway for which it was named. After the East Coast Line Canal Company opened the canal, both vessels navigated the Indian River for several years. The *Haulover* was removed to the west coast of Florida in the late 1880s, but the *Indian River* remained. For several years it maintained a schedule of two round trips weekly from Titusville to Eau Gallie and Melbourne and, later, Sebastian. In early 1885, the steamer *Ino*, a stern wheeler built on the Halifax River, was brought through the canal after "quite a large amount of excavating." It was to run on the Indian River in connection with another vessel which operated out of New Smyrna. H. Q. Hawley's *Frostline* also plied the Indian River in the 1880s.[7]

There was almost as much enthusiasm for an inland waterway along the east coast as for a railroad. Such a waterway had been envisioned in the 1850s when the Internal Improvement Act was passed and small vessels had crossed the Haulover at the northern end of the Indian River by one means or another for years. During the late 1860s and early 1870s, William Henry Gleason had organized the Southern Inland Waterway and Navigation Company with the ostensible purpose of opening an inland waterway from Jacksonville to Biscayne Bay as well as a canal connecting the upper St. Johns at Lake Washington with the Indian River at Elbow Creek. Little work was ever done on either of these projects, although Gleason was granted several tracts of state lands for his efforts. Gleason's activities in these matters languished in the mid-1870s, but interest in both waterways continued.[8]

In 1879 several citizens of Titusville and others along the river as far south as Lake Worth formed a company for the purpose of widening the Haulover canal, but they could not raise the necessary funds. The 1879 legislature chartered the Haulover Tram Railroad Company headed by Phineas D. Wesson of Titusville to construct a railroad which would transport river craft from the Mosquito Lagoon to the Indian River and back to facilitate transportation. Although this firm would have been eligible for land grants, it was never able to begin work.[9]

Unable to raise private funds for opening the waterway, citizens turned to Congress. J. F. LeBaron, an engineer who lived at Titusville, reported to that body in 1881 that improvement of the Haulover canal would be beneficial.

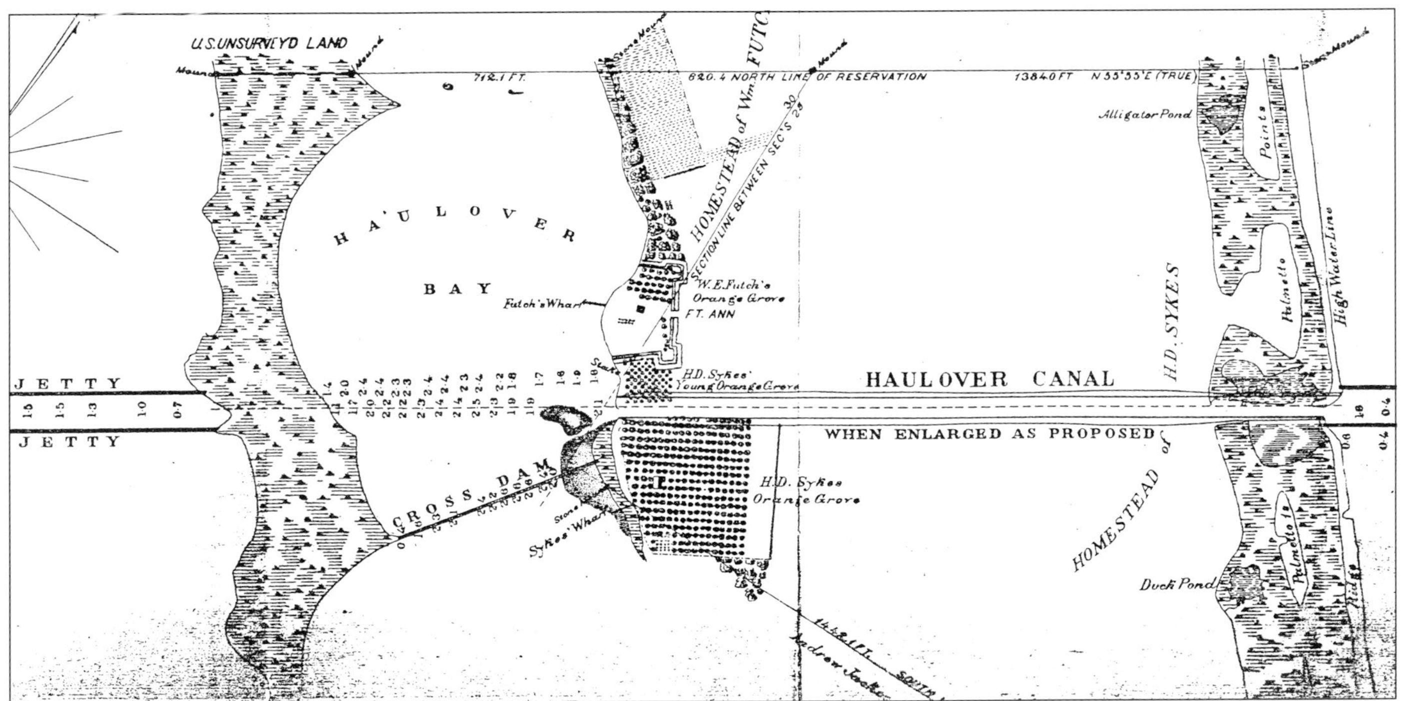

J. F. LeBaron, an engineer who lived at Titusville, reported to Congress in 1881 that improvement of the Haulover canal would be beneficial. (*Brevard County Historical Commission Archives*)

Craft which were then navigating the Indian River were limited to sailboats, sloops, and small schooners, most of which had been built on the river. Five small schooners averaging 40 to 45 feet in length and ten to 14 feet beam were carrying freight and mail through the canal, but they were often subjected to great delays. One schooner was obliged to make its semi-weekly trips on the outside because it was unable to pass through the canal at all. Not only was it difficult to maintain sufficient width and depth of the channel because of the shoals which accumulated at each end, but navigation was also impeded by the current. Usually, the Indian River waters were two or three feet higher than the Mosquito Lagoon with the result that a strong current made it difficult for vessels trying to move against it. LeBaron thought that the canal could be made more adequate to the needs of the citizenry for about $66,000.[10]

Congress did not act on the LeBaron report because the Florida Coast Line Canal and Transportation Company was granted a state charter in August 1881 to build and maintain an intracoastal waterway along the same route. The company began construction in 1883 and eventually received over a million acres of land for completing about 268 miles of canal, but it never really met the conditions of its charter nor were people along the river satisfied with the waterway it ostensibly provided.[11]

Work on the Haulover canal began in 1885 when the Coast Canal Company brought in a group of Italian laborers to clear the way for the dredges. After completing its work at Oak Hill, the steam dredge *Chester* moved to the Haulover. During 1886 it cleared the old canal and moved on to Grant's Farm where it went to work on a channel east of that island. Complaints about the Haulover Canal continued. Two months after the work there had been completed, E. H. Purdy reported that he had been obliged to leave his *Ripple* at the Haulover because of insufficient water.[12] The steamer *Clara* abandoned its trips on the river because of the growing sandbar. The Titusville newspaper complained that the canal was filling up rapidly and "the Coast Canal Company seems to have forgotten that the canal needs any attention at all." It argued that the company should not be allowed its land grant. Meanwhile, plans were underway to relocate the canal and the United States Coast Survey recommended a new site about a half mile away. While the company was relocating the canal in the late 1880s, the legislature took up the larger question of the entire intracoastal waterway.[13]

Brevard County's senator, Gardner S. Hardee, chaired a committee which heard complaints and made recommendations for changes to the 1889 legislature. Recognizing the importance of the inland waterway project, the legislature enacted a measure which seemed to satisfy both the company and the inhabitants of the Atlantic coast. The crucial provision was that the company was obliged to complete the entire waterway from St. Augustine to Biscayne Bay within five years. The Cocoa Public Spirit enthusiastically endorsed the "mammoth enterprise" as "the most important public work that has ever been inaugurated" in East Florida. Enthusiasm was enhanced when Senator Hardee announced that George F. Miles of the canal company had contracted with Rittenhouse, Moore and Company of Mobile, Alabama, to begin work immediately.[14]

Complaints were raised again in 1892 when the Haulover canal was reportedly closed above Titusville and the lower river was filling up so that "communication with Jupiter and Lake Worth may be cut off at any time." Private parties contracted for a dredge to open up the canal between the Haulover and Mosquito lagoon in 1892 so that the steamer J. W. *Sweeney* could get through. Local individuals, backed by New York capital, were interested in this project so that the *Sweeney* could haul pineapples from Eden to New Smyrna and create competition for the railroad and its steamer line.[15]

At about the same time the U. S. Army Corps of Engineers became interested in dredging the waterway.

The steamer Frederick *DeBary was one of the boats that plied the* St. Johns River *in the* 1880's. (*Photo courtesy* Jim Ball)

After about three years of complex negotiations with the Coast Canal Company, the government actually brought its dredge *Suwannee* into the Indian River with a view to opening a channel five feet deep and at least 75 feet wide. A considerable amount of dredging was actually completed, but funds were exhausted before the *Suwannee* finished its task.[16]

By 1895, Henry Flagler had invested about $100,000 in the canal company and had become its president. Its headquarters had been relocated to St. Augustine. George F. Miles was still the general manager and he was still doing dredge work on the southern end of the waterway. Although it is unlikely that Flagler would have allowed the river route to become competitive with his railroad as it was built toward Miami, he had no objection to the formation of the Indian River and Bay Biscayne Inland Navigation Company with A. W. Buie as its Titusville superintendent. Its *St. Augustine* and *St. Sebastian* were advertised as connecting with all trains at Titusville and Rockledge in 1898. By 1905, the Coast Canal Company was claiming a uniform six foot depth all the way from the Haulover to Grant's Farm and its dredge *Florida* was at work opening a comparable channel southward to Jupiter.[17]

The company declared its work complete in 1912 and the state turned over the last of its land grant at that time. It went into receivership in 1923, was reorganized for a brief period, and then closed down completely in 1926. The Intracoastal Waterway was ultimately taken over and completed by the Corps of Engineers in the 1930s.[18]

Most of the railroad companies mentioned in 1881 by the Titusville newspaper never got beyond the paper stage. The Sanford and Indian River Railroad which was chartered by an Orlando syndicate did put about 100 men to work grading from Fort Reed toward Lake Jesup in 1882 and the Leesburg and Indian River Railroad company also progressed to the point that it was hiring laborers, but neither of them seem to have laid any track. The most promising undertaking for a railroad to the Indian River originated with the Palatka and Indian River Railroad which began planning for a line to Titusville in 1881. Grading started from Buffalo Bluff in early 1882 for a line which was to run southward along the St. Johns River. This road apparently was acquired by the Jacksonville, Tampa and Key West Railroad which eventually reached Tampa in 1886.[19]

With the Jacksonville, Tampa, and Key West road working toward Tampa, plans for a connecting link between Enterprise and Titusville began taking shape in 1883. W. B. Watson who was then managing the DeBary steamship line predicted in January of that year that a road would be completed by way of Lake Harney to Titusville within 18 months. Such a road had Frederick

DeBary's support and he had offered to guarantee the first three years interest on bonds to be issued for that purpose. The Atlantic Coast, St. Johns and Indian River Railroad was chartered in 1883.[20]

Railroad fever accelerated during the next few months and the Titusville paper reported that real estate was booming all along the river, especially at Titusville and Melbourne. Further encouragement came when W. B. Watson resigned his position with the DeBary-Baya Line and accepted the position of superintendent of the Enterprise to Titusville Railroad. Residents of the Indian River settlements readily formed a subscription committee when the railroad company officials offered to build the road and have locomotives in Titusville by the first of January 1886, if they would subscribe $30,000 in land or cash. The money was raised almost immediately by enthusiastic citizens of Titusville and LaGrange.[21]

The railroad officials were as good as their word and construction was begun almost immediately with a view to meeting the January 1, 1886, deadline. Three hundred hands were clearing right-of-way, grading, building bridges, and laying track by early summer. When workers became difficult to find, the company offered $1.25 per day, an incentive which seems to have worked. The Cocoa Indian River Sun enthusiastically reported in late August that grading was completed to within four miles of the LaGrange store. Although there was some concern about the approaching deadline, observers were pleased that track was being laid at the rate of a mile a day. Titusville residents finally heard the whistles of the locomotive as it reached Washington Avenue just in time to meet the deadline. Subscribers were consequently obliged to make good on their $30,000 worth of pledges. Cannon were fired, an elaborate display of fireworks was set off, and everyone seemed satisfied.[22]

In late January the Atlantic Coast, St. Johns, and Indian River Railroad was leased to the Jacksonville, Tampa and Key West Railroad to be operated as a branch of that line. Henry Flagler had about a fifty percent interest in the JTKW RR but he remained a silent partner and eventually severed his relations with that road. His involvement in Brevard County affairs would come in the 1890s from a different direction. In the meantime, the company built a 1500 foot dock into the Indian River and laid track on it so that the trains could run out over the water to meet the steamers which the company would soon be operating. The long-awaited arrival of the railroad made Titusville the transportation hub of the Indian River country for about a decade and heralded the golden age of Indian River steamboating. The Cocoa Sun approved the good fortune of her neighbor, commenting that "the place has no longer the air of an inland town, but that of a railroad point.

The long-awaited arrival of the railroad in 1886 made Titusville the transportation hub of the Indian River country. (Photo courtesy Jim Ball)

Above: The Steamer St. Lucie piloted by Captain C. H. Brock made connections between Titusville, Cocoa, Rockledge and "all intermediate landings from Melbourne to Jupiter." (Photo Florida State Archives)

Left: The Steamer Georgiana was one of the Indian River Steamboat Company's fleet of vesssels that plied the Indian River in the 1880's. (Photo Florida State Archives)

The hotels are crowded and business looking up."[23]

The waterborne extension of the JTKW RR was the Indian River Steamboat Company which was organized in early 1886. Captains Richard P. Paddison, Steve Bravo, and A. W. Buie were among its best known masters. Paddison was superintendent until 1889 when he was succeeded by W. B. Watson, formerly of the DeBary-Baya Line. Paddison was master of the *Rockledge*, a 136 foot side-wheel steamer, when it was brought from the St. Johns and refitted for the Indian River. Too heavy for the shallow waters of the lagoon, it was eventually sold to E. E. Vail who converted it into a floating hotel at Jupiter Inlet. But, in the meantime, the *Rockledge* was the darling of the Indian River inhabitants for several years. With its home port at Melbourne, the steamer made daily runs between that point and Titusville from 1886 through 1888. Among the other vessels in the IRSB Co. fleet were the *Indian River*, *St. Lucie*, *St. Augustine*, *Sebastian*, *Georgiana*, *S. V. White*, and *Cleo*.[24]

Partially because demand varied from season to season and partially because some of the vessels were too large to pass through the Narrows, not all of them travelled the entire length of the Indian River, but these vessels effectively extended the reach of the JTKW RR southward to Jupiter. Residents as far south as Melbourne were enabled to reach Jacksonville in a single day where it had previously taken a three-day trip. The Railway Mail Service made the mail much more reliable at least as far as Titusville and the major towns along the river. The steamers stopped at most of the landings on the river, but independent mail contracts continued to be let for some of the tributary routes. The Colegrove Mail Line was given the contract for delivering mail south of Melbourne after 1893.[25]

The JTKW RR and the IRSB Co. soon extended their services beyond Jupiter to Lake Worth by way of the Jupiter and Lake Worth Railway, popularly known as the Celestial Railroad. Jupiter was only a small village at the time, consisting primarily of a lighthouse and a life saving station near Jupiter Inlet. Passengers who left the IRSB boats there could go outside to Miami by sailboat or overland by stage coach. The JTKW RR purchased the *Chattahoochee* and kept it at Jupiter as a floating hotel for those transients. Those who chose the inland route could take the 8.5 mile Celestial Railroad, so called because it ran from Jupiter to Juno on Lake Worth. From Juno they went by sailboat to Lantana where twice weekly stage connections were available to Fort Lauderdale.[26]

This system served residents along the Atlantic Coast for about a decade after 1886. Several of the larger steamers were quite commodious, offering deck and dining facilities on all of them and staterooms on some. Bands for both listening and dancing were quite common as well. All who could enjoyed at least an occasional trip aboard the river steamers. With very shallow draft, vessels were often poled by the crew through some of the narrower passages, but the compensation was a beautiful view of the waterway with its wildlife and lush vegetation.

With improved transportation, Rockledge's growing reputation as the premiere resort town on the lower east coast was further enhanced. Crowds of visitors left the trains as they pulled onto the railroad dock at Titusville during the winter months. Extra trains were scheduled for the busier seasons and additional steamer trips were added to handle the increased demand. Passengers had stopover privileges at various points along the river and often used them. In January 1891, six trains were running to and from Titusville each day. Direct connections were made with the steamers *St. Lucie* and *St. Sebastian* for Cocoa, Rockledge, Melbourne, and "all intermediate landings from Melbourne to Jupiter." The Titusville newspaper also boasted that there was through train sleeper service to Cincinnati in only 40 hours.[27]

"The tide of tourists to Indian River is larger than ever before," the Titusville Star declared in 1888. It reported several railroad cars crowded with passengers arriving in Titusville every day "and they don't all immediately return

President Grover Cleveland, his new bride, Frances Folsom Cleveland, visited Brevard in 1888. With them were Secretary of State Thomas A. Bayard, Secretary of War Daniel S. Lamont, Navy Secretary William C. Whitney, and their wives (all of whom are not pictured). (Photo courtesy Jim Ball)

either." While many visitors traveled as individuals, packaged tours were not uncommon. The Traveling Passengers Association of the United States and Canada organized groups of about 100 each to visit Rockledge as one of the stops on its Florida tour. The first of a series of excursions organized by the Pennsylvania Central Railway arrived in Titusville in early 1888. The round trip from New York to Florida and return, including meals and sleeper facilities and the privilege of remaining twenty days, was $47.50. Henry Grady, editor of the Atlanta Constitution and renowned spokesman of the New South also brought small groups for "pleasure, hunting and fishing and also feasting on Indian River oranges." Another kind of tourist travel was exemplified by the steam yacht *Vera* which brought a group from Rochester to enjoy a voyage down the Indian River. Pierre Lorillard, whose family had owned one of the first steamer companies in Brevard County, was one of many wealthy individuals who spent time on the Indian River in their luxury yachts. His *Caiman* always attracted attention when it was tied up at the Titusville city dock.[28]

Word of the opening of the inland waterway – however incomplete – and the completion of railroad service to Titusville – which became known as the Tropical Trunk Line – spread throughout the nation by many informal means, but it also had official assistance. With the blessing of the State of Florida, Wanton S. Webb outfitted a railroad car with Florida artifacts and scenery which he assembled by visiting many Florida communities, including Titusville, which were served by railroads. He then attached his Rolling Car Exposition to the trains of northern railroads – which were naturally anxious to increase their own passenger traffic – and visited many of the northern cities. He would have his

Wanton S. Webb outfitted a railroad car with Florida artifacts and scenery. Florida's Rolling Exposition visited many northern cities. (Photo courtesy Doug Hendriksen)

car pulled to cities such as Buffalo, Detroit, or Pittsburgh and have it parked on a siding. He then let local residents know that they could come view his Florida car at no cost. Webb reported that those who visited his exhibits in the northern cities in January and February were most impressed.[29]

One of the most publicized promotions of the Indian River, and especially Rockledge, was the 1888 visit of President Grover Cleveland and his party. The event was planned and staged by state senator Gardner S. Hardee and his Rockledge neighbors. With the president and his new bride were secretary of state Thomas A. Bayard, secretary of war Daniel S. Lamont, navy secretary William C. Whitney, and their wives as well. The party was treated to fine dining and a tour of some of the orange groves. The visit received national news coverage.[30]

The almost euphoric enthusiasm over the new transportation was uninterrupted for about three years, after which some of the natural results of monopoly began to emerge. Since the transportation of pineapples, oranges, and other produce constituted a major source of revenue for the IRSB and JTKW, freight rates were soon being protested by shippers. The Titusville East Coast Advocate joined a growing number of its readers in advocating a competing line which seemed the only means of controlling freight rates. Apparently dissatisfied with the policies of his own company, R. P. Paddison left the IRSB Co. – to be replaced by W. B. Watson – and joined H. J. Tiffin, N. N. Penney, E. S. Wiler, and J. M. Dixon in organizing the East Coast Transportation Company, in 1889. They purchased the steamer J. W. *Sweeney*, a 134 foot vessel which was 34 feet wide and drew 22 inches. Equipped to carry both freight and passengers, the *Sweeney* had staterooms, a fine saloon, and decks equipped for dancing. The vessel became famous on the Indian River for its annual excursion voyages from Titusville to Oleander Point for the famous May Day picnics. But, while passengers were important to the ECT company and people enjoyed its accommodations, the *Sweeney* was primarily a competitor to the IRSB for freight and passengers. Since that firm had a monopoly of the JTKW facilities at Titusville, the ECT made New Smyrna its home port and it was for that reason that it had the Haulover canal dredged in 1890 beyond the dimensions then provided by the Coast Canal Company. Even so, the *Sweeney* was once stuck for several days in the canal while attempting to pass through with 500 tons of citrus aboard.[31]

Noting that most of the stock of the firm was held by "men who pay taxes in Brevard County," the East Coast Advocate gave it full support. When the JTKW denied use of its Titusville dock to the ECT on the grounds that it had been leased to the IRSB, the newspaper chided the railroad company for its short-sightedness. It also noted that the JTKW was losing revenue since the *Sweeney* was hauling freight to New Smyrna which could readily have been shipped over the railroad from Titusville. The railroad company also aroused ire by collecting wharfage fees from boatmen who tied up at its dock. The Titusville town council enacted an ordinance prohibiting the practice. When JTKW officials ignored it, the matter was taken before the new railroad commission which ruled that the company could not collect the fees, "regardless of the terms of its lease." Having lost that battle, the company retaliated by moving its dry docks from Titusville to Eau Gallie.[32]

The East Coast Transportation Company was unsuccessful but the IRSB and the JTKW had their own difficulties. The East Coast Advocate reported in late 1892 that "the JTKW RR co. is in the hands of a receiver, but the ECT Co. is in even worse shape, being in the hands of the sheriff, with a $10,000 execution judgment against it in favor of a Jacksonville bank.[33]

S. F. Gray of Titusville was also unsuccessful with his Titusville, Canaveral and Oak Hill Steamboat Company. Begun in 1891 to operate between those points, the firm lasted until the fall of 1893. That failure brought about a measure by D. S. Ebersole to "accommodate the people up and down the Banana River" with a steam-powered houseboat running between Canaveral and Lotus "until something better" could replace it.[34]

Although both remained in receivership, the JTKW and the IRSB survived for a time. Mason Young was ousted from control of both and was replaced by R. B. Cable of Pennsylvania. An impending sheriff's sale of the IRSB property was postponed indefinitely. New schedules were announced and the *St. Lucie*, *St. Sebastian*, *St. Augustine*, *Georgiana* and *White* were soon carrying mail, freight, and passengers on the river again, but this time the company's role was reversed. With Captain A. W. Buie in charge, the steamers were "capturing a good share of the pineapple shipments" and the shippers applauded the IRSB for its competition with new railroad which Henry Flagler had just built down the east coast.[35]

It was only a brief respite, though. The Flagler road, coupled with the disastrous freezes of late 1894 and early 1895, spelled the death knell of the IRSB. Most of its agencies along the river were closed in April 1895. All that remained was the Titusville office from which the St. Lucie ran twice a week to Sewell's Point and once a week to Jupiter. The Jupiter to Juno railroad continued for a while and the *St. Augustine* was running on Lake Worth. But even then, the bank was loaning additional funds to the struggling company to pay its crews. The IRSB was liquidated in early 1896 and its vessels were sold. First to go was the *Cleo*. R. P. Paddison bought it for $50 and also purchased the firm's dry dock facilities at Eau Gallie. The steamer White brought $500 from a Chicago firm. R. B. Cable, the receiver, apparently took some of the other vessels. Although he lived in Florida only during the winter months, Cable was operating the Indian River and Bay Biscayne Transportation Company with four steamers in 1897.[36]

The JTKW continued in receivership, but adhered to a new schedule which was coordinated with Flagler's line. Flagler bought the Titusville to Enterprise branch of the JTKW in 1899 and incorporated it into his Florida East Coast system.[37]

Even as construction on the Enterprise to Titusville railroad had begun, the Titusville newspaper had noted that "a railroad running parallel with the coast, is what

The first through train from Jacksonville to Rockledge arrived on February 6, 1893. Carriages await passengers at the Rockledge Railway Station. (Photo courtesy Doug Hendriksen)

Rockledge was served by a spur track from the main line to the riverfront at the foot of Orange Avenue between the Indian River and Plaza Hotels. In this photo are Roy Packard, OK Key, Morris Weinberg, Vera Packard and Janet Packard. (Photo courtesy Grace Packard Bryant)

we need and will sooner or later have." Despite his investment in the JTKW company, Henry Flagler moved to provide that road in the early 1890s. Flagler had not built a mile of new track before 1890, but had assembled several existing lines into his Jacksonville, St. Augustine and Halifax Railroad which ran between Jacksonville and Daytona. From 1890 to 1892 his road did a brisk business with steamers operating on the Indian River, leading him to invest in a few small vessels of his own for that trade. People from the Indian River section, especially Rockledge, began trying to convince Flagler to extend his road south of Daytona. Several individuals offered land and other inducements. After pondering the matter for a time, Flagler decided to build southward.[38]

The Halifax and Indian River Railway had been incorporated in 1891 to build from Daytona to Titusville. The Titusville town council had given it a franchise to run tracks on DeSoto Street. In 1892 Flagler incorporated the Florida Coast and Gulf Railway Company and acquired the property and franchises of the Halifax and Indian River company. In October 1892 the name of the Florida and Gulf was changed to the Jacksonville, St. Augustine and Indian River Railway Company, the name which Flagler's company retained while it was building through Brevard County.[39]

Flagler's charter authorized him to build from Daytona to Miami, but one of his biographers declared unequivocally that he had no intention of going farther south than Rockledge when he began construction in 1892. If that is true, he soon

Flagler's new station at Titusville was to have a ticket office, hotel office, and dining room. (Photo courtesy Grace Packard Bryant)

Flagler reorganized the Jacksonville, St. Augustine *and* Indian River *Railway Company as the* Florida East Coast *Railroad.* (*Photo courtesy* Jim Ball)

changed his mind. The JSTA&IR reached Titusville, Cocoa and Rockledge in February, 1893, but his crews were already surveying between Coquina and Eau Gallie in October of the previous year. At that time "The Florida Wizard" was enjoying nothing but praise from Indian River residents and Eau Gallie citizens were congratulated for their generous offers of land and town lots as inducement for him to build to that point.[40]

Flagler arrived at Titusville in December 1892 where he and "a party of his railroad managers" boarded his Silver King for a trip southward to Sewall's Point and back as far as Sharpes where they were able to board the construction train for their return to Titusville. In February it was announced that he would invest $12,000 in a combined railroad station and hotel. The first floor was to have a ticket office, hotel office, and dining room. The second floor would have accommodations for about 75 guests. The first through train from Jacksonville to Rockledge arrived on Monday afternoon, February 6, 1893. Large crowds hailed the first trains as they arrived at each of the Indian River towns. An exuberant Titusville editor reported that the new railroad had increased travel so much that hotels and boarding houses along the river were unable to accommodate more than seventy percent of those looking for places to stay. Explaining that "the [Flagler] railroad came upon us too suddenly," he expressed hope that there would be several additional hotels before the next season.[41]

Flagler's actions were acknowledged with enthusiasm and uncritical approval, but they would prove to be mixed blessings. Rockledge was in the early 1890s enjoying a reputation as Florida's southernmost resort community and its hotels were widely applauded. Rockledge citizens were even pleased to boast that theirs was the only town on the new railroad which was served by a spur track from the main line to the river front. But the railroad was extended to Palm Beach in 1894 and to Miami in 1896. Flagler built great hotels at both locations. While he may have intended to make Rockledge the terminus of his railroad it ended up as a stop on the way to the more southerly resort towns and, in the long run, spur tracks proved more easily removed than trunk lines.[42] But the down side was still in the future when the JSTA&IR was reorganized as the Florida East Coast Railroad and Flagler could say with considerable truth that "my domain begins at Jacksonville."

Another improvement to communications along the Indian River was being advanced by the International Ocean Telegraph Company in conjunction with the United States Signal Service. Lines were being strung between Jupiter and Titusville by the fall of 1887 when the Signal Service sloop Magic passed through the latter town on its way to Jupiter with a load of wire. By the latter part of that year signal offices were operating in several towns between Titusville and Jupiter. The value of this service was emphasized by the Titusville Star when it reported that Sergeant William Davis of the Signal Service was moving his office from the end of the long dock to the downtown area where it would be "accessible to all our business men" and only "two minutes walk from the post office." The paper also noted a merging of past and present when it reported that a party of Seminoles had sold some cattle at Melbourne. Having sold more than they had brought with them, the drovers used the telegraph to alert their tribesmen near St. Lucie to begin another round up and save the time it would have taken them to return to their grazing lands.[43]

In 1894 the Canaveral lighthouse was moved to a sand ridge about a mile inland from its previous location. Inset above: Fresnel lenses were added to the light to intensify the brightness of the kerosene-wick type lamp. (Photos Brevard County Historical Commission Archives)

While most of the Indian River area inhabitants were more concerned with intracoastal travel than the open sea, ocean travel was still important to them. The Cape Canaveral lighthouse which had been almost as much a social institution as a navigational aid during the long tenure of Captain Mills Burnham was still serving a useful function in the late 1880s. The configuration of the cape was such that an identifiable marker was a tremendous aid to seafarers. Cape Canaveral juts out into the ocean in such a way that a shoal is caused to extend from it about eight miles into the ocean. On its southern side, the cape turns southwest, then south, and eventually south-southeast. This configuration created several miles of deep water just south of the cape known as the Canaveral Bight. While the long shoal eastward from the cape was quite hazardous, the deep water in the bight was a relatively safe haven for vessels during storms. The goals of navigators then was to avoid the shallow waters and be able to find the deep water in bad weather. The lighthouse facilitated those goals. In the late 1880s that facility was in danger from serious beach erosion. A half-hearted measure in 1886 had involved shoring up the site with board breastworks and sand bags, but the contractor even at the time expressed doubt that his work "will avail much good. If it should fail the light house will have to be taken down and moved to a more safe and suitable place." Two years later, another project was undertaken. Consisting of a 500 foot seawall and seven jetties extending into the surf, it required 140,000 feet of lumber and an expenditure of $4,500. At the end of another two years, two engineers investigated the site and recommended that the lighthouse be moved inland about a mile. With an appropriation of $80,000, the facility was dismantled and moved to a sand ridge about a mile from its previous location from which point it again safely transmitted its signal to passing mariners.[44]

Not every vessel on the high seas was able to find safe haven during the frequent Atlantic storms, and wrecks sometimes brought unexpected supplies to local residents even as they caused disaster for the shippers and their passengers. One of the more famous wrecks was the *LaDonna* which dumped several hundred pairs of women's shoes on the beach to the delight of Brevard County women. Matching up the shoes was most difficult and mismatched foot wear was the style for some time. A considerable amount of construction in the early years was made possible by wrecked lumber vessels which scattered everything from yellow pine to mahogany along the beach. Large quantities of rum and occasional barrels of French brandy were also salvaged by local beachcombers. The *Joannes*, a Greek vessel beached near Lake Worth in 1884 with a cargo of logwood, parrots and monkeys. The following year, a large steamer bound from Vera Cruz to Boston came ashore near Eden with a cargo of 5,000 bags of sugar. The sixteen crewmen were saved by the keepers of Life Saving Station Number Two. Soon after that, a Spanish ship bound for Cuba was wrecked near Gilbert's Bar with a load of logwood and molasses. All the crew except one man reached the station at Gilbert's Bar. There were occasional incidents of wrongdoing associated with the wrecks. An insurance investigator came to Merritt Island in 1892 to look into the matter of a cargo of lumber aboard the wrecked schooner *Drisco*. Ostensibly worth $20,000 it had been sold by the master of the vessel to a party at Georgiana for $700. The irate insurance man thought this wrong since the vessel was high on the beach so that, not only could the lumber have been saved, but the vessel itself could have been put to sea again. Whatever the nature of individual cases, these wrecks were the reason for the life saving station at Gilbert's Bar and nine other locations between Daytona and Biscayne Bay.[45]

As difficult as it was to obtain suitable water and rail transportation for Brevard County, public roads were even harder to build and maintain. In the early days, people who desired roads simply went before the county commission and asked for a road. If the commission agreed, it appointed a three-member road committee to acquire the right-of-way and lay out the route. There was no public outlay and the resulting roads were quite primitive. After the 1885 constitution was implemented, a state road law was passed requiring all able-bodied adult males to give a certain number of days each year for work on the public roads. The law was singularly unsuccessful and its failure coupled with the increasing demand for decent public roads led to taxes for that purpose, and, finally, to county road departments. But, those were some time in coming. In the meantime, Brevard County inhabitants understandably travelled by boat whenever possible.

One of the earlier common efforts at road building was an 1880 meeting of citizens of Titusville, LaGrange, Mims, and Aurantia to determine the best means of providing a road from Titusville through the Turnbull Hammock to the Volusia County line. Part of that route was eventually covered with shell, but the northern portion was delayed because of the swampy terrain. Examples of county-

By 1895 there was a growing demand for a road to run the entire length of the county along the western bank of the Indian River. Indian River Drive at Rockledge. (Photo courtesy Doug Hendriksen)

approved local roads include one in 1891 from the JTKW mile post 147 to the Indian River through the Garvin grant. A. J. Carter, John W. Huntington and A. S. Dickinson were appointed a committee to lay out and open it. Minor Jones, T. J. Cockshutt, and F. A. Chappell were named a committee to "mark out a road" from LaGrange to Titusville in the same year. R. B. Burchfield, John I. Sanders and James M. Brown were made responsible for laying out a road from Georgiana to Tropic in the summer of that year. The $450 appropriated for opening a road from Fort Pierce to the southern boundary of the county in 1891 was comparatively rare for that early date.[46]

By 1895 there was a growing demand for a road to run the entire length of the county along the western bank of the Indian River. R. B. Burchfield, who had become the county surveyor, was ordered to survey the route and R. A. Hardee was given the responsibility of obtaining the right-of-way. Authority was secured from the legislature to bond the county for the road, and it was decided that $150,000 would do the job. The call for a bond election in October 1895 set off a lengthy debate. The residents of Merritt Island were apparently opposed to paying for a road on the mainland. The Titusville newspaper countered that 75 percent of all the taxes in the county were paid by corporations and non-residents and that people living at Titusville, Rockledge, Eau Gallie, Melbourne, Fort Pierce, Ankona, Eden and Jensen paid another 15 percent. The editor felt if those who paid 90 percent of the taxes wanted the road then they should have it. But he suggested that a portion of the money might be used for a good neighborhood road on the island to placate the opposition. The argument failed. Voters of Brevard County rejected the bonding proposal by a vote of 329 against and 285 in favor. The shell road from one end of the county to the other had to wait.[47]

End Notes

1. Titusville Florida Star, August 2, November 2, 1881.
2. Ibid., January 20, May 11, 1881; April 19, 1882, September 27, 1882, January 4, 11, 1883, February 1, 21, 1884, February 5, 1885, December 1, 1886.
3. Ibid., November 2, 1881, March 1, September 27, 1883, February 5, 19, March 12, 1885; May 19, 1887; Brevard County Historical Commission, History Book, 1830-1920 [Hatch Journal].
4. Herman Herold, Log Book of Travels in the Sunny South, 1884, Mss Box 47, P. K. Yonge Library of Florida History; Tallahassee Floridian, May 7, 1885.
5. Titusville Florida Star, March 8, 15, 1883, February 1, May 1, 1884, July 31, 1889, October 23, November 28, 1890, July 1, 1898; Kyle Van Landingham, Pictorial History of St. Lucie County, 1565-1910 (St. Lucie County Historical Society, n.d.), p. 17; Fred A. Hopwood, Steamboating on the Indian River (Melbourne, 1985), p. 55.
6. Hopwood, Steamboating, p. 8.
7. Tallahassee Floridian, February 10, 1885; Titusville Florida Star, December 26, 1886, February 5, 1909; Hopwood, Steamboating, p. 9.
8. Lewis H. Cresse, "A Study of William Henry Gleason" (Unpublished Ph. D. Dissertation, University of South Carolina, 1975), pp. 69-70, 75-76, 78, 95-96.
9. U. S. Senate, Executive Document No. 33, 47th Cong., 1st Sess., Report of J. F. LeBaron, November 11, 1881.
10. Ibid.
11. George E. Buker, Sun, Sand and Water: A History of the Jacksonville District, U. S. Army Corps of Engineers, 1821-1975 (Jacksonville, 1976), pp. 116-117.
12. Titusville Florida Star, May 28, June 11, August 6,1885, September 29, December 1, 1886, April 17, 1887; Tallahassee Floridian, April 15, July 26, 29, 1886, March 10, 1887.
13. Tallahassee Floridian, June 23, July 28, December 15, 1887, July 19, August 16, September 11, 1888.
14. Ibid., June 4, 11, November 5, 1889; Titusville Florida Star, March 21, 1889.
15. Ibid., May 21, 1892.
16. Ibid., April 23, May 21, 1892; Buker, Sun, Sand and Water, p. 120.
17. Titusville Florida Star, February 8, 1895, April 8, June 10, 1898, December 22, 1899, December 8, 1905; Edward N. Akin, Flagler: Rockefeller Partner and Florida Baron (Kent State University, 1988), p. 178.
18. Buker, Sun, Sand and Water, p. 120.
19. Titusville Indian River Star, October 20, 1880; Tallahassee Floridian, January 17, March 31, April 18, July 25, August 15, 1882, May 29, 1883; Titusville Florida Star, June 29, 1881.
20. Titusville Florida Star, January 4, February 15, 1883; Tallahassee Floridian, March 27, 1883; Seth Bramson, Speedway to Sunshine, p. 26.
21. Titusville Florida Star, May 1, 1884, April 2, 9, 19, 1885.
22. Tallahassee Floridian, May 14, July 16, 30, August 27, December 10, 1885, January 7, 1886; Titusville Florida Star, October 30, 1885.
23. Tallahassee Floridian, January 28, 1886.
24. Ernest Watson, Indian River Steamboats (1936), Mss in P. K. Yonge Library; Titusville Florida Star, December 26, 1886, July 26, 1888; Tallahassee Floridian, April 29, 1886, August 4, 1887; Hopwood, Steamboating, pp. 12-13, 15; Register and Enrollment of Vessels, Department of Treasury, Record Group, National Archives.
25. Hopwood, Steamboating, p. 12; Titusville Florida Star, March 3, 1893.
26. Tallahassee Floridian, March 15, 1888; Hopwood, Steamboating, p. 11; Federal Writers Project, "Ships and Shipping in Florida, Mss in P. K. Yonge Library.
27. Titusville Florida Star, January 15, 1891.
28. Titusville Florida Star, January 12, 26, 1888; Tallahassee Floridian, February 9, March 8, 1888, January 11, 1895.
29. Titusville Florida Star, July 19, August 18, December 8, 1887.
30. Eric Caron, One Hundred Years of Rockledge (Rockledge, 1986), p. 16; Charles A. Hentz Autobiography, Volume 11, Southern Historical Collection, University of North Carolina, Chapel Hill.
31. Hopwood, Steamboating, p. 43; Titusville Florida Star, May 2, 1889, July 17, 1890.
32. Titusville East Coast Advocate, August 29, November 21, 1890, March 6, 1891; Titusville Florida Star, August 17, 21, September 4, 1890.
33. Titusville East Coast Advocate, November 18, December 9, 1892.
34. Ibid., September 8, 1893, August 3, 1894.
35. Titusville Florida Star, January 27, February 3, 10, 1893; June 15, 1894.
36. Titusville Indian River Advocate, July 19, 1895, May 8, 1896, March 26, 1897; Titusville Star Advocate, November 29, 1940; "Timothy Murphy v. Indian River Steamboat Company," September 1895, in Brevard County Miscellaneous Court Records.
37. Titusville Florida Star, February 1, 1895; Titusville Indian River Advocate, April 28, 1899; Seth Bramson, Speedway to Sunshine (Erin, Ontario, 1984), p. 26.
38. Sidney Walter Martin, Florida's Flagler (Athens, Georgia, 1949), p. 137; Bramson, Speedway , pp. 25-27.
39. Martin, Flagler, p. 137; Bramson, Speedway, pp. 25-27; Tallahassee Floridian, June 11, 1885.
40. David Leon Chandler, Henry Flagler (New York, 1986), p. 142; Martin, Flagler, p. 137; Titusville Florida Star, October 28, 1892.
41. Titusville East Coast Advocate, February 10, March 3, 1893; Titusville Florida Star, December 16, 1892, February 17, 1893.
42. Caron, Rockledge, p. 15.
43. Titusville Florida Star, September 8, 1887; Tallahassee Floridian, September 15, November 3, 1887, September 11, 1888, June 4, 1889.
44. Buker, Sun, Sand and Water, p. 191; Tallahassee Floridian, August 19, 1886, May 3, 1888; S. M. Stockslager to Chairman, Light House Board, March 18, 1889, and James G. Green and J. C. Mallory to ibid., February 3, 1891, Light House Site Files, and R. D. Hitchcock to Chairman, Light House Board, Correspondence of Light House Board, Department of Treasury Record Group, National Archives; U. S. House, Executive Document No. 98, 50th Cong., 2nd Sess.
45. Bessie Wilson DuBois, Shipwrecks in the Vicinity of Jupiter Inlet (Lantana, 1975), pp. 8-9; Tallahassee Floridian, December 30, 1884, February 26, November 5, 1885, May 6, 1886, January 16, 1892.
46. Titusville Florida Star, January 12, 1880; Brevard County Commission, Reports, July and August, 1891.
47. Brevard County Commission, Reports, June 1895; Titusville Indian River Advocate, February 15, June 17, August 8, 1895.

Page 98 Map: Jacksonville, Tampa and Key West System map, 1891.
(Brevard County Historical Commission Archives)

ALACHUA
Gainesville
Bronson
LEVY
Ocala
MARION
Palatka
PUTNAM
ST. JOHNS
VOLUSIA
Daytona
Port Orange
New Smyrna
Mosquito Inlet
Enterprise
Sanford
ORANGE
Orlando
Titusville
BREVARD
Cape Canaveral
Melbourne
Eau Gallie
Micco
Sebastian
Fort Capron
Indian River Inlet
St. Lucie
Eden
Waveland
Jupiter
Little Lake Worth
Lake Worth
Figulus
SUMTER
Sumterville
HERNANDO
Brooksville
HILLSBOROUGH
Tampa
Plant City
POLK
Bartow
Kissimmee
Lake Kissimmee
Lake Tohopekaliga
Fort Meade
MANATEE
Manatee
Sarasota
Pine Level
Arcadia
Fort Ogden
Punta Gorda
Charlotte Harbor
Lake Istokpoga
Fort Bassinger
LAKE OKEECHOBEE
Fish Eating Cr.
Lake Hicpochee
Caloosahatchee
Myers
Olga
Alva
Thompson
Gasparilla Island
Cayo Costa Island
ATLANTIC OCEAN

9

Towns, Villages and Settlements in Late 19th Century Brevard

When the Indian River was the major avenue of transportation in Brevard, a long line of settlements from Shiloh to Waveland made the area a viable community where people all along the waterway considered each other neighbors.

Lawrence P. Allen waits on the public dock at Courtenay for his Uncle Ned's launch, c. 1899. (Photo courtesy Margaret Funsch, Florida State Archives)

The Titusville East Coast Advocate wrote with satisfaction and little exaggeration in late 1890 that "Indian River communities are becoming attractive to settlers. We have many communities between Titusville and Lake Worth with churches, schools, society and physicians, as well as stores, stocked with almost everything that could be found in Jacksonville." While they varied greatly in size and even permanence, there were communities spread all along the Indian River on the mainland and on Merritt Island from one end of the county to the other.

Aurantia was settled for the second time about 1880 when E. L. Quinby started a sawmilling operation there. Described as a "village just started" with an estimated adjacent population of 50 to 60 it had a post office in 1882 with Quinby as postmaster. The JTKW built a depot there in 1887 about the same time that J. M. Brown opened his cigar factory. There were no stores there at the time, but, in addition to the sawmill and cigar factory, there was a grist mill owned by A. J. Carter, and a school whose single teacher was Mrs. Irene Chandler. E. B. Carter offered teamster services and Elijah Sackett was the local contractor.[1]

Arrival of the railroad in late 1885 gave impetus to the village of Mims. Its depot was adjudged "as fine as any" when completed in 1886, only a few months after the first trains began running. The Hiawatha Hotel was then receiving guests and serving as a community center. There was also a skating rink and dance hall. Two grocery and dry goods stores were run by C. D. Puryear and the Mims Brothers (Britton J. and Robert E.). The Mims brothers also erected a two-story packing house in 1888 to handle the increasing orange crop.[2]

Located about two miles from Titusville, LaGrange was also on the JTKW line. One of the oldest settlements in northern Brevard County, it boasted the oldest church building on the Indian River between St. Augustine and Key West. Built in 1868, the church was the site of quarterly conferences for many years. Charles A. Hentz of City Point regularly attended those conferences and always stayed in the home of Thomas Johnson Cockshutt, one of the community's first settlers. Owner of the Pioneer Cooperage, which shipped barrels by the schooner load to customers all along the east coast, Cockshutt was also a justice of the peace and notary public. Although he used his full name in his official capacities, he was known to most of his neighbors simply as Tom Johnson, preferring not to use the rest of his name which he regarded as "uneuphonious."[3]

The two general merchandise establishments at LaGrange were managed by W. M. Thomas and E. L. Brady. The latter was also postmaster and railroad station agent. He formed a partnership with W. N. Hendry about 1886, but they soon went their separate ways. Hendry remained at LaGrange and Brady moved to Titusville where his business became known as E. L. Brady and Brother. Adhemar Brady, then a LaGrange resident who later moved to Titusville was superintendent of schools at the time. Although the LaGrange church was a social center for many years, and the Pioneer Cooperage continued through most of the 19th century, LaGrange residents seem more and more to have looked to Titusville as their commercial center.[4]

Titusville was the great beneficiary of the arrival of the JTKW railway in 1886, but it had already enjoyed considerable growth as the primary transfer point for travelers to and from the Indian River before that. With the county courthouse, the Lund House, the Titus House, James Pritchard's real estate agency, and several stores, it was enjoying a considerable reputation as a commercial center by the mid-1880s. But it was the railroad which was the catalyst for Titusville's expansion in the late 1880s. The local newspaper editor reported nine new buildings nearing completion within view of his office window three months after the first train whistles were heard. The town was incorporated later that same year. By early 1887 it claimed 20 businesses, three real estate agents, two lumber yards, two newspapers, and had plans for a bank. Its population was then about 200.[5]

One of the oldest of those businesses was the restaurant which Andrew Gibson, a black man, had been operating across the street from the Titus House since 1881. It was famous for fresh oysters and seafood. Gibson also found time to run a barber shop catering entirely to white customers. F. E. Joyner, W. B. Moore, J. C. Norwood and Company, P. E. Wager, and E. L. Brady and Brother were the major merchandise establishments. John M. Dixon was the druggist. G. W. McKenzie and R. C. Scrimgeour both sold notions and fancy goods. Scrimgeour was also a taxidermist and sold sporting

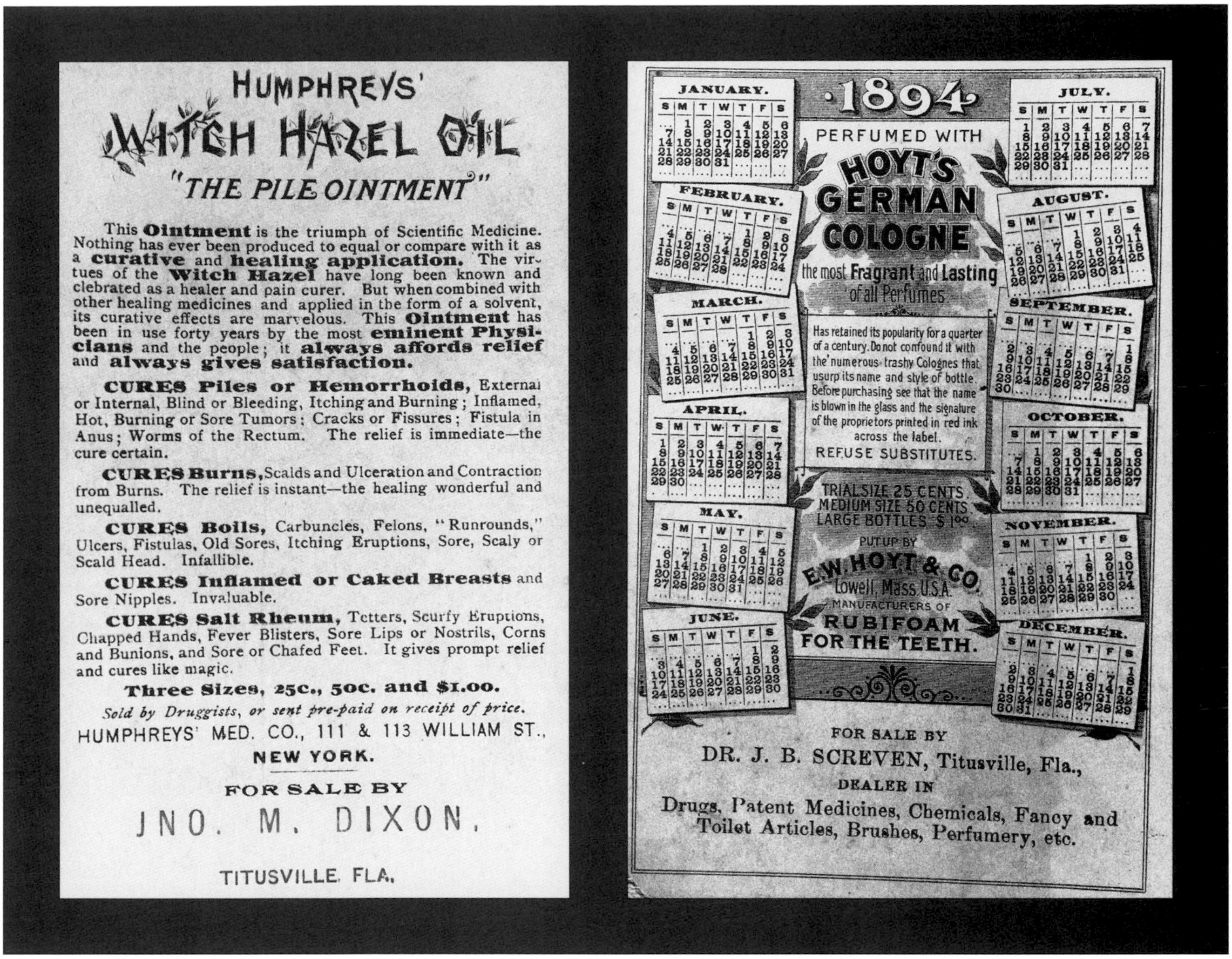

HUMPHREYS'
WITCH HAZEL OIL
"THE PILE OINTMENT"
This Ointment is the triumph of Scientific Medicine. Nothing has ever been produced to equal or compare with it as a curative and healing application. The virtues of the Witch Hazel have long been known and clebrated as a healer and pain curer. But when combined with other healing medicines and applied in the form of a solvent, its curative effects are marvelous. This Ointment has been in use forty years by the most eminent Physicians and the people; it always affords relief and always gives satisfaction.
CURES Piles or Hemorrhoids, External or Internal, Blind or Bleeding, Itching and Burning; Inflamed, Hot, Burning or Sore Tumors; Cracks or Fissures; Fistula in Anus; Worms of the Rectum. The relief is immediate—the cure certain.
CURES Burns, Scalds and Ulceration and Contraction from Burns. The relief is instant—the healing wonderful and unequalled.
CURES Boils, Carbuncles, Felons, "Runrounds," Ulcers, Fistulas, Old Sores, Itching Eruptions, Sore, Scaly or Scald Head. Infallible.
CURES Inflamed or Caked Breasts and Sore Nipples. Invaluable.
CURES Salt Rheum, Tetters, Scurfy Eruptions, Chapped Hands, Fever Blisters, Sore Lips or Nostrils, Corns and Bunions, and Sore or Chafed Feet. It gives prompt relief and cures like magic.
Three Sizes, 25c., 50c. and $1.00.
Sold by Druggists, or sent pre-paid on receipt of price.
HUMPHREYS' MED. CO., 111 & 113 WILLIAM ST., NEW YORK.
FOR SALE BY
JNO. M. DIXON,
TITUSVILLE, FLA.
1894
PERFUMED WITH
HOYT'S GERMAN COLOGNE
the most Fragrant and Lasting of all Perfumes
Has retained its popularity for a quarter of a century. Do not confound it with the numerous trashy Colognes that usurp its name and style of bottle. Before purchasing see that the name is blown in the glass and the signature of the proprietors printed in red ink across the label.
REFUSE SUBSTITUTES.
TRIAL SIZE 25 CENTS.
MEDIUM SIZE 50 CENTS
LARGE BOTTLES $1.00
PUT UP BY
E.W. HOYT & CO.
Lowell, Mass. U.S.A.
MANUFACTURERS OF
RUBIFOAM FOR THE TEETH.
JANUARY.
FEBRUARY.
MARCH.
APRIL.
MAY.
JUNE.
JULY.
AUGUST.
SEPTEMBER.
OCTOBER.
NOVEMBER.
DECEMBER.
FOR SALE BY
DR. J. B. SCREVEN, Titusville, Fla.,
DEALER IN
Drugs, Patent Medicines, Chemicals, Fancy and Toilet Articles, Brushes, Perfumery, etc.

The EVERETT PIANO.
THE JOHN CHURCH COMPANY GENERAL FACTORS. CHICAGO, CINCINNATI, NEW YORK.
INCOMPARABLY THE BEST.
Sold by P. E. Wager, Titusville, Fla.
For cash or on easy monthly payments.
THE STROBRIDGE LITH.CO.CIN.O.
COPYRIGHT 1893 BY THE JOHN CHURCH C

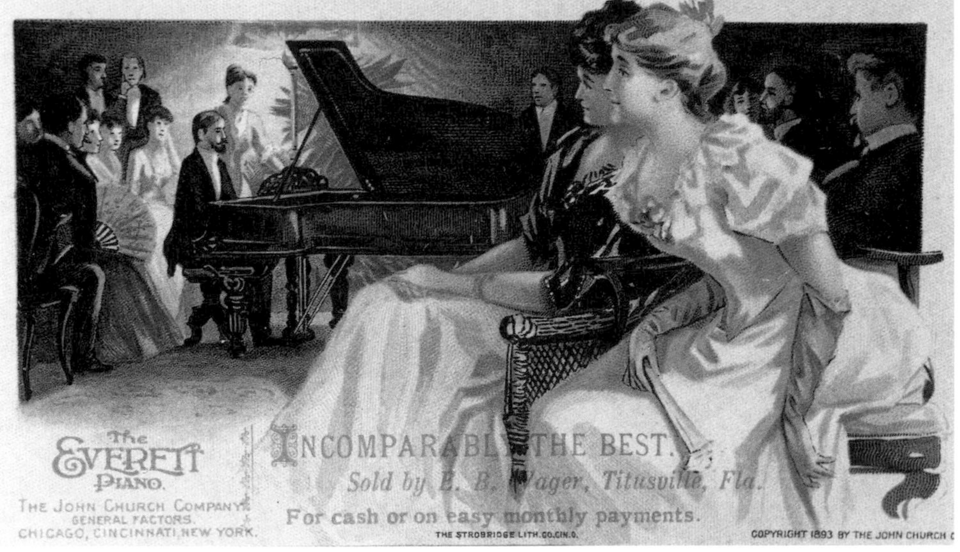

Above: Advertising cards from two of Titusville's druggists in the 1890's, John M. Dixon and J. B. Screven. (Photos courtesy Jim Ball)

Left: A card from P. E. Wager's store advertises the Everett piano. (Photo courtesy Jim Ball)

goods. G. W. Tyler sold furniture and bedding, Mrs. Valentine Gailer was the local baker, and George Warren, another black man, ran a restaurant. During the mid-1880s, Thomas W. Smith operated a boarding house while Joshua Lewis managed the Titus House and S. J. Hodges had charge of the Lund House.[6]

The Indian River Real Estate Agency was owned and operated by James C. Pritchard. Milton Grover also dealt in real estate. Attorneys were Digby Howard, George M. Robbins, D. L. Gaulden, and Minor S. Jones. R. E. Hartford did surveying and engineering work. G. W. Martin and E. T. Redding were building contractors. Stanley G. Montague was a dentist and Benjamin R. Wilson was a physician. A saw and planing mill was operated by Atkinson, Atkinson and Wolf while Robert Ranson was a painter.

James Pritchard had a real estate office and was also president of the new Indian River State Bank, Titusville's first bank. (Photo courtesy Jim Ball)

Ranson subsequently entered the lumber business as well. A. Parkinson made orange wine and George W. Scobie dealt in oysters, fish, and other seafood. Simonson's dry dock and boat repair was in business in the early 1880s with J. E. Enders in charge. As river traffic increased in the latter years of that decade, Robert Sneedley came from Georgia to set up dry docks with capacity for steamers the size of the *Rockledge*. Simonson continued to service smaller craft such as J. J. LaRoche's *Pathfinder*.[7]

Several changes were made by the early 1890s. Pritchard was still handling real estate but he was also president of the Indian River State Bank with W. M. Brown as cashier. W. B. Barnett of Jacksonville was the correspondent banker and a director. Both hotels had undergone structural as well as ownership changes. The Lund House was renamed the Bay View House by Phineas D. Wesson until it was expanded and again renamed the Grand View Hotel. D. S. Hutchinson of New Jersey purchased the Titus hotel and called it the Indian River House. Expanded to a three-story affair with about 60 rooms it offered free salt and sulphur pool bathing in 1890. By 1891 it was being managed by I. M. Babbette.[8]

Some of the new businesses in Titusville in the 1890s included A. Froscher, furniture and undertaking, J. Birnbaum, clothing, S. J. Norton, proprietor of the Indian River bakery, Goldsmith Brothers, clothing, Frank T. Budge, building materials, and J. B. Screven, drugs. Both J. W. Rogers and George B. Rumph sold men's clothing. J. S. Watson and Company was a commission and forwarding merchant with offices on the city dock. Another firm which handled the shipment of citrus and other produce was Furman and Page of New York. T. J. Eaton and Wagoner and Co. were among several merchants who sold Sour Mash Whiskey and other such beverages.[9]

Robert E. Mims built wagons and sold harness and tack while wagon repairs and general blacksmithing was carried on by the Hand Brothers and Blount and Anthony. The Indian River Fibre Company was chartered in 1894 to manufacture palmetto mattresses and similar products. The Phoenix sawing and planing mill had opened the previous year under the direction of Robert Ranson and

S. G. VanLandingham. That firm employed ten men. The Indian River Bottling Works came about the same time. A local branch of the National Railway and Building and Loan Association was organized in 1894 with J. E. Bowman as president, F. W. Miller as vice president and M. E. Gruber as secretary. Directors were T. B. Walker, C. Hale and J. B. Thompson. The association had 21 members in Titusville.[10]

View of downtown Titusville in the early 1890's looking northward on Washington Avenue and showing the new electric street lights. (*Photo courtesy* Robert Hudson, North Brevard Historical Society)

There were some reverses as in the case of Samuel Ray who had migrated from Quincy in the early 1880s and opened a general merchandise store and several other enterprises. He apparently expanded unwisely and was bankrupt in 1893. Advertising "my entire Titusville property for sale," he offered a ten room residence for $3,000, four stores "all on principal streets" for about $1,200 each, one lot with a house for $150 and one without improvements for $100. He also wanted to sell a fish house on the city dock for $100.[11]

The town began urging improvements shortly after it was incorporated. Noting that ten tons of ice were being shipped into town each week, the council encouraged someone to build an ice factory. S. G. Gladwin responded in 1888 with the Titusville Ice Factory. Gladwin formed a partnership in 1890 with T. T. Wetmore who eventually became the sole proprietor of the ice factory. The voters approved a water works in 1887, and water was made available to businesses and residences in 1893. In 1888 the council began discussions about an electric plant and two years later the Titusville Electric Company was organized with a capital of $10,000. Two years later there was such demand for light on the streets and in private homes that the street lights had to be turned off for a few weeks until a larger engine could be installed. Even before the town was incorporated, citizens had cooperated in building a 600 foot city dock into the river on land which was donated by Mrs. Henry Titus. It was at the foot of Main Street. The dock was maintained by the town council until well into the 20th century.[12]

The matter of removing animals from the streets was more difficult than providing utilities. Not only did some residents covet their freedom to allow cattle, horses, and mules to roam at will, but the many open range cattlemen of the county were reluctant to build fences to control their herds. An ordinance applying only to horses and mules was introduced in 1890, but Judge Minor Jones and E. H. Rice, another prominent resident, were vigorously opposed. The stock ordinance failed in 1890, but the nuisance remained. It was not until 1900 that a strong stock ordinance was finally enacted. Owners of cattle, horses, and other stock were notified that after June 11, their animals would be impounded at their expense.[13]

Local newspapers were vital to rural communities in the 19th century and Titusville had its share. The Star, which was first published by Charles Coe at New Smyrna in 1877, was brought to Titusville in 1880 by Ellis B. Wager.

Competitive papers soon appeared. The Titusville Indian River News began publishing a seven column paper in 1882. Edited by Minor S. Jones and J. A. McCory, both of whom were judges, it favored "a constitutional reformation of the State government" but promised to "condemn any resort to Spanish American methods." That paper was soon sold and moved to Cocoa and in 1888 Judge Jones was suing it for libel. The Titusville East Coast Advocate was started in 1890 with Walter S. Graham and C. H. Walton as editors. The firm was dissolved in 1895 when Graham moved to Miami, but the paper continued as the Indian River Advocate until 1900 when the name was changed to the East Coast Advocate and Indian River Chronicle. Several changes were made in the early 1900s, including one which moved the paper to Cocoa, but it eventually was merged with the Star.[14]

Like most of its central Florida neighbors, Titusville suffered economic losses from the great freezes of 1894 and 1895, but its problems were greater than just the adverse weather. It was at that time that the Indian River Steamboat Company was closed and its property sold. If that were not enough, most of the business district was burned by a fire which was probably started by two arsonists – a matter which will be discussed in a later chapter. The growth of the town and its surrounding countryside was interrupted for several years.

That did not mean that business was entirely halted. When the firm of Pace and Doyle closed, the Jacksonville firm of Baker and Holmes opened a branch in Titusville to be operated by Arthur J. Doyle of the failed firm. Frank T. Budge, whose hardware firm survived the depression, sold out in 1898 and moved to Miami. His business was sold to Pritchard and Son to be managed by Boudinot Pritchard who had worked for Budge for several years. The Florida East Coast Telephone Company was organized in 1898 with a capital stock of $10,000 to begin building a telephone line between Jacksonville and Cape Sable. Several Titusville residents were investors.[15]

The Titusville Board of Trade was active in 1900 with Minor S. Jones as president, George M. Robbins as vice president, and J. M. Dixon as treasurer. J. B. Bast was secretary. The board proudly announced that year that the "progressive business men of our town" had discarded kerosene oil lights where they were still in use and

B. C. Willard *opened a store in Cocoa in the early* 1880's *and ran it until his death in* 1888. *This* 1885 *photo also shows* William Jarvis's Delmonico *hotel.* (*Photo courtesy* Daniel *family*, Florida State Archives)

replaced them with incandescent lights.[16]

City Point was about 16 miles south of Titusville and began to emerge about 1880. A post office was established in 1881 with A. J. Whitlock as postmaster. One of its earliest settlers was Dr. George W. Holmes who lived there for many years and delivered many of the children born along the Indian River in the late 19th and early 20th centuries. He was joined in 1881 by Dr. Charles A. Hentz who came from Quincy and lived at City Point for a dozen years before returning to his north Florida home. Hentz practiced medicine but was also involved in developing a grove which was once described as the "paradise" of the countryside. J. C. Norwood and B. C. Willard first had a store there to which they brought supplies from Enterprise by way of their dock on Lake Poinsett. The dock was used by several hack and steamer lines. A. L. Hatch also opened a store which was eventually taken over by his son, George Hatch. Mrs. William H. Sharpe, whose husband was developing citrus groves and busying himself in county politics, ran the Rocky Point House. Other City Point residents who were active in county affairs were school superintendent John H. Sams, tax collector D. W. McQuaig, and tax assessor W. R. Sanders. There was a Methodist Church with Rev. W. A. Simmons as pastor. By 1890 another post office had been opened at the Sharpes' place about a mile and a half from City Point.[17]

In 1895 Titusville had a new and stylish post office complete with brass mailboxes. (Photo courtesy Robert Hudson, North Brevard Historical Society)

About four and a half miles north of City Point, R. A. Hardee had a sawmill at which a post office known as Hardeeville was opened in 1887. The mill was operated by Howard and Ferris who built a long wharf into the river. The post office was in a store on the wharf. It was estimated that about 100 people would receive their mail there. Walton W. Winthrop was the postmaster and one of his patrons was W. W. Westhof.[18]

Platted in 1882 as Indian River City, Cocoa was being called by that name in 1884 when William Barton Smith became postmaster. He estimated that the office would then serve about 80 people. Since it was only three miles from City Point and less than two miles from Rockledge there was considerable overlapping of the addresses of residents and businesses in the three communities. D. W. McQuaig, for example, was shown by the same gazetteer as a resident of City Point and operator of a general store at Cocoa. Gardner S. Hardee was shown as a grocer at Cocoa as well as a grove owner – and subsequently mayor – of Rockledge. His wife's Hardee House was one of the earlier hostelries of Cocoa. Perhaps that is why Cocoa and

Rockledge were often identified as the twin cities.[19]

In addition to his duties as postmaster, Barton Smith also edited the Cocoa Indian River Sun which boosted the town as well as the entire Indian River region. The Mirror, sometimes attributed to Cocoa and sometimes to Rockledge, was being published by Julius King by 1887. King changed its name to the Public Spirit in 1888 and added R. N. Andrews as editor. It was succeeded in 1897 by J. F. Wooten's Cocoa and Rockledge News. B. C. Willard opened a store in Cocoa in the early 1880s and ran it until his death in 1888. Other general stores were those of S. F. Travis and John M. Sanders. Edward Stiling sold hardware and novelties and also had a ship chandlery. Joyner and Booth operated the Lake Poinsett Wharf Company and built boats and steam yachts. Mackey and McMillan was another boat building firm. O. K. Wood had a furniture store next door to the Dixon Brothers store. The Indian River Drug Store was operated by Dr. W. L. Hughlett – a physician – and L. T. Daniel – a dentist. E. E. Hill and Gardner Hardee had grocery stores and A. W. Battle had a candy store. Charles Hammon was a blacksmith who also dealt in guns. D. W. McQuaig ran a dry goods store and a transfer line between the Indian River and Lake Poinsett. C. A. Willard also ran a transportation service between those points. Samuel Chiles was a mason, Hamilton Collier and Frank Fowler were painters, and Lyman Barnes was the local attorney. T. K. Dixon dealt in real estate as did A. A. Taylor and James Holmes whose firm was the Indian River Real Estate Exchange.[20]

Cocoa's two hotels were the Lyon Hotel – Daniel Lyon – and the Delmonico owned and operated by William Jarvis with the sometime assistance of James Minyard. The Delmonico was a two-story building with the upper level reserved for travelers, one of whom was surprised to see the rooms separated by empty potato bags hung at appropriate places.[21]

The Brevard County State Bank was opened in 1889 in the Hill building. Albert A. Taylor was president, James Holmes was vice president, and R. B. Holmes was cashier. Directors included the three officers, J. M. Sanders, and J. F. Wooten. A destructive fire in 1890 did not deter the growth of Cocoa. A company was incorporated to build a street railway from Cocoa to Coquina and a shell road was built along the river between Cocoa and Rockledge. J. R. Dixon, A. Stiling, E. Stiling and a Mr. McIntyre organized a Cocoa branch of the Atlanta Building and Loan Association in 1893.[22]

The community was set back considerably by the mid-1890s freezes, but it struggled back. The town was

Albert A. Taylor was president of the Brevard County State Bank which opened in 1889 in the Hill Building in Cocoa. (Photo BCHC Archives)

First settled in the early 1870's, Rockledge was a little older than Cocoa. (*Photo courtesy Doug Hendriksen*)

incorporated in 1895 and several new businesses and a number of the older ones were shown in the 1897 city directory. A severe storm in 1897 caused extensive damage, but that, too, was soon repaired. An 1898 newspaper story noted several Cocoa industries that were thriving. Several wholesale houses were shipping goods up and down the river. The Hillside Dairy and poultry farms was operating at full scale. Large shipments of fish and fruit were being shipped and the Bracco charcoal manufactory was working to fill many orders. "Some building and considerable repairs, repainting and other improvements to buildings" as well as several property changes were seen in 1900 as signs of returning prosperity.[23]

First settled in the early 1870s, Rockledge was a little older than Cocoa. Its post office was opened about 1875 with H. S. Williams as the postmaster. Williams and Gardner Hardee, prominent founders of Rockledge, would both become leaders of the county and would at various times represent it in the state senate. Williams was in the senate when Rockledge was incorporated in 1887. L. A. Gingras and Arthur F. S. Williams were attorneys and Dr. W. L. Hughlett was the local physician. A. P. Cleveland had a jelly factory. By the mid-1880s Rockledge was enjoying a reputation as the leading resort town on the Florida coast with three fine hotels all facing the Indian River. The first of these was the Tropical House built in 1878 by Stephen Ryder who succeeded Williams as postmaster in 1882.[24]

The Tropical House was purchased by Frederick F. Taylor in the late 1880s and moved back from the river. A

Left: Guests relax on the veranda of the Indian River Hotel. (Photo courtesy Doug Hendriksen)

Below: The New Rockledge Hotel opened by H. P. Shares was one of the fine hotels that attracted visitors to Rockledge. (Photo courtesy Doug Hendriksen)

Stationery from the Hotel Indian River. (Photo courtesy Doug Hendriksen)

Trafford's Lone Store in Cocoa advertised "Fancy Groceries, Soda Fountain, Fruits, Nuts, Candies, and Miscellaneous Goods." Deliveries were made by boat. (Photo courtesy Robert Trafford, Florida State Archives)

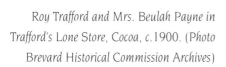

Roy Trafford and Mrs. Beulah Payne in Trafford's Lone Store, Cocoa, c.1900. (Photo Brevard Historical Commission Archives)

new addition was added to the front and the facility was named the Plaza Hotel. A. L. Hatch had built a small hotel in 1881 which became the first Rockledge House. Joseph Wilkinson first purchased a half interest in it and then bought out the rest. He renamed it the Indian River Hotel in 1885. It was J. M. Lee, who had long experience in hotel management in Jacksonville, who turned it into a showplace. The new Rockledge Hotel was opened nearby about the same time by H. P. Shares. The Oaks opened a little later than these three. Offering fine cuisine, large ballrooms with entertainment by their own house bands, beautiful grounds with excellent views of the river, and frequent visits by prominent dignitaries, these hotels became the pride of Rockledge, Brevard County, and the Indian River country during the 1880s and 1890s.[25]

There was rejoicing in 1893 when Flagler's first train steamed into its Rockledge station and discharged passengers who then transferred to another car for the half mile ride to the resort town. Those local residents who had attempted to influence Flagler to build southward were pleased. Rockledge also took pride in being the only town on the railroad with its own spur track. There may have been second thoughts when the Flagler line reached Palm Beach the following year. The Titusville newspaper in early 1895 reported that one of the trains was forty minutes late because of its length – extra cars had been added to accommodate the crowds. "Quite a lot of tourists got off...but the majority were going through to Palm Beach."[26]

The Stewart orange grove at Bonaventure.
(*Photo courtesy Jim Ball*)

The freezes of 1894 and 1895 were more disastrous for Rockledge than its neighboring towns. Apparently because of the decrease in citrus shipments from that point – or perhaps to increase the appeal of his own hotels farther south – the Rockledge depot was closed. Passenger and freight traffic was handled through Cocoa. As the volume of freight increased again in the early 1900s, citrus growers and businessmen of Rockledge asked the Florida Railroad Commission for assistance in getting Flagler to reopen the Rockledge depot. Instead of opening the depot, Flagler brought in a crew on a Sunday and removed the spur track which had connected Rockledge with the main line. Henrietta W. Taylor – the widow of Frederick F. Taylor – was enraged. Her husband had granted to the Flagler company the right-of-way for the railroad to run through his groves and had deeded the land for the station. The case of Henrietta W. Taylor v. FEC Railway Company was argued at great length in 1907. S. F. Travis, J. F. Wooten, A. N. Clarke, and other businessmen testified in behalf of Taylor that Rockledge had been dependent on the tourist business and that Flagler's action had not only deprived the town of a major source of income, but had caused

H. *Bradford's store in* Eau Gallie, *later owned by* W. W. Mullins, *was on the northwest corner of* Highland *and* Ninth *Streets.* (*Photo* Brevard County *Historical* Commission *Archives*)

a drastic reduction in property values. The suit was unsuccessful. Rockledge and its hotels survived, but on a more modest scale than had been the case before Flagler came along.[27]

About two miles south of Rockledge was the Coquina community. It was connected to Rockledge and Cocoa by a shell road and became a post office in 1890. J. Brady Bower was the first postmaster and was still serving in that capacity at the turn of the century.[28]

Bonaventure was slightly less than two miles south of Coquina and its first settler, Israel Stewart, had arrived about 1866. A store was opened there sometime later by E. S. Burton and R. J. White. The community was given a boost by the arrival of the railroad in 1893 at which time a post office was opened near the depot. The post office was named for the 76-acre Bonaventure Grove which had been developed by Britton J. Mims. A large dock accommodated such vessels as the *St. Lucie*, *Georgiana*, and *Sebastian*. Bonaventure at one time boasted a population of nearly 500, a hotel, two boarding houses, at least two citrus packing houses, and a harness shop. There was also a school and a church.[29]

Pineda was some four miles down the river from Bonaventure and was laid out in lots about 1894. Its first postmaster was Virginia W. Parker who was succeeded by J. M. Hopkins. A Star correspondent from Eau Gallie applauded the newly proposed town as "a high and dry site" which was "just a good distance from Eau Gallie." Bovine was a small settlement founded by one of the county's largest cattlemen, Bethel Stewart. Located four miles west of Eau Gallie, it served a handful of cattlemen, lumbermen, and turpentine operators around the Lake Washington area. Belle M. Stewart was the postmistress.[30]

Hartland was a settlement just south of Pineda at which a post office was established in 1890 with John C. Hart as postmaster. It was estimated that about 50 people would use the facility. Bahia was about a mile south of Hartland and its post office claimed about 40 customers. About two and a half miles north of Eau Gallie was the Goshen settlement. A post office was opened there in 1890 with Lura D. Smith in charge. It was expected to serve about 30 people.[31]

First settled by John Houston, Eau Gallie received considerable impetus when William H. Gleason became interested in developing a waterway from Lake Washington to the Indian River by way of Elbow Creek and opening a state agricultural college there. When neither of

The steamer Eau Gallie *and two other boats pause for a view near the headwaters of the* Eau Gallie River. (*Photo courtesy* Doug Hendriksen)

these projects materialized, Eau Gallie languished for a time. Houston remained there, however, and was quite active in county politics. The Gleasons moved there from Miami in the 1880s and William H. Gleason was listed as a local attorney by 1886 even though his main office was in Jacksonville. As late as 1886 Eau Gallie was still listing Rockledge as its shipping point to which place the steamer fare was two dollars. Henry R. Olmstead was the postmaster and mail was delivered three times a week. John Houston was then the mail contractor, having succeeded William H. Gleason who held that position in the 1870s. The Eau Gallie Saw Mill was a steam powered concern owned and operated by Gleason and Brainerd. George W. Hunt was a boat builder in partnership with Gleason whose son, William H. H., was active in the business. Dr. George W. Holmes of City Point made calls to the town. C. J. Young had a meat market from which he used a boat to deliver to customers up and down the river. One of the Seminoles from the interior sold venison in the community in the mid-1880s.[32]

The Indian River Steamboat Company relocated its dry docks to Eau Gallie from Titusville in the late 1880s thus calling attention to the beautiful and well-protected harbor which would make Eau Gallie the delight of boaters on the Indian River and the home of one of the better known yacht clubs on the lagoon within a few years. When Flagler's railroad reached Eau Gallie, the Gleasons wisely agreed to make their dock available to the company rather than risk a competing one. For a brief period, the town enjoyed a boom as the shipping point for supplies used in building the railroad to Palm Beach, but it enjoyed a much longer benefit from the improved transportation which the new road provided.[33]

The State Bank of Eau Gallie opened in 1893 with a paid up capital of $16,000. Directors were John Carey, William Treutler, John McAllister, and John Aspinwall. Officers were Aspinwall, president; Treutler, vice president; and E. G. Vivell, cashier. The Hotel Granada was reported to be "filling up fast" in 1894 with W. T. McCreary of Ashtabula, Ohio, as proprietor. William Treutler also had a hotel there at the time.[34]

The Goode Building in Melbourne housed the Melbourne Post Office and Phone Exchange and Goode and Goode Real Estate and Insurance. Waiting outside is Will Campbell's rig, pulled by Firefly, c. 1895. (Photo by C. F. Conkling, courtesy Harry Goode)

An 1897 Eau Gallie business directory suggests that the town survived the mid-1890s freezes. The Hotel Granada was being operated by George G. Gleason and Captain A. Bennett was offering charter boat services aboard his houseboat *Rochester*. W. J. Nesbitt's Banana River Steamboat Line was carrying the mails to the Banana River communities aboard the steamer *Spartan*. The Hodgson brothers offered steamers and lighters for charter at their ship chandlery and marine railway. They also sold dry goods and groceries. George F. Paddison had a lumber business, William R. Roesch dealt in staple and fancy groceries, hay, grain and fertilizer. W. K. Tombs also sold groceries, dry goods, and men's furnishings, and represented the firm of Wanamaker and Brown of Philadelphia. A. A. Ford was a wholesale and retail dealer in fish and oysters.[35]

A bridge across the Eau Gallie River (formerly Elbow Creek) was completed in 1895. W. J. Nesbitt and John McAllister announced the formation of a social club in 1899 for the purpose of the improvement of Eau Gallie. This was the fifth such club then in existence for the purpose of the "general advancement of our town and citizens."[36]

Just across the river south of town was a large development at which the post office of Sarno was opened in 1894. Only about a mile from Eau Gallie and three and a half miles from Melbourne its postmaster was Charles T. Verbecke, who estimated that it would serve between thirty and forty residents and more than a hundred hotel guests. The new post office was hailed by Eau Gallie residents as a great convenience "since our town is spread over a great deal of ground and we have two passenger stations of the East Coast Line within our limits." The Hotel du Nil on the south bank of the Eau Gallie River boasted a main building and several cottages on eleven acres of beautiful grounds. Originally built by John Green who expected Flagler's road to terminate there, it was taken over by Charles T. Verbecke who then died unexpectedly about a year after the Sarno post office was opened. The property was sold at auction in late 1896 by George M. Robbins as special master. Aaron A. DeGrauw of Jamaica, New York, the mortgagee, purchased it. The Hotel du Nil would figure prominently in local affairs in

Miss Emma Strawbridge ran the Carleton Hotel in Melbourne as well as the Idlewilde Cottage. (Photo courtesy Doug Hendriksen)

Cornthwaite J. Hector became the postmaster with offices in his store. The store, which also had accommodations for guests, was at first on an island in the Indian River, but a causeway was built to connect it with the mainland in the late 1880s. Henry Titus still had the mail contract when the post office was first opened, but the mail was being carried by Peter and Dick Wright. The latter brought the mail from New Smyrna to Titusville where the former took over and delivered to points south.[38]

the early 20th century as the winter home of the Kentucky Military Institute.[37]

Melbourne's first residents had arrived in the 1870s, but the community began taking shape about 1880 when

Melbourne claimed a population of about 70 when Captain R. P. Paddison arrived with the steamer *Rockledge* which made the little town its home port in 1887. Passengers could disembark from the *Rockledge* and other steamers at the city pier which extended 1400 feet into the river, or at Hector's pier which was slightly longer. They could go from the piers to the Carlton Hotel which had recently been opened by Miss Emma Strawbridge, or to the Good House, which Richard Goode had opened about 1884. Miss Strawbridge also had the Idlewilde Cottage. E. P. Branch ran a general store in a two-story building which he had built. D. W. McQuaig had built another two-story structure which was known as the Riverside House. Frank Fee had a hardware store which he subsequently relocated in a brick building which was shared by Ed Nelson's furniture store.[39]

The Melbourne pier extended 1400 feet into the river to welcome steamboats. (Photo by C. F. Conkling, courtesy Harry C. Goode, Sr.)

A dry goods and grocery store was opened by Lewis D. Lockwood in 1890. The Melbourne State Bank was organized three years later with J. H. Phillips as president and E. P. Branch as cashier. In addition to those two, directors were George W. Lyon of Waukeegan, Illinois, P. W. Heins of Olivia, Minnesota, and G. Loutrell Lucas of Eden, Florida. The Izant House was another hotel in the late 1880s. John Beach ran the Indian River Nurseries with stock which he brought from the Bahamas. William Fee was the only physician until about 1894 when Dr. H. D. Brown opened a pharmacy in the town. Captain A. T. Rose moved his boat works from Titusville to Melbourne in 1894 and put up ways on the city dock at a place which had once been occupied by Metcalf's lumber yard.[40]

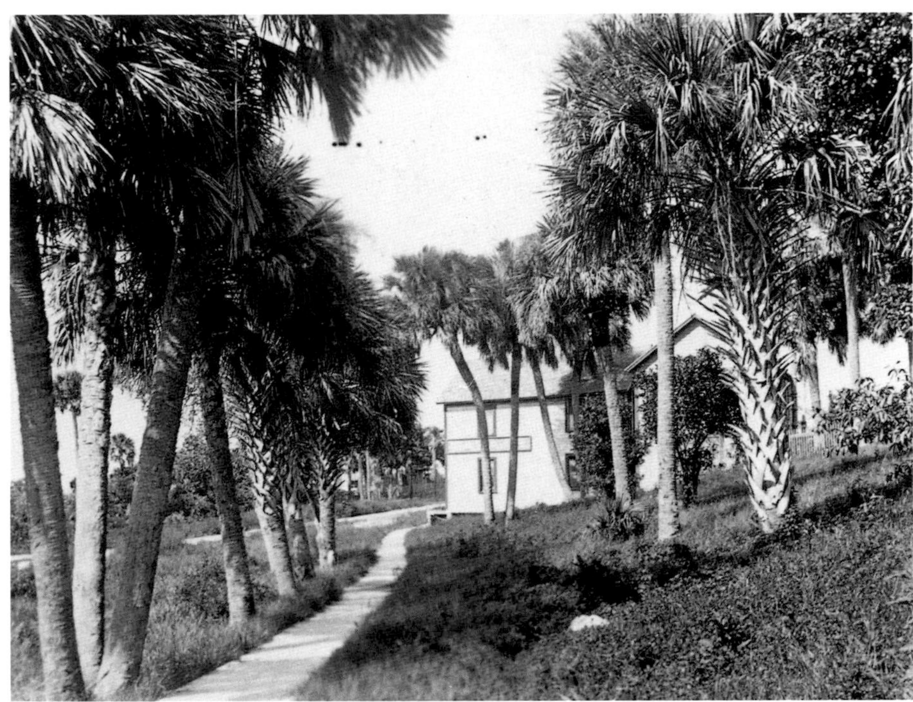

In 1897 Mrs. Charles Campbell was selling millinery goods at The Bazaar in downtown Melbourne. (Photo by C. F. Conkling, Goode Collection, Brevard County Historical Commission Archives)

Guy Metcalf began publishing the Melbourne News in 1887. He later moved to Jupiter but E. D. Oslin then started the Melbourne Times in 1894. His offices were above Frank Fee's hardware store. When he moved to North Carolina in 1899, his brother, Charles, took over the paper. The Melbourne East Coast Republican also began publishing in 1898. Its owners were W. T. Wells, Charles Vickerstaff Hines, and James T. Hogg.[41]

Melbourne was incorporated in 1887. It was an orderly town which boasted that it did not need a jail. However, vagrants were not particularly welcome. When several of these visitors appeared during the winter of 1892-93, they were promised "the opportunity to do some work on the streets" if they remained.[42]

A bridge was built across Crane Creek in the latter 1880s and the Melbourne and Atlantic Railroad was built to Melbourne Beach in 1889. R. W. Beaujean became its first postmaster that year. Before the road was built, the Beaujean ferries offered transportation using a system of semaphore signals by which service could be requested.[43]

Although the Flagler railroad was a welcome improvement to Melbourne's transportation, it was not without some costs. Melbourne had long been the transfer point between the upper and lower portions of the Indian River. Freight was transferred there and passengers often stopped over in town. That changed somewhat as trains replaced steamers as the primary carriers to southern Florida. The mid-1890s freezes also had a deleterious effect on the community. Even before the bad weather, however, the town was shocked to learn that C. J. Hector – one of the larger merchants who was then serving as county commissioner – declared bankruptcy. He had expanded his business interests considerably and perhaps over-extended himself by building an expensive yacht. A serious national depression was beginning to be felt by

Near Haulover was the community of Clifton. One of its first inhabitants was Butler Campbell, a former slave who settled there in 1872. (Photo Cocoa Tribune 1983)

1893. Heavily indebted, Hector was concomitantly unable to collect from a number of people who owed him money. About three weeks before the first freeze in late December 1894, he closed his business and his entire stock was sold. George B. Rumph of Titusville bought the inventory and sent John Walker to take over and manage the business at Melbourne.[44]

The two years following the freezes were austere times for Melbourne, but the town was still intact in 1897. The bank remained in business and was then the only one in the southern portion of Brevard County. Mrs. Charles J. F. Campbell was selling millinery goods at The Bazaar, Harlan D. Brown's Melbourne Pharmacy was open, and A. E. Lyman was the resident dentist. Charles T. McBride was selling groceries, meats, produce, hay and grain. Goode and Goode were dealing in real estate and making loans. James T. Hogg was also in real estate and insurance and was serving as the U. S. Commissioner. Frank Fee's hardware business was still open and Branch and Nicholson were selling pine lumber.[45]

East of the Indian River and extending nearly 40 miles from the northern boundary of the county to a point just across from Eau Gallie, Merritt Island was also being settled. There were small communities on the barrier island east of the Banana River as well. The northernmost settlement on the island was Shiloh. Settled in the 1880s, it was so situated between Brevard and Volusia counties that its trade and social affairs were divided between them. The Kuhl, Griffis, Taylor, and Pattillo families were among its few inhabitants. Just south of Shiloh, the communities of Clifton and Haulover were almost intermingled. In 1886 Charles H. Nauman became postmaster at Haulover and subsequently became a grove owner and county leader. The post office had previously been opened and closed several times, but in 1886 it enjoyed daily mail. J. D. Vann ran a store and restaurant there for a time. The place was renamed Clifton in 1889 and Thomas R. Crook became the postmaster. One of its first inhabitants was Butler Campbell, a former slave who settled in 1872 and purchased land from the state. It was from Campbell that Andrew Jackson, Douglas Dummett's black son-in-law, bought the land on which he developed his celebrated orange grove. Wade Holmes was another substantial black resident of Clifton. In addition to the Crooks and Naumans, the William Watton family from England was also among the white neighbors of Butler, Campbell and Holmes. Although the neighborhood was apparently integrated in many ways, M. R. Mahaffey, a black man, was the teacher of the "colored School " at Clifton.[46]

Heath was at the site of the Dummett Grove and was named for the manager of that property in the 1880s. On the east bank of the Indian River just north of Banana Creek, it was made a post office in 1887. Estimated to

Oceanus was settled in the 1890's when people from the mainland first began making excursions there to enjoy the ocean beach. In this photo the Packard family enjoys an outing in 1917. (Photo courtesy Grace Packard Bryant)

serve fewer than 20 people, it had weekly mail delivery. F. B. Sackett, who had a large apiary at the place, was the postmaster. The Heath office was closed but was reopened in 1891 as Mortonhurst. George W. Morton was then postmaster. Another office was opened at Honeywell in 1891, about five miles north of Canaveral. Luella L. Hanna was postmistress.[47]

Mills Burnham, his son-in-law, Henry Wilson, and a few others lived at Canaveral, a few miles west of the lighthouse near the Banana River. They were receiving their mail at Titusville about 20 miles away until a post office was opened there in 1882. The mail was first delivered twice each week, but that was reduced to a weekly delivery in 1884. Henry Wilson was postmaster there for about 30 years. Just south of Canaveral on the barrier island was Artesia which was made a post office in 1891 with John Henry Hogan as postmaster. The site of Artesia is now the city of Cape Canaveral. Just south of Artesia at the present site of Cocoa Beach was Oceanus which was settled in the early 1890s when people from the mainland first began making excursions there to enjoy the ocean beach. In 1894 the community boasted two boarding houses, one operated by Mrs. Phoebe A. Black and the other by A. S. Norton. There was also a store, a restaurant, a post office, a bakery, a laundry, and "lots of sociable people," according to a local booster. Norton ran a sailboat several times each week to Lotus which was on Merritt Island just south of Georgiana. According to Phoebe Black, Oceanus was practically destroyed by the depression following the 1894-95 freezes.[48]

Several miles south of Banana Creek on the east bank of the Indian River was Courtenay. First called Island City,

Titusville's Washington Avenue looking south, c.1895. (Photo courtesy Robert Hudson, North Brevard Historical Society)

By the 1890's Indianola had its own school.
(Photo courtesy Clyde Field)

Samuel J. Field became the first postmaster of Indianola when an office was opened there in 1887.
(Photo courtesy Clyde Field)

Oak Cottage, Indianola, was the home of A. S. Humphrys.
(Photo courtesy Doug Hendriksen)

H. T. Smith ran a hotel at Merritt known as the Island House, which later became the Merritt Island Hotel. (Photo courtesy Doug Hendriksen)

Courtenay became a post office in 1885 when John Houston had the mail contract. The first postmaster was Milledge B. Sams, a dentist who had recently come from South Carolina. Several of the LaRoche brothers, who had first settled at the Narrows, made their homes at Courtenay and proved up on homesteads there. Several members of the Sams family and E. P. Porcher were among the other early settlers of Courtenay. By the mid-1880s the community claimed a community house, a school, and the first Episcopal church on the island. It was estimated that about fifty people would be served by the post office in 1885.[49]

Indianola was south of Courtenay. Samuel J. Field, a member of one of the first families on the island, became the postmaster when an office was opened there in 1887. With a long wharf – Indianola Landing – it was served by the Indian River steamers and mail was delivered six times each week. By the 1890s, the community was prospering with two stores, a church, a school, and a club house. Boasting that it was free from malaria, the Indianola House was managed by Mrs. G. W. Schuyler. Less than three miles south of Indianola was Merritt, a tiny community which was first settled about 1870. It was estimated that about 25 people would be served by the post office which was opened there in 1884 with Samuel J. Frost in charge. The post office was in the De Frost Hotel which its proprietor had built in 1880. H. T. Smith also ran a hotel, apparently the Island House, which later became the Merritt Island Hotel. Despite its proximity to Indianola, Merritt had its own school. Merritt got a substantial boost in 1891 when

New York Fire Chief Thomas F. Nevins spent his winter vacations at his citrus groves on Merritt Island. Nevins is second from the right as he watches friends feeding ducks at the Cocoa City Dock, 1910. (Photo courtesy Grace Packard Bryant)

Top: Ryder's Landing, photo c. 1880. Stephen Ryder was proprietor of the Tropical House in Rockledge. (Photo courtesy Doug Hendriksen)

Center: It was common for loads of tourists from the hotels at Rockledge to visit Lotus in naptha launches. (Photo courtesy Doug Hendriksen)

Below: Joseph and Louise Cannata with their daughter at their home in Georgiana, c. 1900. (Photo courtesy Clyde Field)

Left: Rufus Stewart built this home at Brantley. He was elected to serve two terms in the Florida legislature in 1909 and 1911. (Photo courtesy Jim Ball)

Below: Charles D. Provost was the first postmast at Lotus in 1893. Later the Dobson family lived there and ran the store and post office. (Photo courtesy Doug Hendriksen)

Thomas F. Nevins, the popular fire chief of New York City, purchased the Frost Hotel, refurbished it, and expanded it to a 50-room capacity. It was managed by Mrs. Peter Nevins.[50]

Chief Nevins spent his winter vacations developing his citrus groves and shipping parcels of the fruit to friends in New York. As his groves came into full production, he capitalized on his home town popularity and began marketing his Nevin oranges on a commercial scale. He even advertised his citrus on the sides of his official carriage and spread the word as he dashed around the streets of New York City. The fruit was packed at a house on a dock at Merritt, transported to Cocoa on barges, and loaded on FEC cars. The barges were pulled by a tug called the *Mystic*. With a black captain named Dennis Sawyer at the helm, the *Mystic* was a well-known part of Indian River traffic.[51]

Footman was a small settlement on the east bank of the river almost directly across from Rockledge. Horti was almost directly east of Footman on the tip of the peninsula between Newfound Harbor and the Banana River. It became a post office in 1887 with Jesse J. Fox as postmaster.[52]

Georgiana was a substantial community on the east bank of the Indian River about five miles south of Rockledge . The area was first settled just after the Civil War by the Wittfeld brothers. William Wittfeld developed beautiful groves and gardens on the famous Honeymoon Lake. Known as Fairyland, the Wittfeld place became one of the county's showplaces in the 1880s. Residents and tourists alike enjoyed their visits to Fairyland. Peter Wittfeld ran a store and a boarding house at Georgiana until he sold out to W. A. Hall in 1894. The Georgiana Hotel was managed by Mrs. S. A. Allen and F. C. Allen was postmaster. The latter also ran a general store near the steamboat landing until he rented it to Weyther and Wagner. Cultivation of vegetables, pineapples and oranges was the major economic activity but both C. B. Magruder and A. A. Stewart ran sawmills. With an excellent boat landing the place was easily accessible to the Indian River steamers and mail delivery was daily except Sunday. An important improvement was made to Georgiana in 1894 when an avenue was opened across the peninsula from the Indian River to the Banana River. Plans were underway in 1894 for a building to house the Georgiana school. The Rev. M. Black, who had first settled on Turkey Creek and sailed up and down the river as an itinerant minister for several years, was instrumental in building the Georgiana Methodist Church. He was the first pastor and Mrs. Black took in boarders. When the pastor died she moved to Oceanus where she ran a boarding house until 1895.[53]

Lotus was about three miles south of Georgiana. Like

Near the southern tip of Merritt Island, just across the river from Eau Gallie, *was Tropic, first settled about* 1880. (*Photo courtesy Doug Hendriksen*)

May Pierson taught at the Malabar district school. (*Photo courtesy Doug Hendriksen*)

most of those on Merritt Island, the groves at Lotus were usually less affected by cold weather than those on the mainland. This sometimes gave the community an advantage when tourists desired to see green trees with fruit on them. It was common for loads of tourists from the hotels at Rockledge to visit Lotus in naptha launches during the colder winters. Charles D. Provost became the first postmaster at Lotus about 1893 when it was estimated that he would serve about 75 patrons. The place then had a general store which was the only one on the island south of Georgiana. People from Hartland, Banyan and Brantley also shopped there. Shortly after the post office was established, a road was opened across the narrow peninsula to the Banana River and it was soon being used by mainland residents and tourists who wished to take advantage of the ocean beaches.[54]

Brantley, a neighborhood about three miles south of Lotus, was named for a man who had planted a pineapple field there about 1860. By the time a post office was opened in 1887, in the charge of Jesse Temple Simmons, Brantley was the center of an extensive pineapple growing area. With landing facilities on the river, it was served by the Indian River Steamboat Company which delivered mail six times weekly. The Rev. A. V. Hiscock of Georgiana held Sunday School there every other week, causing Brantley to proclaim its "lead in moral and religious interest". On the eastern shore of the Banana River, almost due east of Brantley, the community of Atlantic was striving to have a post office established in 1892. John Carson was its leading proponent. He and his handful of neighbors were asking for a "special office" to be supplied from Tropic. On the Indian River, about three miles south of Brantley, Banyan obtained a post office in the early 1890s.[55]

At the southern tip of Merritt Island just across the river from Eau Gallie was Tropic, first settled about 1880. When a post office was opened in 1883, Preston A. MacMillan was in charge. There were about 100 people there in 1886 when M. E. Storms was postmaster. The office was held in 1900 by T. A. Campbell. J. Casper ran a hotel at Tropic and D. G. Gaulden offered legal services. Pineapples, oranges, vegetables and bananas were grown and shipped by local residents. The leading grower and longtime proponent of Tropic was George F. Ensey who imported pineapple slips from the West Indies for resale in Brevard County.[56]

South of Melbourne was a continuing line of settlements of varying size. Tillman was a small community about three miles south of Melbourne where John M.

A view of Sebastian's main street from the roof of the Kitching Building. (Photo by Rodney Kroegel, Brevard County Historical Commission Archives)

nursery, H. C. Starck operated a cigar factory, and J. Briscoe was a carpenter and grove owner. May Pierson taught the Malabar district school. Two miles northwest of Malabar on the east bank of the Indian River was the tiny settlement of Averill at which a post office was established in 1887 with Stephen B. Craft as postmaster.[57]

About four miles south of Malabar, Valkaria was made a post office in 1890 with Edward Cecil as postmaster. He claimed that more than 50 people would be served. Three miles further south, Grant was given a post office in 1891 with Edwin Nelson as postmaster. It was expected to serve about 30 people at that time. George W. Scobie, who was one of the pioneers of Indian River fishing, had a fish house there in the 1890s.[58]

The Micco post office was opened in 1884 with John Bowie as postmaster. About three miles south of Grant, the settlement had mail twice each week. Micco was best known for the Oak Lodge which was run by C. F. Latham just across the river from the post office. The lodge became the winter residence of Professor J. W. Jenks, a Brown University naturalist who frequently brought with him colleagues interested in the rare plants on the many

Minor became the first postmaster in 1887. Its residents preferred that Tillman be recognized as a separate community but it was "always claimed as a suburb of Malabar" where its citizens went to attend church and school. Malabar was only about two and a half miles south of Tillman and was first settled in the 1870s by E. B. Arnold. Its post office was opened in 1883 with R. A. Ward as postmaster. He anticipated that between 60 and 75 people would use the facility. By 1886 it had two hotels, the Malabar House and the American House. John E. Chapin had a general store and a

Fishing was the major industry of the town of Grant which was given a post office in 1891. (Photo courtesy Grant Historical Society)

islands near Micco. People all along the Indian River lamented the 1893 fire which destroyed the lodge, but it was apparently rebuilt because Professor Jenks was staying there again in early 1894.[59]

One of the businesses in Sebastian was the barber shop. (Photo by Rodney Kroegel, Brevard County Historical Commission Archives)

New Haven was settled about 1880 by Thomas New who became its first postmaster in 1882, claiming that about 150 people would use his facility. New fled the area in 1884 after U. S. authorities accused him of having abused the privileges of his office. That post office was closed and another was opened at Sebastian about a mile to the south. Sylvanus Kitching was the new postmaster. With an estimated population of about 90 in 1886, Sebastian had Kitching's store, a saw and planing mill run by W. J. MacMillan, and a hotel known as the Sebastian House. Dr. H. C. Hill was the local physician. Mail was delivered twice weekly by steamer from Titusville. In 1889 S. B. Carter built a hotel near Sebastian on the Fleming Grant. This was apparently the Ercildonne, a hotel frequented by prominent sportsmen, one of whom was Theodore Roosevelt. The community was given a boost in the late 1890s when the Roseland Inlet Company was formed to cut through the barrier island opposite the mouth of the Sebastian River. Incorporated in New York, the company's directors were W. W. Bissell, Thomas S. Drake, H. H. Todd, and Alice P. Hudson. All residents of New Rochelle, New York, they were joint owners of the nearby Fleming Grant. Another

Home of Frank Foster at Sebastian. Sebastian had an estimated population of 90 in 1886. (Photo by Rodney Kroegel, Brevard County Historical Commission Archives)

By 1889 Fort Pierce boasted three hotels and a thriving lumber company. (Photo courtesy Doug Hendriksen)

director was W. W. Russell, manager of the Cincinnatus Farms, about whom more will be said in another chapter.[60]

In some places post offices were so close together that geographic designations became confusing to the uninitiated. That seemed the case with the post offices of Orchid, Enos, and the Narrows. The Titusville newspaper carried an explanation that "geographically the Narrows extends from Barker's Bluff to the north line of Township 33, but for postal purposes the name includes only that portion...which receives its mail from the Narrows post office on Gem Island." Orchid and Enos were distinct and separate. The post office at the Narrows was opened in 1884 with Lewis B. Damon as postmaster. Daniel, James, Ben, Frank, and John LaRoche were among the ten grove owners there at the time, although they later relocated to Courtenay. With fewer than 50 inhabitants the community boasted a school and a library. The library was built in the early 1890s with lumber donated by E. L. Gray. By 1894 it claimed a holding of 1,500 volumes and a patronage which extended for miles along the river. Its board of directors, for example, included G. C. Mathews of Palm Beach, G. A. Saeger of Ankona, W. F. Richards and E. J. Shattuck of Eden, S. F. Gibbs of Melbourne, O. Stypman of Potsdam, and J. Sorensen of Jensen. Orchid was about three miles north of the Narrows where Mrs. Susan M. Mohr served about 37 people. Enos was two and half miles south of the Narrows post office and James E. Dodge was in charge in 1897.[61]

Woodley was a few miles south of the Narrows and Vero was a short distance below that settlement. Both were on the west bank of the river and on the Flagler railroad. Hickory was about six more miles south of Vero when John William Hodge was postmaster. Just south of Hickory was St. Lucie, one of the oldest settlements in the county. James Paine was still living there in the 1880s and serving as collector of the port of St. Lucie. Benjamin Hogg was engaged in a general merchandise business and Minor S. Jones was providing legal services there until he moved to Titusville. Mrs. Jones was running a boarding house. The community was quite excited when Pennsylvania's senior senator, Matt Quay, visited St. Lucie on a

Fort Pierce was a favorite spot for fishermen because of its location near the fishing grounds at Indian River Inlet. A catch of sawfish at Ft. Pierce city dock, c. 1900. (Photo courtesy Colin Campbell)

fishing trip in 1889. He liked the place so well that he built a large winter home nearby. He spent several years there and a settlement eventually grew up around his residence and became known as Quay.[62]

About a mile and a half south of St. Lucie and not far from Fort Pierce, a handful of settlers asked for a post office in 1885. First asking for the name of Portsmouth and then Atlantic City, they were obliged to settle for Bass. Cornelia L. Bass was the postmistress. While Bass claimed about 500 residents, its better-known neighbor just a mile to the south estimated a post office clientele of about 100 when P. P. Cobb became the Fort Pierce postmaster in 1887. A house of refuge was opened there a year earlier with James Bell as its first keeper. Cobb's store was then the center of activity for the settlement which had been known as Cantown in the earlier 1880s. The town seems to

The Seminoles often traded at B. F. Hull's store in Jensen. (Photo by C. F. Conkling, Goode Collection, Brevard County Historical Commission Archives)

A Seminole Indian poses in Jackson Park at White City. (*Photo Brevard County Historical Commission Archives*)

have prospered during the next few years. A. G. LaGow opened his Edgar House in 1889 and it became a favorite spot for fishermen because of its location near the fishing grounds at Indian River Inlet. By 1895 the place boasted three hotels. W. P. Hatchett had a thriving lumber company. P. P. Cobb continued to deal in general merchandise, hay, and grain in the late 1890s. Alderman and Raulerson – both large-scale cattlemen – were wholesale dealers in meat. Another cattlemen, I. L. Carleton, also had a store in Fort Pierce. He advertised beef, pork, and mutton as well as butter, hay and grain. C. P. Platts was a physician and A. J. Lewis was an attorney. J. T. Bevill offered livery services and catered especially to "hunting and traveling parties." T. J. O'Brien was a wholesale dealer in fish, oysters, and green turtles. Fort Pierce was a major trading post for the Indians from the interior in the 1890s and A. C. Swearingen ran a traveling store which visited their camps periodically.[63]

Named for Dr. J. F. Ankeny, Ankona was another settlement which dated back to the 1840s, although it had been dormant for some time until about 1880. Located approximately halfway between Fort Pierce and Eden on a high bluff it was made a post office in 1886 under the name of Ankona Heights. Comfort E. Chaffee was the postmaster and was succeeded by Cora P. V. Chaffee. By the time the post office was opened the community had two hotels, the Romainia House and the Ankona House. C. T. McCarty offered legal services and money to loan in the early 1890s until he relocated to Fort Pierce. A major storekeeper was William H. Tancre, whose business house usually served as the polling place for local elections. The community boasted a considerable growth of both its pineapple acreage and its citrus groves in the late 1890s. Among the growers were W. C. Rawlinson, Mrs. L. B. Abdill, Mrs. J. F. Ankeny, L. S. Eldred, Mrs. James Callahan, and C. T. McCarty.[64]

Nearby Tibbals evolved around L. P. Tibbals' Beulah Plantation. A hotel was built there in 1900 and it was renamed Walton. Viking was first settled in 1892 by B. Daniels. Jens Helseth began planting pineapples there in 1895 and several other Scandanavians soon joined him. The Eden and Tibbals Telephone Company was organized in 1898. Its seven terminals were in the homes of the pineapple growers between the two places.[65]

Thomas E. Richards settled in 1879 at the place which became Eden. Its post office opened in 1882 under the name of Eden Grove. Richards was postmaster and proprietor of the Eden Grove House as well as the largest of several pineapple growers for which Eden became famous. He was also engaged in a general merchandise business. His competitors were Lucas and LeTourneau. Dr. J. F. Ankeny was the physician for Eden and adjacent communities until his death in the 1890s. Charles F. Moise was a painter and H. W. Richards was a carpenter.[66]

Only two miles south of Eden was Jensen, although its residents had first wanted it to be called Mt. Washington or Naples. They settled for Jensen after John L. Jensen, a pineapple grower who settled there in 1883. John Sorensen was the first postmaster when the office opened in 1890. With the Al Fresco and Seminole hotels, Jensen reminded tourists that good accommodations and excellent fishing were available there.[67]

Almost at the southern boundary of Brevard County on the peninsula was Waveland, where a handful of people had lived for some time before a post office was established there in 1891. Anson J. Olds kept the office in his home for about 75 people. There were enough people there, however, that the Rev. B. F. Brown was able to lay the cornerstone for All Saints Church in 1898.[68]

Near Waveland, Stuart – first called Potsdam – was beginning to take shape in the late 1890s. The Florida East Coast Railroad Company built a depot on the south side of the St. Lucie River in 1897 with a dock which permitted trains to go out over the water to meet surface vessels for transferring freight. Walter Kitching retired from the trade boat business and built a large store there. The post office of Rio San Lucie had a brief existence on the banks of the St. Lucie River near Stuart in the mid-1890s.[69]

Seminole Indian family circa 1890. (Photo courtesy Vera Zimmerman)

About five miles north of Rio San Lucie and an equal distance southwest of Fort Pierce was one of the more ambitious efforts at community building in the county. Inspired by the Chicago Exposition of 1893, Louis Pio organized the Florida Cosmopolitan and Immigration Company to settle a group of about 800 Scandinavians and Danes at White City, which was intended to be patterned after the World's Fair model city of the same name. The enterprise fell on hard times when Pio suddenly died. A large amount of its property was sold at auction in 1895, but the community survived with an infusion of funds from Henry Flagler. White City never attained the goals envisioned by its founder, but it became a substantial farming community and lasted into the 20th century.[70]

About eight miles west of Fort Pierce on the road to Fort Drum was Rosenhayn, established as a post office in 1888. William Wilson Layfort was the postmaster. A post office was reestablished at Fort Drum in 1888 as well. Thirty-five miles from Fort Pierce, the place claimed about 26 inhabitants that year. Henry L. Parker was the postmaster and Henry L. Parker and Son was the major merchandising firm for the area. He and the other merchants there did a sizable business with the Indians and shipped large numbers of pelts through Fort Pierce. There was both a school and a church there in 1894 when Joel Swain announced that he was laying out a new development at Fort Drum. He offered a lot to "any white person" who would build on it a house worth $100. Swain based his hopes for success on his belief that the countryside was a sportsmen's paradise and would be a "splendid summer resort for the Indian River people."[71]

Many of the settlements and post offices which sprang up so abundantly in the county during the last quarter of the 19th century have since disappeared or have been absorbed by neighbors. All of those south of Sebastian, of course, were detached when St. Lucie County was formed in 1905. But, in the 19th century, when the Indian River was the major avenue of transportation in Brevard County, they formed a long line of settlements from Shiloh on the north to Waveland on the south which made the Indian River country a viable community where people all along the waterway considered each other neighbors.

End Notes

1. Post Office Site Location Reports, Microfilm 1126, Roll 88, National Archives. Hereinafter cited as PO SL. Titusville Florida Star, September 29, 1880, April 7, 1887, January 26, 1888. Hereinafter cited as Titusville Florida Star. R. L. Polk's Florida Gazetteer and Business Directory, 1886-1887. Hereinafter cited as Gazetteer.
2. Titusville Florida Star, September 29, December 8, 1886, August 9, November 29, 1888.
3. Charles A. Hentz, "Autobiography, Volume 11," Southern Collection, University of North Carolina.
4. Titusville Florida Star, February 1, 1884, January 5, 1888, April 23, 1891, December 23, 1893; Gazetteer, 1884-1885, 1886-1887.
5. Tallahassee Floridian, March 11, 1886; Titusville Florida Star, April 17, 1887.
6. Gazetteer, 1886-1887.
7. Ibid, 1884-1885, 1886-1887; Tallahassee Floridian, March 8, 1888; Titusville Florida Star, January 5, 1891.
8. Titusville Florida Star, February 9, 1887, July 3, 1889; Tallahassee Floridian, February 2, 1888; Titusville East Coast Advocate, November 14, 1890.
9. Titusville Florida Star, April 23, 1891.
10. Titusville East Coast Advocate, January 27, 1893; Titusville Florida Star, April 27, May 4, 11, 1894; Titusville Indian River Advocate, April 2, 1896.
11. Titusville Florida Star, June 30, 1893.
12. Tallahassee Floridian, July 21, August 14, 1887; Titusville Florida Star, February 2, 9, March 15, 1888, January 31, 1889, January 9, 1890.
13. Titusville Florida Star, June 5, 1890, October 2, 1892, June 8, 1900.
14. Tallahassee Floridian, November 7, 1882; Titusville Florida Star, September 15, 1887, May 17, 1888, January 30, August 29, 1890, October 15, 1894; Titusville Indian River Advocate, December 13, 1895, June 1, 1900.
15. Titusville Florida Star, February 11, 1895, February 3, May 6, 1898.
16. Ibid., January 5, May 25, 1900.
17. Ibid., June 1, November 2, 6, 1881, December 14, 1882, 1888, March 16, 1890, July 13, 1894; Gazetteer, 1884-1885; Brevard County Commission, "Hatch Journal."
18. PO SL; Titusville Florida Star, July 21, 1887, November 11, 1888.
19. PO SL; Gazetteer, 1886-1887; Titusville Florida Star, December 8, 1886.
20. Titusville Florida Star, February 9, July 7, December 29, 1887, September 13, 1888, October 23, 1890; April 29, 1891, December 9, 1897; Gazetteer, 1886-1887.
21. Herman Herold, Log Book of Travels in the Sunny South, 1884, MSS Box 47, P. K. Yonge Library; Gazetteer, 1886-1887.
22. Titusville Florida Star, February 9, September 4, 1890, April 21, 1893, April 6, 1894.
23. Ibid., January 1, September 24, 1897, November 25, 1898, May 26, 1899, May 25, 1900.
24. Gazetteer, 1884-1885; Eric Caron, 100 Years of Rockledge (Rockledge, 1986), pp. 13-14; U. S. Post Office, Appointment of S. Ryder as Postmaster of Rockledge, MSS, Box 50, P. K. Yonge Library.
25. Caron, Rockledge, pp. 13-14; John M. Hawks, The East Coast of Florida (Lynn, Massachusetts,1887); Titusville Star Advocate, June 20, 1924.

End Notes

26. Caron, Rockledge, p. 15; Titusville Florida Star, January 25, 1895.
27. Titusville Florida Star, November 14, 1902; Henrietta W. Taylor v. FEC Railway Co., in Brevard County Miscellaneous Court Records; Caron, Rockledge, pp. 28, 32.
28. Titusville Florida Star, February 6, 1890; PO SL.
29. Melbourne Times, August 3, 1977, p. Lb; Broadside of R. E. Mims (Successor to Mims Brothers), in Dr. Robert Dean Collection, New Smyrna Beach, Florida.
30. PO SL; Titusville Florida Star, July 13, 1894; Titusville Indian River Advocate, March 13, 1896; Melbourne Times, August 8, 1977, p. Lb.
31. PO SL.
32. W. H. Hunt to William H. Gleason, May 11, 1885, Gleason Papers, Box 1, P. K. Yonge Library; Titusville Florida Star, January 12, 1887, January 15, 1891; Tallahassee Floridian, November 19, 1885; Gazetteer, 1886-1887.
33. Titusville Florida Star, April 12, 1893.
34. Ibid., September 18, 1889, April 28, 1893, December 21, 1894, January 25, 1895.
35. Ibid., January 1, May 21, 1897.
36. Ibid., July 20, 1894, February 1, 1895, January 20, 1899.
37. PO SL; Titusville Florida Star, February 15, 1895; Titusville Indian River Advocate, December 11, 1896.
38. PO SL; Fred A. Hopwood, Melbourne, Florida Postal History, 1880-1980 (Melbourne, 1980), p. 3.
39. Gazetteer, 1886-1887; Titusville Florida Star, June 28, 1888, July 20, 1894; Amey R. Hoeg, Thy Lighted Lamp (Melbourne, 1958), p. 11.
40. Titusville Florida Star, February 2, 1887, October 15, 1890, April 23, 1891, April 14, 1893, December 21, 1894.
41. Ibid., October 6, 1887, October 5, 1894, February 26, 1898, January 20, 1899.
42. Ibid., January 20, 1893.
43. Ibid., January 14, 1892; Hoag, Lighted Lamp, p. 12; No Author, Melbourne Beach: The First 100 Years (1983); Frank P. Thomas, Early Days in Melbourne Beach, 1888-1928 (Cocoa Beach, 1968), p. 5.
44. Titusville East Coast Advocate, December 7, 1894.
45. Titusville Florida Star, January 1, 1897.
46. PO SL; Weona Cleveland, "History of a Black Community," Melbourne Times, February 2-23, 1982. This four part series by Ms. Cleveland is the story of the black community at Clifton as well as that of two generations of Butler Campbell's exceptional family. The difficulties of a highly literate black family living in a racially segregated world make poignant reading today.
47. PO SL; Gazetteer, 1886-1887; Tallahassee Floridian, March 29, 1888; Titusville Florida Star, March 3, 1887.
48. PO SL; Gazetteer, 1884-1884; Titusville Florida Star, July 13, 1894; Phoebe Black, Letter.
49. PO SL; Titusville Florida Star, January 5, 15, 1894, August 6, 1897.
50. PO SL; Gazetteer, 1886-1887; Titusville Florida Star, January 1, 1885, January 1, 1897; Tallahassee Floridian, January 29, 1889.
51. Titusville Star Advocate, 75th Anniversary Edition, 1955.
52. PO SL; Titusville Florida Star, April 17, August 18, 1887; Charles Vickerstaff Hine, On the Indian River (Chicago, 1891), p. 134.
53. Gazetteer, 1884-1885, 1886-1887; Titusville Florida Star, July 20, 1894, May 24, 1895; Phoebe Black Letter, 1927; Hine, On the Indian River, p. 133.
54. PO SL; Titusville Florida Star, February 1, 1885, February 9, July 6, 1894, January 2, 1895.
55. PO SL; Titusville Florida Star, August 9, 1888.
56. Gazetteer, 1886-1887; PO SL; Titusville Florida Star, October 28, 1892, July 20, 1894; Titusville Indian River Advocate, February 9, 1900; Hine, On the Indian River, p. 226.
57. PO SL; Gazetteer, 1886-1887; Titusville Florida Star, December 28, 1894; Hine, On the Indian River, pp. 163-182.
58. PO SL; Titusville Indian River Advocate, May 18, 1900; Hine, On the Indian River, p. 163.
59. Tallahassee Floridian, June 17, 1884; J. W. P. Jenks to William Morton, January 28, 1893, MSS Box 30, P. Y. Yonge Library; PO SL; Gazetteer, 1886-1887; Titusville Florida Star, September 28, 1893, January 5, 1894.
60. PO SL; Tallahassee Floridian, June 17, 1884; Titusville Florida Star, January 11, 1885, August 14, September 18, 1889; Gazetteer, 1886-1887; Titusville Indian River Advocate, April 28, 1897.
61. PO SL; Gazetteer, 1886-1887; Titusville Florida Star, January 30, 1890, January 1, 1891, December 2, 1892, January 19, 1894.
62. PO SL; Gazetteer, 1884-1885; Titusville Florida Star, July 31, 1889, September 28, 1894; Titusville East Coast Advocate, October 17, 1890.
63. PO SL; Kyle VanLandingham, Pictorial History of St. Lucie County, 1865-1910, p. 17, 23; Titusville Florida Star, January 30, 1890, April 6, 1894, January 11, 1895, April 9, 19, May 21, 1897.
64. PO SL; Titusville Florida Star, December 1, 1886, February 21, 1889, April 24, 1890, November 8, l898, January 20, l899.
65. Titusville Indian River Advocate, December 9, 1898, January 20, 1899, April 13, 1900; Kyle VanLandingham, Saint Lucie County, p. 28.
66. PO SL; Gazetteer, 1884-1885, 1886-1887; Titusville East Coast Advocate, February 3, 1893; Titusville Florida Star, July 23, 1893; VanLandingham, Saint Lucie County, pp. 16, 28.
67. PO SL; Titusville East Coast Advocate, March 3, 1893, January 12, 1894; VanLandingham, St. Lucie County, p. 28.
68. PO SL; Titusville Indian River Advocate, February 16, 1898; Titusville Florida Star, July 23, 1897, December 9, 1898.
69. Titusville Florida Star, May 4, 1894, June 18, 1897; PO SL.
70. PO SL; Titusville Florida Star, January 26, July 23, 1894; Titusville Indian River Advocate, February 8, 1895, April 5, 1895.
71. PO SL; Titusville Florida Star, July 6, 1894, January 8, 1897.

Page 118 Map: Rand McNally & Co. 1880. (Brevard County Historical Commission Archives)

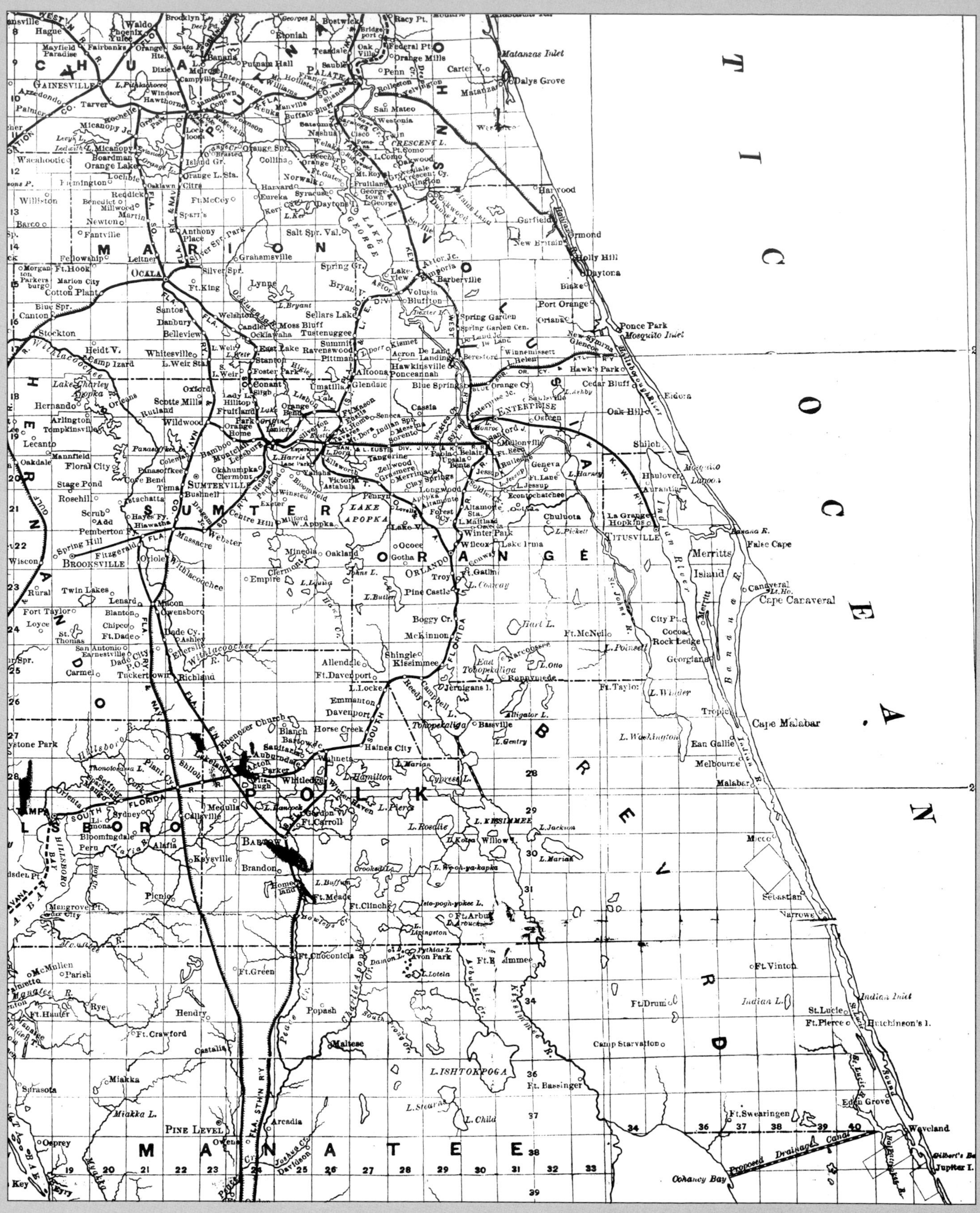

ATLANTIC OCEAN
ALACHUA
PUTNAM
ST. JOHNS
VOLUSIA
MARION
SUMTER
ORANGE
BREVARD
HERNANDO
HILLSBORO
POLK
MANATEE
GAINESVILLE
PALATKA
OCALA
SUMTERVILLE
BROOKSVILLE
ORLANDO
ENTERPRISE
TITUSVILLE
TAMPA
BARTOW
PINE LEVEL
Waldo
Hague
Brooklyn L.
Bostwick
Racy Pt.
Micanopy
Citra
Orange Lake
Fellowship
Leitner
Silver Spr.
Ft. King
Belleview
Ocklawaha
Weirsdale
Crescent L.
Lake George
Ormond
Daytona
Holly Hill
Port Orange
Ponce Park
Mosquito Inlet
New Smyrna
Matanzas Inlet
Dalys Grove
De Land
Blue Springs
Orange City
Sanford
Mellonville
Geneva
Chuluota
Oviedo
Winter Park
Maitland
Apopka
Lake Apopka
Oakland
Ocoee
Gotha
Pine Castle
Kissimmee
Lake Tohopekaliga
East Tohopekaliga
Conway
Ft. Gatlin
Mosquito Lagoon
Indian River
Banana R.
Merritts Island
False Cape
Cape Canaveral
Cocoa
Rockledge
Cape Malabar
Eau Gallie
Melbourne
Malabar
Sebastian
Ft. Pierce
Indian Inlet
St. Lucie
Jupiter I.
Waveland
Eden Grove
Hutchinson's I.
Okeechobee Bay
Proposed Drainage Canal
Ft. Bassinger
Camp Starvation
Ft. Drum
L. Istokpoga
Lake Kissimmee
Avon Park
Ft. Meade
Homeland
Brandon
Lakeland
Auburndale
Haines City
Winter Haven
Plant City
Dade City
Leesburg
Tavares
Eustis
Mt. Dora
Lake Harris
Wildwood
Withlacoochee R.
Spring Hill
Fort Taylor
Arcadia
Ft. Ogden
Sarasota
Miakka
Osprey
Manatee R.
Ft. Hamer
Hendry
Ft. Green
Popash
Peace Cr.
Charlie Apopka Cr.
Pease Cr.

10
Indian River Society and Social Affairs

As Brevard citizens worked to earn their livelihoods they also built a new society with churches, schools, fraternal orders and other social organizations. Along the way they found time to entertain themselves with boat races, dances and picnics.

Dr. W. L. Hughlett, wife Nannie Wilkinson Hughlett and daughters, Allie and Elizabeth, on the porch of their home in Cocoa, c. 1896. (Florida State Archives)

The people who came to Brevard County in the late 19th and early 20th centuries brought with them the ideas, values, customs, and aspirations which they had acquired in the communities of their origins. Those who came first endured hardships and privations which were ameliorated for those who followed. But, wherever a few families settled, they soon formed communities and began building the churches, schools, fraternal organizations, and governing institutions with which they were familiar and which would serve their social needs in their new homes.

Building a new society on the frontier had been the American way since the early 17th century and these new arrivals

The Taylor, Peck, and Seelbach families gather in Cocoa, c.1895. (Photo Brevard County Historical Commission Archives)

on the Indian River were as adept and adaptable as their ancestors. Some came to stay and did; others had the same intentions but changed their minds. Still others came to visit and decided to stay. A large number kept their old homes in more northerly areas and made winter homes in Brevard County. All of them contributed to the development of the Indian River community which evolved in the half century or so following the Civil War. There were good times and others which were not so good, but these residents and their numerous visitors formed a society which found satisfaction and enjoyment in the hard work of earning their livelihoods and building their social institutions. Along the way, they found time to entertain themselves. Because religious beliefs were so important to the majority of the early settlers, churches were probably the primary institutions which bound people together. While most of the denominations sent travelling ministers to the frontier both as circuit riders and as assistants in starting churches, the people themselves were the prime movers. People of differing denominations frequently worshipped together in private homes, heard lay readers, held services with vacationing ministers who happened to be in the area, and improvised in various ways, but their intentions were always to build their own houses of worship and secure regular ministers at the

The community gathers for an outdoor triple wedding c.1880. (Photo courtesy Jim Ball)

Bishop Weed presided at the first service at St. Gabriel's Episcopal Church in Titusville in 1888. (Photo c. 1930 courtesy Jim Ball)

earliest possible times. Nearly all of the places mentioned in the last chapter had church congregations of one or more denominations, although not all of them were able to erect buildings and some were obliged to rely on circuit riders and lay readers.

The first church building in the county was built at LaGrange in 1869 and its services were attended by Titusville residents until they established their own

Both Baptist and African Methodist Episcopal congregations held baptisms in the Indian River at Oleander Point in Cocoa. (*Photo courtesy Jim Ball*)

churches. Its Sunday School was started in 1870 and was also the first in the county. By the early 1880s, annual picnics were being held to celebrate the anniversary of that Sunday School and to provide opportunity for entertainment. Its 30th (Pearl) anniversary in 1900, for example, was held in the oak park on B. F. Ives' property. There was a fish fry and speeches by the Rev. W. N. Chaudoin as well as B. F. Ives. People from several surrounding communities attended. The LaGrange Baptist Church was organized in 1874 by the Rev. S. F. Gove, who started many of the Baptist churches in peninsular Florida during the last quarter of the 19th century. The Rev. W. N. Chaudoin was its minister for many years.[1]

The Mims Methodist Church was not only a place of worship but an active social center as well. Its Epworth League was one of the earlier ones in the county and its Sunday School was quite active. The Tennyson entertainment given by the pupils of Miss Susie F. Brown in 1896, for example, was attended by visitors from surrounding communities as well as Mims residents.[2]

Services were being held by several denominations at Titusville by the early 1880s and churches were being organized and buildings erected. The evolution of St. Gabriel's Episcopal – first known as St. John's – is perhaps exemplary, if not quite typical, of the growth of churches all along the river. Services were being held by various ministers at the Titus House or Wager's Hall by the mid-1880s. Mrs. Mary E. Titus donated a lot in 1886 which was large enough for an Episcopal church as well as a school and a cemetery. Captain R. P. Paddison, master of the steamer Rockledge, conceived the idea of placing on his vessel a receptacle with a card saying "This is to build a church in Titusville." Visitors were apparently favorably impressed and he was able to turn over to the building fund a substantial contribution after every trip downriver. A contract was made in late 1887 with L. R. Decker who agreed to build the church for $1,687. While construction was underway, St. John's Episcopal Church was incorporated after a Sunday service at Wager's Hall in late December that year. Bishop Weed presided at the first services in the new building in September 1888. By 1890, the Titusville Episcopal Church was being called St. Gabriel's and the Rev. B. F. Brown had begun his tenure as rector. People frequently came from other river towns to attend special services as was the case when the steamer Kathleen arrived from Eau Gallie with a capacity crowd pulling a sharpie carrying the overload to a church bazaar on Christmas Eve in 1891.[3]

The Presbyterian Church started much the same way with the Rev. John Foy, recently from Missouri, leading the way. Services were held in public halls in Titusville and bazaars and other fund-raising efforts helped start a building fund. By September 1887 the Presbyterian Church was declared in operation, "complete with a bell tower and bell." Some of the finishing touches were still being added in 1888, but the worshippers apparently did not mind. The Rev. Foy held Union Sunday Schools at the courthouse before his church was completed. There were 46 members from various denominations at the first service in January 1887. Titusville Methodists first met in the courthouse, but they "got busy to erect their own building" after the county commissioners "turned them out" in 1889. The Methodist Episcopal Church, South rotated its ministers, but the Rev. C. S. Byrd was at Titusville in 1891 and the Rev. George J. Kenelly was pastor in 1893. About twenty people organized a Baptist congregation at Titusville in 1889, with the peripatetic Rev. S. F. Gove in charge. The county commissioners seem to have relented by 1890 since the Baptists were allowed to hold services in the courthouse that year. Construction of a building was soon underway. The Rev. A. D. Cohen was the first minister of the church, holding that position until 1894. The Indian River Baptist Association, of which the Rev. Cohen was secretary, held its convention in Titusville in 1892 and the railroads offered special rates for those attending. A Catholic Church was active in Titusville by 1893 with the Rev. J. F. O'Boyle as rector.[4]

Variously called Brooklyn or Colored Town, the black section of Titusville was separate from the white residential areas although some of the town's earliest business men were black and there was frequent mixing of blacks and whites at church socials, weddings, and other gatherings. Separate black churches had been common throughout the South since emancipation and that was the case in Brevard County. Large numbers of blacks had worked on the railroad as it reached Titusville and a number of them remained. This infusion of black residents made possible the formation of both Baptist and African Methodist Episcopal congregations in Titusville in the late 1880s. A Colored Baptist Mission was organized in 1889 when the Rev. W. N. Chaudoin of LaGrange ordained ministers and deacons. Bethlehem Baptist Church was holding baptisms on the Delespine Grant by August of that year. The Rev. Butler C. Reed, a prosperous property owner of Titusville, was one of several ministers of the church during the 1890s. The Rev. N. W. Robinson officiated at the wedding of James Hawkins and Matilda Brooks at that church in 1899 and several white residents attended both the service and the reception which followed.[5]

The Rockledge Presbyterian Church was organized in 1877 and was chartered in 1884. The building was started in 1885 on land donated by George B. Magruder. (Photo courtesy Doug Hendriksen)

Elizabeth Phelps hosts a picnic for all of the children of Cocoa on the grounds of St. Marks Church, 1904. Elizabeth was the daughter of a slave and part Indian, born 1850 on Johns Island, South Carolina. Pictured: Leland Daniel, Dorothy Daniel, Harrison Daniel, Dick Hardee, Lee Geiger, Anita Travis, Bob Travis, Ryan Cooper, Gladys Johnson, Hazel Johnson, Willard Gould, Amos Wooten, Albert Travis, Johnny Paterson, Merwin Wooten, Bob Hardee, Clarence Jones, Blanche Baumgarten, Elizabeth Childs, Gracie Tucker, Ethel Gore, Amy Geiger, Bertie Gibert, Vera Hardee, Allie Hughlett, Lucille Singleton, Dixie Singleton, Nellie Cooper, Rachel Tucker, Carl Geiger, Raymond Johnson, Maude Hardee, Cecil Hardee, Leland Hardee, Billy Heaton, Albert Travis, Albert Booth. (Florida State Archives)

1888. The Rev. A. T. Sharpe was holding services there in 1890. South of that place at Georgiana, the Methodists began raising funds for a church in 1884. F. C. Allen donated a lot and the Rev. M. Black led the move to erect a building the following year. Other ministers who served there included the Rev. J. C. Sullivan and the Rev. J. B. Hawk. The Methodists of Cocoa and Rockledge were holding services by the mid-1880s and built a church in 1889. The Rev. James Bolton was the minister at the time and was followed by the Rev. C. F. Blackburn, the Rev. J. C. Sullivan, and others. Dr. W. L. Hughlett was president of the Indian River Sunday School Association which held its convention at Cocoa in 1891. An unusual event occurred at the City Point Methodist Church in 1894 when the Methodist Episcopal Church, South, and the Methodist Episcopal Church, North – which had been separate since 1844 – held their quarterly conferences at the same time. The Revs. C. F. Blackburn, A. E. Householder

The African Methodist Episcopal Church was formed a little later than the Baptist institution. Isaiah Gorey and Willie Gibson were among the early trustees who struggled unsuccessfully with its finances during the mid-1890s, but its resourceful members were busily raising funds again by the latter years of the decade. Its Busy Bee Club held a cake walk and entertainment in 1898 which was well attended by both black and white supporters. Assisted by E. B. Bartlett, J. H. Davis, W. H. Walstine, and Willie Gibson, Pastor W. G. Fields held another successful fund-raiser in 1899. Titusville was the site of several AME conventions in the 1890s and early 1900s. The railroads offered special rates for the occasions and the local newspaper estimated that as many as 2,000 people attended them.[6]

Just across the river at Courtenay, St. Luke's Episcopal Church was organized and a building was completed in

Eau Gallie Methodist Church and High School. (Photo courtesy Doug Hendriksen)

and J. C. Sullivan were present.[7]

Cornelia Magruder was instrumental in starting the Rockledge Presbyterian Church in 1877. The church was chartered in 1884 and a building was started in 1885 on land donated by her son, George B. Magruder. The Women's Missionary Society of the Methodist Episcopal Church, South, held its first meeting in that church in 1888 about a year before the Methodists completed their own building.

Mrs. Delannoy donated a lot for an Episcopal Church at Cocoa in 1886. The ladies of Cocoa and Rockledge started raising funds shortly thereafter with a bazaar. They were assisted by several ladies from Melbourne. St. Mark's was completed in 1888 and services were being conducted with lay readers later that year. It was apparently difficult to retain the services of a regular rector in the early years, but in 1898 E. E. Johnson was ordained and given full charge of the Episcopal churches at Cocoa and Merritt.

By the early 1890s there were black Baptist and African Methodist Episcopal churches in Cocoa. Blacks of Cocoa celebrated Christmas of 1898 with Christmas Tree celebrations at the Baptist Church on Sunday night and the AME Church on Monday night.[8]

John Mellor was the primary promoter of the Baptist Church at Eau Gallie. Its building was constructed with support from Eau Gallie residents with substantial contributions from Chicago residents. The land was donated by the Gleason family. The edifice was used by both Methodists and Episcopalians, but St. John's Episcopal was ultimately erected in 1897. The first church services in Melbourne were held in the Goode House in 1884. Hector's store was also used at times. An Episcopal Church was completed in 1886 with assistance from Lucy Boardman of Connecticut who wintered at Georgiana. Mrs. Boardman also contributed funds for the Episcopal buildings at Cocoa and Titusville. Like most of the churches of that denomination, Melbourne's Episcopal Church was served by missionary ministers most of the time in the late 19th century. Winter rectors were often

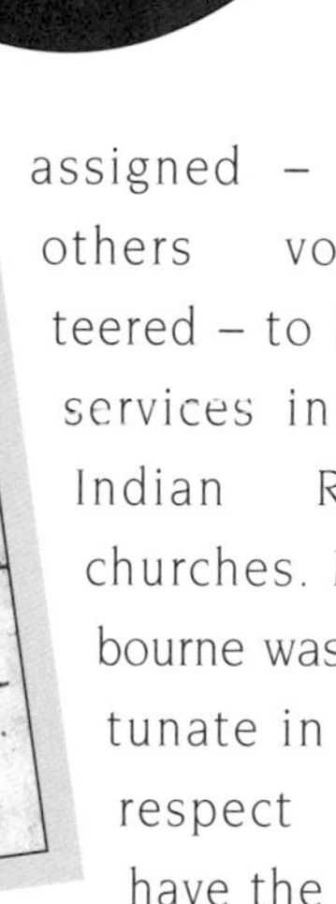

Maria Stewart was one of Brevard's early school teachers. In 1876 she taught at Ten Mile Creek, just west of Fort Pierce. (Photo and document courtesy Jim Ball)

assigned – and others volunteered – to hold services in the Indian River churches. Melbourne was fortunate in this respect to have the Rev. William P. DuBose as a regular winter visitor. From the late 1880s to 1917, Rev. DuBose, who was Dean of the Theological Seminary at the University of the South, preached many times at Holy Trinity. The Methodist Church building was opened for services in 1887. A Congregational Church was built at Melbourne in 1893. Both Merritt and Cocoa had churches of that denomination about the same time. A community chapel was built at Melbourne Beach in 1892. There were AME churches at both Eau Gallie and Melbourne.[9]

The Rev. S. F. Gove officiated at a new Baptist Church at Sebastian in 1895. The Rev. W. T. Laine was pastor there in the late 1890s. Like most of the men of the cloth in the county in the early years, the Rev. Laine frequently visited

St. Marks Episcopal Church, Cocoa, Fla.

St. Mark's Episcopal Chuech in Cocoa was completed in 1888. (Photo courtesy Doug Hendriksen)

other communities. In 1898, for example, he held services at Brantley while the Rev. J. B. Hawk, then assigned to the church at Melbourne, preached at Georgiana. Religious services were being held at Micco in the 1890s in the homes of several of the residents. The Rev. R. N. Andrews officiated in 1892 at the funeral services for Peter Wright, Jr., at the Melbourne AME Church. Wright, a prominent leader of the church and its Sunday School teacher, had accidentally shot and killed himself in his new store. The blacks of Banyan built a structure in the late 1890s in which both church services and school were conducted. The building was the site for frequent social gatherings, such as the Sunday School entertainment and ice cream festival held in July 1899.[10]

Stuart – originally called Potsdam – had both Methodist and Congregational churches by 1897. Baptist missionaries were travelling by steamer to preach at Fort Pierce in the 1880s and the Rev. S. F. Gove helped organize a Baptist congregation there in 1890. Methodists began holding services in the school building in 1889. The Episcopalians started raising funds for a church in 1895.[11]

The temperance movement was gaining momentum in the 1880s. Titusville was a wide open town where several saloons did a thriving business and both Indians and whites came considerable distances to buy liquor. Trade boats regularly peddled liquor along the Indian River and several other towns had establishments which dealt in alcoholic beverages. It was only natural, perhaps, that a Women's Christian Temperance Union chapter was organized by the women of the Titusville Presbyterian Church in the late 1880s. The often-presented "Ten Nights in a Bar Room" played to an audience in 1887 whose members paid 35 cents for general admission and 50 cents for reserved seats. Lively music was heard and a luncheon enjoyed by those who attended the 1889 temperance meeting at Oleander Point where the question "Should Brevard County be wet or dry?" was debated. The Revs. R. N. Andrews and S. F. Gove officiated at the meeting. Both Drs. W. L. Hughlett and George W. Holmes wrote and spoke against the sale and use of alcohol. The temperance movement did not succeed in the 1880s. According to the Titusville Florida Star, the local temperance society was obliged to disband "on account of the non-interest which was manifested." After several turbulent years, however, the movement was renewed. The Brevard County Anti-Saloon League was organized in 1906 with the avowed goal of "making Brevard a 'dry' county." It secured the services of the Rev. W. A. Myers, "a leading temperance lecturer," to speak "at Eau Gallie, Melbourne, Cocoa, Titusville, Indianola, Cocoa again, [and] Titusville four more times." It would appear from this itinerary that the county seat was of special concern to the temperance advocates.[12]

The early settlers in Brevard County were just as

Early Titusville classes met in temporary quarters for several years until the first school was built in 1887. (Photo courtesy Jim Ball)

Students pose on the porch of the new Titusville School in 1888. (Photo courtesy Robert Hudson, North Brevard Historical Society)

In 1888 Melbourne students attended classes in this one room schoolhouse. Charley Don Martin, Will Ely, Claude M. Beaujean, Fred Fee, Kitty Martin, Don R. Beaujean, Roy Shere, Edith Izant, Tottie Ely, Suzie Johnson, May Metcalf, Ed Izant, Essie McQuaid, Sam Martin, Mable Izant, Helen Miller, John Admas, Fred Izant, Teacher Mollie Hitchens. (Photo Goode Collection, Brevard County Historical Commission Archives)

anxious to provide schools for their children as they were to build churches. Only a handful of settlers were in the county when the state enacted its first school law in 1869. That statute made Brevard County a school district to be governed by an appointed board of three members. Schools were to be administered by a superintendent who also acted as ex-officio secretary of the board. The county board had the power to levy taxes and to issue "certificates of competency" to teachers, and to appoint three-member boards of trustees for individual schools. Schools could be opened where there were at least seven children who would attend. Since the population was small and scattered about the county, schools opened and closed with some regularity, although they attained some permanence in the larger communities.

Taxes were permissive but by the early 1890s, Brevard County was levying five mills on property for the support of schools. In many cases, tuition was levied at the rate of about a dollar a month per pupil to pay the teachers' salaries. Taxes gradually replaced tuition in this regard, but children were required to pay for their own books until well into the 20th century. The state began publishing lists of acceptable books in the 1880s and it was only natural that the lobbying of publishers to get their books included became a matter of controversy. Schools were often held in church buildings, but church was also conducted in school buildings at times. Homes or empty buildings, such as the one belonging to Mrs. Roberts at Mims, also housed schools. In any event, schools were quite informal in the early days, terms were short – usually three or fourth months – and attendance was sometimes sporadic. But, many children, as well as their parents, thought that learning was important. Some rode horses to school, while others came by boats. School was often an experience better remembered after the fact than endured at the time. However that may have been, schools were important parts of the communities and served as social and entertainment centers just as did the churches.[13]

By 1880 there were seven schools in Brevard County with 130 pupils. Teachers' salaries were averaging $260 per year for terms of about four months. There was considerable activity and improvement during the next decade or so. Adhemar Brady of LaGrange, who later relocated to City Point, was one of the first superintendents of Brevard County schools. A somewhat visionary intellectual who frequently wrote or spoke about his sometimes controversial views, he became embroiled with the school board and submitted his resignation in 1884. The next superintendent to gain prominence was John H. Sams who remained in that office for a number of years.[14]

In the early 1880s, the state superintendent of public instruction began urging teacher training institutes during the summers. One of the first was held at LaGrange in 1882 with 22 teachers attending. The institutes continued although the numbers at each varied greatly. The 1892 institute was attended by teachers from Titusville, City Point, Fort Pierce, Shiloh, Malabar, Cocoa, Turnbull, Melbourne, Georgiana, Mims, Eau Gallie, LaGrange, St. Lucie and Merritt. Both men and women taught, but most went on to other careers after a time. It may be hoped that the Eau Gallie teacher who became dissatisfied in 1882 and shipped out as first mate on a schooner was an exception, however.[15]

Then as now, school activities were newsworthy. Notice was given when Miss L. D. Joyner opened a new school for blacks in Titusville. A Miss Holden started a private school in the T. W. Smith building in the same town in 1886. Tuition was $1.50 per month for beginners and $2.00 for advanced students. John Goode built a one-room school in Melbourne where racially integrated classes were first conducted in 1883. Separate schools were implemented shortly afterward and by 1889 R. R. Carlson was the teacher of the Melbourne "colored school." The Turnbull community reported the completion of a successful school year in the spring of 1888. Mims residents proudly announced the dedication of a new school building that same year. From Malabar came word that lumber was on the ground for a school in 1890. Waveland's first school opened in 1889. Another was opened in the mid-1880s at Taylor's Creek near Fort Pierce. A palmetto-thatched affair, it was replaced by a frame building at Edgartown in 1888.[16]

Titusville schools were conducted in temporary quarters for several years until the Titusville School Building Association obtained a loan – one of the first made by the new Indian River Bank – for a building in 1887. Completed that year to the satisfaction of local residents, it was transferred by the private association in 1889 to the board of public instruction as that agency assumed a greater role in the administration of local schools. When Henry Flagler built his railroad through Titusville, the school was so close to the tracks that the entrepreneur agreed to bear the expense of moving it back in 1893. All seemed to be going well until it burned in May 1900. The school was kept in operation in temporary quarters until the school board, in cooperation with the residents of Titusville, agreed on a site for a new school.[17] Superintendent Sams reported in 1892 that Brevard County had 42 schools, 31 of which were then open. Four of them were for black children. The inactive ones could be opened on demand from the patrons. The 1892 budget for schools was $12,300, which included the salaries of teachers and school officials, construction of school buildings, and furniture. The state had increased its standards for teacher certification by that time and

Dr. B. R. and Julian Wilson operated a drugstore as well as having a medical practice in Titusville. (Photo courtesy Robert Hudson, North Brevard Hiistorical Society)

examinations were required before certificates of competency could be issued to prospective teachers. Another private institution was opened in Titusville in 1893. Apparently sponsored by the Presbyterian Church, the Indian River High School was a boarding school for boys and girls. The Rev. W. H. McMeen was in charge. Room and board could be arranged with good families at reasonable rates by McMeen or the Rev. John Foy, pastor of the Presbyterian Church.[18]

By the time R. E. Mims became superintendent of public instruction in 1901, Brevard County was following the trend in Florida toward consolidation of schools. The state empowered school districts to bond for school construction in the early 1900s, but in the meantime, smaller schools were being consolidated for greater efficiency and improved instruction. While children had long been obliged to go to school in boats or on horseback on their own, consolidation involved the school board in the matter of transportation. School wagons and school boats were more and more tax-supported as the new century replaced the old. It was estimated that about 75 pupils would attend the consolidated school which replaced local ones at Cocoa, Rockledge and Dixon's Point in 1900. In that same year the Fort Pierce consolidated school was expected to serve about the same number of children.[19]

Both medical training and medical care were quite rudimentary in early Brevard, but there were both doctors and dentists who not only had offices in the larger towns, but also travelled up and down the river to care for patients. Two of the early medical practitioners were Drs. D. Cowie and B. R. Wilson, both of whom were in Titusville in 1880. Cowie apparently moved on, but Wilson, whose offices were in J. M. Dixon's drug store, remained for many years. In 1900 he and his son, Julian, purchased the drug store then belonging to Fred Chaffee and operated it as B. R. Wilson and Son. Dr. George W. Holmes was also practicing as early as 1879. He lived at City Point in the early days, but he saw patients at Georgiana and other points on the island and at least as far south as Eau Gallie. He also travelled as far as Mims in the other direction. Dr. Holmes is remembered for having delivered many of the babies born in Brevard County during the last part of the 19th century and he was still busy well into the 20th. Dr. W. L. Hughlett came a little later and set up a practice in Cocoa where he remained for many years. Dr. E. M. Price was at Titusville before 1880, but he moved to St. Augustine that year. At the urging of the Walton Brothers of Eau Gallie he returned in 1886, but apparently set up his offices in Titusville. Dr. B. L. Willis opened offices above J. W. Rogers and Co., in 1891.[20]

Melbourne's first physician was Dr. William Fee who died in 1895 by which time medical services were also being delivered by Dr. H. D. Brown who also ran a drug store. Since the doctors mixed most of their own medicines in those days, it was not uncommon for them to be druggists as well as medical doctors. In the early 1900s, Dr. W. J. Creel came to Melbourne as a railroad doctor and then remained to build a practice as well as to become one of the town's political leaders. Dr. Creel also had offices in Eau Gallie. Dr. Sarah Hodgson was already practicing in Eau Gallie when Dr. Creel arrived.[21]

According to the Titusville Florida Star there were seven physicians licensed to practice in Brevard County in 1890. They were B. R. Wilson, J. B. Screven, and W. S. Graham of Titusville; G. W. Holmes and C. A. Hentz of City Point; and J. O. Scofield and W. L. Hughlett of Cocoa. Dr. Clyde P. Platts came to Fort Pierce from the midwest because of his health and opened a practice in 1895. He was the only physician there until the early 20th century. Dr. Charlotte Norton had a practice on Merritt Island in the 1890s but she also saw patients at Cocoa on Tuesdays and Fridays in the Wade cottage. Dr. Norton left Brevard in 1900 and moved to New York City.[22]

Medical men along the east coast who were affiliated with the Jacksonville, St. Augustine and Indian River

The Cocoa Library Committee c. 1895: *Mrs. Thompson, Mrs. J. Powell, Mrs. J. D. Trafford, Mrs. Booth, Mrs. Sophia Dixon, Mrs. Paterson, Mrs. Harrison and Mrs. Wilson. (Photo Brevard County Historical Commission Archives)*

Railroad – later the Florida East Coast – organized the East Coast Line Surgical Association in 1893. Brevard County members were B. R. Wilson, George W. Holmes, W. L. Hughlett and H. D. Brown. C. P. Platts joined a little later. They met periodically and presented scholarly papers. Like Dr. Brown's paper on "railway shock," the presentations often created great interest and discussion. The membership sometimes attempted to influence policy and just as often discovered that such action could be controversial. When the organization recommended in 1894 that the FEC discharge all employees with venereal disease, the company was not pleased. The recommendation was rescinded at the next quarterly meeting in December of that year.[23]

Dental services were available from Dr. A. B. Hawley at Titusville in 1884. He was joined two years later by B. B. Smith. Dr. L. T. Daniel arrived at Cocoa a bit later and offered dental services in his office above the drug store which he operated in partnership with Dr. W. L. Hughlett. Dr. D. L. Dodson was a Titusville dentist in 1891. Several dentists travelled from town to town along the coast, announcing their services for a specific period before moving on to the next location. Dr. F. H. Houghton offered a slightly different travelling service. In his *Dentos* he visited the Indian River towns performing his specialty on board in his "floating Dental Apartments."[24]

Patients often went to considerable lengths to receive medical care. In 1897, Sherman Singleton was carried from Horti on the Banana River on a cot to Eau Gallie. There, he was put on board a Florida East Coast car and taken to Titusville. His wife and father-in-law lodged him in the Indian River Hotel where he was attended by Dr. B. R. Wilson. It was at least as common for the doctor to travel to the patient, but house calls could also be challenging. A call came from Mills Burnham in 1884 that he needed medical attention at the lighthouse. Neither Dr. Holmes nor Dr. Hughlett were available, so Charles A. Hentz responded, expressing pleasure "at the prospect of seeing the Light House." He went to Georgiana in F. C. Allen's sailboat, took time to visit Fairy Land, crossed the lake on Dr. Wittfeld's place in a rowboat, and eventually met Orlando Quarterman, a relative of Burnham's, who was waiting for him on the Banana River. Embarking on a sail boat, they "bumped along with a good breeze," making the 25 mile voyage by about one in the morning. Quarterman ran up a flag to let people at the lighthouse know they had arrived and the party retired. After a "hearty breakfast" Hentz left the house at Burnham's Grove aboard a mule-drawn cart driven by one of the old man's grandsons. The doctor eventually reached the lighthouse, and presumably treated the patient. He recorded in his diary a detailed account of the terrain along the five miles between Burnham's Grove and the lighthouse, the old man's fondness for whiskey, Hentz's purchase of a turkey gobbler and four pineapples, and the return voyage, but he made no reference to the illness for which Burnham was treated. The patient apparently survived since he lived nearly two more years. Hentz spent three days on the round trip and returned in time for the turkey to serve as the main course for Christmas dinner.[25]

Hentz was more careful in his account of his and Dr. Holmes' efforts to collect their bills from H. S. Wilkinson, a hotel owner and storekeeper at Rockledge. Both had tended the old man over a period of about three years during a serious illness. Holmes had once remained at bedside for many weeks. Hentz charged $140 for his services and Holmes about $360. Both, according to Hentz, dreaded the encounter "having heard so much of the over bearing and unreasonable ways of the old gentleman." Apparently Wilkinson lived up to his reputation and so offended Hentz that he left Holmes to complete the negotiations. They eventually settled for about two-thirds of their original bills and were apparently glad for that. On another occasion, Hentz attended John Sanders when he encountered a sting-ray. The doctor administered morphine but the patient "suffered dreadfully all night." He was confined to bed for months and then walked on crutches for a long time. "Although he was an ungodly, wicked man," Hentz wrote, "he bore his suffering...with remarkable patience and uncomplaining cheerfulness."

Hentz did have a few routine calls, as in the case of Mrs. Gardner Hardee, who was in confinement. He was called at three in the morning and reached her bedside "just in time to render professional service."[26]

The greatest threat to public health was the yellow fever epidemic which spread across the Florida peninsula in 1887-1888 and laid virtual waste to Jacksonville's population. According to the Tallahassee Floridian "Quarantine is now the order of the day" in the summer of 1887. "Well known men living in sight of Titusville cannot go to that town for a sack of flour...without the regulation certificate," which cost $2.50. The paper concluded that "the yellow fever scare is going to cost the people quite a sum of money." That was probably the case, but at least the Indian River country was spared the loss of lives which other areas suffered. The board of health, in cooperation with the county commission, set up strict quarantines on all routes leading into the county. Railroad passengers were stopped at Mims. There was a check point at the Haulover and others "down the river." Robert Ranson was made quarantine officer at a temporary station on Canaveral Bight because of the vessels leaving Jacksonville and St. Augustine for points south. There was also a quarantine point at Salt Lake where T. W. Lund and his entire family were stopped. Even after they had stayed the required fifteen days, they were still not permitted to take their baggage to Titusville. The Indian River remained free of "this dread pestilence" but the quarantine was still in effect in November 1888 and "a great many northern visitors" were being deterred from their annual visits." The ban was finally lifted when cold weather came.[27]

Fraternal orders and other social organizations came to Brevard County with its first settlers. The Indian River Lodge, F&AM, was meeting on Fridays at LaGrange in early 1886. It apparently moved to Titusville a little later. Cocoa had an active Masonic Lodge by 1889 when it was meeting every Friday night. It sponsored an entertainment and oyster supper at Stiling's store in January 1891 which was attended by 450 people representing nearly every town on the river. Melbourne Lodge No. 143 came a little later and held its meetings on Wednesday. Eastern Star chapters were active in most of the communities by the turn of the century. Several communities had Colored Masonic Lodges. The Knights of Pythias came to the Indian River in the 1890s. The Seminole Lodge, for example, gave a benefit concert by the Dewey Heywood Concert Company in 1895 to which admission was 75 cents. The Daughters of Jericho was an organization of black women at Cocoa. It invited both blacks and whites to attend its installation of officers at Richardson's Hall in that town in October 1894. Admission was ten cents. A chapter of the YMCA was formed in Titusville in 1893. Its officials were John R. Walker, president; George W. Scobie, first vice-president; L. E. Munn, second Vice-president; C. A. Gardner, secretary; and G. P. Anthony, treasurer. A camp of the United Confederate Veterans was organized at the Titusville courthouse in December 1892.[28]

Dr. Peek, Bob Mattox, Mr. Ellis and Jim Bird show off a 16' 8" sawfish with 10 babies. (*Photo by* C. F. *Conkling, Goode Collection, Brevard County Historical Commission Archives*)

A different kind of society was the Independent Order of Truthtellers organized at Titusville in 1894. Blackballed by that order, Arthur Doyle organized an opposing group known as the Ancient, Reckless and Independent Order of Prevaricators. The Truthtellers met in room 57 of the Indian River Hotel and Doyle's group met just across the hall at the same time.[29]

More serious, perhaps, were the literary societies which were formed in most of the communities in the county. One of the earliest was the Palmetto Literary Society of LaGrange which was meeting at least as early as 1880. By the 1890s some of the more active groups were at Cocoa, Melbourne, Malabar, and Sebastian. All of them were influenced by the Chautauqua movement which swept the nation in the late 19th century. Florida headquarters for the Chautauqua was at DeFuniak Springs, but Melbourne became the site of annual meetings which attracted visitors from all along the east coast for many years. Many of them stayed at the Chautauqua Home which was built in the late 1880s. Attendance was sometimes a challenge as in the case of

Known as the Canaveral Club and the Boston Club this hunting lodge was started by C. P. Horton of Boston. Presidents Benjamin Harrison and Grover Cleveland were guests at the club. (Photo courtesy Jim Ball)

the Malabar residents who went to Melbourne in March 1900. The lucky ones took the train, but the crowd which went by boat arrived cold and soaking wet. The meeting was hailed as a success despite the storm. Offices of the Chautauqua that year were Drs. W. L. Davidson, R. H. Palmer, and G. W. Holmes. W. T. Wells, E. W. Butler, E. P. Branch, R. W. Goode, C. H. Stewart, F. H. Fee, Charles Campbell, and W. B. Hainlin also took leading roles. Beginning in the 1890s an important component of the annual Chautauqua meetings was a regatta. In 1900, it was judged by J. E. M. Hodgson, J. Minor and C. J. F. Campbell. Most of the communities had libraries and two of the earliest and best-known were at Cocoa and the Narrows. The Melbourne Women's Club also maintained a library in the early years.[30]

Brass bands, cornet bands, string bands and all forms of musical entertainment were enjoyed by all the communities. The Titusville string band was frequently asked to perform at various places in the 1880s. The Cocoa Cornet Band was also popular beyond the limits of that town. The Jensen Band, directed by E. D. Young, was active around 1900. Music was offered at most of the social affairs and celebrations. The Christmas tree entertainment at the Banyan House in 1901 was typical. Both vocal and instrumental music, recitations by the school students, and exchanges of gifts were enjoyed by all. Debating societies and spelling bees were common and competition was as keen as in baseball, horse races, boat races, and similar physical activities.[31]

In 1881 *the self-proclaimed Duke of Castalucci built the Villa de Castalucci at Dummett's Cove with lumber salvaged from shipwrecks. It was known locally as Dummett's Castle.* (*Etching* © *Vera Zimmerman* 1987)

Outdoor activities abounded. Yacht clubs were numerous with Cocoa, Eau Gallie and Gilbert's Bar having some of the earliest and more active. When the Daytona entries in an Indian River race won all the events, the steamer *Clara* cleared the Titusville docks with a broom waving from the flag staff, a token of the "clean sweep." Noting that the Daytona vessel blew its whistle until it was out of sight, the Titusville newspaper commented that "they ought to crow," since it was the first chance they had in 16 years. Boat races were both organized and spontaneous. One of the many of the latter was between the schooner *Ruby Dye* and the sloop *Frost Line* which was run on the Titusville course in 1888. The *Ruby Dye* won. The fishing fleet at Grant decided to celebrate a successful season with a boat race. George W. Scobie alone entered six boats. Races and regattas were common all along the river, but Cocoa and Eau Gallie emerged as the sites of some of the best known annual events.[32]

Fish were so numerous in the Indian River that their movement left a visible phosphorescent glow at night. Fishing for sport, for food, and for sale was extensive. Visitors as well as residents boasted good catches from the docks as well as from boats. Fish were also abundant in the lakes along the St. Johns River and fresh water fishing was equally popular. It was for such reasons that Henry Grady brought his annual fishing parties from Atlanta. Grover Cleveland and Matthew Quay were only two of the prominent national figures who fished and hunted during the winters in Indian River country. Fishing for food was a major contribution to local diets. Fresh fish could be taken for meals almost all the time, but groups frequently went to the southern end of Merritt Island for mullet runs. In her fictionalized account of her childhood on the Indian

River, Sally Magruder tells of her family's mullet fishing parties as well as some of the boating hazards accompanying them. C. A. Hentz tells of annual expeditions with several boatloads of neighbors to net the mullet when they were moving. It was not uncommon for each member of the party to take 300 to 400 fish in a day. These were then cleaned and stored in salted barrels for home use and sometimes for shipment. Commercial fisherman also used barrels and preserved their fish in salt until ice became available.[33]

Nearly everyone hunted as well. It was quite common for a resident to tend his groves or gardens during part of the day and hunt the rest. Ducks abounded on all the waterways, although Sykes Creek was an especially good hunting site. Deer were plentiful. One man killed 80 deer in a single season while clearing land for a farm. People also hunted bear as they were easy prey during the turtle nesting seasons when they dug along the beaches for eggs. In the early 1890s bear were still so plentiful that Brevard County placed a five dollar bounty on them Alligators were sometimes shot for the sport, but their hides were valuable and they formed the basis of a brisk trade for many years.

It is little wonder that people from all over the country came to the Indian River to hunt and fish. Neither natives nor visitors were much interested in conservation, however. Numerous diaries of visitors record almost unlimited target shooting of pelicans and other birds as well as alligators. There were some early efforts to control such waste. A seine law enacted by the legislature in the mid-1890s was efficient enough to raise the ire of many commercial fishermen. There was also some concern for plume birds about the same time. Howell Titus reported that birds were being taken illegally on the St. Johns River for their plumes and that the sheriff was reacting "in a very loose manner." Game wardens were employed by the counties in the early days and they were usually paid on a fee basis. Manatees created great interest and several were taken for show at such places as the Chicago World's Fair, but the county was quite conservative in issuing permits for their capture and exploitation.[34]

Gun clubs were numerous. One of the earliest was the Titusville Sportsmen's Club, incorporated in 1887 by R. C. Scrimgeour, George W. MacKensie, George W. Scobie, James Lowden, and Howell Titus. Charles Campbell attended one of their meetings in 1892 with a view to organizing a similar one for Melbourne. A frequent winner of the competitions was Charles L. Stewart of Tropic. In 1899, J. G. Bast, proprietor of the Indian River Hotel at Titusville was lessee of the Royal Buck Hounds Hunt Club of Courtenay. It was managed by F. P. Harper.[35]

There were numerous such organizations, but perhaps the most famous was the Canaveral Club formed in 1890 at the initiative of C. P. Horton of Boston who had been hunting on the Indian River since 1870. Composed entirely of members of the Harvard University class of 1890, its members agreed to limit membership to themselves and their eldest sons who could fill the places left by their fathers when they died. The club would remain in existence until the last member of the class of 1890 died. It would then be sold and proceeds distributed to the heirs. With a $5,000 membership fee from each of the 14 members, George H. Reed began buying up land in 1890. He eventually purchased 18,000 acres, including several miles of Atlantic Ocean frontage as well as many of the finger streams along Banana Creek. Its 22-room clubhouse was located on Home Port Lake and boasted the first concrete swimming pool in the southeastern United States. The club was open about six months of the year. Passengers, mail and supplies were transported on the steamer Canaveral and other vessels over the years. The arrival of the members was always newsworthy and the various managers of the club were prominent members of Brevard County society. Presidents Benjamin Harrison and Grover Cleveland and other prominent dignitaries were guests at the club. A coast guard station was built on club

A tram took visitors from the pier to the ocean at Melbourne Beach. On the left is the Villa Marine Hotel and the Rykman House. (Photo courtesy Doug Hendriksen)

Above: The tennis courts of Melbourne's Bellevue Hotel were headquarters for a Racquet Club where annual tournaments were social events. (Photo Brevard County Historical Commission Archives)

Left: Joe and Louise Field, third and fourth from left, and friends enjoy an outing at the beach, c. 1910. (Photo courtesy Clyde Field)

Fourth of July was the occasion for picnics in many communities. This one was held in Malabar in 1899. (Photo Brevard County Historical Commission Archives)

married to E. L. Dwyer of Oregon in the Indian River Hotel at Titusville in January 1895. Accompanied by Dr. W. L. Hughlett, who had been treating her for an illness, she left for New York in March of that same year and died in August. The old Dummett Grove went through several changes of ownership after that and the villa, or "castle" as it became known, was the center of great controversy in Brevard County in the 20th century.[37]

Not all visitors were as newsworthy as the Canaveral Club members or the prominent owners of the Dummett property, but they were important to Brevard County residents both socially and economically. Many stayed in the large hotels where there were bowling alleys, fine dining, dancing, swimming, tennis, croquet, hunting, fishing, and many kinds of excursions. The tennis courts of Melbourne's Bellevue Hotel were headquarters for a Racquet Club whose annual tournaments of February 22 were social events. Wittfeld's Fairyland was a frequent destination for excursions from the hotels. Beach parties were often organized for Oceanus on the Atlantic beach. Other visitors stayed in smaller hotels and boarding houses, and still others roomed in the private homes of people anxious to supplement meager incomes. These visitors enjoyed many of the outdoor pleasures and the frequent holiday celebrations and picnics. They were welcomed as genuine additions to the community, but some were also glad when the season ended and they went back to their homes. One woman, whose family had migrated from Thomasville, Georgia, in the 1870s to develop a farm, spoke for some of her neighbors when she wrote from City Point in 1884. "A crowd of boarders

land during World War I and it later became headquarters for a beach patrol during World War II. By the terms of the original agreement and the passage of time, activities at the club were diminishing by the early 1920s. Club property deteriorated during the depressed 1930s and some of it was sold for taxes. The remaining land was purchased by Arthur K. Reading who had plans in 1945 to develop a town to be called Surfside Beach.[36]

Somewhat earlier than the Canaveral Club, the Dummett Grove again made the news. Having been sold to George W. Schuyler of New York after Dummett's death, it was again sold in 1881 to Ecole Tamajo. Although there is absolutely no evidence that he was a titled nobleman, Tamajo created quite a stir when he announced himself as the Duke of Castalucci. With his Duchess, a native of New York, he busied himself building the Villa de Castalucci in 1881. Lumber from a wrecked vessel near Daytona Beach was rafted down the river and used to build a unique, octagonally designed house. J. J. Coward of New York did the work. The villa became a showplace for a number of years and the grove was kept in excellent condition during the "Duke's" ownership. He died in 1893 and his widow was

were here until last week when they left to our pleasure," she wrote. "We liked them all, but we get tired of such a crowd."[38]

Many travelling shows came to the county. The Templeton Opera Company made its first tour in early 1888, followed shortly by Professor Ferguson of Boston who played the violin at Wager's Hall in Titusville and at other towns. Mr. and Mrs. Harrie Dixie made the Indian River tour each year after 1887, but they fell out of favor when their shows became repetitious. Emma Thursby, a prominent vocalist of

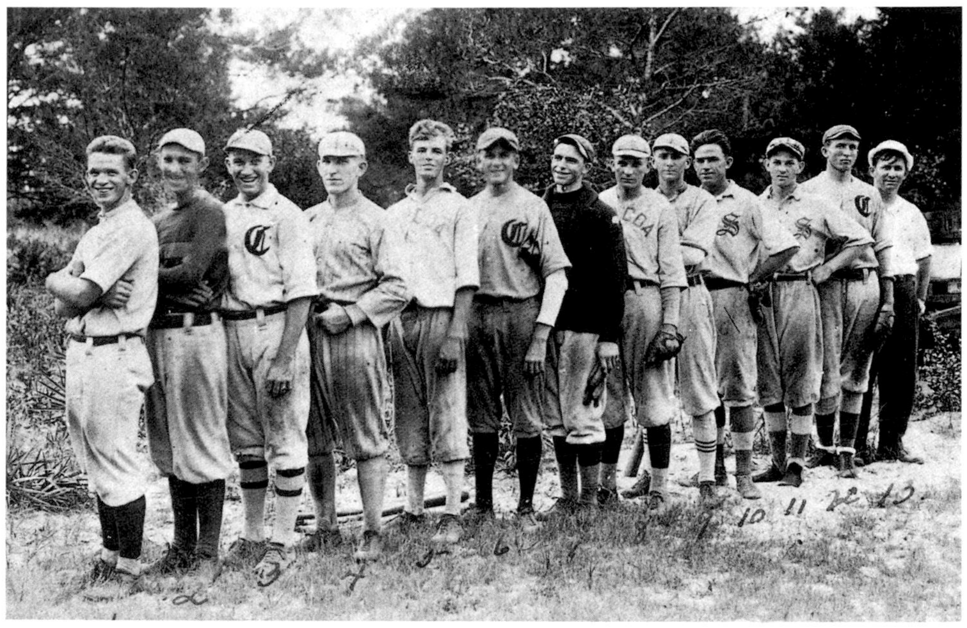

Cocoa baseball team, John Paterson, Carl Geiger, Speck Jones, Chubby Chalker, Cracker Hindle, Unknown, Lefty Forester, Rex Sosebee, Leland Daniel, Lawrence Abney, Minor Jones, Frank Forester, Gator Travis. (Photo Brevard County Historical Commission Archives)

Bicyclists wait for the start of the race in front of Stiling's Hardware in Cocoa, 1895. (Photo Brevard County Historical Commission Archives)

The bicycle was first introduced in the early 1890's and bicycling clubs were soon numerous. Misses Sudie Hoke, Viola Horton and Lucille Drake bicycle near the Trysting Stairs in Melbourne. (Photo Brevard County Historical Commission Archives)

the day, frequently wintered at Cocoa. She gave occasional performances which were well-attended by people from Titusville, Courtenay, City Point, Indianola, Melbourne and other river towns. She also created quite a sensation when she performed at nearby Orlando. A different form of entertainment came when Wanton S. Webb brought his "Florida on Wheels" railroad car to Brevard. The first circus to visit the county was Bingley's which performed under the canvas in 1889. Cooper and Company was another circus which came in the 1890s. It competed with Harris' "gilt edge circus" which was exceptionally well-received in 1895. According to the newspaper, it was the first of its kind to visit the river towns and "conquered all hard times" when it played just two months after the 1894-1895 freezes. Both the Dora Bloom Minstrels and Gorton's Minstrels played Brevard County. Whether they felt any competition from the local Indian River Minstrels is unknown. Thomas J. Keogh's troupe of comedians played at about the same time. There were apparently limits to the amount of professional entertainment which the county's inhabitants could support. Writing in 1895 the Indian River Advocate complained that "our town cannot stand more than two...or three...shows per month. When they come at the rate of two or three per week, they are bound to lose money, and may get stranded; that would be very unfortunate, for the walking between here and Jacksonville is by no means good." They continued to come. Circuses were playing to crowds again that year and in 1897 "Woodward's floating art studio" was at

Cocoa bicyclists Kate Eyer, Florence Gingras, G. A. Paterson, Joe Wilkinson, Hattie Wilkinson, Emma Hardee Skelly, George Gingras, Ollie Holmes, c. 1895. (*Photo Brevard County Historical Commission Archives*)

the Banyan wharf and "bean money [was] finding its way into the coffers thereof."[39]

Neither residents nor visitors waited for visiting entertainers. Social hops were held with great frequency at Wager's Hall in Titusville, Hill's Hall in Cocoa, the casino at Eau Gallie, in most of the hotels, and in private homes. Some were announced to mark special occasions; others were impromptu. At a birthday party given by J. B. Snell for his wife, musicians were brought in from Micco to entertain guests from Bovine, Tropic, Melbourne, Rockledge, and a few other places. A reception and ball in honor of the A. C. Storms at Indianola in 1895 was attended by guests from both sides of the river. When a dance was announced by W. R. Sanders of Courtenay in honor of his daughters' departure for school in 1894, young men from Titusville and other mainland towns attended. Mills Burnham's golden wedding anniversary celebration at Cape Canaveral in 1885 was attended by a large crowd from all along the river. March 16, 1900 was the day set aside for a picnic and ball to mark the 32nd anniversary of the arrival of Mrs. John R. Field at Indianola.[40]

Ring tournaments, adaptations of the medieval jousts, in which young men donned the colors of their ladies and attempted to hit small rings with their spears while riding at breakneck speed, were sometimes held. One was held in Titusville in 1887 and was followed by a dance in the evening at Wager's Hall. A month earlier at the same place a Fireman's Ball had been held to benefit the volunteer fire department.[41]

All of the national holidays were occasions for celebrations. These usually included such activities as speeches by local or visiting dignitaries, parades, shooting matches, ring tournaments, greased pig chases, tub races, sumptuous lunches, baseball games, regattas, and always a dance in the evening. Sometimes there would also be a circus. In later years, bicycle races and sometimes balloon ascensions were added. In the early years, Washington's Birthday, May Day, the Fourth of July, and sometimes Columbus Day were celebrated by individual towns and this sometimes caused conflicts. In time, a loose coordination seems to have developed, so that each of the celebrations was held in the same place each year. May Day, for example, was celebrated for many years at Oleander Point. It was a great festive occasion for those who boarded the steamer *Rockledge* for a river trip to the picnic and celebration. Titusville had a number of Fourth of July celebrations, but that day was eventually reserved for Melbourne. Eau Gallie was the site of the Washington's Birthday festivities. All were well-attended by neighbors from towns up and down the river, as well as winter visitors.[42]

Emancipation Day was a special celebration for black residents. A successful one was held at Melbourne in 1890 although the guests from Titusville were delayed when the steamer had boiler trouble. The one held at Rockledge included a sumptuous meal, several speeches, a baseball game and a shooting match. Titusville was the scene of another in 1902 which was held on the picnic grounds of the "Colored People's Association." Stuart also had an Emancipation Day celebration that same year.[43]

There were also special festive occasions such as the one at Titusville in 1893 when business men of that town chartered the steamer *St. Lucie* to provide a free excursion "from points down river to the county seat." A program included bicycle races, football matches, fire works, and a grand ball in the evening. The Danish constitution of 1848 was celebrated at White City in 1894 by a crowd from several points in the county. The usual festivities were augmented by the formation of a mutual benefit association by the local residents. The Georgiana Women's Christian Temperance Union marked Columbus Day of 1892 with a celebration featuring presentations by the local school children and the Georgiana Brass Band.[44]

Two of the earliest baseball teams were organized at Titusville and City Point in the early 1880s, but most of the communities soon followed suit. Before long, baseball matches were being scheduled with a regularity that almost suggested league play. Teams travelled considerable distances to compete and these trips often amounted to festive outings with picnics and dances included. One of the earlier football games was played at Titusville in 1888.[45]

Everyone enjoyed swimming in the Indian River waters. Wager's dock at Titusville was a favored spot because it was a short walk to deep water whereas the Indian River Hotel dock required "a tiresome distance of wading or rowing out in a boat." The ladies of Tibbals apparently did not mind a boat ride since they formed the Yacht Irene Saturday Afternoon Bathing Club which boasted 17 members.[46]

Western Union brought in a new form of social activity which coincided with civic affairs. The telegraph company agreed to provide 1892 general election news to a crowd at the Titusville opera house. Those who subscribed in advance were admitted free; others were assessed 25 cents for admission.[47]

Other modern innovations were coming to the county. The bicycle was first introduced in the early 1890s and bicycling clubs were soon numerous. These groups incidentally contributed to the demand for improved public roads which was beginning to be heard in Florida and elsewhere in the country. They were not pleased at the notice they received from Cocoa, which established regulations for cyclers in the late 1890s. The first showing of "moving pictures by Kinetoscope" occurred at the Titusville opera house in 1893. Julius Smith of Rockledge drove one of the first cars in the county in December 1900.[48]

End Notes

1. Titusville Florida Star, March 15,1883, May 3, 1888, March 16, 1900; Titusville Star Advocate, November 29, 1940.
2. Titusville Indian River Advocate,April 17, 1896, May 14, 1900.
3. Joseph D. Cushman, Jr., A Goodly Heritage: The Episcopal Church, 1821-1892 (Gainesville, 1965) pp. 184-185; Titusville Star Advocate, May 18, 1934; Tallahassee Floridian, April 15, 1886, October 20, 1887, December 29, 1887; Titusville Florida Star, August 4, 1886, July 7, 1887, July 7, 1888, June 5, 1890, January 8, 1891. Joe Cushman is a native of Titusville and a longtime professor of history at the University of the South.
4. Titusville Florida Star, January 12, March 3, September 15, 1887, May 5, 1888, July 17, August 14, 28, 1889, January 9, 1890, November 11, 1892, July 7, 1893, July 27, 1894; Tallahassee Floridian, January 12, 1888; Titusville East Coast Advocate, January 16, 1891.
5. Titusville Florida Star, June 6, September 7, 1889, October 14, 1892, October 24, 1899, June 15, 1900.
6. W. H. Maxwell v. Isaiah Gorey and Willie Gibson (Trustees for AME Church), Miscellaneous Brevard County Court Records; Titusville Florida Star, November 11, 1898, November 24, 1899.
7. Tallahassee Floridian, May 7, 1884; Titusville Florida Star, October 27, 1887, August 14, 1889, February 20, 1890, April 10, 1890, January 15, 1891, July 13, 1894, August 13, 1894, February 8, 1895, May 13, 1898; Cushman , A Goodly Heritage, pp. 185-186; Phoebe Black Letter, 1927; Clara Edwards, History of Rockledge Presbyterian Church, 1877-1954 (Cocoa, 1953).
8. Titusville Florida Star, January 7, 1886, February 9, 1887, January 19, November 9, 1888, October 5, 1890, May 13, December 4, 1898; Edwards, Rockledge Presbyterian.
9. Cushman, A Goodly Heritage, pp. 181-184; Amey R. Hoag, Thy Lighted Lamp, pp. 14, 58-59; Melbourne Area Chamber of Commerce Centennial Committee, Melbourne. A Century of Memories (Melbourne, 1980), p. 1; N. A., Melbourne Beach, The First 100 Years (1983), p. 9, Titusville Florida Star, February 2, 1888, August 16, 1888, April 14, 1893; Elaine Murray Stone, From Cape of the Canes to Space Coast (Northridge, California, 1988), p. 28.
10. Titusville Florida Star, January 22, 1891, November 25, 1892, February 1, 1895, February 24, March 18, 1898, July 14, 1899.
11. Ibid., February 1, 1895, June 18, 1897; VanLandingham, Saint Lucie County, pp. 23-24.
12. Ibid., June 9, 1887, February 2, 1888, September 18, 1889, April 14, 1893, November 30, 1906.
13. Brevard County Commission, Reports, August 3, 1891.
14. Titusville Florida Star, December 6, 1883; A. Brady to William H. Sharpe, June 30, 1884, Series 24, Carton 6, Record Group 150, Florida State Archives.
15. Titusville Florida Star, February 4, March 29, 1882, December 23, 1892.
16. Ibid., November 16, 1882, December 26, 1886, July 7, 1888, October 28, 1889, November 28, 1889, October 23, 1890; Melbourne: Century, p. 1; VanLandingham, Saint Lucie County, p. 23.
17. Titusville Florida Star, December 15, 1887, May 11, 1900; Titusville Indian River Advocate, May 18, 1900.
18. Titusville Florida Star, December 23, 1892, September 15, 1893, May 11, 1894.
19. Ibid., June 15, 1900 February 8, 1901; R. E. Mims to Callie, July 18, 1904, Dr. Robert Dean Collection;
20. Ibid., January 12, December 1, 1880, December 1, 1886, June 25, 1897, January 5, 1900.
21. Ibid., February 1, 1895; Melbourne: Century, p. 83.
22. Ibid., February 20, 1890, July 23, 1897, April 13, May 25, 1900; VanLandingham, Saint Lucie Country, p. 33.
23. Minutes of the East Coast Line Surgical Association, M76-168, Manuscript Collection, Florida State Archives.
24. Titusville Florida Star, January 8, 1885, February 10, 1886, April 23, 1891; Titusville Indian River Advocate, January 5, 1900.
25. Titusville Florida Star, June 25, 1897; Charles A. Hentz, Autobiography, Volume 11, pp. 270-275.
26. Ibid., pp. 235-236, 243-246.
27. Tallahassee Floridian, June 23, 1887, August 16, September 13, November 8, 1888.
28. Titusville Florida Star, February 10, 1886, September 13, 1888, August 14, 1889, January 18, 1891, December 16, 1892, July 20, August 10, October 19, 1894, January 18, 1895, January 4, 1901.
29. Ibid., July 20, 1894.
30. Ibid., January 12, 1880, May 24, 1882, December 1, 1886, August 14, 1889, May 5, 1893, February 1, 1895, March 11, 1898, February 1, February 23, March 30, 1907; Harry Winter, et al, to Governor F. P. Fleming, August 20, 1892, RG 101, Series 580, Record Group, Florida State Archives.
31. Titusville Florida Star, August 2, 1883, October 6, 1887, August 28, 1889, October 19, 1894, April 19, 1897, March 9, May 25, 1900, January 4, 1901.
32. Ibid., August 16, 1888; Tallahassee Floridian, May 19, 1887; Titusville Indian River Advocate, January 8, 1897, March 23, 1900.
33. Sally I. Magruder, Young Pioneers in Florida (Lynchburg, Virginia). Hentz Diary.
34. Thomas Barbour, That Vanishing Eden: A Naturalist's Florida (Boston, 1945), pp. 130, 187, 194. Henry Titus to Governor, April 14, 1894, Series 581, Box 14, Record Group 101, Florida State Archives; Titusville Florida Star, January 26, 1888, July 7, 1899, November 28, 1902; Brevard County Commission, "Reports," November 6, 1893, passim.
35. Titusville Florida Star, January 12, 1888, October 28, November 25, 1892, June 18, 1897; Titusville East Coast Advocate, November 28, 1890; Titusville Indian River Advocate, February 1899.
36. Titusville Florida Star, January 12, 1888, October 28, 1892; Titusville Indian River Advocate, February, 1899.
37. Titusville Florida Star, March 2, 1881, March 1, 1895; Titusville Indian River Advocate, August 9, 1895 Titusville Star Advocate, January 27, 1928; Indian River Hotel, Cash Book, 1895.
38. Phoebe Black Letter, 1927; Aunt Caroline to Henry, March 22, 1884, Henry H. Bryant Correspondence, Bryant-Stephens Collection, P. K. Yonge Library; Hoag, Lighted Lamp, p. 12.
39. Titusville Indian River Advocate, January 4, 1895; Titusville Florida Star, May 28, 1885, December 26, 1886, December 29, 1887, February 9, 1888, January 24, 1889, March 13, 1890, March 3, 1893, January 18, March 22, 1895, May 21, 1897, June 30, 1899, March 9, 1900.
40. Tallahassee Floridian, September 24, 1885; Titusville Florida Star, September 18, 1889, October 19, 1894, January 25, 1895, March 9, 1900.
41. Titusville Florida Star, November 25, December 29, 1885.
42. Ibid., May 24, 1882, June 7, 1883, April 26, 1888, June 5, 1890, April 20, 1894, May 7, 1897, July 7, 1899; Titusville Star Advocate, June 28, 1929.
43. Titusville Florida Star, May 29, 1890, May 25, 1900; Titusville Indian River Advocate, May 23, 1902.
44. Titusville Florida Star, October 28, 1892, December 15, 1893, June 8, 1894.
45. Ibid., June 1, March 2, August 2, 1883, November 8, 1888, May 4, 1894, January 1, 1897.
46. Ibid., August 27, 1891; Titusville Indian River Advocate, May 18, 1900.
47. Ibid., November 4, 1892.
48. Ibid., June 18, July 30, 1897, December 16, March 4, 1898, December 14, 1900.

Page 152 map: Charles Granville's Railroad and Township Map of Florida, 1886, South Publishing Co. (Brevard County Historical Commission Archives)

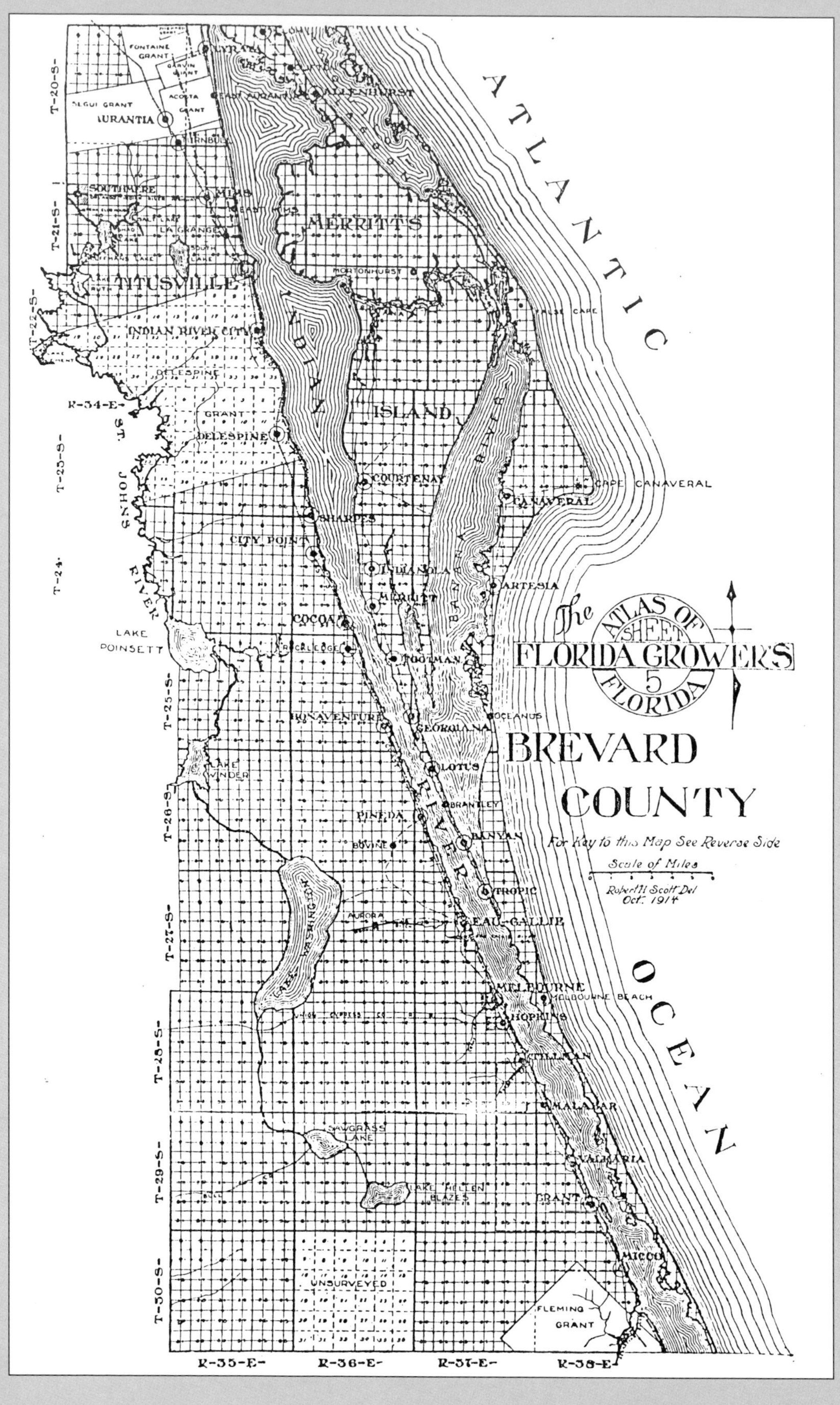

The Atlas of Florida Growers
Sheet 5
Florida
BREVARD COUNTY
For Key to this Map See Reverse Side
Scale of Miles
Robert M. Scott Del
Oct. 1914
ATLANTIC OCEAN
INDIAN RIVER
BANANA RIVER
ST. JOHNS RIVER
MERRITT'S ISLAND
TITUSVILLE
INDIAN RIVER CITY
DELESPINE
DELESPINE GRANT
COURTENAY
SHARPES
CITY POINT
INDIANOLA
COCOA
ROCKLEDGE
ROOTMAN
BONAVENTURE
GEORGIANA
LOTUS
PINEDA
BOVINE
BANYAN
TROPIC
EAU-GALLIE
MELBOURNE
MELBOURNE BEACH
HOPKINS
STILLMAN
MALABAR
VALKARIA
GRANT
MICCO
FLEMING GRANT
UNSURVEYED
LAKE POINSETT
LAKE WINDER
LAKE WASHINGTON
SAWGRASS LAKE
LAKE HELLEN BLAZES
CAPE CANAVERAL
CANAVERAL
ARTESIA
OCEANUS
BRANTLEY
AURORA
MORTONHURST
ALLENHURST
AURANTIA
SEGUI GRANT
FONTAINE GRANT
GARVIN GRANT
ACOSTA GRANT
T-20-S-
T-21-S-
T-22-S-
T-23-S-
T-24-
T-25-S-
T-26-S-
T-27-S-
T-28-S-
T-29-S-
T-30-S-
R-34-E-
R-35-E-
R-36-E-
R-37-E-
R-38-E-

11
A Diversified Economy

Although citrus would emerge as the paramount crop, the landowner with a small grove, a garden with one or more varieties of vegetables, and perhaps some pineapples, sugar cane or guavas was more representative of his neighbors than one who specialized in any of these.

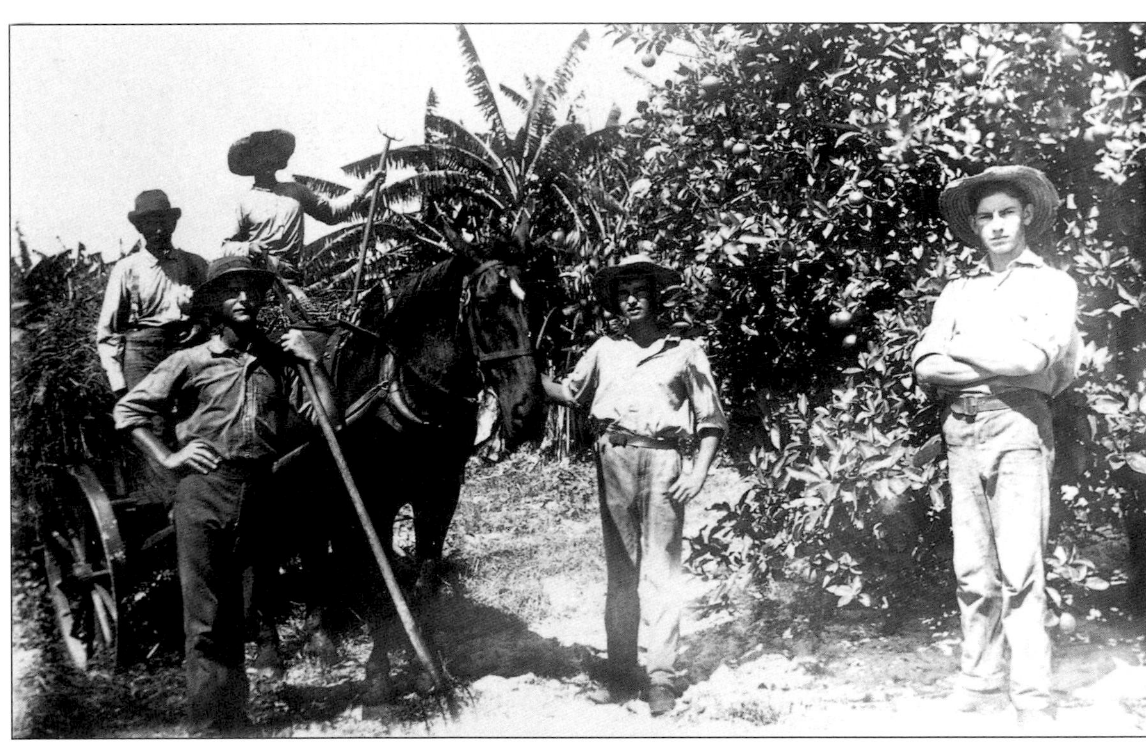

R. O. Conkling and his three sons with H. Yowell farm land at Turkey Creek. (Photo Brevard County Historical Commission Archives)

"Taking the whole number of people who are tilling the soil along Indian River," declared the Cocoa Public Spirit in 1889, "it is probable there are more of them cultivating five acres or less than there are cultivating more than five acres."[1] Although that would change markedly over the ensuing decades, it was probably true when written. With a few exceptions hopes were more abundant than financial resources among Brevard County's early settlers. Clearing the land was a difficult task and labor was scarce even for those who could have afforded it. But, whether they were professional men, merchants, craftsmen, or sailors, nearly everyone engaged in some kind of agriculture. Most grew more than one kind

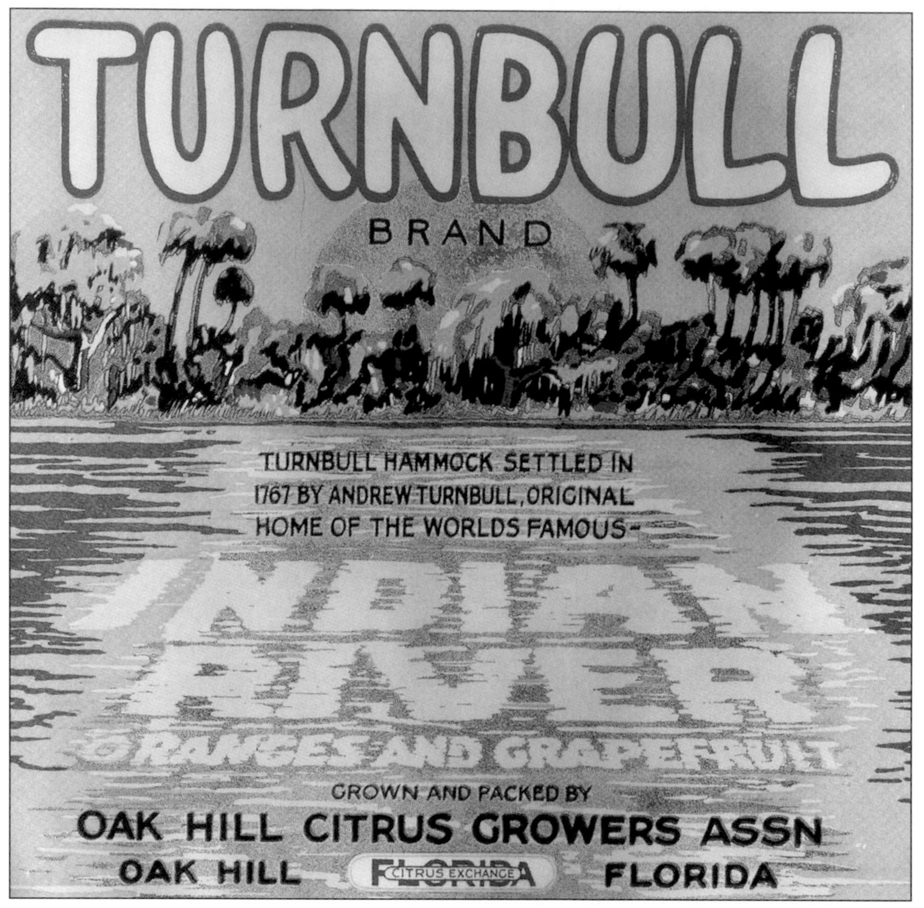
TURNBULL
BRAND
TURNBULL HAMMOCK SETTLED IN
1767 BY ANDREW TURNBULL, ORIGINAL
HOME OF THE WORLDS FAMOUS-
INDIAN
RIVER
ORANGES AND GRAPEFRUIT
GROWN AND PACKED BY
OAK HILL CITRUS GROWERS ASSN
OAK HILL
FLORIDA
CITRUS EXCHANGE
FLORIDA

Many groves and growers associations used distinctive labels to identify their fruit. (Florida Citrus Exchange)

of crop. The landowner with a small grove, a garden with one or more varieties of vegetables, and perhaps some pineapples, sugar cane, or guavas was more representative of his neighbors than the one who specialized in any of these. Some of them would eventually build up sizable holdings, but that was after years of hard work and more than a little disappointment from time to time.

Citrus would one day emerge as the paramount crop and it enjoyed a large share of the attention of the early settlers. In his 1881 survey of agricultural production, J. F. LeBaron reported 204 orange groves along the Indian River. Of their 87,000 trees, 15,000 were bearing and had produced 14,000 boxes that year.[2]

The famous Indian River orange had its origins in one of the groves of sweet oranges which had survived since Spanish days. According to W. S. Hart, who lived at Hawks Park, John D. Sheldon found one of the sweet orange groves in the Turnbull Hammock in what is now Volusia County and transplanted some 6,000 trees to what later became the Packwood place near Oak Hill. Most of the Indian River fruit came from those trees by way of Dummett's grove. The variety was being propagated all along the Indian River by the time LeBaron submitted his 1881 report. Gardner Hardee and his neighbors at Rockledge had producing groves which were so beautiful that they were tourist attractions as was William Wittfeld's grove at Fairyland. Nearly all the first settlers had producing trees by that time. Those who arrived later usually cleared land and started their groves, but some bought land on which trees had already been planted.[3]

One of the latter was Charles A. Hentz who became interested in the Indian River country about 1880 because of reports from many of his northern Florida neighbors who had moved there. Arriving at Titusville that year, he was advised by Henry Titus to look at the DeSoto grove. Said to be older than Dummett's grove, it was located on Banana Creek on the barrier island east of Titusville. Although the grove had many large trees, they were so dilapidated that Hentz was not interested in a purchase, although he noted that it "would make a splendid place for market gardening, if transportation was available." He soon settled on a young grove of 400 trees at City Point for which he paid Lafayette Wooten $400. A year later he bought an adjoining ten acre tract for $500. This composite grove constituted what one observer described a little later as "a paradise." Because he was an elderly man in the 1880s and still spent some time at Quincy, Hentz may not have been a typical Brevard County settler, but his experience in citrus culture was exemplary of that of his neighbors. During his absences, he was able to hire others to tend his grove. Grove tending for absentee landlords would eventually assume professional proportions, but at City Point in the 1880s, Hentz usually relied on neighbors, some of whom were more efficient than others. One of the more satisfactory was Jim Robinson who was paid $40 per month to care for Hentz' grove.[4]

R. T. Smith *and workers pack fruit at* Mullet Creek *using willow withes for strapping.* (*Photo* Grant Historical Society)

Hentz usually managed to be present during harvest. He was there in 1886 when the temperature fell to 27 degrees on January 10, 11, and 12, and ice formed on the edge of the river. The older trees were not hurt, but most of the fruit was frozen. Since the fruit seemed good to eat and others were shipping theirs, he decided to send 57 boxes to W. J. Duncan of New York. The proceeds of the

Many packing houses were located on the river where fruit was loaded directly onto boats for shipment north. The Porcher Packing House *at* Cocoa. (*Photo courtesy of* Doug Hendriksen)

Joseph Cannata and family show off their oranges while picking at Cannata Groves, Georgiana, c. 1900. (Photo courtesy Clyde Field)

shipment was 44 cents worth of postage stamps. The next crop was considerably better and brought $1550.57.[5]

Marketing and transportation soon proved more vexatious than the weather. Growers at first resorted to a variety of informal methods of selling their fruit. Some even shipped small quantities to be sold by friends in northern cities. It was not uncommon for growers to sell their crops on the trees, but that caused problems because buyers sometimes picked and shipped green fruit to the distress of those trying to establish a reputation for high quality. More common was the commission merchant who handled the crop for a percentage of the gross. There were variations in the way they operated. L. J. Carlisle of LaGrange and Titusville took his 2,500 boxes of fruit to New York and sold them to T. G. Furman and Company. Several of his neighbors placed their crop in his hands. Both J. A. Gibson and W. B. Moore, Titusville merchants, handled citrus on consignment just as they did syrup and hides. Both accepted boxed or barreled fruit, but Moore built a packing house next to his store where that additional service was available to those who desired it. B. F. Ives of Philadelphia, who had a grove of his own at LaGrange, handled "a good share of the Indian River fruit." J. S. Watson, another Titusville merchant, was the local agent for E. L. Goodsell of New York. P. Ruhlman, "one of the largest commission merchants in New York City" came to Brevard County and worked out of the Titus House in harvest season.[6]

Increasing fruit production created secondary activities. While many individuals sized their own fruit, wrapped it, packed it, and hand-stamped the crates, someone had to provide the supplies. The Titusville Star printed the paper for wrappers. Several sawmills specialized in making orange boxes and barrels. J. F. Reed, manager of the Titusville Cash Store, offered boxes for 15 cents each, and hoops for 75 cents per hundred. The young ladies of LaGrange organized as the LaGrange Orange Wrappits in 1886 to wrap fruit for five cents per box. One of the more ambitious derivative industries was undertaken by A. Parkinson who began making orange wine from sour oranges in 1884.[7]

As more and more fruit was produced each year, there were difficulties with both marketing and transportation.

The famous Indian River citrus was featured in the Brevard display at the Florida Subtropical Exposition in Jacksonville in 1890. (Photo courtesy Jim Ball)

Several modest efforts at cooperation had begun in the early 1880s, but the Indian River Fruit and Vegetable Growers Protective Association was the first to address the specific problems of the growers. In early 1888 its members met at the residence of A. L. Hatch at City Point to effect an organization. A new constitution and by-laws were adopted and standing committees were named. G. S. Hardee, E. P. Porcher, A. L. Hatch, A. Brady and Dr. G. W. Holmes were made responsible for dealing with delayed shipments and related difficulties. A committee composed of W. H. Sharpe, A. J. Whitlock, John Sanders, Julius King, H. S. Williams and L. A. Gingras was to handle complaints about freight rates and report them to the railroad commission.[8]

Freight rates and poor handling of shipments were continuing problems, but they were over-shadowed by more pressing ones in the 1890s. Indian River fruit had gained such a favorable reputation for taste and quality that other producers were marketing their own fruit under fraudulent Indian River labels. The situation crested in 1891-1892 when 300,000 boxes of Indian River fruit were sold while only 100,000 boxes had actually been produced by Indian River growers. Suffering the possible loss of reputation, the local growers searched for ways to protect their trademark. The result was the formation in November 1892 of the Indian River Orange Growers Association.[9]

Organized at City Point, the association was composed of Adhemar Brady, George W. Holmes, A. L. Hatch, William H. Sharpe, C. H. Brock, C. L. Faber, A. Faber, H. S. Black, E. W. Hall, George E. Chester, A. N. Mather and George H. Rumph who collectively purchased 47 shares at $100 each. C. B. Magruder was president, W. H. Sharpe was treasurer and A. L. Hatch was general manager. The association's linchpin was an agreement to sell through one manager – E. P. Porcher – operating out of Cocoa. The members would set the price and the agent would receive a five percent commission.[10]

While the commission houses complained of the competition from the new organization, Porcher made arrangements with the Flagler railroad which was then building through the county. It handled approximately 50,000 boxes of the 90,000 produced in 1892-1893. He was able to report an overall five percent reduction in freight rates between the Indian River groves and the northern markets. Prior to the arrival of the railroad the Indian River Steamboat Company had transported the crop; some shipments going over the Jacksonville, Tampa and Key West branch from Titusville and others going through the Haulover Canal to Daytona. The faltering IRSB continued to provide some competition for the Flagler road until the great freezes.[11]

Albert Taylor, Mr. Blodgett, Adrienne and Grace Taylor walk through E. P. *Porcher's greenhouse in Courtenay.* (*Photo Brevard County Historical Commission Archives*)

Transportation ceased to be a major problem during the 1894-1895 season. A cold wave just after Christmas in 1894 dropped the temperature to about 35 degrees for two successive days. Then the temperature dropped to 18 degrees and remained there for several hours. By January 4, people were reporting that "trees have sustained equally as much, perhaps more, damage than in 1886." But the weather was extremely warm over the next month. The Titusville newspaper reported on January 25 that "the freeze is not proving so disastrous as at first thought to be." It even reported that the Indian River region "has regained its prestige as to weather" and observed that the favorable weather was helping the trees which were rapidly budding and "putting forth every effort to clothe their leafless branches." Although it could not have known at the time, that was the worst thing that could have been happening.[12]

On February 7, the temperature again plunged to 19 degrees and remained below freezing for two days. Within a few weeks it was clear that the back-to-back freezes had severely damaged most of the Indian River groves, although the destruction was uneven. By March the newspaper was reporting that "Merritt Island and Banana River have proven to be the favored sections for oranges." On the Waveland peninsula, oranges were reported to be "still hanging on trees, untouched by the freeze," and even the lemon trees were undamaged. From Ankona came the observation that the "recent freezes have settled the question of the real orange belt." The Titusville newspaper declared that the year 1895 had been "a disastrous one." Frozen groves, the end of the Indian River Steamboat Company, and a dwindling population were causing adversity, but "still we are not discouraged." That may well have been the case, but it was to be a long time before the citrus industry recovered from what is still referred to as "the great freezes." The economic impact was summed up by A. L. Hatch who commented wryly that "the Hatch store went the way of the orange trees.[13]

One did not have to travel as far south as Ankona to find surviving groves. While some people abandoned the river, most others began replanting. Much of the bud wood they used came from the groves of Dempsey Cain and L. C. Moore's Ercildonne plantation at Roseland. There were also some surviving trees on Merritt Island. But, unfortunately, there was more to come. There were two severe cold waves in January and February of 1898, another in February 1899, and still another in early January 1900. The February 1898 freeze brought the first snow ever recorded in Brevard County.[14]

One enterprising individual tried to provide relief from the freezes while earning a profit. W. H. McFarland organized the McFarland Fruit Protection Company to make tents for orange trees. It was apparently a serious enterprise with offices in Titusville and Jacksonville. E. J.

Seymour, one of his partners and salesmen, published the *Freeze or No Freeze* touting the tents as protection against freeze for oranges, pineapples, and even vegetables. With W. H. English managing his Jacksonville office and W. M. Brown in charge at Titusville, McFarland reported orders for his product from several places along the coast. He actually made some tents in 1899 and said that he was expecting to employ 150 people at Titusville. That was apparently an over-estimation. While offering tents for sale as late as 1902, he was also trying to sell the company as well. Nothing more was heard of the Fruit Protection Company after 1902, but McFarland left town with a traveling show, an enterprise for which his talents may have been better suited. Another freeze in January 1902 saw M. S. Sams, E. P. Porcher and others on Merritt Island firing their groves, a more conventional form of protection.[15]

The recurring freezes were a problem with which the growers would have to contend, but as production increased – reaching pre-1894 levels by about 1907 – green fruit shipments, high freight rates, and general problems of marketing large quantities of citrus demanded attention. In 1907 William H. Sharpe was among those urging a meeting to look into ways of improving the "present rotten system of distributing and selling our fruit."[16]

With the overall state citrus crop amounting to about six million boxes in 1908, everyone decided that it was time for common action. Recognizing that California orange growers had developed a successful marketing arrangement, the Floridians sent a committee to the west coast to study their methods and report back to a convention of Florida growers. The convention met in Tampa in 1909 and organized the Florida Citrus Exchange with power to implement a system of common advertising and marketing. The Exchange was also empowered to set standards of quality of the fruit which was shipped out of the state. Sub-exchanges would process the fruit of individual growers. Representing Brevard County at the convention, E. P. Porcher and H. S. Williams voted to adopt the plan.[17]

Porcher and Williams brought news of the arrangement back to Brevard County and the growers responded almost immediately. Within weeks several groups were

The Field family's cane mill at Indianola was used to grind syrup from sugar cane from the 1880's until the 1950's. (Photo courtesy Clyde Field)

Thomas E. Richards, who came to Eden from New Jersey in 1878, is generally called the founder of the Indian River pineapple industry. Eden, Ankona, and Jensen had the greatest concentrations of pineapple fields, but the fruit was spread all along the sand ridge from Sebastian to the southern boundary of the county. There were also commercial fields at Melbourne and on Merritt Island. In fact, the first growers' organization was the Indian River Pineapple and Coconut Grove Association formed at Eau Gallie in 1886 with C. B. Magruder as president and W. H. Gleason as secretary. But, although pineapples were grown in those areas throughout the 19th century, the heaviest concentration was in the southern part of the county.[22]

Slips were first brought in from the offshore islands by the thousands and planted in the sandy soil. Fertilizer was used and cultivation was intensive. The plants made a beautiful site with their red leaves, especially when they were in bloom. Each plant had from one to three pineapples. They provided a serious challenge for those who worked the fields. They were tough, fibrous and sharp-edged. The leaves could be vicious to the bare skin and field workers were obliged to wear heavy clothing. However, profits could be great. Market prices naturally varied for many reasons, but pineapples seem to have brought from four to seven dollars per crate in the northern markets. They sometimes sold for two dollars in Jacksonville and for slightly less in the fields. Still, some growers claimed that they netted from $400 to $600 per acre in good years. The variations in prices between the field and the northern markets emphasize the difficulty of transporting and marketing the fruit.

In the early 1880s, shipping was as uncertain as it was ingenious. Thomas Richards' daughter, Lucie, described one such method in 1884. She was on her way to her old home in New Jersey and her father put her in the care of Mr. and Mrs. Edward Arnold who happened to be going to New York at the same time. While the Arnolds looked after Lucie, she watched out for Richards' pineapples. Richards and his daughter took the crop from Eden to Rockledge in a sailboat. There, both passengers and pineapples were put on board a steamer for Jacksonville. At that place, Lucie was to be sure that the pineapples were loaded on the train for Savannah. She was to repeat the process at Savannah and again in New York and then report to her father how the shipment was handled all along the way.[23]

Richards may not have been too happy with his daughter's report. During the 1885 season, he harvested about 25,000 pineapples. He shipped only 4,000 of those and made the remainder into wine. The entire crop of the southern part of the county was less than 75,000 pineapples that year. Most of them were shipped

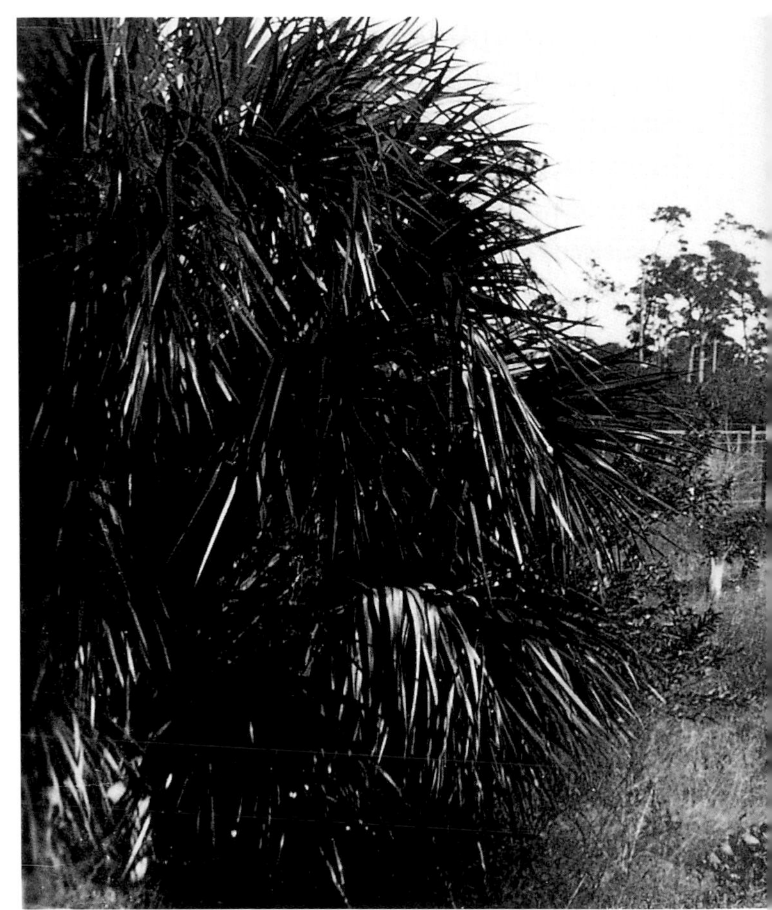

from St. Lucie to Jacksonville.[24]

Many new growers were planting more and more acres of pineapples by the mid-1880s, but marketing was still uncertain. Richards shipped 10,000 pineapples from Titusville in July 1886 but expressed his intention of canning most of his future crops in the belief that more money could be made "from canning than shipping." He was more optimistic in 1888 when he reported a good crop and the shipment of over a thousand barrels "with steamer and sailboats" up to July l. The shipping season usually lasted through August. The inauguration of the Indian River Steamboat Company's service seems to have been the cause of his improved outlook. He wrote that "we are just learning how to manage pineapples and I think the acreage will be greatly expanded. We want to build up the Steamship line as there is no satisfaction in the sailboat shipping perishable goods, but with steamers you can send one crate or 100 and you know just when they will go."[25]

He was correct about the increasing acreage. He and others at Eden alone planted over a half million slips in 1889. Jensen and Ankona farmers were equally active. Between Fort Pierce and Ankona another million plants were set out in 1890. F. P. Hassler and John Henry were among several Melbourne residents who brought in slips from the Bahamas for resale in 1891. They were filling a number of different orders, one of which was for 300,000 plants. Pineapple land was then selling at prices ranging

One effort to diversify the economy may have been ahead of its time. This 1890 photo shows an ostrich farm at Courtenay on Merritt Island. (Photo Library of Congress, Clark Ensminger Collection, Florida State Archives)

from $45 to $100 per acre.[26]

He was less accurate in his enthusiasm over the steamers, however. While one newspaper reported that "returns for this season [1890] have been very flattering...still netting seven dollars and up per crate" in late August, there were others who were less sanguine. Another paper reported that pineapples were being shipped in large quantities, but "many are going in sailboats" because of the exorbitant rates being charged by the IRSB.[27]

A group met at Thomas Richards' home in February 1892 and formed the Indian River and Lake Worth Pineapple Growers Association. The members reconvened at Sewall's Point in December and agreed to attempt a common marketing method through the Florida Fruit Exchange. Transportation also took a different turn the following year when Henry Flagler promised the growers that his new line would ship their crop northward from Eau Gallie which was the railhead that year. In January 1894, Thomas Richards, president of the new association, appointed W. H. Parkin, W. F. Richards and John L. Jensen a committee to draft resolutions endorsing the Exchange as marketing agent for the year.[28]

The year 1894 was not a good one for the growers. They were being adversely affected by competition from foreign growers, a problem which would become much more serious in the future. The Pullman car strike at Chicago caused several large losses by tying up their shipments. And, the marketing arrangement with the Florida Fruit Exchange proved unsatisfactory. The great freezes of 1894 and 1895 did some damage to the pineapples, although it was not nearly as serious as that done to citrus. The demise of the IRSB at the same time was probably a greater loss since it left the Florida East Coast Railway without serious competition.[29]

There was much discussion in 1894 about abandoning the shipping of pineapples in favor of selling in the fields to commission men and canning the surplus. That plan never materialized and the growers turned to E. P. Porcher, who was then marketing much of the Indian River citrus for the Orange Growers Association. At the Al Fresco Hotel in Jensen in 1895, Porcher explained how the citrus operation worked. He was named general agent for the pineapple growers with offices at Jacksonville. At the sixth annual meeting of the Indian River and Lake Worth Pineapple Growers Association at Jensen in January 1897, Porcher reported to members from the area between Biscayne Bay and Melbourne that he had handled about 97 percent of the 1896 crop. In other matters, Charles T. McCarty, a prominent Ankona grower and attorney, was designated to go to Washington and lobby against the provisions of the Dingley Tariff which was about to lower the duties on foreign pineapples. McCarty was unsuccessful and that problem soon became threatening.[30]

In 1900 the pineapple crop was about 130,000 standard crates with Porcher handling about 87,000 of them for the association. About 43,000 were sold independently. The White City Agricultural and Horticultural Association, organized in 1897 with Edward Pitts as president, Hans Christensen as vice president, and J. M. Orrell as secretary, was one of the groups which was not cooperating with the main association, but there were numerous others by 1900. There seems to have been dissatisfaction with Porcher. Meeting at Jensen in 1901, growers of 101,000 crates of pineapples pledged their crops to J. A. Williamson as general agent. Growers of another 20,000 crates, while unwilling to pledge, were sympathetic with the change. Officers of the association that year were W. H. Robinson of North Ankona, George Saeger of Ankona, Harry Jennings of Tibbals, W. F. Richards of Eden, John L. Sorensen of Jensen, W. W. Bessey of Stuart, and F. J. Magill of Jupiter.[31]

Foreign competition was causing difficulty for mainland growers by the early 20th century. The problem originated from the fact that offshore growers could produce and ship to the United States market more cheaply than could the Florida growers. The Dingley Tariff rates, adopted in 1897, were apparently too low to make up the difference. The Florida East Coast Railway got most of the blame for the problem. It was the FEC which was charging Floridians high freight rates while also shipping foreign pineapples. The situation became serious enough by 1906 that J. P. Beckwith, FEC traffic manager, spoke to the growers about it. He explained that the tariff was at the bottom of the problem, but that the steamship company which brought the foreign pineapples to Miami had refused to cooperate with the railroad and raise rates from Havana to put domestic producers on an equal footing with Cubans. He explained that the FEC had been operating at a loss for three years in order to keep its Florida customers competitive with the foreigners. Beckwith obviously had a serious public relations problem and was attempting to put the railroad's case in the best possible light. And he may well have been doing all that was in his power to do. But it should also be remembered that the steamship line to which he referred was also owned outright by Henry Morrison Flagler.[32]

Both Thomas Richards and his son, W. F., died in 1902 and Charles McCarty was shot to death on a Fort Pierce street in 1907, but the hundreds of pineapple producers along the lower Indian River continued to ship pineapples for several more years. They were eventually driven out of business by the foreign competition which had long plagued them, higher costs of production, and diseases that plagued the varieties of pineapples which they grew. It was fortunate for the region that oranges and grapefruit did well on the same soil which had produced the pineapples for nearly two generations.

Open range cattle grazing was about as old as the county, having begun in the 1850s. It continued through the post-war era and survived the murderous range wars of the late 1860s and early 1870s. Even the great flood of 1878 was endured. The entire country between the Kissimmee and St. Johns rivers north of Lake Okeechobee was described as "a vast sea of water and floating forests." Alligators had left the rivers and were attacking cattle on the prairies. The flooding thinned out the herds and left the cattlemen struggling into the 1880s, but they survived and were joined by others during the last two decades of the 20th century.[33]

F. M. Platt and his large family operated from headquarters near the St. Johns River west of Melbourne and grazed cattle for miles. When Calvin Platt died, he left an estate including 100,000 acres of land. He also left a legendary reputation. He was noted for keeping all of his business affairs in his head, making large and small contracts with a handshake and customarily carrying about $10,000 on his person just in case he might need it.[34]

Reuben Carlton was an early settler near Fort Pierce and became one of the largest cattlemen in that area. Others who made Fort Pierce their home were K. B. Raulerson and David L. Alderman. Raulerson's East Coast Cattle Company had holdings near Fort Bassinger and at LaGrange. He slaughtered and shipped beef from pens at the latter place after rail transportation became available. John M. Pearce, Eli O. Morgan and his son-in-law, E. L. Lesley, and some of the Raulersons and Aldermans grazed cattle in the Fort Bassinger area. Henry Parker, his son, and several of his brothers were among the larger cattlemen around Fort Drum. Arch Bass first settled at Kenansville but his large family ultimately spread out over Central Florida. Most of them drove cattle to Punta Rassa or Tampa for sale well into the 20th century. Many of the herds went from those points to Cuba, but Tampa eventually became a fairly good market in its own right. The Lykes Company was an early buyer of beef on the hoof for slaughter. After railroad transportation became available, alternative markets were opened, but the drives to the west coast lasted many years. In 1899, about 100,000 head of cattle were sold for the Cuban market in a single week. It started with Allen Chandler of Fort Drum selling 1,400 head to Eli Morgan. Morgan made a few other purchases while rounding up his own herds. Within a few days, he sold 700 head to R. E. Whidden of Arcadia who had a contract to deliver beef to Cuba. They also sold 5,000 head to W. H. Towles who chartered a steamer from New York to transport them to Cuba. The 100,000 was rounded out from other herds on the range between the Kissimmee and St. Johns rivers, including 600 head from K. B. Raulerson. It was an unusually large drive because of demand in Cuba following the Spanish-American War, but it was representative of the range cattle industry at the turn of the century.[35]

The stories of the simplicity in the way the early cattlemen did business are nearly endless. Calvin Platt was only one of the men who carried large sums of money and shook hands over deals involving thousands of dollars. All of those who dealt in the Cuban market carried quantities of gold doubloons back home in their saddle bags. For the most part they were free from interference. One reason for that was the readiness with which they were able to defend themselves, but most of their associates were honest about dealing with money. One of the better stories comes from E. L. Lesley who rode with E. O. Morgan to settle up after a cattle sale to Ziba King, a legendary cattleman of the lower Peace River Valley. They met at an isolated spot on the prairie east of Kissimmee. King turned the papers over to the younger Lesley and said, "Sonny, you go ahead and figure out how much Col. Morgan owes me while we two talk." King accepted Lesley's figures without question and paid up. While they were talking, Irving Lockler, a Kissimmee banker rode up and loaned King $10,000 and took a hand-written IOU for collateral. Business is no longer transacted that way.[36]

This is not to say there was no crime. It is just that some acts were socially less acceptable than others. While retribution was swift and severe if someone were caught stealing another man's cattle, that practice did not end with the Mizell-Barber confrontation. Many people carried running irons, and the official charged with registering marks and brands was an important personage. But, cattle rustling seems never to have reached the proportions that it had assumed just after the Civil War. A few cattle subjected to an iron near a hot fire by an occasional rustler was more common. Another way of taking cattle was to drive off young unbranded stock and hide it away for several months. The larger yearlings would then be brought to market and sold, sometimes to the original owners. Such an operation was brought to light near Fort Pierce in the early 1890s and the perpetrators were punished. Not all of the cattlemen were guiltless in the matter of rustling and sometimes disputes arose over the innocent misbranding of a few mavericks. It was also not

Fishing was the main industry for many of the people in Grant and fish houses were common along the river in that area. (Photo courtesy Grant Historical Society)

uncommon for cattlemen to look the other way when needy families occasionally butchered a beef not their own, but they took a different view if they thought profit was the motive.[37]

A large amount of the open range was taken from Brevard County when Osceola County was created in 1887 and more went to the new St. Lucie County in 1905, but the cattle industry remained – and still remains – important in the county. In later years there would be great improvement in the quality of the herds, much attention to upgrading the grasslands, and even fencing of the range, but that was not the case in the early years of the 20th century. The herds were still made up mostly of scrub Florida cattle, they ranged freely on the open lands, and they soon began irritating grove owners and townspeople by their uninhibited ways of disregarding property lines.

With the exception of the catching of green turtles and a single group from Connecticut fishing at Indian River Inlet and shipping the catch to Savannah in the 1870s, the commercial fishing industry was started in the early 1880s when George W. Scobie arrived at Titusville with his sharpie and began taking oysters from the Indian River. His inaugural shipment of five gallons of oysters left Titusville on the first train on the new railroad in January 1886. Scobie expanded until he had numerous vessels fishing out of Titusville, Grant, and other points on the river. He ultimately became a major supplier of fish barrels for the Florida east coast. Scobie's expansion southward was typical of the fishing industry in general. The best method of shipping the catch was in barrels packed with ice by way of the railroad.

The industry naturally moved south as the railroad advanced after 1893. By 1895 there were 254 Brevard County residents and 19 firms engaged in the fishing industry. Operating from Titusville, Cocoa, Eau Gallie, Melbourne, Grant, Sebastian, Fort Pierce, Eden, Jensen and Stuart, they shipped 2,659,815 pounds of fish which brought $37,657 in 1895. Although mullet was by far the largest portion of the catch at 1,610,869 pounds, it sold for only $12,251. At the same time 149,000 pounds of pompano brought $9,475.[38]

A United States government team investigated and reported on the Indian River fish population in 1897 and found it to be holding its own. Mullet remained in ample supply and did not seem threatened. Pompano and some of the more prized specie had never been abundant in the river but natural reproduction seemed to be keeping up with the annual catches. There was some concern about the sea trout, red drum, and sheepshead which were not only desirable for commercial purposes, but were also popular among the numerous sport fishermen. The government officials noted that the only Florida law governing fishing was an 1893 statute which forbade all seines and nets except the common gill net within one mile of any of the four inlets from the ocean. They thought the limit should be extended a greater distance from the inlets and that a closed season should be imposed during spawning season, but they were not otherwise overly concerned about immediate danger to the Indian River fish supply.[39]

The investigators did note that there had been an increase in the number of people engaged in fishing since the citrus industry was destroyed by the freezes of 1894-1895, but they thought that only a temporary situation. They noted also that many of the fishermen were so employed only part-time while engaging in other activities such as replanting groves or growing vegetables.[40]

Oysters were increasing in importance in the mid-1890s. The county issued permits to many landowners along the river to plant artificial oyster beds. Among the many so engaged were D. M. Egerton, R. E. Mims, M. C. Salman, and A. A. Stewart. By the early 20th century George Scobie and a few others were also taking oysters from the ocean near Cape Canaveral.[41]

Fishing firms came and went with considerable

Lars Jorgensen and wife Marie with daughters Carrie, Laura, Inger, Anna Jorgensen Fredericks, and grandson, H. Edmond Fredericks, c. 1892. Natives of Denmark, the Jorgensen family emigrated first to Minnesota then to Grant in 1892. (Photo courtesy Grant Historical Society)

regularity and they sent their fleets to different points along the river depending upon the season and the habits of the fish. At Fort Pierce, for example, four firms were fishing there in 1895, but two of them closed and pulled out their boats in the late spring. That left F. B. Everett and Company and Robinson and Richardson who were there all year. J. F. Olmstead sold out to Robinson and Richardson and moved to Miami. Four fishermen from Cocoa moved their operation to Grant for the season of 1897-1898 and occupied an already existing fish house on the community dock.[42]

One of the larger fishing firms was started by the Ricou brothers who came to the St. Lucie area in 1882 about the same time that Scobie arrived. They gradually extended their operations to include 15 fish houses. By 1905 the wholesale house of R. R. Ricou and Sons was located at Jensen. The Ricous then formed a partnership with J. V. Gutermath at Grant where they built a new fish house on a long wharf and operated 12 boats, all equipped with Bridgeport motors. Gutermath was soon supervising the operation at Grant and another at Stuart. The company also operated at Fort Pierce as Ricou and O'Brien. Another fishing enterprise was formed when R. G. Hardee and A. M. Sample joined forces as the Sebastian Fish Company. They had 20 boats operating between that point and Fort Pierce. L. W. Doolittle founded the Atlantic Fish Company at Titusville in 1900. Other fish houses included Lars Jorgensen's at Grant and J. W. Rossiter's at Eau Gallie. Rossiter also supplied barrels for fish as well as other products after 1913.[43]

One of the great fish stories arose in 1901 when the legislature prohibited the use of seines in the Indian River. The new law brought an outcry of opposition from county residents who complained that their livelihood was being taken away. First the freezes destroyed the citrus and now the government was preventing them from fishing. Judge Minor S. Jones, the consummate politician even while wearing his judicial robes, brought temporary relief. When one of his neighbors appeared in court for having violated the law against seining, the judge decided that the mullet in question was not a fish. Before all onlookers he reportedly dissected a mullet, claiming that it differed from other creatures of the sea in that it had a gizzard. The accused had not, therefore, violated the law because he had caught mullet which more resembled chickens than fish. The ruling did not withstand the scrutiny of the Florida Supreme Court, but it abated the crisis while the case was awaiting review. It also caused mullet to be referred to for years as "Indian River Chicken."[44]

Like their neighbors in agriculture, the fishermen had difficulties with transportation and markets. To better their chances in these regards, most affiliated in the late 1890s with the Florida Fish Company, a Jacksonville based trust which marketed most of the fish from the Florida east coast. Supply and demand still fluctuated in mysterious ways. A number of fishermen were laid off in 1901 because the market was glutted. A year later the fishing industry was "paralyzed" for several weeks because of the scarcity of fish. It was a difficult job and a risky business, but many of Brevard County's early residents earned their living from the river. In later years even more would do so when the opening of new inlets gave them easier access to the ocean.[45]

The county had extensive stands of virgin pine which provided excellent raw material for another major industry. In the early days, people imported lumber or used that which could be salvaged from wrecked vessels, but sawmills were soon cropping up to supply the demands of local construction. The Gleason mill at Eau Gallie was typical of the early sawyers. The Phoenix Mill at Titusville provided lumber and added some novelty work. The Mims Brothers started a sawmill at Mims in 1886 with an order for lumber for the new schoolhouse. But, despite such local enterprise, lumber was still being imported in the late 1880s. T. Hatchett and D. L. Gaulden were selling

The county had extensive stands of virgin pine which provided excellent material for the lumber industry.
(Photo Brevard County Historical Commission Archives)

George Paddison started his lumber business in the 1880's. This building was on the corner of Columbus and Pineapple in Eau Gallie, c. 1892. (Photo courtesy Ruth Wynoma Paddison Gordon, Brevard County Historical Commission Archives)

"Georgia Yellow Pine Lumber" in late 1888. More and more, however, local mills handled the demand. L. C. Oliver bought out George F. Ensey and L. B. Bigelow in 1888 and cut locally. Joyner and Booth used logs from the Brevard County forests after 1889. The Indian River Lumber Company, managed by Robert Ranson after 1890, sold both local and imported products. Tom Johnson at LaGrange specialized in barrels for over 30 years. He was later joined by George W. Scobie, J. W. Rossiter, E. B. Sembler and B. W. Munshaw. George Paddison started a lumber business at Eau Gallie in the 1880s and soon had branches at Titusville and Fort Pierce. In 1902 the East Coast Lumber and Supply Company was incorporated with capital stock of $25,000. J. B. Conrad was president, Frank E. Bond was treasurer, and George F. Paddison was general manager. Chartered to "manufacture and sell lumber and builders' supplies," the firm has continued to do that along the Indian River.[46]

Forest industries changed by the 1890s as the demand for both yellow pine lumber and naval stores increased. The favored building lumber in earlier years had been

In 1902, East Coast Lumber and Supply was incorporated with George Paddison as general manager. Ruth Paddison Gordon writes, "Tissue paper for wrapping citrus fruit was in a building on the dock and it would get in the propellers of boats to the annoyance of the operators." (Photo courtesy Ruth Wynoma Paddison Gordon, Brevard County Historical Commission Archives)

white pine from the Great Lakes region, but that was being cut out by about the time of the Civil War. It was replaced by yellow pine which covered much of the southeastern United States. Large lumber firms had been working their way toward Florida and reached Brevard County in the latter years of the 19th century. The same was true of naval stores. The industry had started in North Carolina in colonial days and gradually spread southward. Large firms were acquiring extensive timber tracts in the county for both naval stores and lumber by the 1890s. Some firms concentrated entirely on saw timber, while others were concerned only with turpentine and rosin, but many of them worked both. It was not unusual for a timber firm to secure a large tract of pine land and work the trees for turpentine for three years or so. When the trees became weakened from the extraction of their sap, they would then be cut for the lumber that remained. All of these methods were applied in Brevard County. Whatever their specific product, most of them set up "company towns," often far out from any settlements. Employees lived in houses built by the company, bought supplies from the company store, and generally lived under the tutelage of the company managers. It was a difficult life for those who engaged in it willingly and it was especially onerous for the "convicts" who were leased by both state and local governments to the companies.

Although he cut cypress as well as pine, George Washington Hopkins was representative of the southward movement of the lumber industry. First cutting timber in Michigan, this Virginia-born entrepreneur later moved to South Carolina. After cutting out there he moved in 1900 to Brevard County where he acquired 104,000 acres of timber west of Melbourne. He erected a huge mill and company town and called it Hopkins. Company houses were built, a commissary was established where employees could purchase supplies with Hopkins Company scrip with which they were paid. The town had its own churches and school and the company furnished a doctor. Hopkins built a railroad upon which logs were hauled to the mills. The road eventually reached Deer Park in Osceola County where another company town was established. Spur lines were built as needed to reach the

G. W. *Hopkins erected a huge mill and company town called Hopkins west of Melbourne.* (Photo courtesy Weona Cleveland)

ever-diminishing supply of virgin timber. Huge quantities of pine and cypress lumber were cut and shipped by Hopkins' Union Cypress Company during the first quarter of the 20th century. The pine mill burned in 1923, but the cypress operation continued for a time. The mills are gone but much of the land is still in the possession of family members.[47]

The Pritchett brothers came from Dublin, Georgia, about 1904 and bought out an existing turpentine operation from Mrs. A. A. Monroe. They eventually had three large turpentine camps at Turnbull, Coquina, and Delespine, but they were also engaged in lumber on a large scale. In 1908 they bought the interests of Frank S. and George S. Battle in the Titusville Lumber Company. That purchase included a large milling operation valued at about $100,000 which could cut about 50,000 board feet a day. On a strip of land between the Florida East Coast Railway and the Indian River, they built a company town with about 60 houses for their white and black employees. With the large mill and work force, the Pritchetts expected to cut 130,000,000 board feet from a 20 mile stretch of timber land west of Titusville. Lumber was shipped over a ten mile company railroad to the Titusville-Sanford branch of the FEC.[48]

The Florida East Coast Turpentine Company came to Brevard in 1899. Owners were L. F. Durham, Frank E. Bond, and E. L. Bond, all of whom had extensive experience in the timber business. They expected to start work in 1900 with forty crops.[49] Other large turpentine operators included D. W. Munroe who worked a tract of the Delespine grant, using mostly convict laborers, and T. J. Shave and Company who started at Eau Gallie about 1903 with an initial 30,000 acres of virgin pine. McNair and Wooten was a large firm which leased 40,000 acres on the Delespine grant from the East Coast Realty Company and later worked the entire Segui grant on the northern edge of the county. Many other tracts were turpentined or logged by both large and small operators, but one other must be mentioned. Consolidated Naval Stores, one of the largest firms in the state of Florida bought a tract of more than 100,000 acres in the early 1900s. Located between the St. Johns and Kissimmee rivers, the tract was in both Brevard and Osceola counties.[50]

The Florida Extract Company got its product from a different kind of native plant. Organized by William Brown, cashier of the Bank of Titusville, C. A. Willihan, Allan N. Medd, and W. S. Branning, the firm extracted tannic acid from palmetto and sold it to firms in Germany as well as Chicago and other places in the United States. The fibre, which was a natural by-product of the operation, was once used by George M. Robbins to build a road on land that he was opening on the Delespine grant.[51]

Several real estate firms in the county were beginning to handle large tracts by the 1890s. One of the largest firms was James Pritchard's Indian River Real Estate at Titusville. C. B. and G. M. Magruder were at Rockledge and David Wingood had offices at Cocoa. B. J. and R. E. Mims had offices in Mims as well as Savannah, Georgia. Walter S. Graham and George M. Robbins were attorneys as well as real estate dealers. With A. A. Stewart and Minor S. Jones, they constituted the Brevard Abstract of Title Company. Graham subsequently moved to Miami, but the firm continued. One of the first drainage projects was a 2,000 acre tract west of Mims known as Long Swamp. The tract was acquired by the Indian River Loan and Investment Company through Robbins and Graham. Robbins and Graham also cooperated with Dwight W. Tuttle and Sidney Wilburt to form the Canaveral Land and Harbor Improvement Company with a capitalization of $5,000.[52]

A group of Orlando investors – including C. E. Cecil, Willis Palmer, and Matthew R. Marks – bought 112,000 acres of Brevard land from the Internal Improvement Board in 1891 for fifty cents per acre. They agreed to spend an additional $50,000 within the next six years in draining and reclaiming this "swamp and over-flowed land." A. D.

Russell's Cincinnatus Farms on the Fleming grant – mentioned earlier – was being drained by 1896. W. W. Russell, son of the owner, had 200 men working on a ten-mile railroad which was to carry the necessary drainage equipment to the site. Expected to be completed in two years, the project was hailed as a great boon to Sebastian and Brevard County. More will be said of this project and many more like it which began changing the topography of Brevard County in the early 20th century.[53]

End Notes

1. Tallahassee Floridian, February 12, 1889.
2. United States Senate, Executive Document No. 33, 47th C., 1st Sess., p. 14.
3. H. Harold Hume, Cultivation of Citrus Fruits (New York, 1951), pp. 57-58.
4. Charles A. Hentz, Autobiography, Volume 11, pp. 195, 202, 231, 315.
5. Ibid, p. 277, 315.
6. Titusville Florida Star, January 4, 1883, February 5, 1885, January 8, December 22, 1886, March 20, 1890.
7. Ibid., December 16, 1884, February 12, 1885, December 1, 22, 1886.
8. Ibid., January 5, 1888.
9. Jerry W. Weeks, "Florida Gold," (University of North Carolina Ph. D. Dissertation), p. 206.
10. Titusville Florida Star, October 28, December 16, 1892; Weeks, "Florida Gold," p. 206; Brevard Historical Commission, "Hatch Journal."
11. Titusville Florida Star, January 20, April 14, 1893.
12. Ibid., December 28, 1894, January 4, 25, 1895.
13. Ibid., February 8, 1895, March 8, 1895; Titusville Indian River Advocate, February 22, 1895, January 3, 1896; Brevard Historical Commission, "Hatch Journal."
14. Titusville Indian River Advocate, April 17, 1896, February 17, 1898, February 17, 1899; Titusville Florida Star, January 5, 900.
15. Titusville Florida star, September 22, November 17, 1899, January 5, June 29, August 10, 1900, February 22, November 8, 1901, January 17, 1902.
16. Ibid., February 1, 1907.
17. James T. Hopkins Fifty Years of Citrus: The Florida Citrus Exchange, 1909-1959 (Gainesville, 1960), pp. 1-5.
18. Titusville Florida Star, October 8, 1909.
19. Tallahassee Floridian, July 18, 1883.
20. Titusville East Coast Advocate, August 22, 1890; Tallahassee Floridian, August 7, 1888; Titusville Florida Star, February 1, 1885, April 28, 1887, January 5, 1888, September 3, 1891, December 28, 1894, January 1, 1897; Titusville Indian River Advocate, February 14, February 21, 1896.
21. Titusville Florida Star, February 8, 1895, January 7,1898, January 5, 1900, August 8, 1902; Titusville Indian River Advocate, January 7, 1898, February 17, 1899.
22. Kyle Van Landingham, Pictorial History of Saint Lucie County (St. Lucie County Historical Society, n.d.), p. 52, Titusville Florida Star, January 27, 1886.
23. Lucie to Mary, June 12, 1884. Copy in possession of Kyle Van Landingham, Riverview, Florida.
24. Tallahassee Floridian, August 16, 1885.
25. Titusville Florida Star, July 8, 1886, July 5, 1888.
26. Ibid., July 3, 1889, September 3, 1891; Titusville East Coast Advocate, August 22, 1890.
27. Titusville East Coast Advocate, August 22, 1890; Titusville Florida Star, May 29, 1890.
28. Van Landingham, Saint Lucie County, p. 20; Titusville Florida Star, December 16, 1892, May 12, 1893, January 19, 1894.
29. Titusville Florida Star, July 13, 1894.
30. Ibid., June 15, 1894, January 11, 1895, January 5, 1897, April 19, 1897.
31. Ibid., June 25, 1897, July 20, 1900, April 19, 1901.
32. Ibid., January 5, 1906.
33. Tallahassee Floridian, April 23, 1878, December 3, 1885.
34. Joe A. Akerman, Florida Cowman (Kissimmee, 1976), p. 129; Tallahassee Floridian, April 23, 1878.
35. Akerman, Florida Cowman, pp. 129, 151, 155; Tallahassee Floridian, October 2, 1883, August 4, 1899; Titusville Indian River Advocate, August 11, 1899.
36. Akerman, Florida Cowman, p. 129.
37. Ibid., p. 212.
38. Titusville Indian River Advocate, April 4, 1897.
39. United States Senate, Document No. 46, 54 C., 2nd S., passim.
40. Ibid.
41. Brevard County Commission, Reports, November 6, 1893.
42. Titusville Florida Star, March 18, April 5, 1895, October 15, 1897.
43. Titusville Indian River Advocate, August 3, 1900; Cocoa Florida Star, April 18, 1913; Titusville Florida Star, March 3, December 15, 1905; Titusville Star Advocate, May 8, 1933.
44. Titusville Florida Star, June 1, 11, 1897, Alfred J. Hanna & Kathryn A. Hanna, Florida's Golden Sands, (NY, 1950), p. 218.
45. Titusville Indian River Advocate, August 11, 1899; Titusville Florida Star, August 30, 1901, December 5, 1902.
46. Titusville Florida Star, November 11, 1885, August 18, 1887, January 5, 1888, October 9, 1890, June 15, 1890, June 27, 1902; Tallahassee Floridian, January 9, 1889.
47. Georgiana Greene Kjerulff, Tales of Old Brevard (Melbourne, 1972), pp. 70-73.
48. Titusville East Coast Advocate, November 11, July 24, 1904.
49. Titusville Indian River Advocate, September 8, 1899. In the turpentine business a crop was 10,200 trees. Each crop was worked by men who cut a face on the trunk of each tree and placed a cup to catch the sap. Each tree was visited weekly for 34 weeks. The extractions were poured into barrels and hauled to a still where they were heated to separate the turpentine and rosin. These products were then barreled and shipped. It was a dirty, difficult, and some times dangerous job, but many thousands of barrels of both turpentine and rosin were taken from the Brevard County forests during the half century or so after 1890.
50. Titusville East Coast Advocate, November 14, 1902, February 27, 1903.
51. Titusville Florida Star, June 18, 1897, January 19, 1900; Titusville East Coast Advocate, November 14, 1902, January 16, 1903.
52. Titusville Florida Star, February 9, 1887, April 4, 1889; Titusville East Coast Advocate, September 12, 1890; Tallahassee Floridian, June 13, 1891.
53. Titusville East Coast Advocate, January 2, 1891; Titusville Indian River Advocate, February 21, May 22, 1896.

Page 178 map: Atlas of Florida Growers map, 1914. (Brevard County Historical Commission Archives)

ATLANTIC
Daytona
Port Orange
Mosquito Inlet
New Smyrna
Hawks Park
Eldora
Oak Hill
Shiloh
Deland
Lake Helen
Orange City
Enterprise
Sanford
Ft. Reed
Geneva
Oviedo
Chuluota
Maitland
Winter Pk.
Orlando
Conway
Pine Castle
McKinnon
Englewood
Kissimmee
Narcoossee
Runnymede
Titusville
False Cape
Nathan
Cape Canaveral
Canaveral
City Pt.
Indianola
Merritt
Cocoa
Rockledge
Hartland
Eau Gallie
Melbourne
Melbourne Beach
Malabar
Orchid
Enos
Woodley
Toledo
Gifford
Indian River Inlet
St. Lucie
Fort Pierce
White City
Ankona
Eden
Stuart
Sewalls Pt.
Alicia
Gomez
W. Jupiter
Silver Springs
Ocklawaha
Astor
Clermont
Minneola
Harperville
Davenport
Haines City
Auburndale
Lakeland
Kathleen
Winter Haven
Eagle L.
Bartow
Pebble
Mulberry
Homeland
Ft. Meade
Bowling Green
Wauchula
Torrey
Avon Park
Scott
Zolfo
Frostproof
Reedy Lake
Ft. Arbuckle
L. Arbuckle
Pabor Lake
Fort Kissimmee
Ft. Vinton
Fort Drum
LUCIE
Camp Starvation
Fort Bassinger
Crewsville
Lake Istokpoga
Sweetwater
Calvinia
L. Frances
L. Stearn
DE SOTO
Arcadia
Phosphate
Lily
Nocatee
Hull
Ft. Ogden Cr.
Shell Creek
Cleveland
Indian Mound
Fish Eating Cr.
LAKE
OKEECHOBEE
Chaney B.
Ft. Van Swearinger
L. Annie
L. Huntley
L. Child
Lake Washington
L. Gentry
L. Winder
L. Conlin
L. Jackson
L. Marion
Whittier
Weahyakapka
Kissimmee River

12
Politics and Public Affairs: 1880 – 1905

Increasing population and decisive issues at both state and local levels kept the political cauldron simmering. Sometimes it came to a boil.

On the evening of December 12, 1895, most of the town of Titusville burned to the ground. View looking north on Washington Avenue. (Photo courtesy Robert Hudson, North Brevard Historical Society)

During the 25 years after Titusville became the seat of government, the county grew in population while it was reduced in physical size. Its great size had been a major reason for the election problems of the 1870s which had caused several local officials to be sentenced to prison. The problem was again emphasized in 1884 when Sheriff M. E. English set out on horseback to distribute "the necessary apparatus to run a well regulated poll." Upon his return to Titusville the sheriff had ridden 800 miles to reach all the precincts along the Indian River and on both sides of the St. Johns.[1] The problem was mitigated somewhat in 1887 when part of the county west of the St. Johns was detached and made part of the

County Judge John McCrory, Clerk of Court A. A. Stewart, and County Prosecutor D. L. Gaulden stand in front of Brevard's first county courthouse built in 1882. (Photo courtesy Jim Ball)

new Osceola County. When St. Lucie was established in 1905 with its northern boundary just abutting the Sebastian River, Brevard assumed its approximate present size.

During the same period, the United States government ceased its effort to support a Republican party in Florida and the Democratic party gradually emerged as the only political entity capable of winning statewide elections. Although the Republicans had always been a minority in Brevard County, the change in the state had its effect on the county. The unpopular 1868 Constitution had empowered the governor to appoint almost all local officials and as long as a Republican sat in the governor's chambers, Republicans had a good chance at local offices. After the Democrats captured the state house in 1877 and seemed likely to retain it, some Brevard Republicans changed their party affiliations.

Minor S. Jones of St. Lucie, for example, moved to Titusville in 1882, registered as a Democrat, and started the Indian River News in partnership with Judge J. A. McCrory to urge a constitutional convention. Jones, McCrory, and others who agreed with them wanted a more democratic document which would allow the people to elect their own local officials. Despite some reluctance on the part of white inhabitants in the northern Florida counties which had large black majorities, the voters approved a convention in 1884 and it met the following year. With Alexander Bell of St. Lucie and Henry L. Parker of Fort Drum representing Brevard County, the convention wrote a new constitution which limited the governors to single terms, made legislative sessions biennial, provided for a poll tax as a condition for voting, and permitted local option elections so that people could decide whether or not to permit the sale of alcohol in local jurisdictions. The governor's power to appoint local officials was curtailed, but he was still empowered to appoint county commissioners and school board members.[2] The poll tax was implemented by 1889 drastically reducing the number of black voters in the state. The Republican party became an insignificant minority party for the next several decades, although Brevard County citizens of that persuasion continued to hold conventions and nominate candidates for office in most elections.

These changes heralded what one historian has called "the era of the Democratic County leader."[3] Since the governor relied on local party members to recommend slates of candidates for appointment to those offices which he still controlled, the person who had the greatest influence on the local Democratic executive committee wielded considerable power in the county. By the 1890s that person in Brevard County was Minor S. Jones. He had the willing assistance of most of Brevard County's early leaders who readily accepted public service as an obligation.

In 1880 county officials included A. A. Stewart as clerk of court, J. Q. Stewart as assessor, and Francis M. Platt as collector. William Archer Cocke of Orange County was circuit judge and Abram St. Clair Abrams was state attorney. A. J. Whitlock was county judge, H. S. Williams was treasurer, and W. F. Richards was sheriff. W. S. Norwood was superintendent of schools while J. H. Sams, J. H. Tumlin, and George W. Holmes comprised the school board. The county commission was made up of P. E. Wager, H. L. Parker, J. H. Tumlin, Alexander Bell, and R. A. Hardee. The Democratic Executive Committee at that time was chaired by B. R. Wilson with Adhemar Brady as secretary. Other members were P. E. Wager, C. R. Carlin, H. L. Parker, and H. S. Williams. Its nominees for elective office that year were W. H. Sharpe for the state senate and H. L. Parker for assembly. Both were elected.[4]

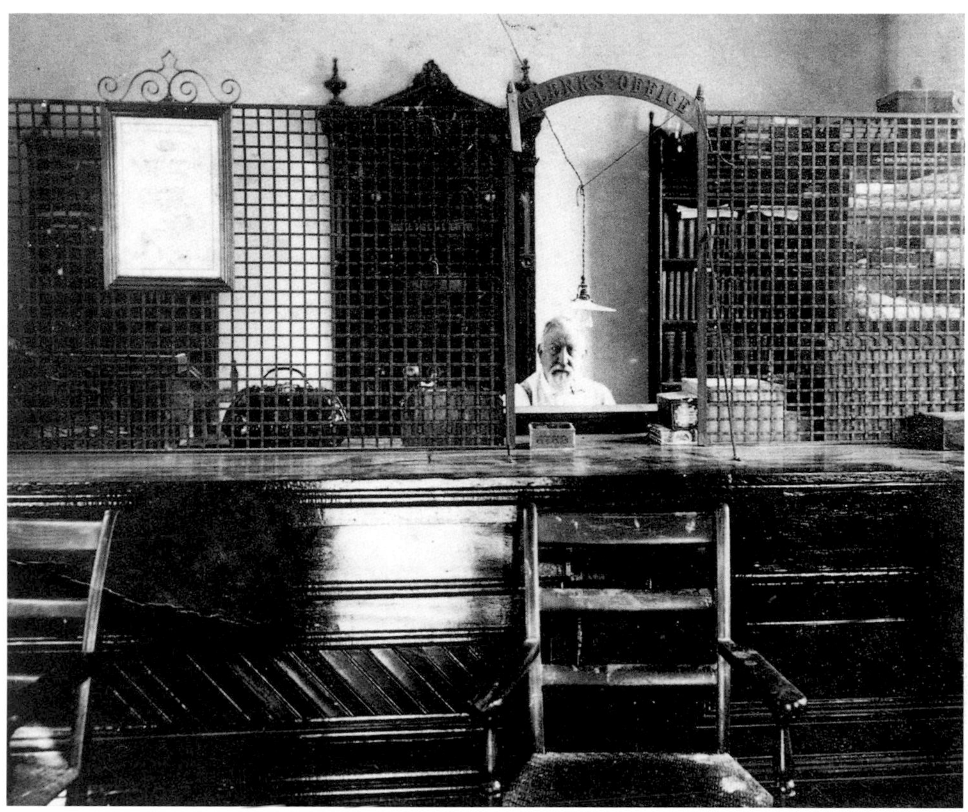

Titusville mayor, B. R. Wilson, *became involved in a bitter feud between Judge Minor Jones and Howell Titus. Mayor Wilson in the Titusville city office,* 1908. (*Photo courtesy Robert Hudson, North Brevard Historical Society*)

Sharpe served in the senate until 1885 when he was succeeded by H. S. Williams. Gardner Hardee was elected to the senate in 1889 and was followed by Robert S. Morrow in 1893. Brevard shared the senatorial district with Dade County and by the mid-1890s that county's population had grown so that the balance seems to have shifted southward. Perhaps that was why the district was represented by E. N. Dimick of Palm Beach from 1897 to 1901. Dimick was then succeeded by Fred M. Hudson of Miami who served several terms in that office after 1901. From 1881 to 1905, Brevard County was represented in the assembly in turn by Henry L. Parker, Francis M. Platt, Riley Johnson, William S. Norwood, H. T. Atkinson, Henry L. Parker, W. R. Sanders, R. A. Hardee, Henry L. Parker, K. B. Raulerson, and C. F. Olmstead.[5]

A county courthouse was completed in 1882 by Peter Fisher and Andrew Froscher. It had been preceded in 1880 by a jail built by F. B. Sackett at a cost of $565. An iron cell was added in 1885 and the county then claimed "as good a jail for the size [of the county] as there is in the state." Sheriff Richards was succeeded in 1883 by M. E. English who served until 1886. His deputy, E. H. Covar then became sheriff, but was removed by the governor for drunkenness the following year. The next sheriff was J. E.

Bowman who, despite some criticism of his activities in the mid-1890s, served until 1900. His successor was Joseph P. Brown.[6]

In 1881 Wallace R. Moses was tax assessor and W. R. Sanders of City Point succeeded him in 1883. D. W. McQuaig was then collector. County finances were beginning to improve by that time. The Titusville Star reported that the county warrants which "went begging for...25 to 30 cents on the dollar" in 1881 were commanding 75 to 80 cents in 1882.[7]

After ratification of the 1885 Constitution, the county was divided into specific commission districts with one person from each district being appointed by the governor. Robert Morrow became chairman of the commission and his colleagues included J. D. Vann, G. S. Hardee, P. D. Wesson, and T. E. Whaley. J. A. McCrory had served as county judge since 1881 and was succeeded by Minor Jones in 1887. Since his relocation to Titusville, Jones had become widely known as an attorney and businessman. He retained the position of county judge until his appoinment to the seventh circuit bench in 1898. He was then replaced as county judge by D. L. Gaulden, a prominent local attorney whose most recent position had been county prosecutor.[8]

Although it was unable to win offices at either the state or county level after 1882, the Republican party continued to hold conventions and sometimes name candidates for office throughout the remainder of the 19th century. Among those who remained with the party out of conviction were T. T. Wetmore and R. C. Scrimgeour of Titusville, C. J. Schoonmaker of Cocoa, Reverend Wilson of Rockledge, William H. Gleason and his sons of Eau Gallie, J. T. Hogg, C. H. Stewart, R. W. Goode, R. W. Ropode, W. M. Fee of Melbourne, C. W. Bolton and H. C. Starck of Malabar, and C. T. McCarty of Ankona.[9]

The political dominance of the Democratic party was not the same thing as political harmony, however. Decisive issues at both state and local levels kept the political caldron simmering and sometimes it came to a boil. One of the disruptive issues was the growing dissatisfaction among farmers and citrus growers about railroad freight rates and the handling of shipments of perishable products. Their discontent was voiced through the Farmers' Alliance which was first organized in Texas, came to Florida in 1888, and reached Brevard County in the early 1890s. The Alliance was originally intended as a social and educational organization with chapters at the county level guided by a statewide headquarters. It was immediately popular because it was open to entire families and featured social gatherings such as picnics and covered dish dinners at which people could gather and socialize. It also featured lecturers who spoke on agricultural improvement and other matters of interest to rural dwellers. Although it was not originally intended as a politically active organization, it was only natural that its meetings focused discussion on common problems. Before long the Farmers' Alliance had adopted a political program and the legislature was responding to it.

Most of Brevard's communities had alliances by 1890. Even tiny Tropic had a sub-alliance with 14 members. Both Mims and LaGrange had active organizations. The Courtenay branch, with Seabrook Sams as president and E. P. Porcher as secretary, was hailed with enthusiasm by its "lady members" who anticipated "some pleasant social evenings during the coming winter [of 1890]." Led by R. C. May, the Cocoa sub-alliance was especially active. Meetings were held by the sub-alliances about twice a month and the county organization met quarterly. The March 1891 quarterly session, for example, was held at the courthouse in Titusville and featured an address by C. B. Collins, the state lecturer for the Alliance. Officers for the year were elected and included R. C. May as president; T. J. Cockshutt vice president; F. G. Schell, lecturer; and M. S. Sams, secretary and treasurer. A committee on legislation and transportation was made up of Cockshutt, M. S. Sams, R. A. Conkling, F. Chappell, and May. Other active members were J. M. Miner, A. A. Stewart, and George Chester. Melbourne was chosen as the site for the June meeting.[10]

The Alliance was influential enough that a railroad commission was created by the 1890 legislature, although its effectiveness was limited because Governor Francis P. Fleming appointed to it men who were overly sympathetic to the railroads. The initial political success caused many Alliance men to call for a break with the Democrats and formation of a People's party. That move was not popular among Brevard County Democrats who maintained a united Democratic front. When the People's Party met and nominated Alonzo P. Baskin for governor and Austin S. Mann for lieutenant governor, most Brevard County Democrats supported the regular nominee, Henry Mitchell of Tampa, who also had been a member of the Alliance. Mitchell easily defeated Baskin and served as governor from 1893 to 1897. A more effective railroad commission was established in 1897 during the last year of his term.[11]

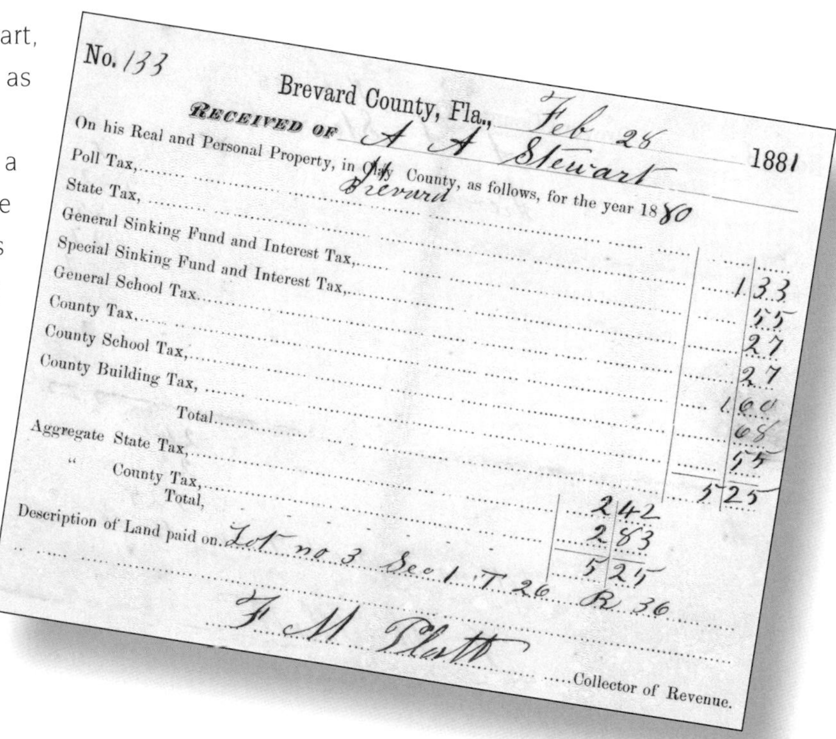

No. 133

Brevard County, Fla., Feb 28 1881

RECEIVED OF A A Stewart

On his Real and Personal Property, in ~~Clay~~ Brevard County, as follows, for the year 1880

Poll Tax,

State Tax,

General Sinking Fund and Interest Tax,

Special Sinking Fund and Interest Tax, 1.33

General School Tax, .55

County Tax, .27

County School Tax, .27

County Building Tax, 1.60

Total .68

Aggregate State Tax, 2.42 .55

" County Tax, 2.83

Total, 5.25 5.25

Description of Land paid on. Lot no. 3 Sec 1. T 26 R 36

F M Platt Collector of Revenue.

The $5.25 *tax receipt of clerk of court* A. A. *Stewart was signed by* F. M. *Platt, Tax Collector. (Courtesy Jim Ball)*

More complex and much closer to home was the controversy which erupted over county finances and the Brevard County Reform Association in 1892. Although there seem to have been several personal conflicts involved, the catalyst for the protest organization was the county commission's expenditure of $8,000 on the county jail and the resulting treasury deficit for 1892. The commission was made up of Robert S. Morrow as chairman and Adhemar Brady, William H. Sharpe, Cornthwaite J. Hector, and Comfort E. Chaffee as members. Brady wrote Governor Francis Fleming in late 1891 that Morrow was dominating the commission and pursuing a spending policy which was running the county into debt. Brady, who had a reputation for controversy, weakened his case with the governor when he complained that he could not muster the votes to deter Morrow. Fleming wrote then-Senator Gardner Hardee asking about the situation. Hardee explained his understanding of the Brady complaint and defended Morrow, saying that the two had settled on the Indian River at the same time in 1868 and that he [Gardner] had "known him favorably ever since." His letter was accompanied by an affidavit signed by most of the prominent leaders of the "Titusville Commissioner's District (Number Two)," expressing confidence in Morrow.[12]

The matter was not settled. Brady seems to have touched a tender spot in the county's political alignment since the Brevard County Reform Association was soon holding tempestuous meetings at several communities as far south as Malabar. The major complaint was the specific expenditures on the jail and the general criticism that more money was being spent than was being taken in. The discrepancy was not great. Tax Assessor W. R. Sanders reported that the assessed property evaluation of the county for 1892 was $1,657,836 which had produced revenues of nearly $50,000. Of that amount, $18,000 was for state purposes and the remaining $37,000 belonged to the county. The county shortfall was only about $1,200. That did not deter the complaints. There was little the reformers could do since the Democratic Executive Committee controlled nominations for the county commission. That body, with W. S. Norwood as chairman, Minor Jones as treasurer, and Henry B. Archibald as secretary, agreed with Morrow and the majority of the county commission.[13]

Unable to influence the governor to alter the county commission, the Brevard County Reform Association turned to the election for the state senate in which Robert Morrow was the regular candidate. Its membership hurriedly named E. P. Porcher – apparently without his knowledge – to oppose Morrow. Porcher wrote a letter to the Star declining the nomination. "I am not before the voters of this district for political preferment, or any office on any ticket," he declared. "I feel that we are under the heel of a clique in our own party and that proper 'reform' would have my sympathy...but the method adopted by the present 'reform party' of working in the dark and springing a ticket at the last moment...is not the way to go to work ...Those of us who are dissatisfied should have spoken up before. Now it is too late..."[14]

Morrow won the senate seat. His commission colleagues declared their pleasure at his election but bemoaned the loss to the commission. The reform association continued its campaign. At the Malabar school house an animated discussion of the complaints ensued in February 1893. Some of the spokesmen were R. A. Conkling, Frank P. Hassler, and Charles W. Bolton. A committee of H. C. Starck, C. W. Corbett and C. W. Arnold presented a resolution endorsing the Brevard County Reform Association and calling for the appointment of E. G. Vivell in place of C. J. Hector in that district. Another meeting at the Eureka Hotel in Eau Gallie was organized by Mayor Treutler and W. Wilson. The major speaker was John Aspinwall, and other participants included D. S. Bryan, John Carey, John Green, W. Roesch, and A. Bennett. They adopted a resolution condemning C. J. Hector.[15]

It is not clear that much was accomplished by the reform association. Apprised of the controversy in Brevard County, newly inaugurated Governor Henry Mitchell wrote a strong letter expressing his support of the Democratic Executive Committee and calling for a harmonious "Democratic Phalanx" in the county. Mitchell quickly approved the local committee's new slate of candidates for the county commission. It included Frank T. Budge in place of Robert Morrow who had gone to the state senate. Joseph Mendel in place of Adhemar Brady who had presumably caused the controversy, and William H. Sharpe, Cornthwaite J. Hector, and Comfort E. Chaffee, all holdovers from the previous commission. Hector was retained apparently because most of his vocal opponents were registered Republicans.[16]

The "Democratic Phalanx" did not last long. About the time that Governor Mitchell approved the new county commission, a bitter feud erupted between Judge Minor Jones and Howell Titus, his county prosecutor and erstwhile protege. All three of the elder Henry Titus' sons and his two daughters were still living in Brevard County in 1893. One daughter was married to George F. Ensey and lived at Tropic. Pierre Titus lived quietly at Titusville. Henry Titus was the town marshal there and, while he had a reputation for gambling and sympathy with the saloon keepers – a major issue at the time, he was generally respected for the way he carried out his official duties. Howell Titus had earned an unsavory reputation for his irresponsible conduct in his earlier years, but had made a marked change for the better in the late 1880s. Judge Jones had taken an interest in him, helped him obtain admission to the bar, and had backed him in a successful campaign for the prosecutor's office in 1892. Their relationship deteriorated rapidly after April 1893, when Howell Titus seems to have resumed the conduct which had earlier earned him a reputation as a "bulldozer."[17]

On April 13 Judge Jones, Senator Robert Morrow, and Representative Henry Parker wrote Governor Mitchell that they thought Titus was guilty of "conduct toward Mr. H. R. Olmstead, an old and inoffensive citizen of Eau Gallie, not only unbecoming an attorney and officer of the court, but also in gross violation of law."[18] When Jones wrote Titus suggesting that he resign his office, the battle was on. The "vigorous young man," as one observer described him, obtained affidavits from Olmstead and his wife which ostensibly exonerated him. The way in which the affidavits were obtained caused the judge to discount their value and he persisted in his efforts to oust Titus from office. In the meantime, Sheriff J. E. Bowman filed a complaint that Titus had accepted a bribe to drop a charge against Cullen Rhodes, a resident of Georgia, who had been arrested in Brevard County. The sheriff relented when Titus confronted him, and swore to a second affidavit which cast doubt on his original charge. In early September, Titus was drinking in the Losely and Renaker saloon and billiard room when one of Judge Jones' sons entered. The prosecuting attorney launched into a tirade of abuse toward the judge and several other prominent officials and then physically assaulted the younger Jones. Several patrons managed to separate the antagonists and Henry Titus, the town marshal, got his brother to go home.[19]

With both Judge Jones and the prosecuting attorney firing off lengthy letters to Governor Mitchell, the chief executive must have had a difficult time deciding how to respond. The judge, all of the attorneys in Titusville, and many prominent men of the county were warning that Howell Titus should be removed from office. At the same time, Mayor B. R. Wilson, who was then engaged in a heated re-election battle with William R. Sanders, the candidate of Judge Jones, sided with Titus. William S Norwood, chairman of the Democratic Executive Committee, also opposed the judge, who was by that time the most influential member of the committee. The Jacksonville Florida Times-Union even entered the affair on the side of Titus. In an apparent quandary, Mitchell wrote William H. Sharpe, a personal acquaintance, for an opinion. Sharpe replied candidly. He said that Jones was "a slate maker and in the conventions and primaries we fight each other and [he] having a strong influence with the saloons he downs me, but for all that we remain personal friends and I want to see the fair thing." He recounted the formerly close association of Jones and Titus, the apparent falling out, and Titus' propensity for bullying witnesses and those who disagreed with him. Sharpe concluded his letter with the comment that Jones was "a good officer and I think has no other object than that of the public good."[20]

In early November, J. D. Beggs, state attorney for the seventh judicial circuit, sent an urgent letter to the governor about Titus. "He is just terrorizing the people," Beggs wrote. The latest episode involved D. L. Gaulden, one of the attorneys of the county, whom Titus had assaulted on the street and then leveled a pistol at him threatening to kill. Beggs continued that "there are 3 Bros of them and of course they have a few sympathizers or hangers on, and they make it dangerous to those who differ from them. The sheriff is afraid (so I am informed) to take a positive stand and is afraid to perform his duty...I would not be surprised to hear...of persons being killed in Titusville." Beggs promised to report more fully from there.[21]

He need not have bothered. The governor had already dodged a decision. On November 11 he had decided there was not sufficient evidence to make out the charges against Titus. He stipulated that there had been a clear case of bribery in State vs. Cullen Rhodes, but the sheriff's conflicting affidavits clouded the charge. The governor went on to say that Titus' assault on "young Mr. Jones" was reprehensible but not to the extent that would warrant

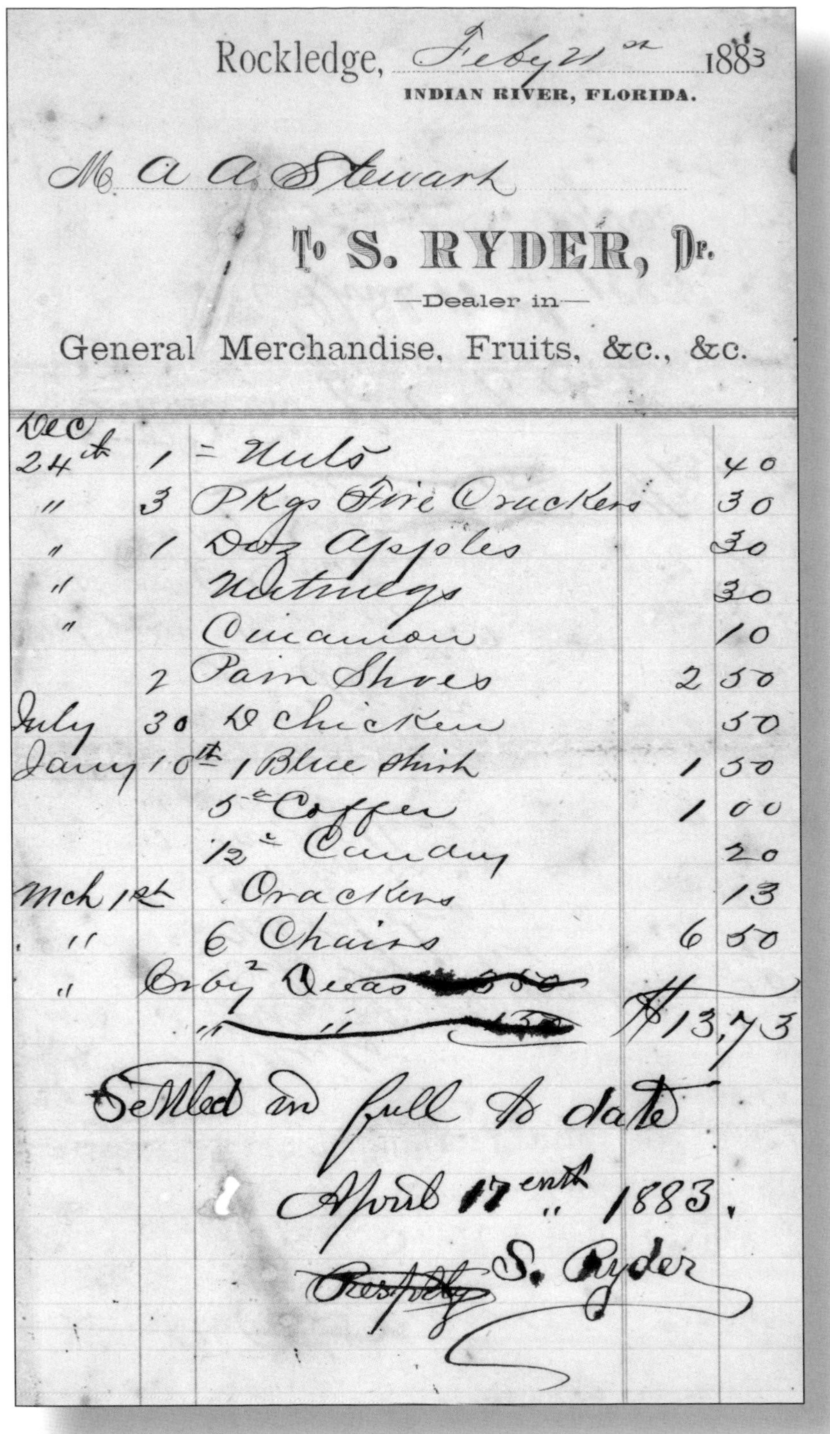

Rockledge, Feby 21st 1883
INDIAN RIVER, FLORIDA.

M A. A. Stewart

To S. RYDER, Dr.

—Dealer in—

General Merchandise, Fruits, &c., &c.

Dec 24th	1	Nuts	40
"	3	Pkgs Fire Crackers	30
"	1	Doz Apples	30
"		Nutmegs	30
"		Cinnamon	10
	2	Pair Shoes	2 50
July	30	Chicken	50
Jany	10th	1 Blue Shirt	1 50
		5 Coffee	1 00
		1/2 Candy	20
Mch 1st		Crackers	13
"		6 Chairs	6 50
			$13,73

Settled in full to date
April 17th 1883.
S. Ryder

1883 *prices are reflected in this bill from* T. S. *Ryder's store.* (Courtesy Jim Ball)

suspension from office. He concluded that there were insufficient charges for him to remove Titus, but there was need for a thorough investigation by the grand jury which could decide the issue. The grand jury did investigate and found no case against Titus. In a boastful letter to the governor on December 6, Titus castigated Jones for his role in the affair and promised that "he will never run this County anymore for the people are largely aware of his past rascality...[and] when the voice of the people shall be heard he will be relegated to private life for all time to come." The young attorney had his prognosis backward. Five years after this episode Minor Jones was elevated to the seventh judicial circuit bench and Howell Titus was reportedly living in Tennessee.[22]

Titusville was probably the most unruly town in Brevard County in the late 19th century and the period from 1892 to 1895 was certainly the most turbulent time in that town, but the problem of law enforcement was as broad as the county. One of the few cases involving both state and United States authorities occurred in 1884 when Sheriff English and Deputy Marshal Thomas arrested Postmaster Thomas New of New Haven for the state crime of selling liquor without a license and what the Tallahassee Floridian called "some post office crookedness." With all his problems, New was better off than Micco Postmaster John Bowie who was found in 1886 lying on the post office floor with a fatal gunshot wound in his head. He had been robbed and killed by Nathan McDonell and Thomas E. Brennan who were apprehended in Cocoa the next day and bound over for trial. E. H. Rice was obliged to resign as justice of the peace in 1885 because he was busy answering charges of manslaughter but he assured the governor that "I can prove my innocence."[23]

Brevard County was one of the first jurisdictions to call a "wet-dry" election after the 1885 Constitution became effective. With elections scheduled for September 1887, a sensational murder seems to have helped decide the outcome. A Titusville carpenter named Hoyt, described as "a good inoffensive man" was busy in his shop when a man named Cook, a "bartender in Purdy's Whisky Saloon," accosted him because his wife played the piano too loudly. When Hoyt demurred, Cook shot him dead. "A strong element of miserable whisky drinking men," as one indignant observer wrote, prevented Cook's arrest. Citizens from all along the river rushed to Titusville to see that justice was served. Amidst great excitement Cook was eventually arrested, convicted, and sentenced to prison. The Brevard County voters decided by a majority of 356 to 75 to stop liquor sales in the county. J. E. Bowman succeeded E. H. Covar who resigned as sheriff at that time. In his letter of resignation, Covar admitted his drunkenness, but explained that some one had spiked his drink.[24]

The sale of liquor became legal again in the early 1890s, and Titusville was quite generous in issuing licenses for saloons. In the meantime, the closing of Brevard County's saloons had created a new business which was difficult to eradicate. While the Melbourne News and Titusville Star were exchanging charges over Titusville's "reputation for saloons," County Commissioner C. J. Hector of Melbourne opened one of the county's numerous "blind tigers" on shore and sold liquor on his trade boats. He was still in business in that line at least as late as 1895. The Licensed Saloon Keepers' Association organized in the early 1890s to help suppress the illicit sale of liquor, but it apparently enjoyed only limited success. Meanwhile, Titusville regained its reputation as a wide-open town.[25]

In his 1928 memoirs, Robert Ranson described Titusville as a "tough town" in the 1890s, but he also explained that the railroad construction of that period added to the disorder in the county seat as well as the entire county. He estimated that there was approximately one murder for every mile of track built through Brevard County between 1892 and 1894. Perhaps the largest pitched battle in Titusville's history occurred in October 1892 when a large band of black railroad workers literally stormed the town. Trouble started when several blacks protested the arrest of one of their number for disorderly conduct. They began shooting up the town and robbing citizens of their money on the streets. The militia was called out immediately and a battle resulted in several deaths. As it turned out, one of the dead men was the notorious Jake McCulloch, who had been a fugitive from justice for several years. The riot had occurred on Saturday night and the fighting carried over to Sunday. It was unfortunate that several residents began drinking on the following Monday evening and decided to shoot up the black section of Titusville, even though the offenders had been from the railroad camp. The Star reported that "luckily no white man or inoffensive colored man were harmed."[26]

Shortly after the excitement over the Howell Titus affair subsided, Judge Jones was again obliged to take precipitate action. A black man had killed a white man at a sawmill near the Narrows and the sheriff had brought him to the county jail. Unfortunately, the murdered man's son also came to town and had instigated a lynch mob by early evening. Since the local militia was holding a meeting in a room above the jail, Judge Jones and Mayor B. R. Wilson asked Captain A. T. Feaster if he would keep his company in the hall throughout the night. While the guard held the attention of the mob, Jones and the sheriff took the prisoner to the railroad station from which the sheriff escorted him to the DeLand jail. Jones explained that he was aware that only the governor had authority to call out the militia but that "a lynching here would greatly injure our country and, besides, it is not certain that the negro is guilty." The governor concurred in the judge's action.[27]

Not every prisoner was so lucky. Charley "Kid" Harris, a black man accused of raping a six-year-old white girl in September 1896, was being taken by Sheriff Bowman and two deputies in a buggy to the Volusia County jail when they stopped for water at the Carlile home at Mims. They were surrounded by a crowd of men who took Harris from the sheriff's custody and shot and hanged him at Wolf's Crossing near LaGrange.[28]

On the evening of December 12, 1895, most of the town of Titusville burned to the ground. Most of the business district was destroyed and a total of 42 buildings were lost. The fire had started in the furniture and dry goods store of Simon Hamberg. While everyone was in shock at the loss, it was learned that Hamberg and J. B. Garner, his employee, had once been indicted for burning a building in Chicago. Rumors immediately circulated that the two had set fire to the store for the insurance. The town was soon in an uproar. Sheriff J. E. Bowman searched the home of the two men and apparently abused and insulted their wives in the process. Both men returned to their home early in the morning and surrendered to the sheriff and L. T. Coody, the town marshal. Discussion of lynching was rampant on the Titusville streets the next day and by nightfall Judge Jones once again decided to take the initiative. With Garner and Hamberg lodged in the county jail under charges of arson, Jones discovered that Sheriff Bowman was "so drunk that he had to go to bed and did not appear any more that night." Before the sheriff retired, Judge Jones had him deputize Marshal Coody and

The Indian River Guards, Company C of the 5th Battalion, State Militia, were mustered for local defense during the Spanish American War. (Photo courtesy Robert Hudson, North Brevard Historical Society)

several other citizens to guard the prisoners. Both the judge and Titusville Mayor William M. Brown remained with the deputies at the jail all night. The sheriff remained in an intoxicated state throughout the week-end and temporary deputies stayed on duty until Tuesday, December 17.[29]

Governor Mitchell then ordered the two prisoners removed to the Orlando jail, but that did not settle the matter. Fifty-nine Titusville citizens signed a petition to the county commissioners denying that the two men were in danger and demanding that they be returned to Titusville. The commission, then composed of William H. Sharpe, R. D. Hoke, Frank T. Budge, John Houston, and J. Mendel wrote the governor that they had investigated and had decided that the sheriff had never been incapacitated from drink and that there was no mob or unlawful assembly which ever threatened the safety of the prisoners. They assured the governor that there was no reason for keeping the prisoners in another county as they would be perfectly safe in "our own jail." Mayor Brown also wrote the governor that the threats of lynching were real enough and that the people who had circulated the petition only wanted to get their hands on the prisoners. Simon and Hamberg apparently remained in the Orlando jail and Titusville residents eventually returned to the task of rebuilding their decimated town.[30]

Caldwell "Clad" Stewart, Captain of the Indian River Guards, and Ellis Mims, c.1898. (Photo courtesy Jim Ball)

J. F. Wooten (1860 - 1909) moved to Rockledge in 1874 and was tax assessor for Brevard County in 1900. (Photo Florida State Archives)

While Brevard County was still struggling with the depression following the devastating freezes of the mid-1890s, news circulated that A. T. Feaster, the county treasurer and scion of one of the oldest families of LaGrange, was over $10,000 short in his accounts. That set off another furor. The Star castigated Feaster for allowing his expenditures to run so far behind his receipts. Others thought the difficult economic situation was partially to blame. State Attorney J. D. Beggs reviewed the situation and recommended Feaster's removal from office. Feaster had told Beggs that he "has nothing in the world...[and] would have to rely on friends." But Beggs was "afraid

Surveyor Elmer Robb of Fort Pierce, with crew Bruce Ryall, Arthur Kroegel, Gottlob Kroegel, Robert Ryall, George Vickers, all of Sebastian, circa 1910. (Photo courtesy Rodney Kroegel, Brevard County Historical Commission Archives)

his friends are in the same condition." Feaster was removed and the Democratic Executive Committee named Tom Johnson, N. N. Penney, and M. S. Sams a committee to recommend a successor. John Henry of Eau Gallie was their choice. Feaster was charged with embezzlement and was tried in January 1899. Admitting that he had handled his account carelessly, Feaster denied that he had wilfully embezzled the missing money. The jury found him innocent.[31]

The onset of the Spanish-American War caused considerable excitement in Brevard County and perhaps diverted attention from the austere economic conditions. About 50 Cubans with a "large stock of arms and ammunition" passed through Titusville in April 1897 on a train bound for Palm Beach where they intended to board a vessel for Cuba. The United States Coast Guard prevented them from going to sea and they returned to Titusville where they spent a day on their way back to Jacksonville. Most of the local citizenry was sympathetic with the men and their cause. Whether or not it was equally sympathetic, the coast guard was thorough in its search for vessels suspected of smuggling to Cuba. Charles Philipsen reported in early 1898 that torpedo boats were anchored in Canaveral Bight watching him closely as he worked his fish pound.[32]

When war was declared against Spain, coastal communities all along the Atlantic expressed alarm and asked for defense. The Star was laconic in reporting the war department's denial of aid: "Come to the East Coast of Florida if hostilities begin, as you will then be certain of absolute safety." The communities along the railroad were obliged to watch as one train after another transported soldiers from as far away as Montana and Texas to an encampment at Miami. Crowds cheered the troops as they stopped briefly at various Brevard County towns, but there were some drawbacks. The Star observed that "the war is firing the people's patriotism and the fires set by passing trains are firing more tangible things." It seems that four houses were burned at Malabar by fires from the trains and several other communities reported damage. When the state adjutant general called the state militia to active duty at Tampa, the Indian River Guards – Company C of the 5th Battalion – marched off 29 strong under the command of Captain C. R. Stewart. Home guards were organized in all of the river towns. The closest any of them came to action, however, was when a detachment from Miami came looking for deserters and found two at Sarno. The Spanish-American War was over late in the summer in which it began. The Spanish were defeated, Cuba was liberated, and everyone had their attention diverted, however briefly, from their economic woes.[33]

By the turn of the century there were signs of economic recovery, the legislature was enacting laws making it possible for local governments to bond themselves for public improvements, and the people seemed ready and willing to pay for better roads and schools. State laws had also removed the appointive powers of the governor and voters were able to vote directly for their own officials. The school board had been made elective in 1894 and county commissioners followed them in 1900.

The last appointive county commission was composed of J. R. Walker as chairman and William H. Sharpe, Joseph Mendel, John Houston, and J. N. Waller as members. Other county officials as of 1900 were D. L. Gaulden, county judge; M. Goldsmith, prosecuting attorney; A. A. Stewart, clerk of court; J. F. Wooten, tax assessor; E. W. Hall, tax collector; John Henry, treasurer; J. O. Fries, county surveyor; T. J. Cockshutt, supervisor of voter registration. J. H. Sams was still superintendent of public instruction, soon to be succeeded by R. E. Mims. J. P. Brown had recently replaced J. E. Bowman as sheriff.[34]

The move to elected commissioners was accompanied by a redistricting to reflect recent population changes. With about 1,400 voters in the county, lines were drawn to place about 280 in each district. The first district included the LaGrange, Titusville and Haulover precincts. District two was made up of City Point, Cocoa, Merritt, Canaveral and Georgiana. District three comprised Eau Gallie, Melbourne, Malabar, Micco, Banyan and Sebastian. The fourth district was Narrows, Woodley, Fort Pierce and Fort Drum. The fifth included Eden, Ankona and White City.[35]

There had long been concern for better public roads, but plans for a county road had been interrupted by the great freezes. Interest resumed in the late 1890s. At that time, each of the five county commissioners' districts also constituted a road district. A three mill tax was being levied for public roads, but individuals were still expected

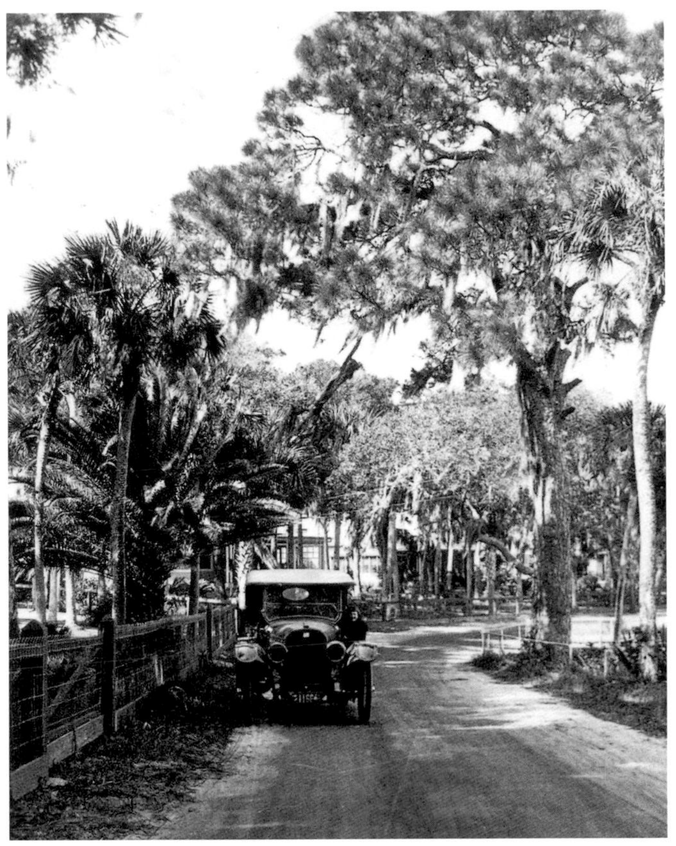

At Cocoa and Rockledge a drive was opened along the bank of the river which soon became a tourist attraction. (Photo courtesy Doug Hendriksen)

to donate rights-of-way without compensation. If a community desired a road, it was still customary for a delegation to ask the commission for it. If approved, a three-member committee of local citizens were still expected to become a road commission for that particular purpose. The county road running the entire length of the county was built and maintained for a time in the same fashion. The issue in the late 1890s involved, not only new roads and route changes, but improvement in the quality of the roads whether new or already existing.[36]

The commission sent C. A. Robinson of Eden; E. B. Wager and C. H. Walton of Titusville; J. F. Wooten of Cocoa; and E. D. Oslin of Melbourne to the second Good Roads Convention at Orlando in February, 1897. They returned with high hopes and urged local road organizations which

Shell from the Indian mounds along the river was the most common paving material. Here the last of Barker's Bluff mound is removed in 1912. The shell from this one mound paved 75 miles of road. (Photo courtesy Rodney Kroegel, Brevard County Historical Commission Archives)

were soon meeting. Fifty-nine property owners met at Fort Pierce soon after the Orlando convention and encouraged opening of a public road between that town and Waveland at the southern border of the county. A few days later a road association at Eden called for legislative action to permit bonding for a shell road. A Malabar group appointed H. C. Starck, F. W. Comstock, and G. W. Washburn a committee to lay out their part of a public road. They urged the laying of a shell surface from Malabar to Tillman. At Cocoa and Rockledge a drive was opened along the bank of the river which soon became a tourist attraction. R. A. Hardee began building a road with private funds to run westward from Sebastian. It was hailed as a competing route to the Sebastian and Cincinnatus Farms railroad which had been opened in the 1890s.[37]

By 1900 shell had been decided upon as the most desirable road material which was available in Brevard County. A 14-mile shell road was completed from Titusville to Hardeeville along the banks of the Indian River that year. Noting the "evidence of returning prosperity," the Star applauded those who were pushing completion of the extension of that road from Hardeeville to Cocoa "before the return of the winter visitors in 1901." It also reported an extension of the road for a half mile between Sharpes and the Florida East Coast station and thanked the FEC for changing the station's name from Faustina to Sharpes. Taxpayers of the 5th district arranged for an advance of money against a 1902 special road levy and shelled their part of the road between Fort Pierce and Waveland (about 15 miles) with an extension to Tibbals to the north. Having previously used shells from the numerous Indian mounds along the river, the commission in 1902 delegated C. T. McCarty as its agent to purchase 20 acres of rock land in Dade County. The rock was intended for use on future county roads. By that time the county road leading from the north to the south boundaries of the county was open and there were bridges across all the streams as well. In 1905 the county boasted "more completed miles of good road along the coast than Volusia." There was a continuous good road for 125 miles "and only at intervals here and there is there a break."[38]

The school consolidation movement was mentioned in an earlier chapter. That move was encouraged by an 1899 school law which allowed the people to decide whether they wished to create special school tax districts in which they might levy additional taxes of three mills to add to the regular county levy. Every precinct in Brevard County approved the measure. Consolidated schools were shortly in operation at Titusville, Cocoa and Fort Pierce, although the building at the latter place was destroyed by fire in

1901. This change necessitated "a regularly employed conveyance to bring the pupils to school in the morning and take them home." "School busing" has a venerable heritage in Florida and it had its critics even in the early days. Because 24 pupils were obliged to crowd into the school wagon at Eden, it was called the "Sardine Express." Some difficulties seemed ageless. At a 1901 meeting the school board announced that it had no objection to use of the school building for religious services where there were no church edifices, but it "positively prohibited anyone from using our school buildings...for dancing."[39]

A school bus took students to the newly consolidated school in Cocoa after 1901. (Photo courtesy Grace Packard Bryant)

There had been almost no opposition in 1887 when a portion of the county was detached and made part of Osceola County. The question of creating a new county from the southern portion of Brevard was a different matter. There was talk of county division in 1888 when the Melbourne newspaper attacked Titusville for its reputation as a haven for saloons and disreputable behavior, but that seems not to have been serious. That was not the case when residents in the southern part of the county began talking in 1889 of the rapid settlement of Indian River Narrows, St. Lucie, Fort Pierce, Ankona and neighboring communities along the river. People from the river westward to Fort Drum began voicing their desires for a new county. Perhaps because of the precarious position of Titusville in the northern part of a county which extended many miles to the south, the Titusville Florida Star favored the division of the county at the section line between townships 29 and 30. The paper noted that the valuation of real property south of that line and the Sebastian River amounted to $300,000 which was sufficient to produce revenue for county expenses. A county seat at Fort Pierce, the Star continued, would be advantageous to all residents since Brevard County was obliged to pay mileage for official travel between Titusville and the southern part of the county. Little was heard of county division for several more years, but there was a call in 1895 for rearrangement of commission districts better to serve the growing population in the south. A more strident message came from Fort Pierce in 1897 when a mass meeting resolved that its members were "in dead earnest this time and if Titusville wants to retain the county seat they will second the movement."[40]

The matter reached serious proportions in the early 1900s. By that time residents of the northern part of the county were largely in opposition. Petitions were circulated in the Cocoa and Rockledge area in early 1905 asking Senator Fred Hudson and Representative C. F. Olmstead to oppose legislation calling for division. Sheriff J.P. Brown rode through the entire county gathering petition signatures in opposition. A reporter from Eden expressed surprise at the number of his neighbors who opposed division. The Titusville East Coast Advocate

Merritt Island students arrived at school in Cocoa by boat. (*Photo Brevard County Historical Commission Archives*)

expressed unequivocal opposition because "the county is not populous, and not wealthy." It suggested that the pro-division Fort Pierce News note that 47 of the largest taxpayers south of its town signed petitions against division. But the momentum was too great. Both Senator Hudson who represented the 13th senatorial district and C. F. Olmstead, Brevard's assembly representative, introduced bills in the 1905 legislative session calling for a new county to be called St. Lucie. The legislation passed easily and was signed into law. Brevard's new southern boundary was drawn at the section line between townships 30 and 31 running eastward to the south fork of the Saint Sebastian River, down that stream to the Indian River, south along its eastern shore back to the original section line and then easterly to the Atlantic Ocean.[41]

END NOTES

1. Tallahassee Floridian, October 21, 1884.
2. Proceedings of the Constitutional Convention of Florida, 1885.
3. Edward C. Williamson, Florida Politics in the Gilded Age: 1877-1893 (Gainesville: 1976).
4. Titusville Florida Star, October 13, 20, 1880; Florida Senate Journal, 188l.
5. Florida House Journal, 1881-1903; Florida Senate Journal, 1881-1905; Laws of Florida, 1881-1905.
6. Tallahassee Floridian, August 22, 1882, October 8, 1885; Titusville Florida Star, February 14, October 11, 1882; Titusville Star Advocate, July 1, 1930, October 29, 1940.
7. Tallahassee Floridian, February 7, 1882; Florida State Archives, Record Group 101, Series 577, Box 5, Senate Confirmations, 1881, 1883.
8. Titusville Florida Star, January 12, 1887, June 30, 1887, November 11, 1898; Florida State Archives, RG 101, S577, Box 5, and S578, Box 1, Senate Confirmations.
9. Titusville Florida Star, March 20, 1884, January 12, 1890, May 3, 1898, November 11, 1898, Titusville East Coast Advocate, October 17, 1890.
10. Titusville Florida Star, January 30, October 16, 23, November 6, 1890, January 1, 1891; Titusville East Coast Advocate, October 17, 1890, March 13, 1891.
11. Titusville Florida Star, October 25, 28, 1892; Titusville East Coast Advocate, November 4, 1892.
12. Governor Fleming, December 25, 1892, and A. Brady to Fleming, December 10, 1891; Titusville Florida Star, February 24, 1893.
13. Titusville Florida Star, April 16, October 7, 1892.
14. Ibid., October 7, 1892.
15. Titusville East Coast Advocate, February 17, 1893; Titusville Florida Star, February 24, April 7, 1893.
16. Florida State Archives, RG 101, S581, W. S. Norwood, Minor S. Jones, and Henry B. Archibald to Governor Mitchell, March 9, and April 3, 1893; Titusville Florida Star, April 7, May 26, 1893.
17. Florida State Archives, RG 101, S581, Box 10, William H. Sharpe to Governor Mitchell, October 8, 1893.
18. Florida State Archives, RG 101, S581, Box 10, Minor Jones, Henry Parker and Robert Morrow to Mitchell, April 13, 1893.
19. Ibid., Affidavit of F. A. Losley, September 15, 1893.
20. Ibid., Sharpe to Mitchell, October 8, 1893; Jones to Mitchell, September 25, 1893; Titus to Mitchell, September, 1893.
21. Ibid., J. D. Beggs to Governor, November 16, 1893.
22. Ibid., Governor to Judge Jones, November 11, 1893; Titus to Governor, December 6, 1893.
23. Tallahassee Floridian, August 5, 12, 1884, August 12, 1886; Florida State Archives, RG 150, S24, Box 6, Rice to Governor Perry, March 31, 1885.
24. Charles A. Hentz, Autobiography, Volume II, pp. 289-290; Florida State Archives, RG 150, S24, Box 6, E. H. Covar to Governor E. A. Perry, October 12, 1887, Titusville Florida Star, September 15, 1887.
25. Titusville Florida Star, July 26, 1888, May 11, July 13, 1894.
26. Ibid., October 28, 1892; Titusville Star Advocate, June 12, 1928.
27. Florida State Archives, RG 101, S581, Box 14, Jones to Mitchell, March 14, 15, 1894.
28. Titusville Indian River Advocate, September 18, 1896.
29. Ibid., December 13, 1895; Florida State Archives, RG 101, S581, Affidavit of L. T. Coody.
30. Florida State Archives, RG 101, S581, Box 10, Affidavits of L. T. Coody, John Myers, Henry J. Anthony, Emma A. Hamberg, Agnes Garner, and Dr. B. L. Wills, December 17, 1895, Petitions to County Commission and Governor Henry L. Mitchell, and William M. Brown to Mitchell, December 27, 1895; Titusville Indian River Advocate, January 3, 1896.
31. Titusville Florida Star, October 15, 1897; Titusville Indian River Advocate, January 27, 1899; Florida State Archives, RG 101, S578, Box 9, J. D. Beggs to Governor Bloxham, October 14, 1897.
32. Titusville Indian River Advocate, April 16. 1897, February 18, 1898
33. Titusville Florida Star, April 22, May 13, 1898; Titusville Indian River Advocate, April 29, July 1, 29, 1898.
34. Titusville Florida Star, July 13, 1894, April 20, 1900.
35. Ibid., May 10, 1901.
36. Brevard County Commission, Reports, July 7, 1891.
37. Titusville Indian River Advocate, January 22, 1897; Titusville Florida Star, January 29, February 5, May 21, June 11, 1897, May 13, 1898; Florida State Archives, RG 101, S581, Box 2, W. C. Braddock and James A. Grove to Governor, June 30, 1890.
38. Titusville Florida Star, November 10, 1899, April 6, 1900, May 10, 1901, December 26, 1902, January 13, 1905; Titusville East Coast Advocate, October 24, 1902, Titusville Indian River Advocate, May 5, 1900.
39. Titusville Florida Star, June 29, 1900, February 22, April 5, May 10, 1901; Titusville East Coast Advocate, January 19, 1904.
40. Titusville Florida Star, March 2, 1889, January 29, 1897.
41. Ibid., March 24, May 26, 1905; Titusville East Coast Advocate, April 21, 28, 1905; Laws of Florida, 1905, p. 404; Kyle Van Landingham, Pictorial History of St. Lucie County, 1565-1910, p. 42, (St. Lucie County Historical Society, n.d.).

Page 200 Map: The 1907 Rand McNally map shows Brevard County's new southern boundary set in 1905 at the Sebastian River. (Florida State Archives)

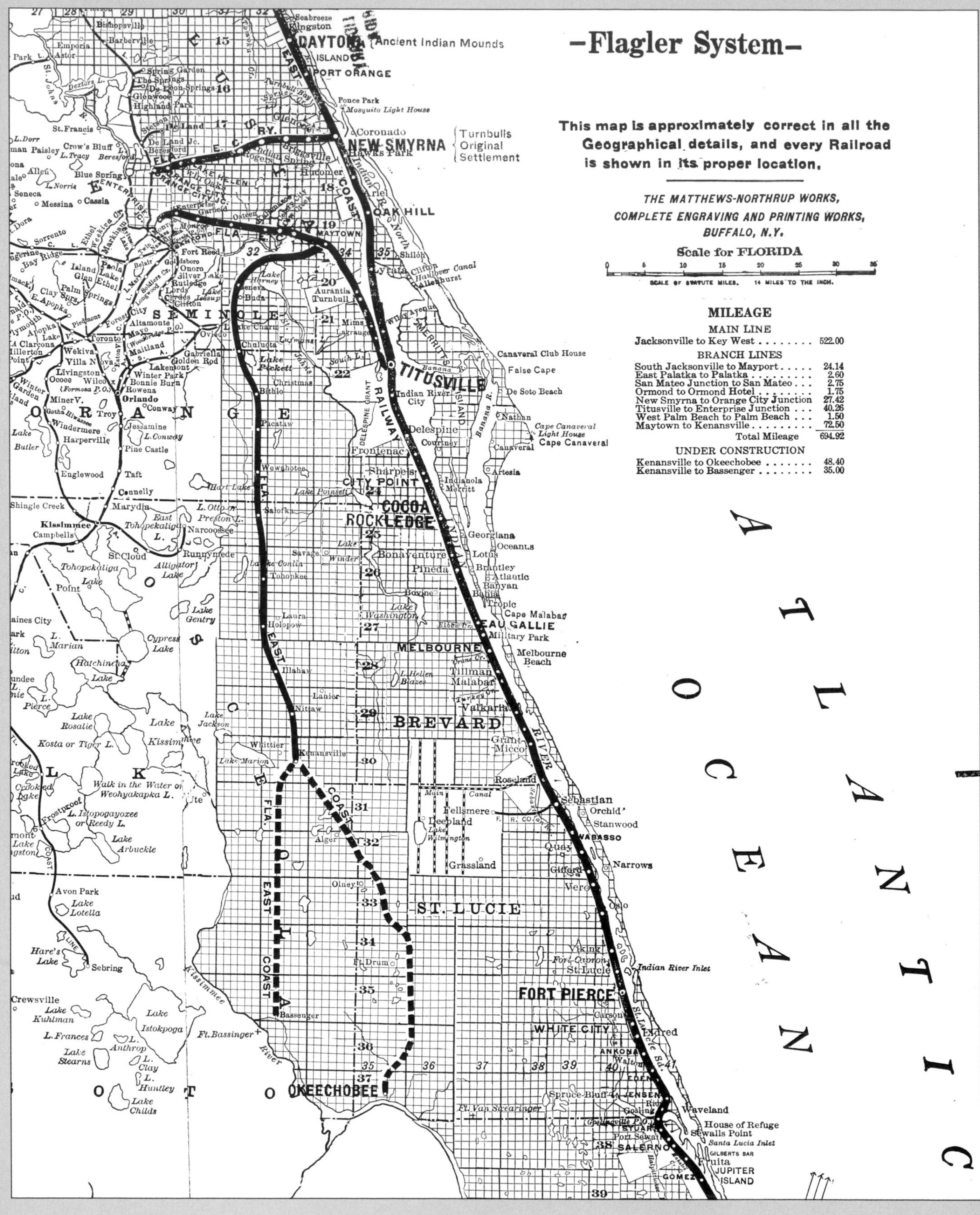
-Flagler System-
This map is approximately correct in all the Geographical details, and every Railroad is shown in its proper location.
THE MATTHEWS-NORTHRUP WORKS,
COMPLETE ENGRAVING AND PRINTING WORKS,
BUFFALO, N.Y.
Scale for FLORIDA
0 5 10 15 20 25 30 35
SCALE OF STATUTE MILES. 14 MILES TO THE INCH.
MILEAGE
MAIN LINE
Jacksonville to Key West 522.00
BRANCH LINES
South Jacksonville to Mayport 24.14
East Palatka to Palatka 2.60
San Mateo Junction to San Mateo ... 2.75
Ormond to Ormond Hotel 1.75
New Smyrna to Orange City Junction 27.42
Titusville to Enterprise Junction ... 40.26
West Palm Beach to Palm Beach ... 1.50
Maytown to Kenansville 72.50
Total Mileage 694.92
UNDER CONSTRUCTION
Kenansville to Okeechobee 48.40
Kenansville to Bassenger 35.00
ATLANTIC OCEAN
DAYTONA
Ancient Indian Mounds
PORT ORANGE
Mosquito Light House
NEW SMYRNA
Turnbulls Original Settlement
OAK HILL
MAYTOWN
TITUSVILLE
COCOA
ROCKLEDGE
EAU GALLIE
MELBOURNE
BREVARD
ST. LUCIE
FORT PIERCE
WHITE CITY
OKEECHOBEE
SEMINOLE
ORANGE
OSCEOLA
Orlando
Kissimmee
Cape Canaveral
Sebastian
Jupiter Island

13
Politics, Progress, Work and Play: 1905 – 1920

The railroad, automobile, telephone and other technological innovations were transforming the Indian River area into a more complex society with a need for expanded government services.

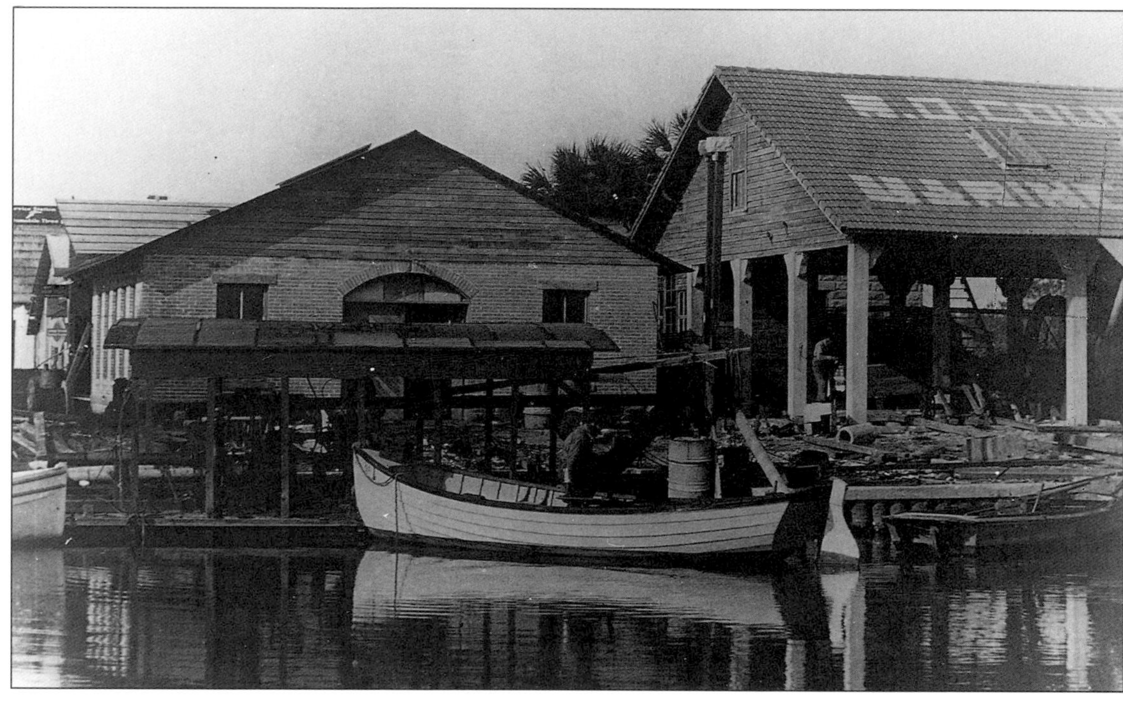

In addition to fishing, boat building and repair became important industries in Brevard County. Couch Manufacturing Company installed marine engines at Grant. (Photo by Hollis Bottomley, Grant Historical Society)

The early years of the 20th century were optimistic ones for the United States. Progress was the spirit of the time. People believed that they could improve themselves and their society by the hard work and self-reliance which were traditional to Americans and by adapting the plethora of technological innovations which were becoming available. The automobile, the telephone, and a constant array of new uses for electricity were transforming a society which eagerly accepted the new innovations. Greater reliance on these inventions increased the complexity of society and augured for a greater degree of collective action. People began looking toward government at all levels to provide the coordination

Paul Kroegel (1864-1948), *citrus grower and boat builder, was the first ranger of* Pelican Island. *Paul Kroegel with his wife* Ila Lawson Kroegel, *c.* 1910. *(Photo by* Rodney Kroegel, Brevard County Historical Commission Archives)

for a more complex society. While these meant some restraints on personal choice in exchange for expanded government services, most people in the early 1900s thought it a worthwhile concession. An early example was the 1903 creation of the wildlife refuge at Pelican Island. Accidentally catapulted into the presidency by the assassination of William McKinley, Theodore Roosevelt soon became the national symbol of early 20th century progressivism. He not only called on Americans to increase the scope of their governments to provide more services, but he also began a program of conservation of forests, wildlife, and other natural resources. Pelican Island was one of the first of many tracts which the national government set aside for our common benefit and represented the arrival of the progressive movement in Brevard County.

While Roosevelt's energetic leadership provided an impetus, progressivism was nevertheless more of a grass roots movement than a national one. It was at the local level that governments began to expand their services beyond the traditional limits of the previous century. The changes were already underway when Brevard County was reduced in 1905 to near its present size. There was no sudden departure, but change was comparatively rapid and by the end of the first world war in 1919, the county had changed considerably from the way it had been at the turn of the 20th century.

Many familiar names filled the rosters of Brevard County government in 1905. A. A. Stewart was still clerk of the court after 25 years of service. B. R. Wilson had become the county judge in place of D. L. Gaulden who resumed his old position as county prosecutor. Joseph P. Brown was still sheriff. John Henry retained the office of treasurer while E. W. Wall was collector and P. A. MacMillan served as assessor. W. S. Norwood was supervisor of voter registration, a position in which he alternated over the years with Thomas Johnson Cockshutt, the longtime LaGrange resident. County commissioners were W. R. Walker, first district; John R. Miot, second district; R. A. Conkling, third district; J. C. Jones, fourth district; and J. F. Bell, fifth district. The entire county school administration was new. The old school board members, J. M. Dixon, R. N. Andrews, and J. E. Fultz, all stepped down in 1905, along with Superintendent R. E. Mims. J. R. Walker

In 1903 President Theodore Roosevelt named Pelican Island as a National Wildlife Refuge. (Photo *by* Paul Kroegel, *courtesy* Rodney Kroegel, Brevard County Historical Commission Archives)

resigned from the county commission to become the new school superintendent. The new board consisted of A. J. Carter, R. E. Mims and E. B. Arnold.[1]

In 1905 Cocoa began urging the relocation of the county seat and offered itself as a suitable site. (*Photo Brevard County Historical Commission Archives*)

Shortly after the reduction of Brevard County's boundaries in 1905, Cocoa began urging the relocation of the county seat and offered itself as a suitable site. The issue was placed on the ballot in 1908 and Cocoa citizens raised $5,000 toward a new county building if their city were chosen. Eau Gallie residents then argued that their town should be the new county site since it was the most centrally located. Situated just at the mouth of the Banana River it was accessible to the people of that section "which is destined in the near future to be a thickly populated section." A vigorous registration drive increased the number of voters to more than 1,000 out of a population of about 4,000. Many blacks, deprived of the opportunity to vote in the Democratic primaries since 1901, availed themselves of the opportunity to take part in this non-partisan election. The contest was quite exciting and 955 votes were cast. With 498 votes to 372 for Cocoa and 85 for Eau Gallie, Titusville retained the county seat. The northern precincts voted overwhelmingly for Titusville while some of the southern precincts split. Melbourne, for example, cast 22 votes out of 55 for Titusville and Eau Gallie, oddly enough, voted 20 to nine in favor of leaving the county seat where it was. Although the issue was largely one of north Brevard versus south Brevard, the votes from Melbourne and Eau Gallie gave Titusville its majority of 41over the two other towns. "Some unpleasant feeling" was expressed at Cocoa "in connection with the building of a new court house" in 1912. The new edifice was turned over to the county in March 1913 at a cost of $30,566.[2] The new court house was scarcely finished before the Arnolds, Platts, and a few other south Brevard residents began calling for a county of their own with Melbourne as the seat of government. The movement failed primarily because many citizens felt the population simply too small to support another division.[3]

Elections were quite frequent in 1908. As soon as the county seat question was settled in August, voters turned to the general elections. The most important race was between William Jennings Bryan and William Howard Taft for president. Assisted by a two to one majority from the voters of Titusville, Bryan carried the county, but Melbourne and Cocoa both gave majorities to Republican Taft. Melbourne had frequently voted for Republican presidential candidates, but 1908 was the first time that Cocoa had done so. There was some surprise that the Canaveral precinct gave a plurality for the electors of the minority Socialist Party. The final count gave the Democrats 294 votes while the Republicans received 225 and the Socialists 50.[4]

The general elections were followed shortly by another "wet-dry" decision. When a petition for such an election received the requisite number of signatures in September,

The new courthouse was turned over to the county in March 1913 *at a cost of* $30,566. (*Photo courtesy* Doug *Hendriksen*)

an election was called for late December. As president of the Brevard County Anti-Saloon League, Dr. George W. Holmes called on the membership to "keep the county dry." The November vote was about five to one in favor of a continued dry county.[5]

Although black Brevard citizens continued to vote in non-partisan and general elections, they were denied the right to help select most of the county and state officials after 1901. The Democratic party had ruled in 1900 that only white people could vote in its primaries. The legislature of 1901 followed with a law requiring primary elections for the nomination of party candidates. Since the Republican party was a distinct minority in the county and the state, the two measures meant that Democratic primaries would decide who filled the offices and that only white voters could participate in them. Brevard County participated in the development of a system of "Jim Crow" laws which prescribed rigid segregation of the races in almost all aspects of daily life. The extent of that separation was emphasized in 1906 when the grand jury called on the county to separate "white and colored prisoners" in the county jail.[6]

Racial distinctions were less clear in the case of Asians. When several Japanese families began settling on farms west of Eau Gallie in 1909, the school board members voted to deny their children access to the public schools. Their constituents rebelled. Thirty-five patrons of the Eau Gallie school signed a petition demanding that the Japanese children be admitted. The board relented, but ruled that a special school would be created as soon as there were ten Japanese children of school age.[7]

Schools were receiving increasing support at all levels of government. The state was urging longer school terms, improved curricula, mandatory attendance, and better

Schools were receiving increasing support at all levels of government. This 1912 photo shows students in Eva Wooten's class, Cocoa. (Photo by Merwin Wooten, Florida State Archives)

teacher training. The national government added its effort with provisions for agricultural and home economics courses in the schools. With United States government assistance, County Agent Alf S. Nielsen promoted Corn Clubs and Pig Clubs in the schools to encourage students to learn about improved farming and animal husbandry methods. A companion program enabled Mrs. Walter Gay of Melbourne to become the county demonstrator. Her duties were to visit the schools and organize canning clubs and courses relating to food preparation in the homes.[8]

It was the local school boards who assumed the greater tasks. They were the ones obliged to match the federal funds for courses in the school. It was their responsibility to provide funding for the longer school terms, enriched curricula, and teacher salaries. They also had to raise money for larger and more costly school buildings. Brevard residents responded enthusiastically to calls for increased appropriations for schools. When it was explained that the 1905 county division had left Brevard County with two-thirds of the schools and only about half of the money, the special school districts approved a three mill tax to meet the situation. Several of

The new Cocoa High School "of reinforced concrete" was built in 1916 at a cost of $40,000. (Photo courtesy Doug Hendriksen)

Cocoa's 1919 graduating class included Ruth Swinson, Robert Young, Julia Rembert, Robert Hatch, Maimie Parrish, Lewis Fay, Emily Jones, Lang Roberts, Lillian Owens, William Heaton, Nannie Cooper, and Chester Stackhouse. (Photo Julia Rembert Alexander Collection, Brevard County Historical Commission Archives)

them bonded themselves for school construction. An example was the 1915 vote in special district number one which approved a $100,000 school construction bond by a "handsome majority." Sixty thousand dollars was for a new high school in Titusville. About $20,000 more was for a new school at Mims. Elated by the vote, an enthusiastic editor predicted that the two new schools would "advance education in the county by 20 years." One year later, Cocoa contracted for a new school building "of reinforced concrete" at a cost of $40,000. Other districts throughout the county were equally active.[9]

In a continuing effort to use its financial resources in the most efficient way while providing greater services, Brevard County followed a national trend in caring for the county's poor people. It had long been customary for county officials to maintain "pauper lists." Persons knowing of someone in need would notify the county commission and it would routinely place that individual or family on the list to receive a few dollars each month. By the early 20th century, the list was extensive enough that the commissioners looked for alternatives. Like many other counties across the nation, Brevard turned to a "poor farm." Supervised first by John Gore and then by James F. Prevatt, the Brevard County Industrial Farm was established to provide a habitat for destitute residents. No "invalids or paupers" would subsequently receive public money unless they were residents of the farm. The farm received annual appropriations and was inspected regularly by members of the board of county commissioners. A 1910 grand jury evaluated the institution and concluded that its costs "could be used to better advantage to the poor by abolishing it." The commissioners apparently disagreed, however. The farm was still being maintained well into the 1920s.[10]

When the county jail burned in 1908, it was soon rebuilt, but not all prisoners were housed there. Following the lead of the state and other counties, Brevard adopted the convict leasing system by which prisoners were let to the highest private bidders. The successful bidders paid the county a specified amount for the labor of the prisoners and, in return, provided room and board for them and kept them in secure situations until their sentences were served. While the system reduced the county's costs for maintaining its jail facilities, it also opened up opportunities for abuse. A typical lease was consummated in 1905 when Pritchett and Company, a firm with extensive turpentine operations in the county, obtained the lease for all county convicts. The company agreed to pay Brevard County $15 per month for "every able bodied man convicted in the courts of the county." William Pritchett and Company agreed to pay the amount for each prisoner from "the date he [was] notified by the sheriff either verbally or in writing" that a prisoner was available. Such an arrangement meant that a private employer assumed the responsibility for keeping prisoners in custody while deriving a profit from their labor. One of the unfortunate results of such a system was demonstrated in 1905 when four "negro convicts" escaped from the Pritchett camp on the Delespine Grant. Three of the escapees were quickly brought back into custody, but one Henry Williams remained at large. Seven days after the escape Williams was overtaken by two of the camp guards "in the sawgrass north of Mims and shot." A similar incident occurred at a Pritchett camp near Turnbull about two months later. Edward Screve was shot while trying to flee the camp by a guard named J. J. Mobley. A jury was quickly impanelled from the citizens of Mims and Turnbull and a verdict of "justifiable homicide" was routinely returned.[11]

When the county jail burned in 1908, it was soon rebuilt. (Photo courtesy Jim Ball)

The leasing system was still in place in 1916 when the board of county commissioners announced that it would "receive bids for hire of the Colored County Convicts at their regular February meeting." By that time convict leasing was receiving extensive criticism for its abuses of common civil rights. The practice was outlawed at the state level in 1919 and at the county level in 1923. It was perhaps fortunate for Brevard County that a better use of its prisoners was emerging. As the county assumed increasing responsibility for the building and maintenance of its roads, the need for a better way of managing its prisoners and the concomitant demand for labor on the public roads seemed naturally to converge. By 1920 the convicts were being maintained by the county and roads were being maintained by the convicts. In early 1920, the Titusville Star Advocate reported that the convicts were to be under the supervision of Philip Roberts, commissioner for the Mims district, to work on the Dixie Highway north of Titusville. They were to go next to G. G. Brockett's district where they would continue to work on the Dixie Highway. Thereafter they would be placed under the direction of Lige Johnson of Cocoa, chairman of the board of county commissioners, who would put them to work on roads between Sharpes and Eau Gallie. John B. Rodes of Melbourne would then supervise their work south of Eau Gallie to the county line.[12]

Road building had made great progress by that time and the Good Roads Associations had been busy. A meeting at Titusville in early 1905 was presided over by S. H. Peck in place of L. W. Battenfield who was absent. The secretary for the meeting was A. H. Mckeown. A similar meeting occurred in 1907 at Cocoa with E. P. Porcher presiding and John A. Fiske acting as secretary. Both meetings had been concerned with better financing of a county road department. A bill was enacted by the 1907 legislature which permitted money accumulated in the fine and forfeiture fund to be used for general road construction and maintenance. Another measure empowered Brevard County to levy an additional two mill tax for purchasing road machinery. The two enactments enabled the county to purchase twelve mules and six dump wagons and to employ personnel to use them.[13]

As more and more automobiles appeared, there was a move not only to build more roads, but also to widen them and coordinate routes to facilitate long distance trips. It was noted in 1906 that "folks who have horses that are afraid of autos should widen their roads." Since county roads were at that time too narrow for two horse-drawn vehicles to pass safely, it was deemed only sensible to begin making them wider to accommodate both kinds of transportation. At the same time, Brevard County responded to a move toward a "Montreal to Miami Highway." Excitement was created in 1911 when the Titusville board of trade entertained a convoy of "automobilists" who were passing through to promote such a highway. At a 1912 election, Brevard voters approved a special taxing district and the borrowing of $20,000 to provide hard surfaces on the unfinished parts of the main county road from the northern boundary line to the southern part of the Delespine Grant. St. Lucie and other counties along the way were upgrading their roads at the same time to assure completion of the Montreal-to-Miami route. One of the drawbacks was the marshy land at the head of the Indian River which necessitated a lengthy detour to the west or a ferry boat ride. J. H. Allen of Allenhurst was operating a ferry boat which could carry five cars at a time between Oak Hill and Shiloh, but Volusia and Brevard counties were combining their efforts to improve the road across the swamp between Oak Hill and the Brevard line. It was finished in 1912.[14]

The Indian River was both a means of transportation and a barrier to it in the early 20th century. Mr. Rogero was operating a yacht service between Eau Gallie and Courtenay, stopping at all intermediate points on the island to carry freight and passengers to the railroad stations at Cocoa and Eau Gallie. About the same time, the Cocoa town council gave a group of Indianola citizens the authority to build and maintain a wharf at the foot of Willard Street and a right of way for a tram road to the railroad depot. Cocoa boosters applauded the neighborly act but then expounded on the desirability of extending

Viewing the new Sebastian River Bridge in 1911 are Paris Lawson, Mrs. Bamma Lawson, Jesse Yongue, Mrs. Paul Kroegel and children. The large boat is Kroegel's Audubon. *(Photo by Paul Kroegel, courtesy Rodney Kroegel, Brevard County Historical Commission Archives)*

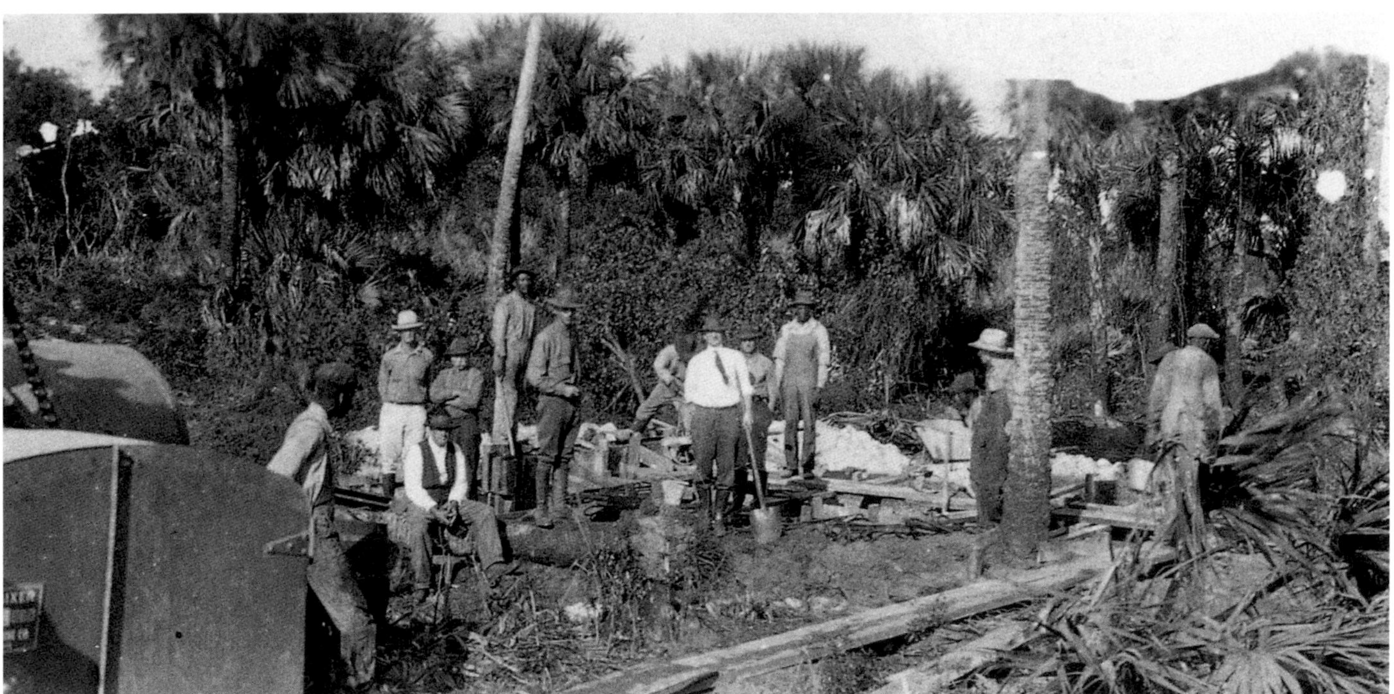

A *convict leasing system was in use during the building of the* Dixie Highway. (*Photo* Brevard County Historical Commission Archives)

the wharf and making a bridge across the river. "What a development for Cocoa and the Island would follow" completion of a bridge and a "road from one end of the island to the other," they said. The idea became a serious consideration about 1913 when a mass meeting was held at the Cocoa town hall to discuss it. Eau Gallie residents favored the bridge but wanted it built by private companies rather than with county taxes. The Rockledge-Cocoa Yacht Club was concerned that it would hinder boat traffic on the river. All differences were worked out by 1916 when Cocoa and Brevard County authorities announced plans to build a Merritt Island-Cocoa Bridge which would be 5,840 feet long with a draw bridge affording a 55 foot clearance. At a cost of about $75,000, a narrow bridge without side rails was opened in 1917. It must have been a thrill to cross such a bridge in the automobiles of the day.[15]

Automobiles were on their way, but railroads were not yet finished. The Florida East Coast Railroad Company contracted in 1911 for a branch line to run from Titusville through Maytown in Volusia County to Lake Okeechobee, a distance of 135 miles. The first 20 miles of this Kissimmee Valley Railroad were completed in February 1912 and trains were running to Chuluota in Orange County. When the line was completed, the Titusville East Coast Advocate predicted that "hustlers" would soon be developing "natural resources as yet almost untouched." Regular round-trip fares from Titusville to Okeechobee were $8.30 in early 1915, but excursions were available for only $4.25. Tickets were available at the Palmhurst Hotel. While that road was being built, the Florida East Coast Hotel Company – companion to the railroad firm – was operating a line of automobiles between Ormond and Palm Beach. Three 40-horsepower cars had been acquired for the route from the American Locomobile Company.[16]

While the Montreal-to-Miami highway was making progress, Carl Fisher announced plans for a Dixie Highway to run between Chicago and Miami. Brevard County joined many other local governments in a scramble to have the route run through their communities. After lengthy

The Cocoa-Merritt Island bridge which opened in 1917 was 5,840 feet long. A draw bridge afforded 55 foot clearance for boat traffic. View east on Harrison Street, Cocoa, c. 1920. (Photo Brevard County Historical Commission Archives)

lobbying and negotiations it was decided that there would be two routes – one to run through Jacksonville to Miami and the other to wind through Gainesville, Ocala, and Orlando, eventually rejoining the main line at Palm Beach. When W. S. Gilbreath of Chattanooga and A. S. Belcher of Miami, representing the Dixie Highway Association, suggested that it would be necessary for Brevard County to "fix up several gaps" in its part of the road, county residents quickly approved funds for the project by a majority of 257 to 11. A. F. Harley was appointed engineer to begin work in August 1916. By September tourist traffic was "very brisk, 50 to 60 automobiles every day."[17]

The idea of an automobile route to Orlando from the Titusville area originated about 1913, but it was originally suggested to run from Mims to Six Mile Branch and then through Volusia County to Orlando. Since no one lived in that portion of Volusia County there was understandably little interest in such a road on that side of the county line. After negotiations with Orange County officials, it was agreed that the two counties would build roads westward from Indian River City – just south of Titusville – and eastward from Orlando to meet at the St. Johns River. By the summer of 1915, members of the Brevard County Good Roads Committee were meeting with their Orange County counterparts to work out arrangements for a bridge across the St. Johns River. A barbecue picnic was held on June 2, 1916, to celebrate the opening of the Indian River-Orlando Highway. Although it would require some rerouting and much improvement over the next few years this route, known as the Cheney Highway, eventually became today's State Road 50.[18]

By 1920 work was underway on the Brevard portion of a highway between Melbourne and Kissimmee which was part of a cross-state road that would eventually connect the Atlantic Coast and Tampa. As of April that year automobiles could travel over the completed part of the road between Melbourne and St. Cloud in only three hours.[19]

Telephone communications were beginning as early as 1899 with service extending over short distances. Long-distance service was emerging by about 1905 and improved rapidly after that. The Brevard County Telephone Company was extending its services from Cocoa to Bonaventure by March 1905. A firm was running a line between Eau Gallie and Melbourne the following year. About the same time the Titusville Telephone Company was extending a cable from City Point to Courtenay. From that point lines would extend through Indianola, Merritt, and Georgiana to Tropic. In 1911 the Brevard County Telephone Company was acquired by John E. Reed and Arthur A. Buck, both of Merritt Island. It almost immediately built a cable across the river to Eau Gallie where it connected with the Tropical Telephone Company. That firm purchased the Titusville Telephone Company in 1912 and opened a Titusville Central with Mrs. Carl Battle in charge. Telephone service was given a sizable boost in 1916 when the American Telephone and Telegraph Company obtained a franchise to operate in Titusville, Miami, and Key West.[20]

Expansion of the road system rekindled demands for animal controls which had been voiced from time to time since the 1880s. After nearly a decade, Titusville had managed to enact an ordinance in the late 1890s aimed at keeping horses and mules off its streets. Although challenged in the courts by the cattlemen, the town's cattle ordinance was upheld in 1910. Titusville citizens then called on the legislature for a "no-fence law" for the entire county. Such a measure meant that cattlemen would be obliged to fence in their ranges rather than other property owners having to build fences to keep animals out. Brevard County ranchers were able to prevent an unlimited "no-fence law," but the 1913 legislature did make it unlawful for hogs to run loose in the county. Hogs running at large in violation of the law could be impounded and sold by county officials. The question of cattle on the open range again became a heated issue in the early 1920s.[21]

While the county never endured the lawlessness of the 1890s again, the sheriff had more to do than impound hogs. The advent of automobiles brought a new form of crime. Sheriff Joseph P. Brown apprehended two thieves in 1916 after they stole a new Oldsmobile belonging to George W. Hopkins, operator of the Union Cypress Company. The thieves were captured at a sawmill at Hastings in St. Johns County. The newspaper announced that the addition of the two car thieves gave the sheriff "only 28 boarders at the county bastille." Most of the inhabitants had been caught running "blind tigers" but one John Alexander had been apprehended with a kit of burglars' tools and two bottles of nitroglycerine. Although he no longer lived in Brevard County, residents were shocked in 1907 to learn that C. T. McCarty of Fort Pierce had been shot to death as he emerged from a barber shop by W. C. Rawlinson of Ankona. Five years later news reverberated through the county that Lars Jorgensen, a leading citizen of Grant for 25 years, was shot and killed on the road toward Valkaria. Sheriff Brown soon arrested Charles L. Scott for the offense. Rufus M. Robbins, another prominent county citizen, was found guilty of mishandling the funds of William Treutler's estate at Eau Gallie.[22]

The sheriff's office itself became an issue in 1917. Brown was succeeded by L. W. Doolittle, a longtime Titusville fisherman and businessman. Unfortunately for the tranquility of the state, Sidney J. Catts became governor that year. The impulsive Catts interfered in the affairs of many counties, removing local officials both with and without cause. Doolittle became the object of Catts' ire and was removed from office and replaced by Minor S. Jones, son of the famous judge. When he ran for office again in 1920, Doolittle was elected and served the county well until he was succeeded by Roy F. Roberts.[23]

Except for the several large drainage and development projects which will be addressed in the following chapter, economic activity of the early 20th century continued to be focused on the river, the forests, the groves, and the

This car was barged over the Banana River in 1917 before the opening of the Cocoa-Merritt Island Bridge. Merwin Wooten, Bill Hendry, and Coot Hendry at the Packard family cottage in Oceanus. (Photo Robert Trafford, Florida State Archives)

fields. Despite a severe cold wave in January 1905, the coldest since 1895, the citrus industry had largely recovered by the second decade of the 20th century. The Florida Citrus Exchange, organized in 1909, and its several sub-exchanges in Brevard County, were improving their marketing techniques. Many growers had stopped selling their crops on the trees in an effort to reduce the amount of green fruit which continued to appear on northern markets. Growers persuaded the legislature to enact a "green fruit bill" in 1911 which further limited the shipment of immature oranges. Neighbors were saddened by the 1905 death of Burton J. Mims who had spent 35 years developing groves at Mims and Bonaventure. Despite the loss, the Mims Packing House continued to handle large quantities of fruit.[24]

The arrival of J. J. Parrish in 1899 from his Bowling Green birthplace was a valuable addition to the citrus industry in particular and Brevard County in general. Parrish had grove lands in the Mims area and was expanding as far as northern St. Lucie County by 1915. He was advertising in 1916 as the resident buyer and shipper of Fancy Indian River Fruit Crops which he was willing to purchase from growers either in bulk or by the box. When Chief Thomas F. Nevins chartered the Nevins Fruit Co., Inc., in 1915 he took in both J. J. Parrish and the Egan and Fickett advertising firm of New York as partners. By 1920, Parrish had acquired the citrus interests of Chief Nevins and, with his brother, Henry, was operating three large packing houses. The firm retained the Nevins Fruit Company name and marketed its product under the Green Label which enjoyed a favorable reputation in the northern markets. J. J. spent much of his time in public affairs while Henry concentrated on the day-to-day management of the business.[25]

The first automobile in Grant was owned by John Jorgensen, parked here in front of the Grant Grocery and Post Office in 1908. (*Photo courtesy Grant Historical Society*)

A. M. Terwilliger, one of the largest growers in the county by 1909 built a long wharf with a bulkhead and warehouse at the end of Wiley Avenue in Mims from which he operated a steamboat service for shippers from Merritt island and the mainland to markets at Jacksonville and Savannah. When the Florida East Coast Company sent representatives to look into the possibility of establishing a flag station at the Terwilliger wharf, some other citrus packers objected, arguing that a station at East Mims would be less expensive and much more centrally located for shipping "the whole hammock crop." The rich lands of the Turnbull Hammock west and north of Mims were a major source of Indian River fruit by that time. The FEC seems to have satisfied all parties in the long run. Although they may not have had precisely equal access to the main line, all of the major packing houses eventually had railroad sidings for loading fruit. There was even a station named Jay Jay which served Parrish's packing house at LaGrange, a community which was increasingly being referred to as North Titusville. Chase and Company, headed by Sidney Chase of Sanford, had groves in the Turnbull Hammock area and, eventually, throughout the county. Chase, the Mims Packing House, and A. J. Nye and Company were major shippers of grapefruit as well as oranges. William H. Sharpe and several of his neighbors at City Point shipped quantities of fruit through the local sub-exchange as well as several private packing houses. In 1912, not long before his death, Sharpe won a medal for his excellent citrus at the St. Louis Exposition. Sam Osteen of Lotus was awarded first prize for several varieties of oranges at the Florida State Fair in 1920. The excellent quality of Indian River Fruit was well-established by that time.[26]

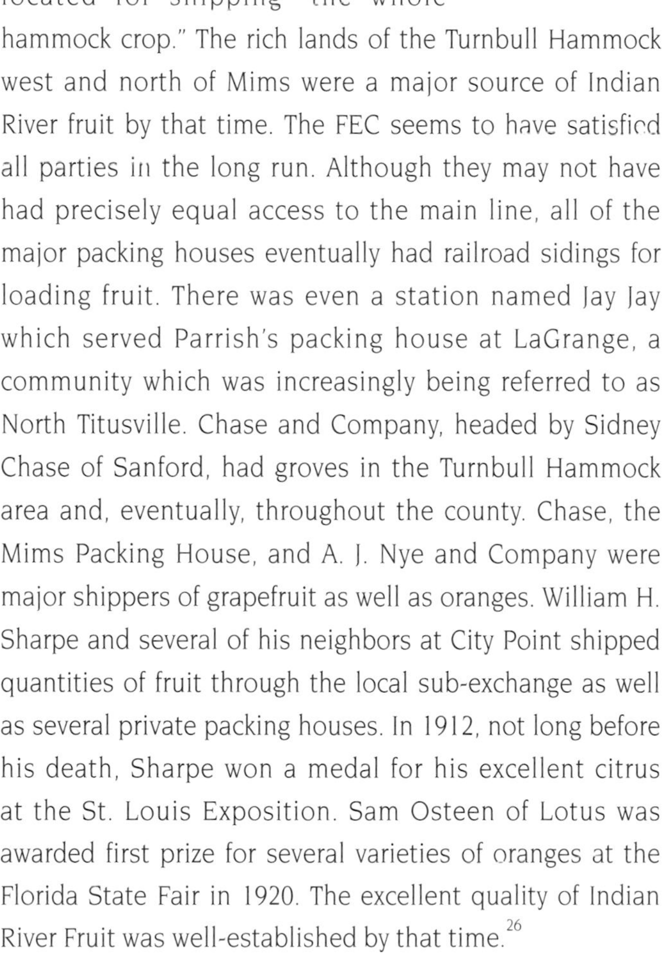

Although access to market was somewhat more complicated for some of its growers, Merritt Island was also a major citrus producer. The packing houses of James A. Taylor, F. P. Ziy, and J. W. Griffis were shipping both grapefruit and oranges by 1912. G. L. Comer was taking advantage of new technology and hauling fruit to the wharves from Shiloh by "auto truck." Orsino growers were obliged to put a crew of men on the roads in 1920 in order to ship "a bumper crop of citrus." By that time there were several crate and box mills manufacturing containers for the crops. One of the largest was the Mims Mills, owned by Hansell and Bevill and operated by O. C. Hansell. Indian River fruit producers were pleased in late 1920 when United States Senator Park Trammell purchased the Happy Alligator orange and grapefruit grove at Courtenay.[27]

The Indian River and Lake Worth Pineapple Growers' Association was still shipping its product in the early 1900s and E. P. Porcher was still its marketing agent. Each summer he moved with his family to Jacksonville for the harvesting and marketing season. As many as 30 carloads per week were still passing through Titusville in 1906.

The boat Shell of Cocoa *waits for passengers at the* Hodgson *Brothers dock in* Eau Gallie, *c.* 1920. (*Photo Brevard County Historical Commission Archives*)

Institutes at Melbourne, Sharpes, and Mims in late 1916. One of the progressive laws of Congress was the Federal Farm Loan Act of that year. Pursuant to that legislation John W. Elkins, cashier of the Bank of Cocoa, announced the opening of a Farm Loan Association for Brevard County. The county agent was a permanent fixture in local government by 1920, but his salary of $175 per month was considered inadequate since his traveling expenses consumed about half of that amount. The county commissioners were considering a separate expense account to supplement his basic salary.[28]

Quantities of watermelons were grown on the mainland as well as on Merritt Island. Fields around the newly established Indian River City were producing lettuce in 1915. Celery was a fairly successful crop there a little later. The Rockdale Nursery Company was large enough by 1915 that the Titusville Hardware Company installed a $10,000 irrigation system for it. The county agent was promoting improved agricultural methods through Farmers'

The Indian River continued to provide income through both commercial fishing and tourism. The Sebastian Fish Company not only shipped fish from that place but also provided considerable business for the Hodgson Company at Eau Gallie which built the boats for its fleet. Hodgson's ways were also used for building and main-

The 88' yacht Victoria *brought* President-elect Warren Harding *and cabinet appointees for a visit to* Brevard. (*Photo courtesy* Doug Hendriksen)

taining the boats of the Florida Fish and Produce Company which operated from Eau Gallie. J. W. Rosseter was operating at least 30 fishing boats on the river. According to E. Svedelius of the Ocean Fish Company at Valkaria, fishermen could find year-round employment at that place. Fishing firms came and went with some regularity at Titusville. D. L. Gaulden, L. W. Haile and Andrew J. Griffis chartered the Eureka Fish Company with a capitalization of $10,000 to engage in general fishing in 1905. The Peninsular Fish Company opened for business on the Titusville city wharf in early 1906. L. Alexander left the Eureka firm to take charge of the new business. The Atlantic Fish Company which operated adjacent to the Peninsular company was taken over by L. W. Haile in the summer of 1906. Calling his business the Cooperative Fish Company, he attracted "several of the best crews" to work with him. The new enterprise did not succeed and was in turn acquired in early 1907 by A. B. Yelvington who called it the Brevard Fish Company. One of the more durable enterprises was the Seaboard Fish Company owned and operated by George and Fred Scobie. All of these firms and others which joined them shipped many carloads of fish to both southern and northern towns in ice-packed barrels. The shipments returned thousands of dollars to Brevard County during the period. In some years, fishing was more valuable than citrus to the local economy.[29]

One of the first automobiles in Cocoa stops at Ronald and Fiske Hardware Store. (Photo courtesy Doug Hendriksen)

In addition to the Hodgson Brothers at Eau Gallie, Sam Martin was building boats on the river. Increasing demand compelled him to add a new building and additional workers in 1905. George Gingras was still in business at Cocoa. The Lorillard Boat Company extended both its main railways in 1906 in order to handle larger vessels. It also added extra help about that time, but the works were sold the following year. Adhemar Brady took over and called his new enterprise the Titusville Boat Company.[30]

One reason for the increased demand for boats was the improvement of the inland waterway. The Florida Coast Line Canal and Transportation Company was still working toward its goal of completing a navigable channel from Jacksonville to Miami and it was enjoying at least temporary success in the early 1900s. By 1910 the Gulf Refining Company was hauling its products from Jacksonville to Brevard County by way of the inland waterway. The Gulf Coast Navigation Company put on a freight and passenger steamer service in 1911 to make scheduled trips between St. Augustine and Palm Beach. By 1913 the Florida Coastal Inland Navigation Company was running the *Swan* and *Emmett Small* between Cocoa and Jacksonville. According to the local newspapers "a regular procession of power boats are found passing along the Indian River, and quite frequently are...making side exploration trips into the numerous rivers and creeks that abound along the route. Future President Warren G. Harding made several trips on palatial yachts, usually stopping at Cocoa to visit relatives."[31]

There were many references during the period to the

fact that Melbourne needed wharves of at least 1500 feet in length to reach deep water while Titusville was much closer to navigable waters. The latter town was proud of its new city dock completed in 1909 with five fish houses, a yacht club house, and the Titusville Boat facilities, in addition to plenty of wharfage for river traffic. But, a hurricane in 1910 demonstrated some inadequacies in the new construction. Wind "blew furiously for over twenty-four hours." There was great damage along the river front which was strewn with wrecked docks and boats. While all of the fish houses were saved, the yacht club house was demolished. Observers concluded that a dock with only two feet more height would have "stood the storm." In 1911 W. G. Hendry was rebuilding the wharf much larger than before, to be able to accommodate large river steamers as well as all kinds of small craft. It was higher than the wharf it was replacing.[32]

Cattle continued to graze on the open range on the mainland as well as the island. Cattle were rounded up twice each year. New calves were branded and marketable animals were sent to market. The issue of free-ranging cattle versus groves and vegetable fields caused occasional difficulties, but the residents of Merritt island worked out an amicable arrangement. The largest herdsmen on the island were the Cleveland and Field families and John R. Miot. With their assistance a fence company was organized to build and maintain a fence across the island just north of Georgiana. Citrus and vegetable growers on the island expressed their pleasure with the cattlemen who were "very fair and have helped to keep up the fence and have allowed all hopeless marauders to be shot at once." Remembering how people on the west side suffer from cattle and hogs, we are very thankful that we live on the island and have such fine neighbors."[33]

The naval stores and lumber industries which were addressed in an earlier chapter continued and probably reached their zenith in the second decade of the 20th century. The huge mills of the Union Cypress Company at Hopkins and Deer Park were quite active in both cypress and pine as has been mentioned. A turpentine operation at the latter place employed more than 200 blacks. The Pritchett brothers, with turpentine stills at Turnbull, Delespine, and Bonaventure, and the Consolidated Naval Stores Company were among the large naval store enterprises. The East Coast Turpentine Company even operated freighters on the river which were maintained by the Hodgson Brothers. J. A. Shipp's saw mill was cutting timber at Merritt in 1906. A. L. Hill opened a saw mill near Delespine in 1916. The Sams Lumber Company of Courtenay worked out an arrangement with the Florida East Coast Company to move its mill to Delespine and cut timber from its extensive lands. The Clark Brothers lumber and milling firm contracted to cut the timber on the G. W. Hopkins ranch west of Eau Gallie. James Pritchard cut timber on a tract near Titusville and retailed most of it through his Titusville Lumber Company. The East Coast Lumber and Supply Company handled all kinds of building supplies and also provided orange boxes, nails, and wrappers to growers all along the river. The Indian River Lumber and Supply Company was formed at Melbourne in 1913 by A. L. Eschbach and D. S. Welch.[34]

While most of Brevard County's economy was agricultural or extractive in nature, there were several manufacturing companies. The Florida Extract Works was still in business in 1907, but was sold to Clinton A. Spencer, H. C. Spencer, and W. V. Carter of Boston that year. Renamed the Acme Fiber Extract factory, the firm sold tannic acid from a plant valued at $12,000. When the plant burned in 1908 its activities were transferred to the company's other facility at Port Orange. The Palmetto Products Company of New York began manufacturing rugs from palmetto leaves in 1914. Two years later John M. Sanders and Fred Baldwin installed machinery for the Hydraulic Stone Company at Cocoa. George W. Michel built a factory near the Titusville Electric Light Plant for manufacturing cement blocks, bricks, and coping. Menhaden were turned into fertilizer at a factory located at Canaveral after 1905. In addition to barrel factories already existing at Titusville and Eau Gallie, C. C. Braddock took over a barrel manufacturing plant at Sebastian in 1910. Melbourne's Martin Dairy prided itself in the quality of its "Jersey milk" delivered twice each day to residents of that town. Another dairy at Georgiana supplied the local citizenry and shipped milk to ten customers at Coquina by the mail carrier.[35]

Everyone was pleased when Fred Scobie arrived in Titusville with his new Mitchell touring car after a ride of only seven hours and 55 minutes from Jacksonville. Complete with a chauffeur who was teaching him how to drive, the 30 horsepower automobile cost $1,500. "Who will be next" the Star asked. "Titusville ought to have a dozen cars this year." Fred's brother, George W. Scobie, Jr., was next. He bought a Mitchell 20 runabout from the Fred E. Gilbert Company within less than a month after his brother's purchase. The two were so pleased with their cars that they made their Seaboard Fish Company the agent for Mitchell cars in Brevard County. That was just the beginning. Four months later, Ellis Wager's Indian River Music House began taking orders for Ford automobiles. A carload of Ford touring cars and turnabouts were anxiously awaited in late November of 1909. Maxwell cars were being sold by 1914. The company made a four-reel movie of its product which was shown at the Magnolia Movie Theater in 1916. By that time, the Indian River Music House had expanded its automobile branch with the addition of Studebakers.[36]

When Julius Kline sold his dry goods and men's clothing business in 1910 after 17 years in business, another change became evident. The purchaser was the Mill-Factory Syndicate, a chain store firm. Although chains would shortly become commonplace, this one was scarcely evident since C.J. Denham bought the store only a few months later. Denham had first arrived in Titusville in 1902 and worked for others. He took over the Kline business in 1910 and was still there in 1929 by which time he owned other stores in Melbourne and New Smyrna. Titusville boasted the Stout Business College as one of its institutions by 1920.[37]

Eau Gallie, described by the Titusville paper as "a pretty little village overlooking the famous Indian River" was enjoying extensive face-lifting by 1907. Streets were being repaired, new walks were being laid out, existing homes were being improved and several new ones were under construction. The lumber and citrus industries surrounding the community, the Hodgson boat works, the Rosseter fish house and barrel factory, several other fish houses, and the Eau Gallie Yacht Club were important parts of the revival, but a new use for the long-defunct Hotel du Nil across the river at Sarno seems to have been the catalyst. Proving that schools as well as individuals could become winter residents of Florida, the Kentucky Military Institute of Lyndon, Kentucky, presided over by Colonel C. W. Fowler, acquired the Hotel du Nil in 1905 and began refurbishing it for winter classes. For more than 20 years, the school conducted its winter term at Eau Gallie, returning to its summer quarters in Kentucky each spring. The 150 or so cadets who attended the school added a tremendous dimension to the social life of Brevard County.[38]

Colonel Fowler resisted lucrative inducements from other localities and improved the campus and housing at Sarno until it was a showplace. The regimen of the military curriculum with daily drills and parades on the spacious grounds as well as the frequent dinners and balls held by Colonel and Mrs. Fowler were the talk of the river. According to the Eau Gallie Record of 1907, the school was expanded to include a naval institute that year, but it continued to be known as KMI throughout its years in Brevard County. The school even had its own post office, known as Military Park.[39]

Several new dormitories and classrooms were added

This float in the 1917 Cocoa May Day parade is pulled by Old Bill and carries a sign saying, "Bread from the Cocoa Home Bakery, Best Nutriment for Young and Old." (*Photo courtesy Grace Packard Bryant*)

to the existing hotel and cottages which had been originally constructed about 1895. After a destructive fire in 1916, the large building and several smaller dormitories were quickly replaced. After nine years as pastor of the Melbourne Methodist Church, the Rev. J. B. Hawk joined the faculty of the Kentucky Military Institute in 1909. The campus also had hotel facilities for people wishing to spend time there during the season and excursions from nearby communities were quite common. An example was the 1915 Washington's Birthday celebration featuring races and a ball game by the cadets. Excursion boats came from Tropic, Melbourne Beach and several other river towns to enjoy the occasion. The cadets not only conducted parades at the school but also participated in many of those held in other towns. The cadets and faculty frequently undertook excursions of their own. A typical one occurred in 1915 when nearly 50 cadets and teachers chartered a cabin cruiser for a trip to Oceanus on the Atlantic. The school and its student body remained popular in the county. When it closed its 17th season in April 1923, the Titusville Star Advocate promised that the students would be "warmly welcomed when they return next winter."[40]

The Chautauqua of the Tropics continued to meet each winter at Melbourne. The 1906 meeting started on March 4 with the Rev. S. D. Paine of the Melbourne Congregational Church in charge. Bible study was conducted by the Rev. J. B. Hawk of the Methodist Church. Children's classes were handled by Miss Bertha Adams. C. Rucker Adams and his wife were in charge of physical culture. Mrs. Clara I. McLean provided music. The opening session featured a moving picture by the American Vitagraph, "the finest moving picture machine to be had" at that time. By the early 1920s, the Chautauqua was branching out. It was held in the Titusville school house for five nights in 1921.[41]

An important annual event in Titusville in the early 1900s was the African Methodist Episcopal Church camp meeting which was attended by as many as 3,000 members from all along the Atlantic Coast of Florida. The railroads extended excursion rates for the occasion and merchants were given special permission to remain open on Sunday. Services were conducted in a "mammoth tent" and whites as well as blacks attended. Everyone enjoyed the meetings and "the exchequers of [Titusville] merchants were considerably added to..."[42]

J. M. Codman continued to be the earliest arrival at the Canaveral Club whose declining membership still enjoyed the famous hunting resort in the early 20th century. H. W. Brown and W. S. Norwood both managed the facility at various times during the period. The Indian River Haulover and Outing Club was established in 1907 on property

The Eau Gallie Yacht Club was not only popular for its boat races, but it also held successful baseball competitions complete with music, dances, and dinners. (*Photo courtesy* Doug Hendriksen)

obtained from J. H. Allen at the Haulover Canal. Organized under the laws of Wisconsin with a paid up capital of $10,000, it was immediately contracting for an "elegant club house." It claimed 30 members from the city of Madison, Wisconsin, alone. Two years later Allenhurst was celebrating the Fourth of July with a flag raising ceremony which featured a new 70-foot flag pole, motor boat races, and a speech by George M. Robbins of Titusville.[43]

Holidays were still important to Brevard County society. May Day celebrations at Cocoa, held at the Forest Avenue Park after 1913, had become a sort of annual reunion of old settlers by that time. Having been observed each year for nearly four decades, it was usually attended by residents from all over Brevard County as well as Fort Pierce and a few other St. Lucie communities. The 76 or so residents of Titusville who attended in 1910 were upstaged by about 100 from Melbourne. Indianola was called a "deserted village" on the 4th of July, 1905, when nearly all of its residents joined people from several towns to celebrate the day at Titusville. Christmas tree socials continued to be held in the churches and homes of the county. Everyone conceded that LaGrange always had the largest tree. Chief Nevins celebrated Christmas in 1909 with a large supper and dance at his new packing house on his dock at Merritt.[44]

The Eau Gallie Yacht Club was not only popular for its boat races, but it also held successful baseball competitions complete with music, dances, and dinners. The Indian River Yacht Club of Titusville was not to be outdone. J. Lorillard, Jr., P. G. Walton, D. B. Pritchard, and H. E. Oxner met with G. M. Robbins in his law offices in 1906 and agreed to solicit new members for the club which had just secured approval from the city to erect a club house on the public dock. It was soon holding oyster suppers and dances at the local opera house. Melbourne was still conceded to have "one of the brightest and best tennis clubs on the East Coast."[45]

It was either an accident or a sign of changing times when the Merritt Island Civic Association held a basket picnic at Courtenay on February 12, 1916 – Abraham Lincoln's birthday. Julian R. Sams was running his 40-foot launch between the Titusville dock and Courtenay to bring passengers over for 50 cents each. Courtenay was applauded for its Women's Progressive Club which was organized in 1913. Mims' citizens were still gathering on the grounds of the Hiawatha Hotel where a picnic and dance were held in 1909. About the same time the Rockledge Presbyterian Church gave an ice cream social at White's cottage. The young men of Titusville formed a social club in 1906 which featured bi-monthly dances at the opera house. The same place was the site of Mardi Gras parties sponsored by the St. Gabriel's Guild about 1915. Dances were also held at Bert Johnson's Magnolia Theater. Indian River City's new Pines Hotel was the place for musical entertainment on such occasions as

Washington's Birthday in 1916. Subscription dances were held at the Bay Crest Pavilion at Micco. People from Rockledge, Eau Gallie, Tillman, Sebastian, Fellsmere, and even Fort Pierce attended.[46]

Traveling shows were still popular. A few examples would include the Beggar Prince Opera Company which played to a packed house at the Titusville opera house in 1908. The Four Pickerts Company was scheduled for the following week. A. G. Allen's Big Minstrel Show made one of several appearances in Brevard County the same year. The "famed Colburn's Minstrels" was one of several such shows to play the new Magnolia Theater in 1915. Boxing matches had proved quite controversial in Florida, but they were making a comeback by the early 20th century. A boxing match was scheduled at Titusville in 1908 between Ed Murphy and G. W. Wood. When Murphy failed to appear, Wood agreed to fight "Professor Joe Fielding" and they fought to a draw in six rounds. The crowd seemed satisfied with the substitution.[47]

The county was treated to another new technological development in 1915 when Charles A. Hermann flew his airplane from Palm Beach and landed at Sand Point after "sailing around Titusville, so that all could see his machine in flight." A number of residents rushed to Sand Point to inspect the "hydro-aeroplane" while it was being refueled before taking off for Daytona.[48]

A Georgiana free library was opened in 1910 for the use of residents at the south end of Merritt Island. Sponsored by Mrs. George H. Bruen of Webb City, Missouri, it was housed at Oak Hammock Camp at Georgiana until the new club house was completed. The library board was soliciting contributions for additional books. Another type of enrichment was offered at the Wilson school on the north end of the island when the first monthly agricultural and literary entertainment convened in the fall of 1915. The program included recitations by the students, singing, music by the local band, and speeches by several farmers. The Woodmen of the World was a new fraternal organization which was organized in the county in 1906 and held its first meeting in the Masonic Hall in Titusville. It also had recitations, music, addresses by local dignitaries, and a box supper. The Independent Order of Odd Fellows, Lodge No. 85, began holding meetings in 1914.[49]

The Brevard County Medical Society met regularly during the period, usually at the Dixie Hotel in Titusville. In 1914, Dr. W. L. Hughlett of Cocoa was president, Dr. L. H. Martin of Melbourne was vice president, and Dr. J. C. Spell of Titusville was secretary and treasurer. New members included Guy S. Peppers, I. F. Bean, B. S. Mullay, and B. A. Burks. Visitors were Dr. Davis Forster of Hawks Park and Dr. A. F. Thomas of Titusville. The same physicians were present at a meeting in March 1915. Others in attendance included M. P. DeBow of Cocoa, and Helen G. F. Mac-Grueby of Boston.[50]

Several national reform movements were attracting attention in Brevard County. Women's suffrage was receiving considerable attention as was the campaign for a constitutional amendment outlawing liquor sales. Temperance lectures were popular even though Brevard County had been a "dry" jurisdiction for years. A Women's Christian Temperance Union was organized in the county and was especially strong at Eau Gallie. Another national concern was for better protection of children. Eau Gallie was also the center of a county Child Welfare League which held meetings during the period.[51]

An account of Brevard County social affairs in the early 20th century would be incomplete without mention of "Billy Long Legs," a sand hill crane known by local residents as the "traffic cop" on the street corner near the Cocoa House where he "held up many automobiles much to the astonishment of Northern tourists." When the friendly crane suffered a broken wing in a traffic accident, he was given a permanent home on the "spacious grounds of the Merritt Hotel at the island end of the Cocoa bridge.[52]

End Notes

1. Titusville Florida Star, January 6, August 11, February 17, 1905; Florida State Archives, Record Group 156, Series 259, Division of Elections, Directory of Commissions, 1905-1909.
2. Titusville Florida Star, July 24, August 7, 21, 1908; Titusville East Coast Advocate, August 16, 1912, March 7, 1913.
3. Titusville East Coast Advocate, April 16, 1915.
4. Titusville Florida Star, November 6, 30, 1908.
5. Ibid., September 25, December 27, 1908; Titusville East Coast Advocate, December 25, 1908.
6. Titusville Florida Star, March 30, 1906.
7. Titusville East Coast Advocate, September 10, 1909.
8. Ibid., November 5, 1915, February 25, 1916.
9. Titusville Florida Star, August 11, 1905; Titusville East Coast Advocate, September 10, 17, 1915, July 28, 1916.
10. Titusville Florida Star, October 6, 1905, February 9, March 30, 1906, April 1, 1910.
11. Ibid.,June 2, 9, August 25, October 6, 1905.
12. Titusville East Coast Advocate, January 14, 1916; Titusville Florida Star, April 8, 1921.
13. Titusville Florida Star, January 27, 1905, March 1, May 17, November 22, 1907.
14. Ibid., September 8, 1906, July 30, 1909, August 25, December 8, 1911, May 3, 1912; Titusville East Coast Advocate, June 11, 1909.
15. Titusville Florida Star, April 28, November 10, 1905, January 3, 1913; Cocoa Florida Star, February 7, 1913; Titusville East Coast Advocate, August 18, 1916; Glenn Rabac, The City of Cocoa Beach: The First Sixty Years (Winona, Minnesota: 1986), p.1.
16. Titusville Florida Star, January 15, 1909, Titusville East Coast Advocate, March 10, 1911, February 2, 1912, February 12, 1915.
17. Titusville East Coast Advocate, July 21, 30, October 22, 1915, September 29, 1916; Cocoa News and Star, May 12, 1916.
18. Titusville East Coast Advocate, April 11, 1913, August 13, 1915, May 26, 1916.
19. Titusville Star Advocate, April 2, 1920.
20. Titusville Florida Star March 23, 1905, April 17, 1908; Titusville East Coast Advocate, June 1, September 14, 1906, February 12, 1911, March 15, 1912, April 28, 1916; Cocoa Florida Star, February 7, 1913.
21. Titusville Florida Star, April 8, June 24, 1910; Titusville East Coast Advocate, October 10, 1913.
22. Titusville East Coast Advocate, February 1, 1907, January 28, 1916; Titusville Florida Star, March 22, 1912; Titusville Star Advocate, April 2, 1920.
23. Titusville Star Advocate, November 29, 1940.
24. Titusville Florida Star, January 27, 1905, September 3, 1909; Titusville Star Advocate, August 25, 1911; Titusville East Coast Advocate, June 25, 1909, October 22, 1915, July 28, 1916.
25. Titusville Star Advocate, 75th Anniversary Edition, 1955.
26. Titusville East Coast Advocate, April 30, 1909, June 10, 1910, January 26, 1912, November 5, 1915, November 11, 1920.
27. Titusville East Coast Advocate, October 25, 1912, December 4, 1914, November 3, 1916, October 29, December 10, 1920.
28. Titusville Florida Star, June 2, 1905; Titusville East Coast Advocate, June 1, 29, 1906, June 4, 1909, August 13, 1915, November 5, 1915, November 3, 1916, December l5, 1916; Titusville Star Advocate, July 16, 1920.
29. Titusville Florida Star, July 14, 1905, January 5, March 23, July 27, August 17, September 14, 1906; Titusville East Coast Advocate, August 4, 1905, February 1, 1907, April 19, 1907; Cocoa Florida Star, October 3, 1913.
30. Titusville Florida Star, August 11, 1905, March 30, November 23, 1906, April 19, 1907; Titusville East Coast Advocate, February 21, 1907.
31. Titusville East Coast Advocate, February 21, 1907, September 30, 1910, January 13, 1911; Cocoa Florida Star, January 31, 1913.
32. Titusville Florida Star, January 15, 1909; Titusville Star Advocate, October 21, 1910; Titusville East Coast Advocate, November 17, 1911.
33. Titusville Florida Star, July l4, 1905, October 30, 1908.
34. N. McKemy, Melbourne, A Century of Memories (Melbourne, 1980), p. 39; Titusville Florida Star, January 12, September 14, 1906, April 12, July 12, 1907, July 24, 1908; Titusville East Coast Advocate, August 11, 1911, October 11, 12, February 4, 1913, May 26, 1916.
35. Titusville Florida Star, October 27, 1905, January 19, 1906, April 5, 1907, March 27, 1908, Titusville Star Advocate, October l4, 1910; Titusville East Coast Advocate, August 7, 1914, January 1, 1915, July 28, 1916, December 15, 1916.
36. Titusville Florida Star, July 2, 1909, November 19, 1909; Titusville East Coast Advocate, July 30, 1909, January 28, 1916.
37. Titusville Florida Star, January 7, February 25, 1910; Titusville Star Advocate, April 23, 1920, June 28, 1929.
38. Ibid., April 20, August 17, 1906; Titusville East Coast Advocate, June 21, 1907.
39. Titusville Florida Star, April 20, 1906, July 12, 1907; Titusville East Coast Advocate, June 21, 1907; National Archives, Microfilm 1126, Roll 88.
40. Titusville Florida Star, August 17, 1906, August 6, 1909; Titusville East Coast Advocate, April 10, 1914, February 5, February 26, 1915, September 29, 1916; Titusville Star Advocate, April 20, 1923.
41. Titusville East Coast Advocate, March 2, 1906; Titusville Florida Star, March 2, 1906; Titusville Star Advocate, May 27, 1921.
42. Titusville East Coast Advocate, November 4, 1904; Titusville Florida Star, October 23, 1908, November 5, 1909; Titusville Star Advocate, October 27, 1911.
43. Titusville Florida Star, January l2, 1906, July 19, 1907, July 9, 1909; Titusville Star Advocate, September 10, 1910.
44. Titusville Florida Star, July 14, 1905, May 6, 1910; Titusville East Coast Advocate, December 31, 1909; Cocoa Florida Star, May 2, 1913.
45. Titusville Florida Star, January 12, October 19, 1906; Titusville East Coast Advocate, January 16, 1915, December 5, 1916.
46. Titusville Florida Star, October 5, 1906; Titusville East Coast Advocate, June 11, August 13, 1909, February 5, 1915, February 4, 25, 1916.
47. Titusville Florida Star, January 3, February 7, 28, 1908; Titusville East Coast Advocate, February 5, 1915.
48. Titusville East Coast Advocate, October 23, 1915.
49. Titusville Florida Star, October 19, 1906, April 30, 1910; Titusville East Coast Advocate, May 1, 1914, December 15, 1916.
50. Titusville East Coast Advocate, September 18, 1914, March 12, 1915.
51. Titusville Florida Star, March 2, 1906; Titusville Star Advocate, October 14, 1910, April 2, 1920.
52. Titusville Star Advocate, November 12, 1920.

Page 218 map: Florida East Coast Railway Map, circa 1912. (Brevard County Historical Commission Archives)

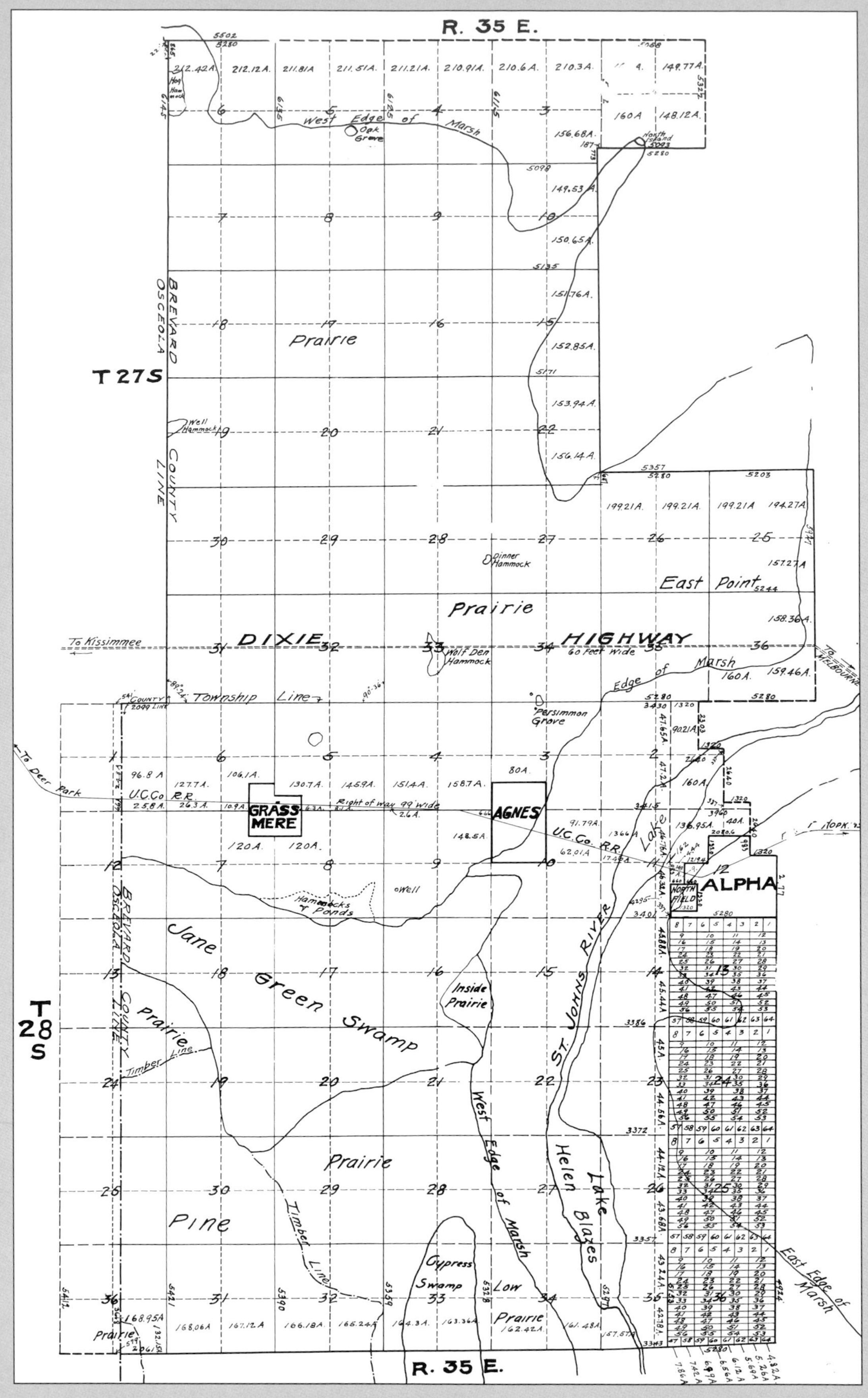
R. 35 E.
T 27 S
T 28 S
BREVARD
OSCEOLA
COUNTY LINE
West Edge of Marsh
Oak Grove
Prairie
Well Hammock
Dinner Hammock
East Point
To Kissimmee
DIXIE HIGHWAY
60 feet wide
Wolf Den Hammock
Edge of Marsh
To MELBOURNE
Township Line
Persimmon Grove
To Deer Park
U.C.Co. R.R.
GRASS MERE
Right of way 99' wide
AGNES
Lake
ALPHA
NORTH FIELD
Hammocks & Ponds
Well
Jane Green Swamp
Inside Prairie
ST. JOHNS RIVER
Prairie
Timber Line
West Edge of Marsh
Lake Helen Blazes
Pine
Cypress Swamp
Low Prairie
East Edge of Marsh
R. 35 E.

14
Old Towns, New Towns, Developers and Dipper Dredges

Growth and boosterism brought large development and drainage projects. By the time World War 1 ended in 1919, Brevard County was ready for the boom years of the 1920's.

World War I paraders pose in front of the Cocoa House Hotel, Cocoa. (Photo Brevard County Historical Commission Archives)

"Brevard County is approximately 70 miles long and has four towns of considerable importance and 26 other settlements on the river, all more or less interested in good fishing," declared the Titusville East Coast Advocate in 1913.[1] The assertion was true, but much more was happening in the county in 1913 than just "good fishing." Growth and development were important components of the "progressive movement" and Brevard County was very much a part of it in the early 20th century. Extensive reaches of the county's lands were available for development which usually meant drainage. Both the financial resources and the necessary machinery were available for the acquisition and reclamation of the land

A dredge digs the main canal at Fellsmere, c. 1914. (Photo by Paul Kroegel, courtesy Rodney Kroegel, Brevard County Historical Commission Archives)

along the Indian River and several sizable developments were already underway by the turn of the century. Both Roseland Park and Fellsmere Farms had begun in the 1890s. The 1899 legislature had revived an old scheme of William H. Gleason's to open a canal between Lake Washington and the Indian River "to drain surplus water." A contract was let in April 1900 to J. N. Whitner, C. W. Goodrich, Sidney O. Chase, and A. T. Rosseter for the project, but little work was completed before it stalled because of doubts about its effect on the water table.[2]

Both Roseland Park and Fellsmere Farms were growing at the turn of the century, although much of the latter enterprise became a part of the new St. Lucie County in 1905. The railroad which had begun in 1896 as the Sebastian and Cincinnatus Railroad was known for a time as the Fellsmere Railroad, but it eventually became the Trans-Florida Railroad, operating across the peninsula until 1952. The Fellsmere Farms Company was reorganized in 1910 with Oscar Crosby of Virginia as president. E. Nelson Fell, also of Virginia, was vice president. Other officers were T. F. Sherwood and W. W. Stanley, both of New York. The largest and most comprehensive drainage project to be undertaken by that time, it was done by the engineering firm of J. G. White and Company. Ernest H. Every was general manager, and R. A. Conkling of Brevard County was in charge of the demonstration work. Roseland Park had also made progress since its inception. By 1910 the Redstone saw mill was running at full capacity to provide building materials for 50 homes then under construction. About 100 men were draining and clearing land. People were arriving from Oklahoma, Missouri, New Jersey, Illinois, and Indiana to purchase and occupy the

Fellsmere Farms which was begun in the 1890's was made possible by extensive dredging and draining. Aerial view c.1915. (Photo courtesy Rodney Kroegel, Brevard County Historical Commission Archives)

new homes. Managers of the firm were running excursions from the midwest through Chicago to the building sites with the intention of bringing in additional settlers.[3]

The land department of the Florida East Coast Railway was doing its part to develop the county. Fifteen families were brought from Aiken, South Carolina, and Augusta, Georgia, in 1908 to take up land near Mims for a cooperative venture in cultivating oranges and truck gardens. The Segui Grant, situated on the boundary between Brevard and Volusia counties had been tied up in litigation for decades. Encompassing about 16,000 acres, its title was cleared in 1905 in the case of Dallam vs. Indian River Manufacturing Company for about $10,000. The entire tract was sold shortly afterward to A. W. Barrs of Jacksonville. Barrs divided the land into smaller tracts and began selling them to parties interested in establishing citrus groves. Edwin B. Lord of Milwaukee, Wisconsin, purchased 2,000 acres just southwest of Titusville in 1910 and advertised it to settlers interested in citrus culture. Ames A. Barlow formed the Brevard County Development Company and purchased 20,000 acres west of Cocoa and City Point. He opened an office in Cocoa "for the purpose of developing and handling this tract." By 1913 he was "making roads and ditches on a large scale" on his land. Barlow's company was also interested in general real estate and offered to "list for sale any improved or unimproved lands...whether on Merritt Island or the west side of the river."[4]

Litigation over title to the Delespine Grant between the Gleason family and several other claimants was finally settled about the turn of the century. Several parties were soon looking into the purchase of portions of its approximately 46,000 acres. One of the first to complete a sale was the Florida East Coast Company (FECCO) of Philadelphia. With 5,100 acres located between the Indian River and the Florida East Coast Railroad, the company was selling land through its Philadelphia office by 1909. At the same time, Harold G. Wilson, secretary and treasurer of the firm, was on the site clearing the land and laying out roads. A 60-foot road to be known as the St. Johns Highway bisected the property from east to west while Riverside Drive paralleled the river. Several tributary roads – 40 feet in width – provided access to lots which ranged from two to 40 acres in size. The Florida East Coast Railway cooperated by closing its flag station at the old Pritchett turpentine camp on the Delespine Grant and building a new passenger and freight station complete with loading dock at the new site to be called Delespine.

The railroad begun in 1896 as the Sebastian and Cincinnatus Railroad was known for a time as the Fellsmere Railroad. (Photo courtesy Doug Hendriksen)

Montreal to Miami Highway celebration, 1914-15. *Back seat*: Bill Myres, Ray Packard, Gus Thomas. *Front seat*: Charlie Turter, Ed Grimes. *Girls*: Anita Travis, Arlene Wooten, Maude Hindle. (*Photo courtesy* Grace Packard Bryant)

An express office was opened there immediately and a post office, located only 150 feet from the station, was established in late 1911. F. H. Black, superintendent of land development for the FECCO, was the postmaster. Delespine was located about 10 miles south of Titusville and four miles from Sharpes. Harold Wilson remained general manager of the enterprise and Miss Wilhemina Wilson managed a store and the railroad ticket office. Delespine got its first telephone in 1912 when a line was extended to Superintendent Black's new home which he called Alpha Bungalow.[5]

Another investor interested in the Delespine Grant was Alonzo Hill, a Californian who purchased 10,000 acres there in 1913. He advertised it as ideally situated on both the Florida East Coast Railway and the Montreal-to-Miami Highway.[6] Hill's development was preceded by the much larger and more ambitious Titusville Fruit and Farm Lands Company, incorporated in 1911 by Edgar W. Ellis, C. J. West, and J. H. Beckwith, with an initial stock offering of $300,000. The firm acquired a tract of 22,500 acres of the Delespine Grant. Starting about three miles south of Titusville, the land extended along the Indian River for about seven miles and stretched all the way to the St. Johns River on the west. Company headquarters were at Indian River City which was located near the river about four miles south of Titusville. A post office was opened there in 1912 with Peter Jepson as postmaster. A 20 room hotel and several bungalows were erected by 1913. The new town also boasted a store with telephone communications, a saw mill, a cement block and brick factory, and a school with 25 pupils. Under a headline reading "Brevard County Not Behind in Development Work," the Cocoa Florida Star enthusiastically reported the company's 1913 purchase of a dipper dredge capable of cutting 12 foot swaths of earth. The new equipment was immediately set to work on a canal from Bird Lake eastward to the Indian River. By 1915, the company's main canal from Rock Cut east to the Indian River was complete with a 20 foot bottom through which "a vast amount of water can now flow ...without any interruption." The Titusville East Coast Advocate applauded the Titusville Fruit and Farm Lands Company for the approaching completion of its "vast drainage system." In an earlier issue, the paper had predicted that development of the huge tract would result in Indian River Heights and Indian River City merging with Titusville into one big city.[7]

The Florida East Coast Fruit Land Company, a Jacksonville firm, acquired a large tract near the old town of Aurantia and began developing it as Indian River Park in

1911. A new town site for Aurantia was laid out, complete with business and residential sections. New streets were graded and a 20 room hotel was built at the town center. With land sales reportedly quite brisk, residents of the new development met in 1912 to establish a school for the 18 eligible children there. W. J. Morrell, J. E. Blakeman and W. T. McCullough were elected as trustees. In the meantime, the company had established a demonstration farm which was producing strawberries, English peas, and other truck crops. An Indian River Park Truck and Fruit Growers Association was formed and, by 1914, it was sponsoring Fourth of July celebrations at Aurantia.[8]

Right: Steam power made land clearing and ditching faster. (Photo by Paul Kroegel, courtesy Rodney Kroegel, Brevard County Historical Commission Archives)

About 12 miles north of Titusville and not far from Aurantia was Lyrata, the site of the Florida Land Sales Company headquarters. The firm was busily cleaning up the streets in 1915 and the Swink and Matson saw mill had relocated there from Aurantia to cut longleaf pine lumber for local use as well as for shipment. Lyrata claimed an FEC station with freight facilities and a post office. It also was situated on the main automobile road and had a dock reaching into the Indian River.[9]

Northwest of Titusville and about seven miles east of the St. Johns River was the new town of Southmere, headquarters of the Southmere Farms and Fruit Company. Backed by northern capitalists, the firm had 30,000 acres of land which was for sale in lots of ten, twenty, and forty acres. With Ward Klingensmith as manager, the firm had cut a road to the land from Mims and heavy machinery was grading roads and digging drainage ditches within the tract by late 1913. The Melbourne based Florida and Indian River Land Company acquired a large tract near the head of Crane Creek and in 1911 "purchased a powerful steam ditching machine" for draining the land.[10]

News of one land transaction in 1912 was received by many Brevard County residents with mixed feelings. For more than 40 years, Dr. William Wittfeld had lived at Fairyland near Georgiana. With its beautiful grounds, expansive groves, and Honeymoon Lake, it had long been a showplace to which local residents and visitors had come in large numbers. The aging Wittfeld sold 100 acres of the place, including Honeymoon Lake, to Thomas A. White of the White Sewing Machine Company about 1912. Persons interested in obtaining the remaining 50 acres were asked to contact John Frey of Bonaventure with whom Dr. Wittfeld was living after that date. Another local institution was also in decline by 1921 when John W. Winslow paid $30,000 for 7,000 acres on the ocean front which had belonged to the Canaveral Club.[11]

Those were exceptions. Most of the land sales were hailed by local boosters with enthusiasm. The Titusville East Coast Advocate exulted in 1911 that "crowds of

Above: Between 1910 and 1914 the Indian River Land Company sold property between Palm Bay and Grant. They often brought in groups of farmers from the midwest on vacation/sales trips. (Photo courtesy Grant Historical Society)

Right: R. T. Smith, Alonzo Pond, Hollis Bottomley, and Charner Smith survey new roads c. 1915. (Photo courtesy Grant Historical Society)

strangers are seen on our streets of late, while carloads of horses, mules and agricultural implements have arrived." The crowds were attributed to the "good work" which was being done by the Florida East Coast Company, the Florida East Coast Fruit Land Company, and the Florida Land Sales Company. Local merchants were "selling goods by the cart-loads" and should appreciate what the land companies were doing.[12]

The momentum of land sales accelerated when a "grand picnic and auction sale of 75 choice homes sites" was held at Melbourne in early March 1911. Conducted by the Cambridge Realty Company which had offices at Melbourne, the auction featured two sites to be given away as door prizes, a brass band, daylight fireworks, and a balloon display. Another such sale was announced for the "Lieutenant Governor Gleason property in South Titusville" in March 1913. "Close in lots" were to be sold to the highest bidders regardless of price. Terms were one-fourth cash on settlement and easy payments for the balance. The "most popular young lady" would receive a diamond ring, a gold watch would be given to the "most popular business man," and the "most popular lodge" was to receive a free lot. There would also be prizes of merchandise, chinaware, and $25 in cash. Everyone who attended was promised a prize "whether you buy or not." There would be a brass band, dinner on the ground, and a balloon display. The Bowman Realty Company of Huntington, West Virginia was the sales agent in charge and Major Thomas F. Combs was the "whirlwind auctioneer." Auctions were still popular in 1915 when the United Realty Company of Wilmington, North Carolina, announced a "big auction lot sale" in the Park Addition of Titusville. There was to be free music by a fine band. Prizes included "one choice lot," bags of gold and silver, and "valuable souvenirs and presents."[13]

Less fanfare accompanied the sale in 1908 of land between Eau Gallie and Lake Washington to a colony of Japanese. By 1909 "the little brown men" had cleared their land and were planning a fall crop. Another quiet sale involved the transfer of 35,574 acres from the Florida Coast Line Canal Company of St. Augustine to the Prudential Land Company of Jacksonville for a consideration of $71,149.66. While all these private sales were underway, the United States Land Office at Gainesville announced that there were still 15,775 acres of vacant government land in Brevard County which had been surveyed and was ready for homesteading.[14]

One of the characteristics of the "progressive era" was the organization of local boards of trade – precursors of the chambers of commerce of the 1920s. Brevard County and its larger communities began forming such boards in the second decade of the 20th century as land sales and development schemes were accelerating. Titusville led the way in 1911 with a board of trade which assessed each member a fee of one dollar. Original members were G. M. Robbins, George W. Scobie, Sr., E. W. Ellis, J. H. Beckwith, L. A. Brady, George G. Brockett, G. L. Mandaville, W. H. Hall, W. E. Bryson, S. L. Paro, J. J. Parrish, George W. Scobie, Jr., J. S. Wilson, E. E. Knox, Rufus M. Robbins, E. H. Paro, E. B. Wager, Charles H. Walton, Adhemar Brady, W. E. Goldsmith, George Schnierle, C. J. Denham, D. B. Pritchard, A. B. Tall, J. N. Waller, C. J. West, A. H. Elliott, J. Cameron, G. F. Duren, B. R. Wilson, M. F. Moore, E. J. Midens, and Fred B. Scobie. A similar organization, calling itself the Business Men's Association of Cocoa, was organized in 1913. Its officers were John A. Fiske, president; W. G. Paterson, vice president; and George L. Wallace, secretary and treasurer. R. O. Wright, T. R. Puckett, and E. D. Oslin comprised the executive board. Other members were Charles Stewart, Rodes and Baggett, Claude Edge, A. J. Byrd, A. J. Frink, and J. E. Field. Edge and E. D. Oslin were from Melbourne; Byrd and Frink were from Eau Gallie, and Field was from Indianola.[15]

The local groups and interested individuals from other communities successfully urged establishment of a county board of trade. It was formed at a meeting at Cocoa in

Fred Travis, Jr. built this home on the Indian River at Cocoa circa 1905. (Photo courtesy Virginia Hankins)

February 1915. At a second meeting at Eau Gallie a month later, John A. Fiske was named president with J. D. Frink as secretary and treasurer. W. H. H. Gleason became the first vice-president. Other members of the executive committee were named from Titusville, Cocoa, Sharpes, and Malabar. Meeting at Malabar in September, the board heard a report from its advertising committee. The county commission had pledged $300 for advertising and the board was asked to match the sum. It was suggested that a booklet be compiled consisting of "write ups" of each town. R. F. Moore was named to describe Titusville as well as the first and fifth commission districts. Mrs. P. C. Watkins was to handle Sharpes, Frontenac, and City Point. Cocoa was the responsibility of Mrs. L. K. Myers. Miss Helen Harcourt would write about Indianola and Merritt Island. Other writers were W. H. Adams for Eau Gallie, R. C. Burns at Canaveral, S. S. Lichty for Melbourne and Tillman, and G. E. Ulman for the communities of Grant, Valkaria, and Micco. Material thus gathered by the board resulted in the circulation of booklets highlighting Brevard communities, a number of special supplements to the East Coast Advocate, and numerous newspaper articles about the several towns of the county.[16] One of the spinoffs of the board of trade movement was Eau Gallie's initiative in organizing a county fair in 1915. The East Coast Advocate congratulated the citizens of that town for their work and called on "every man and woman" in the county to support it with exhibits and attendance. A Brevard County Fair Booklet was compiled for the event and it proudly announced the 1915 census figures showing the county population at 7,270, a gain of more than 50 percent since the national census of 1910.[17]

A number of new communities were started during the period and several older ones enjoyed renewed activity. A post office was opened at Jamestown, six and a half miles northeast of Titusville in 1914. By the summer of that year, a Fourth of July celebration was held at the Jamestown school house. New activity at Allenhurst by the Indian River Company brought a post office there on the grounds that the Clifton post office, about two miles away, was inconvenient. Calling itself "the place that's different," Allenhurst boasted that it could be reached by rail from Chicago by way of Jacksonville and Titusville and by water from Jacksonville. The emphasis on Chicago was a reflection of the Indian River Company's home office in Madison, Wisconsin. A new post office was opened at Audubon in 1914 with A. Fortenberry as postmaster. It was located about two and a half miles east of Sykes Creek and about 250 feet from the "east channel of the Indian River." A post office was reopened at Wilson in the same year. The school house was once again housing students and local residents were doing voluntary road work to make it more accessible. Heath, at the site of the old Dummett Grove, was also experiencing growth. Newcomers were clearing land and planting groves and an Agricultural Improvement Association had been activated. At Orsino, the Blue Hammock Civic Association was advertising for settlers. Mims, which had become an important citrus packing point with about 75,000 boxes annually, advertised itself as one of the most cosmopolitan villages in the state. It claimed residents from England, France, Ireland, Scotland, Germany, Austria, Italy, Jerusalem, Canada, and "nearly every state in the Union."[18]

Down the river at Grant, improvement projects were also gaining support. The county commission in 1909 authorized construction of a dock out into the channel to be built and maintained by Grant citizens at their own expense. It was to be located at the end of the public road running to the river between the stores of Lars Jorgensen and R. T. Smith. The Ridgeland Hotel there had just undergone extensive repairs and was open for guests. The year-round fishing business of Grant was mentioned in the previous chapter. Sebastian, benefiting considerably from the activity at Fellsmere Farms and Roseland Park, boasted four general merchandise stores, a high school with 80 students, two churches and two railroads – the FEC and the short line to Fellsmere Farms.[19] The "four towns of considerable importance" mentioned by the 1913 East Coast Advocate, were "in a more prosperous condition than in many years, owing to the fact that several land companies have been 'booming' things along," according to the same paper. Well before the grand auction of 1911, real estate was "moving in Melbourne." More than 30 lots were sold in 1906, mostly to people from northern states. The town was described at that time as a "northern town in the new South...pulsating with life and energy." The boosterish Advocate declared

A Melbourne ordinance outlawed travel by auto, horse, or mule at more than eight miles an hour. Prescott Wells and Allen Middleton obey the speed limit. (Photo Brevard County Historical Commission Archives)

Comfortable lodging was available in Melbourne at the Brown House operated by G. M. Brown. (Photo Brevard County Historical Commission Archives)

The MacDowell Family at Melbourne Beach: Mr. *and* Mrs. Louis G. MacDowell, Sr., *sons Carl Burr and* Louis, Jr., *and Grandma* MacDowell. (*Photo Goode Collection, Brevard County* Historical *Commission Archives*)

unequivocally that "no village in Florida has more promise ... as this Yankee settlement on the Indian River steamboat route." By that time most of the original stores which had fronted the river had given way to fine homes along the bluff. Stores were moving slightly inland to "a new city" which was springing up with "money and enterprise behind it." Comfortable lodging was available at three hotels, the Carleton, the Bellevue, and the Brown House. Keeping up with modern times, the municipal government passed an ordinance outlawing travel by auto, horse, or mule at more than eight miles an hour. Melbourne Beach, with a good hotel and several cottages, was accessible by way of the Melbourne Beach Improvement Company's motor train.[20]

The revival of Eau Gallie with the advent of the Kentucky Military Institute in 1905 has been mentioned, but there was more. The Eau Gallie Record, with four other newspapers in the county, struggled from time to time, but it kept afloat with its printing business. The Southland and Windsor hotels had just been built and new cement sidewalks were completed by 1912. There were several boarding houses in addition to the two hotels as well as five general stores, a jewelry repair shop, a meat market, a drug store, and an ice factory. Dr. Sarah Hodgson offered medical services. There were three marine railway and machine shops, turpentine companies, an excellent novelty works, a large lumber business, and several fish houses. With its renowned deep and safe harbor, a leading yacht club, and the Kentucky Military Institute, Eau Gallie considered itself a vibrant part of the progressive age.[21]

More and more frequently referred to as the twin city to Cocoa, Rockledge had recovered somewhat from the adversity brought on by the Florida East Coast Railway's removal of its spur line. The litigation with the FEC was ended in 1908. The spur line was not rebuilt, but the company apparently agreed on some compensation for damages. The Indian River, Plaza and New Rockledge hotels were still receiving guests in 1908 and the town was enjoying a revival of activity. New streets were being laid out and real estate offices were busy. The Indian River Hotel was sold in 1910 to S.F. Travis of Cocoa and two New Jersey men who planned to install new elevators and put the establishment in "first class shape."

The Indian River Drug Company opened a pharmacy in 1912 in the building formerly occupied by E. E. Ranck, across from the Rockledge Hotel. Dr. Charles L. Hughlett was in charge. H. M. Lockhart was one of the merchants of the community, but he usually closed each June and spent about three months in his native Michigan.[22]

The younger member of the "twin cities" was enjoying returning prosperity as early as 1905. The business district boasted three general stores, an exclusive grocery store, a hardware business, and a furniture store. There were two drug stores, a meat market, a bank, two tanneries, a jewelry store, two milliners, and a dry goods store, among others. E. D. Oslin of Melbourne acquired the Cocoa and Rockledge News from T. R. Puckett in 1907 but continued to publish it at Cocoa. At that time Oslin was still publishing the Melbourne Times as well as the Eau Gallie Record. T. R. Puckett purchased the Florida Star from Ellis Wager in 1912 and removed it to Cocoa.[23]

The Indian River Hotel was sold in 1910 to S. F. Travis of Cocoa and two New Jersey men who planned to put the establishment in "first class shape." (Photo courtesy Doug Hendriksen)

Right: The Ridgeland Hotel in Grant underwent extensive repairs in 1909. (Photo courtesy Doug Hendriksen)

Below: The Cocoa House continued to serve tourists as Cocoa grew around it. (Photo courtesy Doug Hendriksen)

R. M. *Rembert Building and Grocery, Cocoa, circa* 1915. (*Photo Julia Rembert Alexander, Brevard County Historical Commission Archives*)

secretary and treasurer. Other members were D. G. Rembert, O. K. Key, T. W. Scott, G. N. Hendry, F. M. Heule, J. A. Fiske, E. Hendry, R. A. Schlernitzauer, W. G. Paterson, and T. G. Ronald. Its first order of business was to work toward an equalization of taxes, paved streets, and a water works and sewage system. The Upper St. Johns Drainage District was reclaiming submerged lands west of the city and real estate transfers were accompanied by the construction of a number of new buildings. An undeniable sign of modern times was Cocoa's two moving picture houses by 1914. The street lighting was partially resolved in 1912 when a "great white way" was installed on the west side of Delannoy Avenue.[24]

One enthusiastic Cocoa resident declared in 1908 that people who had not been in his town in a year "would scarcely know the place" because of the many improvements. There were "fine residences, large stores, wide sidewalks, no saloons and nothing lacking now but good street lamps to make our town the nicest one on the river." Another writer boasted a few months later that "our people seem to be in a hurry for fear they will be left, and yet we are moving calmly and steadily..." However paradoxical such boosterism may have been, Cocoa was on the move. A new city charter was approved by the legislature in 1913, compliments of Brevard County Representative John M. Sanders, a local resident. The Brevard County State Bank, with S. F. Travis as president, J. Lapham as vice president, R. B. Holmes as cashier, and M. W. Weinberg as assistant cashier, was showing a capitalization of $50,000 and resources of $300,000. A Cocoa Progressive Club was organized in 1913 with George L. Wallace as president and H. A. Thompson as

Since Titusville remained an important transportation center and much of the county business was transacted there, it was a major beneficiary of the growth of the progressive area. There were 23 residential houses under construction in 1907 and the Titusville Lumber Company was completing $100,000 worth of rebuilding. Two small hotels, the Sterling and the Palmhurst, were being improved to attract tourists. Everyone was pleased when G. F. Duren purchased the aging Grand View Hotel and began tearing it down. Once a popular hotel, it had long since seen its better days and Duren was applauded for removing an "eye sore." The Titusville Hotel Company, capitalized at $25,000 was formed in 1908 to purchase and refurbish the Indian River Hotel and install elevators, salt baths, and other modern improvements. A number of Titusville businessmen bought stock in the company. Among them were J. S. Daniel, George M. Robbins, L. R.

Decker, F. S. Battle, James L. Conner, L. L. Brady, S. A. Rathbun, G. F. Duren, W. S. Branning, J. C. Spell, Julius Kline, Ellis B. Wager, and Charles H. Walton.[25]

Kate Stewart and Ben Warbuton work in an office across from the Brevard County Courthouse in Titusville. (*Photo courtesy Jim Ball*)

New legislation abolished the town of Titusville in 1909 and created the City of Titusville. One of the early ordinances of the city amended regulations dealing with automobiles, motorcycles and bicycles. In the future those vehicles would be required to obey a speed limit of 15 miles per hour and to sound a whistle or horn as they approached each corner or crossing. All vehicles had to have at least one headlight and automobiles were required to have two. The city also contracted for a waterworks in 1912 at an approximate cost of $27,000. In 1916 the city sold its electric light plant to the Southern Utilities Company, owners of the local ice plant, for about $35,000. One of the measures of municipal progress during the progressive years was street lighting. Titusville announced the opening of its "white way" in April 1916 when seven standard electric lamps, each with five globes, were turned on along Washington Avenue.[26]

The Indian River State Bank celebrated 20 years of business in 1909. James Pritchard was still president of the firm. The competing Bank of Titusville opened its doors in September, 1912. Officers were Harold G. Wilson – manager of the FECCO – as president, A. B. Tull as vice president, and Frank V. Raymond as cashier. The Cooperative Building and Loan Association opened for business in 1916 with R. J. Glenn, president; J. R. Walker, vice president; Harry Wilson, treasurer; and H. S. Walker, secretary. In addition to the officers, other directors were N. P. Thompson, Charles H. Walton, and W. F. Hobson.[27]

J. M. Osban was still running a livery stable behind the Robbins' law offices while the Titusville Garage, owned by Wilson and Everitt, continued to serve the increasing number of automobiles on the roads. The Rice Brothers sold their automobile business and garage to Joseph McMurdie from Chicago in 1916. L. Euklenfield, in partnership with Dr. L. H. Bartee opened the New Titusville Pharmacy in 1912 in a building previously occupied by a skating rank. That business apparently replaced the one previously known as the Titusville – or Red Cross – Pharmacy operated by Drs. H. G. Utley and E. R. Blakewood. The Banner Drug Store, owned and managed by D. H. Spell and Dr. J. C. Spell remained in business for many years after its inception in 1907. Titusville also boasted a steam laundry and bottling works in 1913. F. A. Foster opened a branch of the Coca Cola Company there in 1916. Among the other businesses in Titusville, there were Frank Depps' City

The Indian River State Bank celebrated 20 years of business in 1909. (Photo courtesy Robert Hudson, North Brevard Historical Society)

Bakery, J. E. Easterly's wood turning and novelty works, the Titusville Hardware Company, M. Davis' dry goods store, and Winston Branning's clothing store.[28]

In another booster article of 1915, the Titusville East Coast Advocate estimated the city's population at 1,200 with "new settlers coming all the time." It had a new county court house costing $31,000 and a modern brick jail which rarely housed over "two or three inmates." There were shelled streets, electric lights, two reliable banks, seven fine brick business blocks, a water works, a board of trade, five white churches, two opera houses, two motion picture houses, and several law and real estate offices. The article went on to list 11 social organizations, a city telephone office, an express delivery, several hotels and assorted other businesses.[29]

The "four towns of considerable size," most of the other communities – both old and new, and the county as a whole were enjoying growth and prosperity by the second decade of the 20th century. There was an interruption as the United States turned to the war in Europe after 1917. Some Brevard County residents marched off to war while others remained at home, purchased liberty bonds, observed meatless Tuesday, grew vegetables, citrus, and cattle for the armed forces, and otherwise went about business as usual. The war did quell some of the impetus of the boom which was developing in the county prior to 1917, but did not have a severely adverse effect. By the time the war ended in 1919, Brevard County had already experienced much of the boosterism, development, drainage, and growth which was to characterize the 1920s.

End Notes

1. Titusville East Coast Advocate, October 31, 1913.
2. Titusville Florida Star, April 27, 1900.
3. Charlotte Lockwood, Florida's Historic Indian River County (Vero Beach, 1975) p. 49; Cocoa Florida Star, April 18, 1913; Titusville East Coast Advocate, February 17, 1911.
4. Titusville Florida Star, June 9, 1905, January 1, 1908, March 11, 1910; Cocoa Florida Star, January 10, 1913, September 19, 1913.
5. Titusville East Coast Advocate, June 25, 1909, January 26, February 2, 16, September 6, 1912; Titusville Florida Star, September 10, 1910; Titusville Star Advocate, April 12, 1912; National Archives, Microfilm 1126, Roll 88.
6. Cocoa Florida Star, October 31, 1913.
7. Titusville East Coast Advocate, January 27, August 18, 1911, February 4, August 13, November 7, 1913, July 2, 1915, Cocoa Florida Star, August 29, 1913; Titusville Star Advocate, September 16, 1911; National Archives, Microfilm 1126, Roll 88.
8. Titusville East Coast Advocate, November 24, 1911, April 15, July 19, 1912, February 17, 1913, July 10, December 18, 1914, March 15, 1915.
9. Ibid., November 5, 1915, February 25, 1916.
10. National Archives, M 1126, Roll 88; Titusville East Coast Advocate, September 19, 1913, March 5, 1915; Titusville Florida Star, November, 10 1911.
11. Titusville Florida Star, November 22, 1912; Titusville Star Advocate, December 30, 1921.
12. Titusville East Coast Advocate, December 14, 1911.
13. Ibid., February 24, 1911, March 21, 1913, February 12, 1915.
14. Ibid., September 4, 1908, July 23, 1909, August 11, 1911, July 2, 1915.
15. Ibid., August 18, 1911; Cocoa Florida Star, May 23, 1913.
16. Titusville East Coast Advocate, February 5, March 26, September 10, 1915.
17. Ibid., January 29, March 5, November 26, 1915.
18. National Archives, M 1126, Roll 88; Titusville Florida Star, June 19. 1908; Titusville East Coast Advocate, May 24 1911, April 10, July 10, 1914, January 29, August 13, September 3, 1915, February 4, August 18, 1916.
19. Titusville Florida Star, March 9, 1908, August 6, 1909; Titusville East Coast Advocate, January 13, 1911, August 16, 1912.
20. Titusville Florida Star, January 26, October 19, 1906; Titusville East Coast Advocate, February 23, March 16, 1906, August 16, 1912.
21. Titusville East Coast Advocate, September 13, 1912.
22. Titusville Florida Star, June 7, 1907, August 14, 1908, May 28, 1909, February 25, 1910, December 20, 1912.
23. Ibid., May 26, 1905, August 2, 1907.
24. Ibid., May 22, July 3, 1908; Titusville Florida Star, November 29, 1912; Cocoa Florida Star, January 17, September 19, 1913; Titusville East Coast Advocate, February 4, May 30, 1913, January 16, 1914.
25. Titusville East Coast Advocate, November 29, 1907, April 10, 1908, April 16, 1909.
26. Ibid., May 28, 1909, October 4, 1912, November 29, 1912, April 28, September 29, 1916.
27. Ibid., December 17, 1909, September 13, 1912, May 17, 1913, July 4, 1916.
28. Ibid., March 22, November 22, 1907, September 6, 1912, June 13, July 25, 1913, December 4, 1914, January 1, 1915, February 14, April 7, 1916.
29. Ibid., February 5, 1915.

Page 240 Map: Land of George W. Hopkins. 1915-18. (Brevard County Historical Commission Archives)

Bibliography

INTERVIEWS

Ball, Ann, Titusville.
Cardwell, Harold, Daytona Beach.
Cleveland, Weona, Melbourne.
Dean, Dr. Robert, New Smyrna Beach.
Hill, Emily, Merritt Island.
Hiott, Laura, Palm Bay.
Hopwood, Fred, Melbourne.
Hudson, Robert, Titusville.
Grant, Marion, Merritt Island.
Parrish, Henry U., Jr., Cocoa.
Parrish, Ada, Cocoa.
Tucker, Daisy, Melbourne.
Whitney, Robert, Indian Harbour Beach.
Wentworth, Michael, Comprehensive Planning Division, Viera.
Wickham, Joe, Melbourne.
Winstead, Ray C., Jr., Titusville.
Woelk, Mrs. Fred, Orlando.
Zimmerman, Vera, Merritt Island.

MANUSCRIPTS

Black, Phebe, letter, n/d, 1927.
Bryant-Stephens Collection, P. K. Yonge Library of Florida History.
Dixon, Nancy J., letter, March 24, 1896, MSS Coll, PKY.
Dr. Robert Dean Collection, New Smyrna Beach.
Gleason, William H., Broadside, circa 1870s. Box 69 MSS Coll, PKY.
Gleason, William H., Papers. PKY.
Herold, Herman. Log Book of Travels in the Sunny South. Box 47, MSS Coll. PKY.
Hotel Indian River, "Cash Book," 1895.
Jenks, J.W.P., to William Morton, January 28, 1893 (Micco), Box 30, MSS Coll. PKY.
Parsons, George W., Diary, 1873-1875. PKY.
Ryder, Stephen., Appointment as U.S. Postmaster at Rockledge. Box 50, MSS Coll. PKY.
Sidney O. Chase Papers, PKY.
Thompson, George F., Journal ... as Inspector, Bureau of Refugees, Freedmen and Abandoned Lands, on a tour of central Florida and the lower west coast, December 1865.
Hentz, Charles A., Diary. Southern Collection, UNC. Chapel Hill
L'Engle, Edward M. Papers. Ibid.

PUBLIC DOCUMENTS

Brevard County. Board of Commissioners. Minutes. 1891-1949.
Brevard County, Clerk of Board of Commissioners, Official Files.
Brevard County. Miscellaneous Court Records. Case of Henrietta W. Taylor, Albert A. Taylor, and Samuel H. Peck vs. Florida East Coast Railway.
Brevard County. Data Abstracts, 1970-1990.
Florida Laws. 1844-1980.
_________. Journal of the Constitutional Convention of 1865.
Florida State Archives. Department of State Records. State and County Directories, 1845-1945. Record Group 150, Series 1284.
_________. Governor's Correspondence, 1845-1929. Record Group 101.
_________. Governor's Correspondence, 1929-1949. Record Group 102.
_________. Board of Trustees of the Internal Improvement Fund, General Correspondence, 1855-1856. Record Group 593, Series 914.
_________. Manuscript Collection. Minutes of the East Florida Line Surgical Associates. M76-168.
_________. Original Census Schedules, Agriculture, Florida, 1880. Record Group 1020, Series 1203.
_________. Original Census Schedules, Florida,1880, Manufactures. Record Group 1020, Series 1203.
_________. Original Census Schedules, Florida, 1870, Social Statistics. Record Group 1020, Series 1202.
_________. Original Census Schedules, Florida, 1870, Mortality. Record Group 1020, Series 1202.
_________. Original Census Schedules, Florida, 1870, Agriculture, Record Group, 1020, Series 1202.
_________. Original Census Schedules, Florida, 1860, Manufactures. Record Group 1020, Series 1201.
_________. Original Census Schedules, Florida, 1860, Agriculture. Record Group 1020, Series 1201.
_________. Original Census Schedules, Florida, 1860, Social Statistics. Record Group 1020, Series 1201.
_________. Original Census Schedules, Florida, 1850. Record Group 1020, Series 1200.
_________. Correspondence of Ossian B. Hart, Supervisor of Registration, 1867. Record Group 1020, Series 626.

_________. Secretary of State Correspondence. Record Group 150, Series 24.
_________. WPA Roster of State and County Officers, 1845-1868.
Florida State Library. Roster of Members of the Florida House of Representatives and Senate.
National Archives. Microfilm 1126, Roll 88. Post Office Department, Site Locations, Brevard County, Florida.
_________. Record Group 26. Correspondence of Lighthouse Board, Department of Treasury.
_________. Record Group 26. Lighthouse Site Files.
_________. Record Group 41. Register and Enrollment of Vessels (Jacksonville to Jupiter).
_________. Record Group 56. Letters to and from Collectors of Small Ports (Florida East Coast).
_________. Record Group 105. Freedmen's Bureau Records. Letters to and from Assistant Commissioner for Florida.
_________. Record Group 217. Department of Treasury, Reports of the Secretary of Commerce and Navigation, 1880s-1890s.
_________. Record Group 393. Old Military Records. U. S. ArmyCommands. Letters Received, 1854-55.
_________. Record Group 393. Records of United States Army Commands, 1821-1900.
Orange County Circuit Court (Criminal). Moses B. F. Barber Papers, 1868-1870.
_________. Minute Book A.
Original Census Schedules of St. Lucie County, Florida. Population, 1850.
United States. House of Representatives. Document No. 70. 28th Cong., 1st Sess.
_________. House of Representatives. Document No. 90. 29th Cong., 2nd Sess.
_________. House of Representatives. Miscellaneous Document No. 10. 45th Cong., 1st Sess.
_________. House of Representatives. Miscellaneous Document No. 26. 46th Cong., 1st Sess.
_________. House of Representatives. Document No. 11. 47th Cong., 1st Sess.
_________. House of Representatives. Executive Document No. 98. 50th Cong., 2nd Sess.
_________. Senate. Ex. Doc. 49. 31st Cong., 1st Sess.
_________. Senate. Ex. Doc. No. 33, 47th Cong., 1st Sess.
_________. Senate. Ex. Doc. 189. 47th Cong., 1st Sess.
_________. Senate. Doc. 46 (Fisheries of the Indian River). 54th Cong., 2nd Sess.

Newspapers and Periodicals

Cocoa *News and Star*, 1916.
Cocoa *Tribune*, 1917-1949.
Eau Gallie *Journal*, 1961.
Eau Gallie *Record*, 1927.
Florida East Coast Homeseeker, 1898-1899.
Florida Today, 1987-1991.
Florida Today, 1987-1990.
Ft. Pierce *News Tribune*, 1980s passim.
Gazenovia (NY) *Republican*, September 2 - September 30, 1880. (Microfilm in P. K. Yonge Library of Florida History, UF)
Jacksonville *Florida Dispatch*, 1881.
Jacksonville *Florida Times Union*, 1925.
Jacksonville *Metropolis*, 1920.
Melbourne *Times*, 1926-1980.
"Melbourne Centennial", Supplement to Melbourne *Times*, June 11, 1980.
Merritt Island *Daily News*, 1938.
Orlando *Sentinel*, 1967-1992.
Palm Bay *News*, 1984.
Sebastian *Sun*, 1991.
St. Augustine *Examiner*, 1867.
Tallahassee *Floridian*, 1877-1892.
Tampa Florida *Peninsular*, May 25, 1870.
Titusville *Star Advocate*, (title varies), 1880-1949.
Today (Moonwalk Souvenir Edition), July 1969.

Articles, Books and Pamphlets

Akerman, Joe A, *Florida Cowman*. Kissimmee, 1976.
Akin, Edward N., *Flagler, Rockefeller Partner and Florida Baron*. Kent, Ohio, 1988.
Andrews, Evangeline Walker, and Charles McLean Andrews (editors), *Jonathan Dickinson's Journal*. Stuart, Florida, 1975.
Author Unknown, *Melbourne Beach, The First Hundred Years*. 1983.
Bacon, Eve, *Orlando: A Centennial History*, Volume 2. Chuluota, 1977.
Barbour, Thomas, *That Vanishing Eden: A Naturalists Florida*. Boston, 1945.
Barcia, Carvallido y Zuniga, Andre G. de. *Chronological History of the Continent of Florida, 1517-1522.* Gainesville, 1951.
Barrientos, Bartolome, *Pedro Menéndez, de Avilés, Founder of Florida*. Gainesville, 1965.

Behrendt, Lloyd L. (comp.), *Development and Operation of the Atlantic Missile Range*, Volume 2, (Patrick AFB, AFMTC, 1963)

Bell, Emily Lagow, *My Pioneer Days in Florida, 1875-1898.* Privately Published, 1898.

Bense, Judith A., and John C. Phillips *Archaeological Assessment of Six Selected Areas in Brevard County: A First Generation Model.* Pensacola, 1990.

Benson, Charles D., and William Barnaby Faherty, *Moonport: A History of Apollo Launch Facilities and Operations.* (Washington, D.C., 1978).

Bramlitt, E. R. *History of the Canveral District.* Jacksonville, 1971.

Bramson, Seth, *Speedway to Sunshine: The Story of the Florida East Coast Railway.* Erin, Ontario, 1984.

Brevard County Board of Commissioners, *A Brief Description of Brevard County.* 2nd Ed. Titusville, 1889.

Brevard County Historical Commission, *Historical Book, 1830-1920.* (Hatch Journal).

Brevard County Supervisor of Elections, *Voter Registration Information*, 1981-1990.

Brinton, Daniel G., *Notes on the Florida Peninsula.* Philadelphia, 1859.

Buker, George E. *Sun, Sand & Water.* Jacksonville, 1975.

Carter, Clarence E., *Territorial Papers of the United States, 1839-1845*, Volume 26. Washington, 1960.

Caron, Eric, *One Hundred Years of Rockledge.* Rockledge, 1986.

Chandler, David Leon, *Henry Flagler.* New York, 1986.

Cleveland, Weona, "History of a Black Community," Melbourne *Times*, February 2-23, 1893.

Coker, William S., and Jerrell H. Shofner, *Florida: From the Beginning to 1992.* Houston, 1992.

Crepeau, Richard C., *Melbourne Village: The First Twenty Five Years*, 1946-71. Gainesville, 1988.

Cushman, Joseph D., Jr., *A Goodly Heritage: The Episcopal Church, 1821-1892.* Gainesville, 1965.

_______, "The Indian River Settlement, 1842-1849," *Florida Historical Quarterly*, XLIII (I964), pp. 21-35.

Chatelain, Verne de., *Defenses of Spanish Florida, 1565-1763.* Washington, 1914.

Connor, Jeannette Thurber (translator), *Pedro Menéndez de Avilés.* Gainesville, 1964.

Dau, Frederick W., *Florida, Old and New.* New York. 1934.

DeWaard, E. John, and Nancy DeWaard, *History of NASA: American Voyage to the Stars* (New York, 1984).

Edwards, Clara, *History of the Rockledge Presbyterian Church, 1877- 1953.* (Cocoa, 1953).

Edwards, John L., *Gratuitous Guide to Florida.* 1874.

Geiger, Maynard J., *The Francis Conquest of Florida, 1573-1618.* Washington, 1937.

Gold, Pleasant D., *History of Volusia County* (DeLand, 1927).

Griffin, John W., and James J. Miller, *Cultural Resource Survey of Merritt Island Wildlife Refuge* (August 1, 1978).

Hallock, Charles, *Camp Life in Florida.* New York, 1876.

Hartsfield, Annie Mary, Mary Alice Griffin, and Charles M. Grigg, *Summary Report: NASA Impact on Brevard County.* (Tallahassee, 1966).

Hanna, Alfred Jackson, and Kathryn A. Hanna, *Florida's Golden Sands.* Indianapolis and New York, 1950.

_________. *Lake Okeechobee.* Indianapolis and New York, 1948.

Hawks, John M., *The East Coast of Florida, A Descriptive Narrative.* Lynn, Mass: 1887.

Hellier, Walter R., *Indian River, Florida's Treasure Coast* (Coconut Grove, 1965).

Henshall, James A., *Camping and Cruising in Florida.* Cincinnati, 1888.

Hine, C[harles] V[ickerstaff], *On the Indian River.* Chicago, 1891.

Hoag, Amey R., *Thy Lighted Lamp.* Melbourne, 1958.

Holmes Regional Medical Center, *Fifty Years of Service* (Melbourne, 1982).

Hopkins, James T., *Fifty Years of Citrus; The Florida Fruit Exchange, 1909-1959.* Gainesville, 1960.

Hopwood, Fred A., *History of West Melbourne.* Melbourne, 1984.

_________ *Steamboating on the Indian River.* Melbourne, 1985.

Hume, Harold H., *Early Culture of Citrus Fruit.* New York, 1926.

Jarrett, Frank E., *Chronology of KSC and KSC Related Events for 1976 and 1977.* Kennedy Space Center, 1976, 1977.

Johnson, Clifton, *Highways and Byways of Florida.* New York, 1918.

Kjerulff, Georgiana Greene, *Tales of Old Brevard.* Melbourne, 1972.

_________ *Troubled Paradise: Melbourne Village, Florida.* Melbourne, 1987.

Lockwood, Charlotte, *Florida's Historic Indian River County*. Vero Beach, 1975.

Magruder, Sally I., *Young Pioneers in Florida* (Lynchburg, Virginia, 1919).

Maynard, C. J., "A Naturalist's Trip to Florida," *The American Sportsman*, July 11, 1874.

Mahon, John K., *History of the Second Seminole War, 1835-1842*. Gainesville, 1967.

Martin, Sidney Walter, *Florida's Flagler*. Athens, Georgia, 1949.

McKeny, Noreda, *Melbourne, A Century of Memories*. Melbourne, 1980.

Motte, Jacob Rhette, *Journey Into Wilderness: An Army Surgeon's Account of Life in Field and Camp During the Creek and Seminole Wars, 1836-1838*. Gainesville, 1953.

Nail, Ken, *Chronology of KSC and KSC Related Events for 1978 through 1990*. Kennedy Space Center, 1978-1990.

Newman, Anna Pearl, *Early Life Along the Beautiful Indian River*. Vero Beach, 1953.

Office of Information, PAFB, *Air Force Eastern Test Range* (Patrick Air Force Base, 1969).

Olney, George W., *A Guide to Florida*. New York, 1872.

Pritchard, James, and Co., *Descriptive Circular of Indian River*. Titusville, 1885.

Polk's *Florida State Gazetteer*, 1884-1885.

Polk's *Florida State Gazetteer*, 1886-1887.

Purdy, Barbara A. (editor), *Wet Site Archaeology*. Caldwell, New Jersey, 1988.

Rabac, Glenn, *City of Cocoa Beach, The First Sixty Years*. Winona, Minnesota, 1986.

Ranson, Robert, *East Coast Florida Memories, 1837-1886*. Port Salerno, Florida, 1989.

Rouse, Irving, *A Survey of Indian River Archaeology*. New Haven, 1957.

Shelton, William Roy. *Countdown: The Story of Cape Canaveral* (Boston, 1960).

Shofner, Jerrell H., *History of Apopka and Northwest Orange County*. Tallahassee, 1982.

________. *Nor Is It Over Yet: Florida in the Era of Reconstruction, 1863-1877*. Gainesville, 1974.

Stone, Elaine Murray, *Brevard County, From Cape of the Canes to Space Coast*. (Northridge, California, 1988).

Strickland, Alice, "Blockade Runners," *Florida Historical Quarterly*, XXXVI (1957),pp. 85-93.

Solís de Merás, Gonzalo, *Pedro Menéndez de Avilés*. Gainesville, 1964.

Sprague, John T., Origin, *Progress and Conclusion of the Florida War*. Gainesville, 1964.

Swanton, John R., *The Indians of the Southeastern United States*. Washington, 1946.

Taylor, L. B., *Liftoff: The Story of America's Spaceport* (New York: 1968).

Taylor, Theodore, *Fire on the Beaches*. New York, 1958.

Tebeau, Charlton, *A History of Florida*. Miami, 1971.

Thomas, Frank J., *Early Days in Melbourne Beach, 1888-1928*. (Cocoa Beach, 1968).

Thurm, Ann H., *History of Port Canaveral and the Cape Canaveral Area*. Cape Canaveral, 1987.

Van Landingham, Kyle S., *Pictorial History of St. Lucie County, 1565-1910*. St. Lucie County Historical Society, n.d.

Vignoles, Charles, *Observations Upon the Floridas*. Gainesville, 1977.

Wuesthoff Hospital, *50th Anniversary*. Rockledge, 1991.

Williams, John Lee, *Territorial Florida*. Gainesville, 1962.

Unpublished Material

Clark, James C., "Harry T. Moore and Civil Rights in Florida." Typescript in preparation for publication, 1991.

Cresse, Lewis H., Jr., "A Study of William Henry Gleason" (Unpublished Ph. D. Dissertation, University of South Carolina, 1975).

Federal Writers' Project, "Fishing and Fish Along Florida's East Coast." (circa 1935), PKY.

________. "Indian River County," (mss). PKY.

________. "Ships and Shipping in Florida." (circa 1936). PKY.

________. Ernest Watson, "Indian River Steamboats." (1936). PKY.

Author Unknown, "Fort Pierce." (typescript), MI85L. PKY.

Weeks, Jerry W., "Florida Gold: The Emergence of the Florida Citrus Industry, 1865-1895," (Unpublished Ph. D. Dissertation, University of North Carolina, 1977).

INDEX

Contributors

Many thanks to the following generous contributors:

Dr. Jack T. Bechtel

Dr. and Mrs. Kendall Beckman

Brevard St. Johns Realty

Mr. and Mrs. Ernest M. Briel and Patricia H. Briel

Mr. S. C. Brower, Jr.

Ms. Constance Bruce

Ms. Barbara S. Dekalb

EKS Incorporated

Ms. Lisa Gary

Ms. Carey Gleason

Ms. Isabelle L. Gleason

Ms. Evelyn M. Glover

Harry Goode's Outdoor Shop, Inc.

Mr. Richard W. Goode

Grant Historical Society

Ms. Jennie L. Gutermuth

Harris Corporation

Mrs. William W. Kerr

Mr. Thomas D. Lawton, Jr.

Mrs. Margret B. MacNeill

Ms. Mary P. Meeks

In Memory of Gladys Oudshoff

Provost Office Equipment Company

Mr. and Mrs. Adger and Gretelle M. Smith

Ms. Marie Louise G. West

Brevard County Board of County Commissioners

Truman Scarborough, Jr., District 1

Randy O'Brien, District 2

Nancy Higgs, Disstrict 3

Mark Cook, District 4

Scott Ellis, District 5